High-performance Algorithmic Trading using Machine Learning

Building automated trading strategies with AutoML and feature engineering

Franck Bardol

bpb

www.bpbonline.com

First Edition 2025

Copyright © BPB Publications, India

ISBN: 978-93-65893-892

To View Complete
BPB Publications Catalogue
Scan the QR Code:

Dedicated to

*My wife **Vassilina***

*My daughters **Ermance** and **Odile***

About the Author

Franck Bardol is an AI professor, senior consultant, and expert advisor in generative AI and machine learning with over two decades of experience in the intersection of quantitative finance, applied research, and data science. He began his career as a quantitative analyst for hedge funds and proprietary trading desks, where he developed algorithmic trading strategies and predictive models across asset classes. He later expanded his work into industrial and service sectors, applying machine learning to problems in fraud detection, maintenance optimization, customer experience, computer vision and detection of toxic emissions from a factory.

Franck has collaborated with organizations such as Axa, CA-CIB, Equalt alternative, Finaltis Hedge fund, Bouygues, Allianz, Orange Telecom Guinée, LVMH, Banque de France, ITER nuclear fusion project, General Electrics and Airbus. He has also contributed to public policy and ethics through his roles as an independent expert for the European Commission and the French AI Villani Commission.

As an educator, he has designed and delivered AI programs for institutions including the University of Geneva, ISEP, ESME Sudria, and Microsoft AI Campus. His teaching covers supervised and unsupervised learning, generative AI, and data-driven strategy, with a focus on real-world application. He is also a LinkedIn Learning instructor in data science and data marketing, having trained over 50,000 learners through his MOOC courses on the platform. He has delivered keynotes at major events such as Swiss IT Forum, Salon du Trading, and the CEPIC Conference, where he spoke alongside leading international press agencies including AFP, Associated Press, and Xinhua.

Franck holds MSc degrees in artificial intelligence, quantitative modeling, and financial markets, along with a certificate in philosophical ethics. He is the founder of the Paris Machine Learning Meetup, a leading European community of over 8,500 AI professionals and experts.

Acknowledgement

I would like to express my sincere gratitude to all those who contributed to the completion of this book.

I am immensely grateful to BPB Publications for their guidance and expertise in bringing this project to life. Their professionalism and support were invaluable in navigating the complexities of the publishing process.

I would also like to extend my thanks to the editors, technical experts, and the entire team of reviewers. Your thoughtful feedback, careful review, and constructive suggestions have greatly contributed to refining the content and elevating the quality of this manuscript.

Finally, I would like to express my deepest appreciation to my beloved parents, my sister Sylvia, and her husband, Charles Bacon, for their unwavering support and encouragement throughout this journey.

And to the readers who have shown interest in this book — your curiosity and engagement are the true reason this work exists.

Thank you to everyone who played a part in making this book a reality.

Preface

Machine learning has rapidly become a transformative tool in algorithmic trading, offering capabilities that go far beyond traditional methods such as econometrics, technical analysis, stochastic calculus, portfolio optimization, and signal processing. While these established approaches have long been staples in quantitative finance, they often rely on rigid assumptions and handcrafted rules. In contrast, machine learning enables systems to learn directly from data—discovering patterns, adapting to market dynamics, and building predictive models with minimal human intervention. The idea that examples—training sets—could be transformed into models automatically is revolutionary.

This book was written to fill a gap I observed repeatedly: the space between the first steps taken by beginners in machine learning for trading, and the more advanced, often inaccessible, expertise found in academic or institutional settings. Many newcomers begin by trying to classify returns—often unsuccessfully—due to a lack of experience with alternative prediction targets or a deeper understanding of feature engineering. My goal is to bridge that gap by introducing modern machine learning techniques that are both powerful and practical. Whether you're working on your own or within a small team, this book focuses on approaches that are computationally efficient, applicable in real trading contexts, and capable of delivering measurable results.

This book is designed as a hands-on journey through the key techniques of machine learning applied to real-world trading. It starts with the foundations of algorithmic strategy design, then progressively expands into supervised learning, unsupervised models, pattern mining, NLP for financial text, and ends with portfolio construction using advanced ML techniques. The focus is entirely practical—mathematical derivations have been intentionally excluded in favor of code, tools, and examples—making the material accessible without sacrificing technical depth.

You will learn how to apply quantamental methods by integrating accounting data into predictive models, detect structural changes in time series and extract rules automatically, work with alternative and unstructured data, and engineer features that go far beyond basic OHLC inputs, filter out market noise while preserving signal, and construct volume- or volatility-based bars and leverage recent breakthroughs in AutoML and low-code ML, using tools like H2O and Microsoft FLAML. Each chapter combines clear explanations, ready-to-run code, and use cases that reflect real trading problems and constraints.

Chapter 1: Algorithmic Trading and Machine Learning in a Nutshell - This chapter introduces systematic trading strategies, key players in the industry, and how machine learning fits into modern trading systems. Covers traditional approaches and contrasts them with ML-driven pipelines.

Chapter 2: Data Feed, Backtests, and Forward Testing - This chapter explores how to acquire macroeconomic and fundamental data via APIs, and how to prepare data for machine learning workflows. Introduces forward testing concepts and time-aware data pipelines.

Chapter 3: Optimizing Trading Systems, Metrics, and Automated Reporting - This chapter covers feature engineering, metric selection, model boosting, and creating automatic performance reports using QuantStats and other tools.

Chapter 4: Implement Trading Strategies - This chapter focuses on event-driven strategy implementation using Backtrader. Includes end-to-end ML strategy deployment, risk management, and performance evaluation.

Chapter 5: Supervised Learning for Trading Systems - This chapter covers the classification and regression algorithms relevant for trading. Emphasizes model selection, metric interpretation, and prediction targets.

Chapter 6: Improving Model Capability with Features - This chapter explores advanced feature creation: technical indicators, entropy, PCA, UMAP, tree-based features, and feature selection techniques.

Chapter 7: Advanced Machine Learning Models for Trading - This chapter presents ensemble methods (boosting, bagging, stacking), kernel-based regressors, and online learning strategies adapted to financial time series.

Chapter 8: AutoML and Low-Code for Trading Strategies - This chapter shows how to use AutoML frameworks (H2O, FLAML) to build efficient models without manual tuning. Focuses on workflow automation and reproducibility.

Chapter 9: Unsupervised Learning Methods for Trading - This chapter introduces change point detection and clustering for uncovering hidden patterns and structural shifts in financial series.

Chapter 10: Unsupervised Learning with Pattern Matching - This chapter teaches how to use recurrence plots, distance matrices, and matrix profiles to identify motifs and anomalies in time series data.

Chapter 11: Trading Signals from Reports and News - This chapter combines NLP and embeddings to extract trading signals from unstructured text. Covers GloVe, UMAP, similarity graphs, and HRP-based portfolio construction.

Chapter 12: Advanced Unsupervised Learning, Anomaly Detection, and Association Rules - This chapter explores unsupervised anomaly detection, projection-based clustering, and association rule mining for discovering hidden market structures.

Code Bundle and Coloured Images

Please follow the link to download the
Code Bundle and the *Coloured Images* of the book:

https://rebrand.ly/g36hcbb

The code bundle for the book is also hosted on GitHub at
https://github.com/bpbpublications/High-performance-Algorithmic-Trading-using-Machine-Learning.
In case there's an update to the code, it will be updated on the existing GitHub repository.

We have code bundles from our rich catalogue of books and videos available at
https://github.com/bpbpublications. Check them out!

Errata

We take immense pride in our work at BPB Publications and follow best practices to
ensure the accuracy of our content to provide with an indulging reading experience to our
subscribers. Our readers are our mirrors, and we use their inputs to reflect and improve
upon human errors, if any, that may have occurred during the publishing processes
involved. To let us maintain the quality and help us reach out to any readers who might be
having difficulties due to any unforeseen errors, please write to us at :

errata@bpbonline.com

Your support, suggestions and feedbacks are highly appreciated by the BPB Publications'
Family.

Did you know that BPB offers eBook versions of every book published, with PDF
and ePub files available? You can upgrade to the eBook version at www.bpbonline.
com and as a print book customer, you are entitled to a discount on the eBook copy.
Get in touch with us at :

business@bpbonline.com for more details.

At **www.bpbonline.com**, you can also read a collection of free technical articles,
sign up for a range of free newsletters, and receive exclusive discounts and offers
on BPB books and eBooks.

Piracy

If you come across any illegal copies of our works in any form on the internet, we would be grateful if you would provide us with the location address or website name. Please contact us at **business@bpbonline.com** with a link to the material.

If you are interested in becoming an author

If there is a topic that you have expertise in, and you are interested in either writing or contributing to a book, please visit **www.bpbonline.com**. We have worked with thousands of developers and tech professionals, just like you, to help them share their insights with the global tech community. You can make a general application, apply for a specific hot topic that we are recruiting an author for, or submit your own idea.

Reviews

Please leave a review. Once you have read and used this book, why not leave a review on the site that you purchased it from? Potential readers can then see and use your unbiased opinion to make purchase decisions. We at BPB can understand what you think about our products, and our authors can see your feedback on their book. Thank you!

For more information about BPB, please visit **www.bpbonline.com**.

Join our book's Discord space

Join the book's Discord Workspace for Latest updates, Offers, Tech happenings around the world, New Release and Sessions with the Authors:

https://discord.bpbonline.com

Table of Contents

CHAPTER 1
Algorithmic Trading and Machine Learning in a Nutshell

Introduction

This chapter provides an overview of algorithmic trading. It covers the basics of algorithmic trading strategies.

It explains the reasons why ML is being introduced in trading and the potential consequences of its use. This chapter discusses the use of **machine learning** (**ML**) in algorithmic trading, from momentum to statistical arbitrage strategies. It explores how ML can detect trends and mean-reversion patterns for trading and other innovative applications, such as meta-learning.

Structure

In this chapter, we will cover the following topics:

- Systematic algorithmic trading
- Discretionary vs. systematic trading
- Main types of algorithmic strategies
- Understanding machine learning
- Machine learning in trading
- Meta-strategy using machine learning

Objectives

By the end of this chapter, you will have a robust understanding of algorithmic trading, its inception, the driving forces behind its development, and its diverse applications. Moreover, you can differentiate and describe key algorithmic strategies, from momentum to statistical arbitrage and **high-frequency trading (HFT)**, recognizing the distinguishing elements and identifying the various participants in the space.

This chapter aims to provide a comprehensive foundation in algorithmic trading and machine learning applications, empowering you to build upon this knowledge in real-world applications.

Systematic algorithmic trading

The evolution of the financial markets and investment industry has led to the development of various sophisticated trading methodologies. One such method that has emerged and seen considerable growth over the years is systematic, algorithmic trading. Algorithmic trading[1] has captured over 50% of the trading volume in US markets today. The reasons for this proliferation are manifold, with the key drivers being the ability to process large amounts of information rapidly and the elimination of human errors and emotions from the trading process. This approach eliminates emotional biases and subjectivity from trading decisions, providing objectivity.

Historically, trading was primarily discretionary, which involved human decision-making and intuition. However, it became apparent over time that this approach has inherent limitations, particularly in processing vast amounts of data and acting rapidly on market opportunities. Systematic algorithmic trading solved these challenges, introducing a new speed, scalability, and efficiency paradigm.

It was introduced in the 1970s when highly computerized trading systems emerged in the American financial markets.

The systematic aspect comes from the use of explicitly formulated investment rules. These rules express the conduct to be followed. Consequently, the writing and formulation of relevant rules becomes a strategic differentiator between investors, and we will see throughout this book how to achieve this. This book aims to explore methods for generating trading rules using self-learning algorithms.

Before going any further, let us take a moment to illustrate this. Here is an example of a trading rule:

```
"Buy Microsoft share if
the Volume exceeds the previous day's volume and
the closing price is higher the opening"
```

1 https://analyzingalpha.com/algorithmic-trading-history

This rule constitutes a trading strategy, which, when followed, is called systematic or algorithmic trading[2].

The algorithmic trading concept involves applying quantitative models to create, back-test, and implement trading strategies. This approach enables the execution of large orders exceptionally quickly, often resulting in significant financial gains.

Speed and scalability are a natural consequence of using a computer (via programming language) to process these systematic trading rules and send the resulting buy/sell orders to the financial markets. The rule encompasses all the necessary information to make informed investment decisions in each context.

The decision involves selecting the most suitable course of action from the options, such as buy, sell, do nothing, reduce exposure, lighten a portfolio, hedge a financial risk, or protect an investment. The usefulness of a rule is precisely to choose among these actions.

Now let us look at some of the key players in this business and a brief history.

Emblematic players in systematic trading

The narrative of algorithmic trading began in the late 1970s, deeply rooted in quantitative methodologies. *Ed Thorp*[3], a math professor turned hedge fund manager, was one of the pioneers, utilizing his expertise in blackjack strategies to make a lasting impact on Wall Street. His strategies were well-suited for Wall Street, leaving a lasting mark on trading history. He introduced quantitative methods into finance, establishing the foundation for systematic trading. He is considered the first quantitative analyst in history.

Here is how it started[4].

In the late 1970s, the prevailing theory of efficient markets, which posits that financial markets reflect all available information, thus rendering it impossible to consistently achieve higher than average profits, was subject to increasing skepticism. Influential figures like Ed Thorp, renowned for his successful application of probabilistic strategies in blackjack, and *Jerome Baesel*, a distinguished mathematician at *UCI University* and colleague at *Princeton-Newport Partners*, harbored strong beliefs in the existence of market inefficiencies. Their conviction was further buoyed by empirical evidence, including the consistently successful investment strategies of *Warren Buffett*, suggesting that savvy players could indeed beat the market. Thus, the stage was set for the era of systematic trading and the advent of new tools to exploit these inefficiencies.

While at Princeton-Newport Partners, they embarked on a groundbreaking project: studying the impact of various indicators and characteristics on the historical returns of

2 To be quite precise, there is a fine distinction between systematic trading and algorithmic trading. Unlike algorithmic trading, systematic trading offers no discretionary alternative to the trader or manager who applies it. In this book, we will deal mainly with systematic strategies.

3 http://www.fortunesformula.com/EdwardThorpBio.html

4 Ed Thorp, a mathematician on Wall Street, Statistical Arbitrage, part I, https://www.valuewalk.com/1850840

securities. This audacious endeavor involved analyzing factors like P.E. ratios, book-to-price ratios, and company size, and was met with a wave of criticism from the academic world. Yet, they pressed on undeterred.

Then, in a twist of fate, one of their researchers stumbled upon a game-changing idea: statistical arbitrage.

This concept hinged on a single indicator that ranked stocks from best to worst and offered short-term forecasts of their performance relative to one another. They discovered intriguing recurrent patterns by examining the percentage change in price over a recent period, such as the last two weeks. The stocks that experienced significant gains tended to falter in the subsequent weeks, while those that suffered losses often rebounded.

With this newfound insight, they devised a system called MUD, which cleverly stood for most up, most down stocks. Through extensive computer simulations, they were astounded to find that buying the top-performing decile of stocks while short-selling the bottom-performing decile could yield an annualized return of around 20 percent.

At the end of this paragraph, we will return to this system and propose an implementation.

Concurrently with *Ed Thorp*, innovators such as *Richard Olsen* and *Michael Stumm* launched digital forex trading platforms, further preparing the ground for the adoption of algorithmic methods.

Among the other pioneers of algorithmic trading, the most famous is a mathematician specializing in transmission codes and how to break them. Armed with this knowledge of code breaker, he founded Renaissance in 1982. It is the best-known systematic hedge fund globally for its success[5] and the aura of secrecy surrounding its strategies.

Renaissance Technologies was not alone on this new frontier. Other noteworthy hedge funds, including *D.E. Shaw* and *Citadel*, were also at the forefront of the algorithmic trading movement. They were early adopters of systematic algorithmic trading and have reaped substantial rewards from their endeavors.

For instance, D.E. Shaw manages assets worth over $50 billion, with trading systems powered by algorithms consistently delivering market-beating returns. Similarly, Renaissance Technologies, with around $130 billion in assets under management, and Citadel, with assets exceeding $34 billion, have realized remarkable performance from their algorithmic trading operations.

These entities and their significant successes exemplify the substantial potential inherent in algorithmic trading. However, the nuances and variations in algorithmic trading strategies are vast, with each type possessing unique attributes and considerations. We will delve deeper into these strategies in the subsequent sections.

---

5 "Renaissance's flagship Medallion fund is famous for the best track record on Wall Street, returning more than 66 percent annualized before fees over a 30-year span from 1988 to 2018".
Source Wikipedia, https://en.wikipedia.org/wiki/Renaissance_Technologies

Let us take a moment to implement the idea, which is probably the ancestor of modern statistical arbitrage systems: buy the poor performers and sell the best. This forms the basis of trading systems based on the **statistical properties** of mean reversion of financial asset prices.

Implementing the first statistical arbitrage system

The sequence is as follows, starting with installing the **Yahoo finance library (yfinance)** if necessary:

```python
try :
    import yfinance as yf
except ModuleNotfoundError as e:
    !pip install -q yfinance


import yfinance as yf
```

Next, we request a long history of daily quotes for 30 tickers traded on the New York Stock Exchange. Tickers are randomly picked:

```python
# Define the stock tickers
tickers = ['AAP', 'AXP', 'BA', 'CAT', 'CSCO', 'CVX', 'DIS', 'GS', 'HD', \
           'IBM', 'INTC', 'JNJ', 'JPM', 'KO', 'MCD', 'MMM', 'MRK', 'MSFT', 'NKE'\
           'PFE', 'PG', 'TRV', 'UNH', 'VZ', 'WBA', 'WMT', 'XOM', 'MMM']
# Download historical price data from Yahoo Finance
data = yf.download(tickers, start='1990-01-01', end='2023-07-07' , interval ='1d')
```

Compute returns and drop missing values with the help of the Pandas **dropna()** function :

```python
# Calculate the percentage change in price over a recent period (e.g., last two weeks)
ret = data['Adj Close'].pct_change(periods=10)
# Drop `Nan` values
ret.dropna(inplace=True)
```

Then, following the logic outlined by Ed Thorp, we start by sorting the returns (**rank** function) to determine the best (**top_decile**) and worst performers (**bottom_decile**) for each period of history.

```python
# Rank the stocks based on their percentage change
ranked_ret = ret.rank(axis=1, ascending=False)


# Select the top-performing and bottom-performing deciles of stocks
```

```
# x% first
top_decile = ranked_ret[ranked_ret <= len(tickers) * 0.2]
```

```
# worst performers
bottom_decile = ranked_ret[ranked_ret > len(tickers) * 0.9]
bottom_decile.dropna()
```

We buy shares (**long_positions**) from the **top_decile** list and sell those from the **bottom_decile** list.

```
# Open new positions based on the strategy
long_positions = top_decile.loc[date].dropna()
short_positions = bottom_decile.loc[date].dropna()
```

The exit condition is as follows: assets are removed from the portfolio when they are no longer on one of the lists of top or worst performers:

```
if stock not in top_decile.loc[date].dropna().index and stock not in
bottom_decile.loc[date].dropna().index:
```

We apply this system with the following management parameters:

```
# Initial portfolio value
portfolio_value = 10000
total_trades = 0
total_profit_loss = 0
lst_pnl = []
stp_loss = -2/100 * portfolio_value
# Define transaction cost per share, x$  per share ($0.005 : IB Broker)
transaction_cost = 0.01
```

In Interactive Broker Trading Platform[6], the commission for trading US exchanged-listed stocks is $0.005 per share for professional account. We double this amount to $0.01 to account for additional frictions (slippage, etc.).

We add a basic stop-loss that cuts the loss to 2% of the amount of capital traded ($100,000 portfolio).

We obtain the following statistics and profit and loss equity curve:

```
avg return in pct: 7.65%
Total Profit/Loss: 1138014.42
Average Return per Trade: 580.62
```

Our statistical arbitrage system gives promising results in line with the information provided by *Ed Thorp*:

---

6 https://www.interactivebrokers.com/en/index.php?f=49637

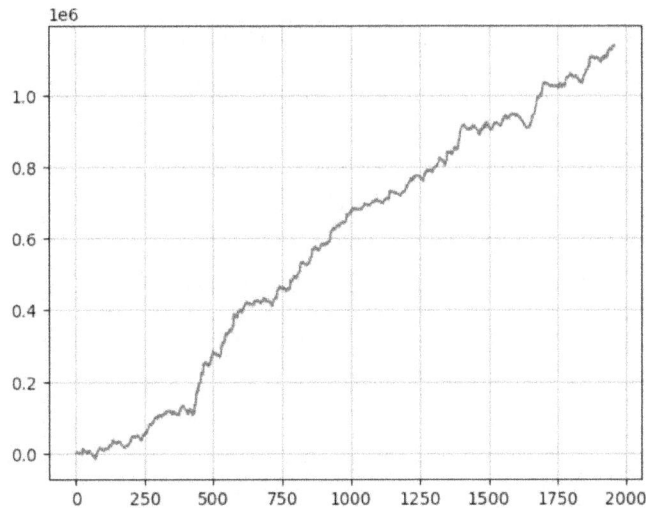

Figure 1.1: *Equity curve for Mean-Reversion strategy*

Now that we have implemented the logic of statistical arbitrage, let us look at the differences between systematic, to which statistical arbitrage belongs, and discretionary trading to fully understand the advantages and disadvantages of the two main investment methods.

Discretionary vs. systematic trading

Systematic trading involves using computer algorithms to make trading decisions based on predefined rules and criteria. This approach eliminates emotional biases and subjectivity from trading decisions, providing objectivity. However, systematic trading may have limitations in unique situations or sudden changes in market conditions, as the predefined rules and algorithms may not always capture or adapt to these changes. You must bear this limitation in mind. The most systematic rules, even the most sophisticated ones, will likely be outdated and ineffective in a wholly unprecedented and improbable situation.

On the other hand, discretionary trading relies on the skills of individual traders or teams to make trading decisions. This approach enables greater flexibility in responding to unique market situations or sudden changes in market conditions.

There is no definitive answer to whether systematic strategies are better than discretionary ones, as it depends on various factors, including market conditions, the specific strategy employed, and the individual trader's or team's skills. Some studies suggest combining both approaches can provide benefits such as improved portfolio diversification and more solid risk management over the entire market cycle.

As far as we are concerned, we will talk about systematic trading in the remainder of this book. Having understood the motivation behind systematic trading, we will now explore the core strategies employed in algorithmic trading.

Main types of algorithmic strategies

As we enter the realm of systematic trading, it is essential to understand the main approaches to systematic trading and what sets them apart. We will outline the statistical arbitrage strategies, detailing the most emblematic and accessible ones in terms of infrastructure (required equipment) and theoretical background.

Momentum and trend-following strategies

This strategy seeks to capitalize on continuing existing market trends, buying securities trending up, and selling those trending down. It is probably the most well-known and intuitive strategy.

In this example, the systematic trading strategy will take advantage of the uptrend (Red line in *Figure 1.2*). To achieve this, you must detect the trend early enough to exploit it and distinguish between false signals (the most numerous) and real opportunities.

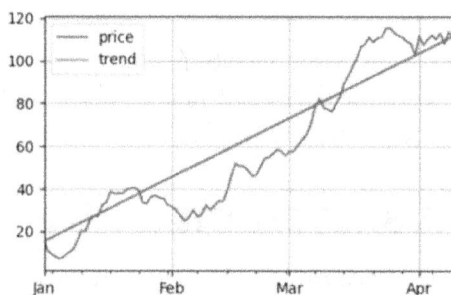

Figure 1.2: *Momentum systematic strategy*

Statistical arbitrage

This strategy involves statistical modeling to identify and exploit market inefficiencies. The two main statistical arbitrage strategies are pair trading and mean reversion.

Pair trading

In the late 1980s, Pair trading emerged at *Morgan Stanley*, led by *Nunzio Tartaglia* and his team. Later, team members established renowned hedge funds, such as PDT Partners and D.E. Shaw, ultimately creating Sigma. Pair trading has become a popular and sophisticated strategy. However, as markets evolved and technology advanced, arbitrage opportunities became scarcer and profit margins narrower. To adapt, the industry underwent an upgrade, and after a period of decline, there has been a resurgence of interest in pairs trading, accompanied by the development of advanced approaches and much-needed change. We will explain the basic principles in this paragraph without going into the details of the most recent research.

Pair trading strategy involves identifying pairs of assets that historically have a strong correlation[7] and then taking advantage of temporary price divergences between them. The algorithm calculates the spread between two assets (or more) and generates trading signals based essentially on crossing predefined thresholds and levels.

Implementing a pair trading strategy requires matching opposite (long and short) positions:

Figure 1.3: *Pair trading strategy between FORD and GM stocks*

There are three stages to a pair trading strategy:

- Firstly, you need to identify the pair among the shares. This is the pair's selection phase.
- In the second stage, we need to model the spread, and finally.
- Deal with the trading rules that give us our intervention strategy.

All these points are covered in detail in the reference works listed in the bibliography.

Here, we show the elements of calculating these three stages that could be used for a pair trading strategy. It will help you understand the logic and sequence of events. In the figure above, the systematic pair trading strategy will capitalize on the relationship between Ford and **General Motors** (**GM**). Indeed, the fluctuations of the two stocks appear to be **synchronised**.

This suggests that Ford and GM shares are correlated by the influence of the joint economic factors that affect them simultaneously. A pair trading strategy takes advantage of this link, even if the correlation is not perfect and fluctuates over time.

---

7 Calculating **correlation** is not enough to measure the link between the two assets in the pair. Pair Trading use a statistical measure called **co-integration** which measures the long-term equilibrium relationship between two or more assets.

This type of strategy considers the pair of stocks as an asset. This is represented in the chart above, which gives us the pair's evolution in the first cadran and the spread between the two individual shares () in the second cadran. Then, the spread is standardized[8] according to the following calculation: .

The thresholds and levels that trigger a trading decision can be identified using elementary statistical calculations based on the z-score, as follows.

Here is a summary of the operations that led to the result. Details and Python source code can be found in the Github notebook. The sequence is as follows: installing the **Yahoo finance library (yfinance)** if necessary. Next, we request a history of the last 900 days of quotes for FORD and GM shares, which we store in the Pandas arrays (dataframes) entitled s1 and s2.

```
try :
    import yfinance as yf
except ModuleNotfoundError as e:
    !pip install -q yfinance


import yfinance as yf


companies = ['FORD','GM']
tickers = yf.Tickers(companies)
tickers_hist = tickers.history(period='900d',interval='1d',)


s1 = tickers_hist['Close']['FORD']
s2 = tickers_hist['Close']['GM']
```

Then, the spread is standardized, using the z-score formula mentioned above, to make it easier to interpret the percentiles:

```
import numpy as np
tmp = s2 - s1
spread = (tmp - np.mean(tmp)) / np.std(tmp)
```

The z-score[9] calculated for a spread between two shares quantifies the deviation of the spread value from its mean, as follows:

---

8 zero mean and standard deviation equal to 1

9 "The standard score is the number of standard deviations by which the value of a raw score is above or below the mean value of what is being observed or measured"

https://en.wikipedia.org/wiki/Standard_score

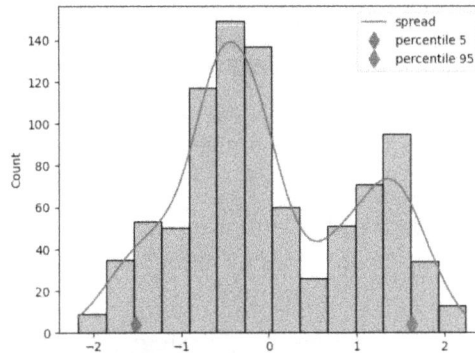

Figure 1.4: *Spread distribution*

A z-score of 0 indicates that the spread is at its mean, while positive and negative z-scores indicate deviations above and below the mean. Fluctuations in the standardized spread are represented in the lower quadrant in *Figure 1.3*.

The 5th and 95th percentiles of the z-score distribution serve as **thresholds** for identifying potential trading opportunities in pair trading strategies. We position these percentiles on *Figure 1.4*, which represents the statistical distribution of spread values over the historical period studied.

```
quantile = [0.05 , .25 , .50 , .75 , 0.95]
qtl = np.quantile(spread , quantile)
qtl
# array([-1.52366456, -0.66268085, -0.2051237 ,  0.88300426,  1.62259108])
```

Trades may be executed when the z-score crosses these thresholds (percentile 5 or 95), indicating extreme deviations from the mean and potential mean reversion opportunities in the spread. Percentile 5 gives us the spread value, so 5% of the calculated spread values are below it. The Python script above tells us that this value is -1.52.

This is the first value in the list **qtl** calculated by the **quantile** function above.

Symmetrically, the percentile 95 gives us the spread value (1.62) such that 5% of the calculated spread values are above it. This is the last value in the list **qtl** calculated by the **Numpy** function **quantile**.

These two levels are shown in *Figure 1.5*:

Figure 1.5: *Spread and thresholds*

Buy undervalued and sell overvalued is the fundamental investment principle we will apply.

In our peer trading strategy, undervalued means that the standardized spread is historically low.

We buy the spread when it falls below **percentile_5** threshold. Buying the spread ( ) means buying GM and selling FORD. We are therefore betting on a return to its central value given by the average, that is, zero.

Conversely, when the spread moves towards unusual values (given by the value of the **percentile_95**), we use the opposite strategy, which consists of selling the spread to bet on a return to lower values.

One of the advantages of the mean-reverting strategy is that it requires no predictions, since the spread is assumed to revert to its mean and fluctuate around it constantly.

The basic principle of a peer trading strategy we have outlined could be improved in various ways. For example, establishing adaptive rather than fixed thresholds or applying more sophisticated quantitative methods.

We have not mentioned that the portfolio of our two stocks must be market-neutral. The reason is that we are trying to profit from the spread, not from the market. A pair trading strategy aims to profit from relative performance while hedging against overall market movements. This is a point that must be borne in mind when putting the strategy.

Now let us look at the essential principles of another statistical arbitrage strategy: the mean-reversion strategy.

Mean reversion strategy

The basic principle of this strategy is that it assumes that prices, or levels of various indicators, will return to their historical averages, asset prices that have deviated significantly from their mean will eventually return to a more normal level and trades are made in anticipation of this reversion.

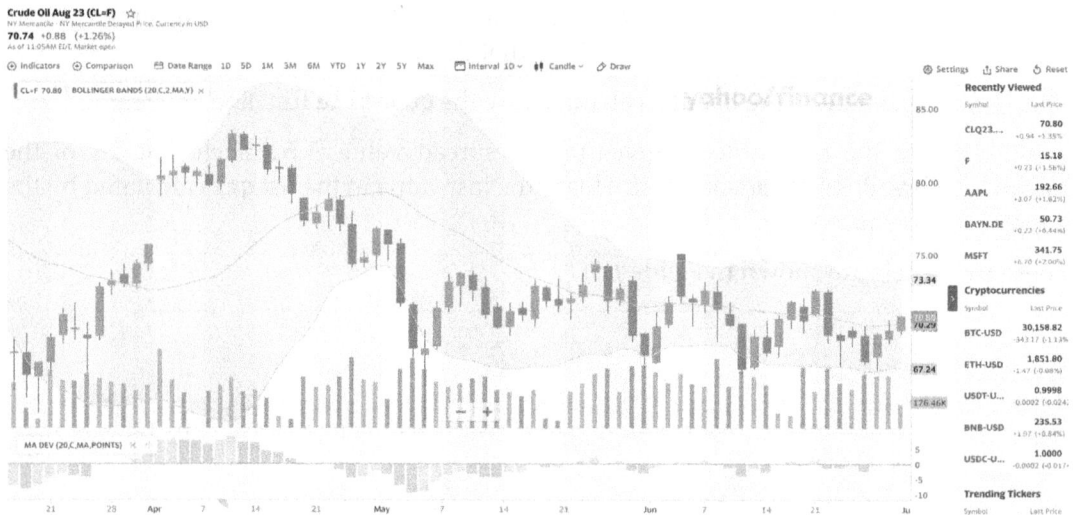

Figure 1.6: *Mean reversion systematic strategy, Crude Oil*

The preceding graph shows the price of crude oil and the moving average (solid orange line) of these prices.

We can see that the price of oil fluctuates constantly around this moving average (moving average or similar quantity). The average is an attractor towards which the price constantly returns.

On the chart, the orange area illustrates the distance separating the price from the moving average. Consequently, this area is large when the gap between the price of the financial asset and its average is also large. These situations are known as overbought and oversold and correspond to abnormal gaps. This is the case when the price of the asset rises too quickly, both upwards (overbought) and downwards (oversold).

This trading strategy corresponds to identifying over-bought and over-sold assets to take an opposite position and a bet on a correction phase that follows extreme periods (buying losers and selling winners).

Major steps to implement mean-reversion strategy

Implementing the strategy will require resolving many technical issues, but the founding principle is simple: uninterrupted fluctuations around a central value.

Let us look at the essential stages of a mean reversion strategy:

- **Asset selection**: Identify suitable assets that exhibit mean-reverting behavior. These assets should have a history of oscillating around their mean values.

- **Mean calculation**: Calculate the mean of the asset's price or another relevant metric. The mean represents the average value over a specific period and is a reference point for determining deviations.

- **Standard deviation calculation**: Calculate the standard deviation of the asset's price or relevant metric. The standard deviation quantifies the dispersion of prices around the mean and helps identify significant deviations.

- **Deviation measurement**: Measure the deviation of the asset's price from its mean. This can be done by calculating the z-score, which represents the number of standard deviations the current price is away from the mean (as calculated in steps 2 and 3).

- **Trading strategy, entry, and exit points**: Define entry and exit points based on the deviations from the mean. Typically, traders look for instances when the price moves significantly away from the mean, signaling a potential reversion opportunity. An entry point may be when the price falls below a certain number of standard deviations from the mean, and an exit point may be when the price reverts to a specific threshold or the mean itself.

- **Risk management**: Establish risk management parameters to control the size of positions, set stop-loss orders, and manage overall portfolio risk. This step is crucial for protecting against large losses and ensuring proper risk-adjusted returns.

Intrinsically, the mean reversion strategy focuses on identifying oversold or overbought conditions of an individual asset based on its historical price patterns. Trades are executed when the price reaches extreme levels, anticipating a reversal towards the mean. This is exactly the statistical arbitrage strategy given in the introduction.

The attentive reader will have noted the similarity between pair trading and mean-reversion strategies. However, there are differences between these two statistical arbitrage strategies. Here is what makes them different.

Difference between pair trading and mean reversion strategies:

- Pair trading identifies correlated **asset pairs** and profits from temporary price divergences, while mean reversion focuses on **individual assets** deviating from their mean.

- Pair trading employs a **market-neutral** approach, capturing the relative performance of assets, while mean reversion targets **oversold/overbought** conditions.

- Pair trading uses **spread** calculation and historical behavior, while mean reversion relies on **price** patterns.

- Pair trading **hedges** against market risk, while mean reversion **exposes** to specific asset risk. Both strategies differ in approach, with pair trading focused on divergences and mean reversion on price reversion to the mean.

Other algorithmic strategies

There are other statistical arbitrage strategies that we will not discuss in detail in this introductory chapter. However, we will learn the main points:

- **Relative value strategy**: Compare the relative valuation of assets within a sector or industry to identify mispriced securities.

- **Event-driven**: Capitalizing on market reactions to specific events, such as earnings announcements or corporate actions.

- **Statistical factors strategy**: Utilizing quantitative models based on statistical factors such as momentum, volatility, and liquidity.

- **Index arbitrage strategy**: Exploiting price discrepancies between the underlying components of an index and the index itself.

- **High-frequency (HFT) and market-making strategies**: These strategies use powerful computers to transact many orders at extremely high speeds.

  Market-making strategies involve continuously buying and selling securities to provide liquidity to the market, profiting from the bid-ask spread.

These last two strategies (HFT and market making) operate continuously and quickly. They require considerable material resources, privileged access to markets, and data flows (low latency trading systems). For these reasons, they are the preserve of professional investors (hedge funds, investment banks, or proprietary trading houses).

Refer to *Table 1.1* for an overview of these strategies:

Strategy	Required a market direction	Horizon and time frame	Single asset vs. Pairs	Professional infrastructure	Profit driver
HFT	No	Sub seconds	Single	Yes	Speed
Market-making	No	Sub seconds	Single	Yes	Bid-ask spread
Pair trading	No	Intraday and longer	Pair	No	Relation between assets
Mean reversion	No	Intraday and longer	Single	No	Return to the mean
Momentum	Yes	Intraday and longer	Single	No	Trend continuation

Table 1.1: Overview of systematic strategies

In the remainder of this chapter, we will introduce machine learning and find out what it is and what we can expect from it in the context of algorithmic trading.

Then, by way of illustration, we will take one of the strategies mentioned and decorate it with machine learning. This will allow us to experiment with a promising area of research known as meta-strategy. This will be our first use case for machine learning.

Understanding machine learning

As we move forward in this chapter, we will unravel the mysteries of **machine learning** (**ML**), its roots, and the exciting potential it holds for the realm of algorithmic trading. At its core, machine learning is a subset of artificial intelligence that enables computer systems to learn from data and improve their performance without being explicitly programmed.

During this time, in 1959, a computer scientist named *Arthur Samuel* gave a name to a growing concept: **Machine Learning**. We owe him the definition of machine learning that we have just quoted, which is still the authority on the subject.

Working in the stimulating environment of IBM, Samuel was shaping the future with his innovative checkers-playing program. Unlike standard programs of the time, Samuel's brainchild stood apart. It was designed to learn from every game it played, incrementally refining its strategy and boosting its performance.

Legend has it that the program soon surpassed its creator's skills, winning games against Samuel. This convinced Samuel of the revolutionary potential of this new field of knowledge.

Interestingly, Samuel's explorations in machine learning were not happening in isolation. The broader field of artificial intelligence was also gaining momentum, with the 1956 Dartmouth Conference serving as a pivotal catalyst. This conference convened thought leaders such as *John McCarthy, Marvin Minsky, Nathaniel Rochester*, and *Claude Shannon*. Together, they debated and dreamt about machines mirroring human intelligence, setting the stage for the transformative world of artificial intelligence we know today.

These conversations were partly inspired by the groundbreaking work of Alan Turing, who laid the foundation for theoretical computer science and artificial intelligence.

However, it is crucial to understand that machine learning and artificial intelligence, while interconnected, are not identical. Artificial intelligence is a broader concept, referring to machines or software that can mimic human intelligence. On the other hand, machine learning is a subset of AI that specifically focuses on using algorithms and statistical models to allow machines to improve at tasks with experience. It is a practical application of AI where systems can learn and make decisions from data without being explicitly programmed (*Figure 1.7*).

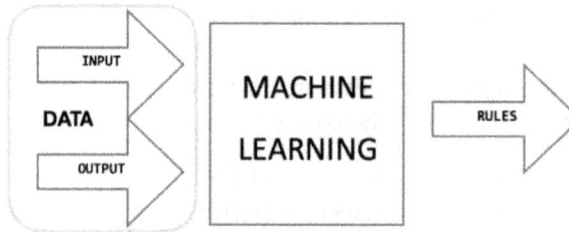

Figure 1.7: Machine learning functioning

In short, machine learning algorithms output rules. This is the crucial point for understanding the essence of machine learning. This contrasts with traditional computer programming, in which the developer, the analyst, is responsible for producing, imagining, and designing the rules that enable him to make decisions informed by their application.

This is exactly the promise of what machine learning is capable of offering: rules extracted from data during a learning phase.

When we use an ML algorithm, we let the algorithm draw its deductions and conclusions in accordance with the data it is presented with. The rules are buried and hidden in the data. The algorithm scours the data for patterns of repetition and complex correlations that will enable it to make the best possible predictions. We will come back to learning in more detail in the next section.

Fast forward to today, machine learning has permeated virtually every sector, from healthcare and logistics to finance and trading. In the context of algorithmic trading, machine learning is a game-changer, offering innovative ways to model and predict market behavior.

As we explore ML's role in trading, we will discover its ability to sift through vast amounts of financial data, identify complex patterns, and make accurate predictions. This capability is particularly beneficial for enhancing established trading strategies, which we will illustrate by applying ML to a trend following strategy. We will then discuss an exciting area of research known as meta-strategy.

In essence, a meta-strategy is a framework that uses machine learning to optimize and adapt trading strategies based on changing market conditions. This approach enables us to extract even greater value from our trading strategies, marking our first venture into applying machine learning in a practical, impactful way within the context of systematic algorithmic trading.

Machine learning in trading

Here is an example of one of the simplest trading rules employed by traders, known as a moving average crossover strategy:

- **Set-up**: The strategy uses two moving averages - a shorter period and a longer period average. The most common lengths are 50 days (around 2 months) for the shorter period average (SMA50) and 200 days for the longer period average (SMA200).

- **Buy rule**: When the SMA50 crosses above the SMA200, it generates a bullish signal, and the trader buys the asset.

- **Sell rule**: Conversely, when the SMA50 crosses below the SMA200, it generates a bearish signal, and the trader sells the asset.

These two rules form a trend-following strategy that seeks to capture the momentum of an asset.

Momentum strategy with machine learning

To implement this moving average crossover strategy using machine learning, we will first have to modify the problem to be suitable for an ML approach. Rather than creating explicit rules for when to buy and sell, we would use ML to learn these rules based on past data.

In fact, this is exactly the promise of what machine learning is capable of offering: rules extracted from data during a learning phase.

Here is an example using supervised learning, and in particular, a classification approach. **Classification** means that we are trying to learn how to predict a category

The following gives an idea of what machine learning can do for trading. We will return to the methodological points concerning implementation in the next section (*Implementing supervised trading systems*).

These are the steps that lead to a trading system powered by a machine learning algorithm:

1. **Preprocessing and data**: First, we download the data, then calculate the same moving averages (SMA50 and SMA200) on historical price data. On the other hand, we use the same data as in the traditional approach (without ML), which is why we calculate the moving averages in the same way to include them in the inputs that will be submitted to the model for the search for recurring patterns. We then create a target variable that is +1 when the next day's closing price is higher than the day before (bullish signal) and -1 for the opposite (bearish signal). This target variable is what we will train our model to predict.

2. **Feature creation**: Next, we create features for our model. These could include the current price, volume, the values of the two moving averages, and potentially many others. A big part of ML is selecting and engineering these features. We will return to this point in *Chapter 6, Improving Model Capability with Features*.

3. **Model training**: We then split our data into a training set and a test set, and train our ML model (for example, a decision tree, logistic regression, to start with, and then move on to more complex models) on the training set. The model learns to predict the target variable based on the features.

4. **Model testing**: After our model is trained, we test its performance on the test set to make sure it generalizes well to new data. We can adjust our model parameters or try different models based on this performance.

5. **Trading rule**: We now have an ML model that, given the current features, predicts whether the short-term moving average will be above or below the long-term moving average in the future. We can use these predictions to trade: if the prediction is +1, we buy, and if the prediction is -1, we sell.

Regarding model training, modern machine learning systems utilize proven and optimized APIs. For our purposes, we have chosen the scikit-learn machine learning library. This is the most widely used machine learning library in the world, along with Google's **TensorFlow**. Furthermore, in addition to its intrinsic qualities, the Scikit-Learn license permits the code to be reused for commercial purposes, and the code is open-source, available for consultation on GitHub.

Here is the code that illustrates each of these points:

The study concerns the General Motors share (GM ticker) over the last 5 years (1000 daily data). Let us start by preprocessing and downloading data from Yahoo Finance:

```
import pandas as pd
import numpy as np
import yfinance as yf
yf.pdr_override()
```

```
symbol = 'GM'
ticker = yf.Ticker(symbol)
#Valid intervals: [1m, 2m, 5m, 15m, 30m, 60m, 90m, 1h, 1d, 5d, 1wk, 1mo,
3mo]
df = ticker.history(period='1000d', interval='1d')
```

The next step is to create the features given as input to the machine learning algorithm. This stage is known as feature engineering:

```
# Compute moving averages
df['SMA50'] = df['Close'].rolling(window=50).mean()
df['SMA200'] = df['Close'].rolling(window=200).mean()
df['MA_cross'] = df['SMA50'] - df['SMA200']


# Create target variable
df['target'] = pd.DataFrame(np.zeros(len(df)))
df['target'] = np.where(df['Close'].pct_change() > 0 , 1 , -1)


df['target'] = df['target'].shift(-1)


# Remove NaNs
df.dropna(inplace=True)


# Create features
X = df[['Open','High','Low','Close','SMA50', 'SMA200' , 'MA_cross']]
```

The ML method consists of providing the ML algorithm with the same ingredients as for the MA-cross over strategy, but without going so far as to give it the rules of this strategy (respective positions of the moving averages). The purpose of the machine learning algorithm is to extract these rules. To do this, it is guided by the output (target column), which represents the goal to be achieved.

During the training phase, the ML algorithm scans the features submitted to it (input) in search of repetitions and complex correlations that will enable it to predict the supervision column (output) appropriately.

Model training: **train_test_split()** function splits the data into a training and a test set. In this way, only the training set is submitted during the training phase of the algorithm.

```
# Train-test split
X_train, X_test, y_train, y_test = train_test_split(X, df['target'] ,
shuffle=False)
```

```
# Create and train decision tree classifier
clf = DecisionTreeClassifier(random_state=42)
clf.fit(X_train, y_train)
```

And, finally, model testing, the output of the function is as follows:

```
from sklearn.metrics import classification_report
print (classification_report(clf.predict(X_test) , y_test))
```

	precision	recall	f1-score	support
-1.0	0.24	0.50	0.33	46
1.0	0.78	0.53	0.63	154
accuracy			0.53	200
macro avg	0.51	0.52	0.48	200
weighted avg	0.66	0.53	0.56	200

It is important to note that all the performance metrics are calculated on data to which the algorithm does not have access during training (X_test). So, it has not been trained with it. These data reasonably illustrate the expected performance on new and unpublished data, such as what might be encountered in a production and live trading environment. This is a crucial point. We will come back later to the meaning and interpretation of the metrics (the higher, the better) we have in front of us.

The percentage of correct predictions for the class positive (+1: rising period) is much higher than the uninformed random prediction (coin toss), which in this case is 0.5. In fact, the precision is 0.78.

However, this is not the case for the other class (-1). The prediction of down periods is not good.

Now, we need to compare it with the metrics of the traditional cross-over system. The trading rule is implemented to calculate the associated performance metrics.

As mentioned in the introduction, the simplest possible rule is the cross-over rule, which can be expressed as follows:

```
# cross-over rules : +1 MA(50 days) > MA(200) ; -1 : MA(50 days) < MA(200)
ma_cross = np.where(X_test['MA_cross']>0,1,-1)
print (classification_report(ma_cross , y_test))
```

	precision	recall	f1-score	support
-1.0	0.55	0.46	0.50	114

1.0	0.41	0.50	0.45	86
accuracy			0.48	200
macro avg	0.48	0.48	0.47	200
weighted avg	0.49	0.47	0.48	200

The cross-over system without the help of ML does not do - significantly - better than a random prediction. Metrics are around 50% (0.5).

Before concluding this initial overview of what ML can bring to the design of algorithmic trading systems, it is worth noting that we have not sought to optimize the system (i.e., we have not conducted a search for optimal parameters). Furthermore, the ML algorithm used (a decision tree) is suitable but falls short of representing the current state of the art. All this means that we can hope to further improve the metrics of future algorithms that we will study together.

Meta-strategy using machine learning

A meta-strategy, within the realm of machine learning, points to a practice known as meta-learning. This concept, also termed as learning to learn, is a niche subset of machine learning. The power of meta-learning lies in its ability to enhance the performance of a learning algorithm by modifying specific aspects of that algorithm based on the results obtained from experiments.

The true brilliance of meta-learning becomes apparent in its ability to substitute hand-engineered algorithms with methodologies learned in a data-driven manner.

Consequently, when applied to trading strategies, meta-learning takes the form of a meta-strategy. The role of this framework is to leverage machine learning not only to optimize but also to adapt trading strategies in response to changing market dynamics. This translates to an adaptive and flexible approach to algorithmic trading, one that evolves in step with the market.

In effect, a meta-strategy has the potential to extract even greater value from our existing trading strategies. A meta-strategy in trading, powered by meta-learning, is a dynamic approach to optimize and evolve trading algorithms based on their performance and changing market conditions.

At its heart, meta-learning is a process that enables a model to learn from its past experiences. This means it not only analyses the input data but also its own performance and adjusts its algorithms based on the insights gained. When applied to trading systems, this concept evolves into a meta-strategy.

Meta strategy in action

Here is how it works, instead of utilizing a static trading algorithm that operates on pre-defined rules, a meta-strategy uses a learning algorithm. This learning algorithm assesses the performance of the trading strategy in different market scenarios, understanding its strengths and weaknesses. It then **adapts the trading strategy based on this learned knowledge**, making it more robust and effective.

For example, a trading strategy may perform well during high-volatility periods but struggle during low-volatility periods. A meta-strategy, using meta-learning, would recognize this pattern and adjust the strategy, perhaps by reducing position sizes or altering entry and exit points during low-volatility periods.

In this manner, meta-strategies can continuously optimize a trading system, enhancing its performance over time and across varying market conditions. They represent the next level of algorithmic trading, where trading systems are not just automated but are also self-improving and adaptive.

Meta trading strategy

Let us take a concrete example to try out a meta strategy written to complement an existing strategy. To do this, let us take the strategy of returning to the mean of detection of overbought and oversold shares. We described the principle in the previous section.

Idea of the strategy with meta-learning:

Check whether the strategy's profit and loss can be predicted as a function of the strategy's input data.

If this is the case, we will predict the sign of the PnL before trading to send only promising trades (those with a predicted positive PnL).

To achieve this, the meta-strategy requires only minor modifications to the initial strategy.

The meta strategy takes as input the data that describes the strategy we are trying to boost. These data are as follows:

- The performance of the strategy (profit and loss)

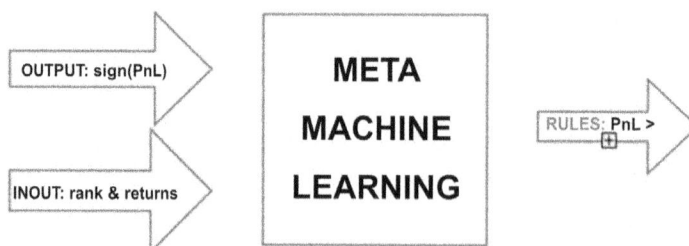

Figure 1.8: Meta machine learning

The input data for the strategy being analysed.

Here are the steps required for the computer code:

1. We need to keep a record of the profits and losses for each period (**ar_pnl** array).

```
# agregated PnL for each specific period :
ar_pnl = pd.DataFrame(np.zeros(len(ranked_ret.index)) , index =
ranked_ret.index , columns=["agg_pnl"] )
```

2. We fill in this table with the PnL for each period.

```
# Calculate transaction cost
# transaction cost in basis point:
# transaction_cost_amount = (open_price + close_price) * quantity *
transaction_cost
# transaction cost per share (broker fee : minimum 1$):
transaction_cost_amount = max(quantity * transaction_cost , 1)
profit_loss = (close_price - open_price) * quantity - transaction_
cost_amount
# apply stop loss
profit_loss = np.max([profit_loss , stp_loss])
lst_pnl.append(profit_loss)
total_profit_loss = total_profit_loss + profit_loss
ar_pnl['agg_pnl'].loc[date] = ar_pnl['agg_pnl'].loc[date] + profit_
loss
```

3. Next, we take the **features (X)** of the strategy, i.e. the returns and the ranking of these returns (rank assigned to each asset according to the size of its return).

```
# features : we merge the ranked returns and array of returns
X = pd.concat([ret , ranked_ret] , axis =1)
```

4. The target is to learn to predict. It is a binary target (**y**) depending on whether the profit and loss generated is positive or not.

```
# target : agregated PnL for each specific period -> ar_pnl
y = np.sign(ar_pnl.shift(-1))
# binary sign is either 1 or -1 not 0
y[y == 0] = -1
# last period, zero to clean missing value
y.iloc[-1] = -1
y = np.ravel(y)
```

5. The learning phase:

```
# Split the data into training and testing sets
X_train, X_test, y_train, y_test = train_test_split(X, y , test_size
=0.025,shuffle = False)


clf = RandomForestClassifier()
clf.fit(X_train , y_train)
```

Here are the metrics associated with predicting the sign of the PnL:

	precision	recall	f1-score	support
-1.0	0.40	0.61	0.48	36
1.0	0.67	0.46	0.54	61
accuracy			0.52	97
macro avg	0.53	0.54	0.51	97
weighted avg	0.57	0.52	0.52	97

The algorithm finds prediction patterns for the positive class (+1 : the positive Profit & Loss). The ratio of correct predictions to false predictions is equal to 2/3 (0.67) which is above average and of course above the random prediction.

All that remains is to plug in the filter formed by the meta-rule.

Before each trade, we check whether the trade has a chance of generating a positive profit. Here is how we proceed, the information about the forthcoming trade is sent to the prediction function (**predict_proba**) associated with the trained algorithm. This function returns a probability that the trade will generate a profit. This probability filters trades (meta-rule) and only allows trades with a winning potential. We send only the PnL that exceeds the 50% threshold (probability of generating a positive profit):

```
# open a trade if the ML model allows it ....
if clf.predict_proba(pd.DataFrame(X.loc[date].values.reshape(1,-1) ,
columns=X.columns))[0,1] > 0.5:
        print("ML OK for this trade")
        lst_pnl_meta_strat.append(profit_loss)
else:
        lst_pnl_meta_strat.append(0)
```

At the same time, we keep track of the PnL of the strategy, which is not filtered by a meta-rule (**not meta curve**). We have these two equity curves in the following graph:

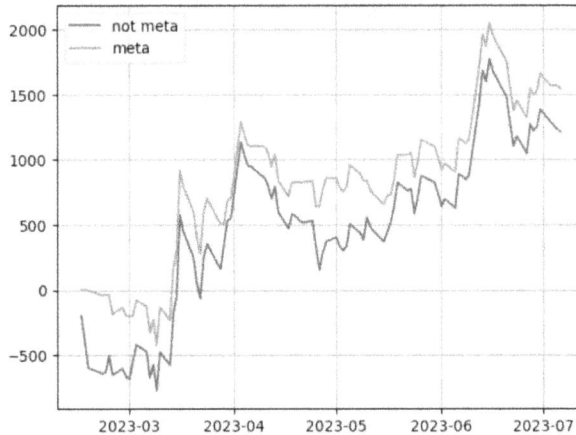

Figure 1.9: *Meta trading strategy*

The meta-rule works. The drawdowns of the filtered strategy are lower, and the profits are higher. The difference between the two curves is not spectacular, but once again, there is no search for optimal parameters or fine-tuning.

Conclusion

By the end of this chapter, it is our hope that you now have a solid grounding in algorithmic trading and the role of machine learning within this space. We have journeyed from the birth and evolution of algorithmic trading, understanding its types and strategies, through to the significance of machine learning and its impact on trading practices.

We have navigated the waters of momentum to statistical arbitrage strategies, recognized the potential of machine learning to discern trends and mean-reversion patterns, and even touched on the emerging sphere of meta-learning. This understanding sets the stage for you to dig deeper into the applications of machine learning within the context of algorithmic trading.

In the next chapter, we will look at the spectrum of data used in AI algorithms for algorithmic trading, emphasizing economic and fundamental numerical data and non-traditional data sources. A key focus of this chapter will be to unravel the basic principles of back-testing, a crucial element for evaluating and refining trading strategies. It aims to equip the reader with a solid understanding of how these principles, coupled with the appropriate use of data, can enhance the effectiveness of algorithmic trading systems.

References

1. *Statistical arbitrage: Algorithmic Trading Insights and Techniques, Andrew Pole.*

2. *Algorithmic trading, Whiley Trading Series, Ernest P. Chan.*

3. *Pairs trading: Quantitative Methods and Analysis, Whiley Finance, Ganapathy Vidyamurthy.*

4. *A Machine Learning based Pair Trading Investment Strategy, Springer, Sarmento and Horta.*

5. *Optimal mean reversion trading: Mathematical Analysis and Practical Applications, Tim Siu-Tang, Xin Li.*

Join our book's Discord space

Join the book's Discord Workspace for Latest updates, Offers, Tech happenings around the world, New Release and Sessions with the Authors:

https://discord.bpbonline.com

## CHAPTER 2

Data Feed, Backtests, and Forward Testing

Introduction

In this chapter, we will discuss the critical aspects of algorithmic trading with machine learning, emphasizing the types of data utilized in feeding AI algorithms and the core principles of backtesting and forward testing.

It pinpoints both economic and fundamental data as well as the price of financial assets traded on the markets, such as high, low, close, and opening prices, as vital inputs. It accentuates the variable time intervals used in trading, highlighting the adaptability required in algorithmic models. Furthermore, it urges readers to think beyond traditional data sources and consider unorthodox data, from social media sentiment to geopolitical events, which can potentially provide unique and predictive insights into market behavior.

It highlights the significance of data preprocessing, the procedure of refining data before feeding it into a model, which includes addressing missing data and outliers and encoding categorical data.

Structure

In this chapter, we will cover the following topics:

- Data feed
- World Bank API

- Federal Reserve Economic Data
- Financial modeling prep fundamental data API

Objectives

This chapter discusses the fundamentals of data feeds, backtests, and forward testing. Beginning with understanding the role of data feeds in financial analysis, the chapter navigates through macroeconomic and fundamental data sources. Recognizing the increasing integration of APIs in data retrieval, it highlights the features of notable platforms like the World Bank API, Federal Reserve Economic Data API, and the Quandl Economic Data API.

The exploration extends to fundamental data, discussing the attributes and benefits of tools such as the Tiingo Fundamental Data API and the Financial Modelling Prep Fundamental Data API. A noteworthy segment introduces the principles of a quantamental investing model, emphasizing the symbiotic relationship between data feeds and quantamental strategies.

The chapter also underscores the relevance of **Open-High-Low-Close** (**OHLC**) price data in financial endeavors. Moving forward, it touches upon the significance and challenges of leveraging reports, studies, and unstructured data. The entire discussion serves as a comprehensive guide for readers to understand the multifaceted world of financial data.

Data feed

The world of algorithmic trading is incredibly diverse, underpinned by a vast array of data sources that form the backbone of trading algorithms. One of the crucial aspects of building robust and reliable trading models lies in understanding and selecting the most appropriate types of data.

The primary data sources utilized in algorithmic trading can be broadly categorized as economic and fundamental numerical data. These datasets provide quantifiable, measurable insights into the economic landscape and company-specific performance indicators, which form the bedrock of many trading strategies.

The other most common type of data used as input for machine learning algorithms is the asset price traded on the financial market (the opening and closing price) and its basic descriptive statistics, such as the highest and lowest prices recorded.

We will describe these two categories of data in more detail in the following paragraphs. Let us start with economic data and fundamental data.

Macroeconomic and fundamental data

Economic data refers to the macroeconomic indicators that reflect the health and trends of a country's economy. These include indicators such as **gross domestic product** (**GDP**), inflation rate, unemployment rate, consumer sentiment indexes, industrial production, and many others. In the financial markets, these figures are watched closely as they can provide indications of future policy actions by central banks, such as changes in interest rates, which can significantly impact asset prices.

Global macro trading strategies use macroeconomic data as their main ingredient. These strategies are implemented by hedge funds and investment funds. The investment vehicles favored by these funds is indices. These can be equity, bond, currency, property, or other indices. This means that these funds do not[1] invest in individual companies but in economic sectors or countries. The most common macro strategies are managed futures, global tactical asset allocation, and currency carry trade.

We will now present some sources of macroeconomic data that can be accessed free of charge via API to feed your automatic systems. We begin with the World Bank, then we continue with Federal Reserve Economic Data, and finally, we end this tour of quality data providers with Quandl.

World Bank API

Let's us examine an example of the World Bank's API[2]. The aim is to show how to query this free, high-quality data source to retrieve economic data for the United States.

First, install the World Bank's API **wbdata** if you do not already have one:

```
try :
  import wbdata
except ModuleNotFoundError as e:
  print(e)
  !pip install wbdata
import wbdata
```

The following code fetches the inflation data (code: **'FP.CPI.TOTL.ZG'**) for the United States (country code: **'USA'**) and stores it in a DataFrame called **data**:

```
# Set the data parameters
indicator = {'FP.CPI.TOTL.ZG': 'Inflation'}
country = {'USA': 'United States'}
```

---

1 Of course, this is not a formal prohibition. Some global macro managers define a strategic process that begins with a choice of countries and then identifies and analyses companies belonging to sectors that, in the light of the macroeconomic outlook, seem solid. This point of view was developed by Jim Leitner (Falcon Management) who is a recognised manager of this type of strategy.

2 World Bank API: Provides access to a wide range of economic and financial indicators for countries worldwide.
API Documentation: https://datahelpdesk.worldbank.org/knowledgebase/topics/125589-developer-information

```
# Retrieve the data
data = wbdata.get_dataframe(indicator, country=country)

# chronological order
data = data.reindex(index=data.index[::-1])
data.info()
```

The **info()** function gives us summary information about this dataset:

```
<class 'wbdata.api.WBDataFrame'>
Index: 63 entries, 1960 to 2022
Data columns (total 1 columns):
 #   Column      Non-Null Count  Dtype
---  ------      --------------  -----
 0   Inflation   63 non-null     float64
dtypes: float64(1)
memory usage: 1008.0+ bytes
```

A basic graph gives us an overview of the information returned by the API, as follows:

```
import matplotlib.pyplot as plt
data.plot(figsize=(5,3) )
plt.grid()
```

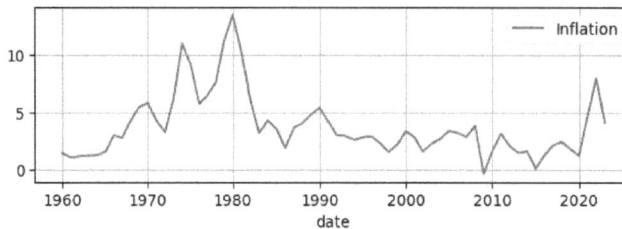

Figure 2.1: *World Bank API inflation data*

Using this example as a template, you can simply replace the economic code and/or the country to access a wide range of data. For example, you can replace the indicator code with other fundamental economic data codes to retrieve different types of data, like GDP, unemployment rate, etc.

The following is an example of using the API to retrieve GDP data for China. For GDP data, the indicator code is '**NY.GDP.MKTP.CD**,' and the country code for China is '**CHN**':

```
# Set the data parameters
indicator = {'NY.GDP.MKTP.CD': 'GDP'}
country = {'CHN': 'China'}
```

The rest of the code is unchanged from the previous example, apart from an appropriate transformation (**logy=True**) to reflect the exponential trend in the data.

The code and graph corresponding to this economic growth dataset are as follows:

```
data.plot(figsize=(5,3) , logy=True)
```

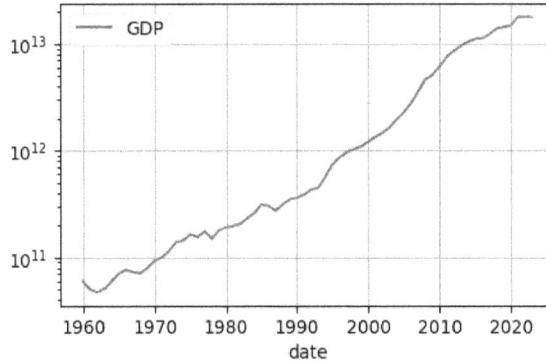

Figure 2.2: World Bank API GDP data

This example shows how easy it is to query this data source, whose reputation is indisputable.

Note: The data is distributed under a Creative Commons License.

This license allows reusers to distribute, remix, adapt, and build upon the material in any medium or format, so long as attribution is given to the creator.

Let us move on to another leading official source of fundamental economic data, the Federal Reserve Economic Data.

Federal Reserve Economic Data API

Federal Reserve Economic Data (FRED) API[3] offers economic data from the Federal Reserve, including interest rates, GDP, employment, and more. Like the previous source (World Bank), this official source offers data of indisputable quality.

First, you need to create a login and then obtain an API key[4] to send requests to this institution's server. Once you have got your key, you will need to include it in all requests, as demonstrated in the following code.

Here is an example of using the FRED API to retrieve the interest rate data for the 10-Year Treasury Constant Maturity Rate.

First, install the API if you do not already have one:

3 API Documentation: https://fred.stlouisfed.org/docs/api/fred/
4 https://fredaccount.stlouisfed.org/apikey

```
!pip install fredapi
```

```
import pandas as pd
import fredapi
```

We request the API with the code (**'GS10**') corresponding to the series you wish to obtain:

```
api_key = 'YOUR_API_KEY'
# Replace 'YOUR_API_KEY' with your actual API key from the FRED website
fred = fredapi.Fred(api_key=api_key)
# Retrieve the interest rate data for the 10-Year Treasury Constant
Maturity Rate
interest_rate_data = fred.get_series('GS10')
# Print the data
print(interest_rate_data)
```

The following is the data (**interest_rate_data**) obtained in return from the API call:

```
1953-04-01    2.83
1953-05-01    3.05
1953-06-01    3.11
1953-07-01    2.93
1953-08-01    2.95
              ...
2023-02-01    3.75
2023-03-01    3.66
2023-04-01    3.46
2023-05-01    3.57
2023-06-01    3.75
Length: 843, dtype: float64
```

Quandl economic data API

Quandl[5] is a universal data platform that effortlessly gathers and formats millions of datasets from various sources, making them accessible and ready to use. Quandl serves as a search engine for numerical data, offering financial, economic, and sociological time series datasets. It combines over 20 million financial and economic datasets from over 500 sources in a single interface. Its open platform aims to become a Wikipedia of time series, empowering users to find, visualize, and share valuable information.

For all these reasons, Quandl is a data source that you need to know about. However, Quandl is not intended to be used with real-time or intra-day data.

---

5 https://demo.quandl.com/tools/python

Here is an example to check these points and show how the API works. You do not need a personal key to get started. However, for advanced use (i.e., more than 50 calls a day), you must identify yourself.

The code for installing and importing the API to query its databases is as follows:

```
!pip install -q quandl
import quandl
```

Note: You need to know the Quandl code of each dataset you download.

```
quandl.get("FRED/GDP")
```

Date	
1947-01-01	243.164
1947-04-01	245.968
1947-07-01	249.585
1947-10-01	259.745
1948-01-01	265.742
...	...
2020-10-01	21477.597
2021-01-01	22038.226
2021-04-01	22740.959
2021-07-01	23202.344
2021-10-01	23992.355

```
300 rows × 1 columns
```

This example concludes this section. We have seen that macroeconomic data is abundantly available on the Internet. We will now look at how to obtain fundamental data relating to the activity of companies listed on the markets and how to use this data in a trading strategy.

Fundamental data

Fundamental data pertains to information about **specific companies** and their financial performance. This includes data like **earnings per share (EPS)**, **price-to-earnings (P/E)** ratio, **return on equity (ROE)**, dividends, revenue growth, and countless other factors. By analyzing these, traders can make informed predictions about a company's future performance and the possible direction of its stock price.

The relationship between these types of data and algorithmic trading is pivotal. Economists and traditional investors have used such data to make investment decisions for decades.

However, algorithmic trading has taken this to a new level, using systematic methods to exploit patterns and trends that may be apparent in these data.

Economic and fundamental data can be accessed and processed in several ways. Many financial data providers offer **application programming interfaces (APIs)** that allow traders to access real-time or historical data directly. Examples of such providers include Yahoo Finance and Quandl, which we have already experienced together. However, other data services still provide fundamental data via their APIs.

Tiingo Fundamental data API

Tiingo[6] provides (among other things) a free fundamental data service. This service only requires authentication (API key) beforehand.

The following is an example of a query that gives us the financial statements for Microsoft (ticker: MSFT) as provided in the declarations:

```
import requests
headers = {
    'Content-Type': 'application/json'
}
requestResponse = requests.get("https://api.tiingo.com/tiingo/fundamentals/
msft/statements?token="+API_KEY, headers=headers)
requestResponse.json()
```

The following is the expected data:

```
[
    {
        "date":"2019-12-31",
        "quarter":4,
        "year":2019,
        "statementData":
            "balanceSheet":[
                {
                    "dataCode":"assetsCurrent",
                    "value":167074000000.0
                },
                {
                    "dataCode":"totalAssets",
                    "value":282794000000.0
                },
```

---

6 https://www.tiingo.com/documentation/fundamentals

```
        {
            "dataCode":"acctPay",
            "value":8811000000.0
        },
        {

            «dataCode»:»assetsNonCurrent»,
            «value»:115720000000.0
        },
        {

            «dataCode»:»accoci»,
            "value":-255000000.0
        },
        {

            "dataCode":"totalLiabilities",
            "value":172685000000.0
        },
        {

            "dataCode":"taxLiabilities",
            "value":31663000000.0
        },
        {

            "dataCode":"taxAssets",
            "value":0.0
        },
        {

            "dataCode":"deferredRev",
            "value":31221000000.0
        }
    ],
    "cashFlow": [...],
    "incomeStatement": [...],
    "overview": [...]
  }
 }
]
```

Financial modeling prep fundamental data API

To complete our tour of quality data services, we can mention SEC-Edgar-downloader[7] or even **Financial Modelling Prep**[8] (**FMP**).

The following is an example[9] [10] of the latter. This service only requires authentication (API key) beforehand, as follows:

```
url = 'https://financialmodelingprep.com/api/v3/income-statement/
AAPL?limit=120&apikey='
import requests


headers = {
    'Content-Type': 'application/json'
}
requestResponse = requests.get(url + API_KEY, headers=headers)
requestResponse.json()
```

The following is the expected data:

```
[{'date': '2022-09-24',
  'symbol': 'AAPL',
  'reportedCurrency': 'USD',
  'cik': '0000320193',
  'fillingDate': '2022-10-28',
  'acceptedDate': '2022-10-27 18:01:14',
  'calendarYear': '2022',
  'period': 'FY',
  'revenue': 394328000000,
  'costOfRevenue': 223546000000,
  'grossProfit': 170782000000,
  'grossProfitRatio': 0.4330963056,
  'researchAndDevelopmentExpenses': 26251000000,
  'generalAndAdministrativeExpenses': 0,
  'sellingAndMarketingExpenses': 0,
  'sellingGeneralAndAdministrativeExpenses': 25094000000,
```

7 https://sec-edgar-downloader.readthedocs.io
8 https://site.financialmodelingprep.com
9 https://site.financialmodelingprep.com/developer/docs/#Company-Financial-Statements-As-Reported
10 https://site.financialmodelingprep.com/login

```
 'otherExpenses': -334000000,
 'operatingExpenses': 51345000000,
 'costAndExpenses': 274891000000,
 'interestIncome': 2825000000,
 'interestExpense': 2931000000,
 'depreciationAndAmortization': 11104000000,
 'ebitda': 130541000000,
 'ebitdaratio': 0.3310467428,
 'operatingIncome': 119437000000,
 'operatingIncomeRatio': 0.302887444,
 'totalOtherIncomeExpensesNet': -334000000,
 'incomeBeforeTax': 119103000000,
 'incomeBeforeTaxRatio': 0.3020404333,
 'incomeTaxExpense': 19300000000,
 'netIncome': 99803000000,
 'netIncomeRatio': 0.2530964071,
 'eps': 6.15,
 'epsdiluted': 6.11,
 'weightedAverageShsOut': 16215963000,
 'weightedAverageShsOutDil': 16325819000,
 'link': 'https://www.sec.gov/Archives/edgar/
data/320193/000032019322000108/0000320193-22-000108-index.htm',
 'finalLink': 'https://www.sec.gov/Archives/edgar/
data/320193/000032019322000108/aapl-20220924.htm'},
 {'date': '2021-09-25',
 'symbol': 'AAPL',
 'reportedCurrency': 'USD',
...}
}]
```

These examples show the impressive ease of use of these remarkable services. The data obtained with these few lines of code is the same as that used daily by investment banks and hedge funds.

Now that we know where to find the data, let us examine how it can be utilized in a machine learning algorithm.

Quantamental investing model

The fundamental data dataset we are going to use contains the financial statements of a set of companies listed on the market. This accounting data is supplemented by the stock market performance of each company. Our objective will be to predict the stock market performance that occurs in the period following the publication of the fundamental data as accurately as possible.

This type of analysis is an example of the **quantamental**[11] approach, which combines quantitative (quant) models with the fundamental (amental) expertise of financial analysts and accountants.

Let us start by presenting the dataset. This dataset can be downloaded from **https://www.kaggle.com**. This is a data science competition site. This dataset contains[12] fundamental data obtained via the FMP API, which we detailed in the previous section. The archive (zip file) contains data from 2014 to 2018. The data for each year is contained in a different dataset (**'2014_Financial_Data.csv'**, … , **'2018_Financial_Data.csv'**).

We will work on the first of these files. It contains the data for 2014. You can then carry out the same analysis on the files corresponding to subsequent years.

This dataset contains hundreds of financial indicators that are found in the 10-K filings that each publicly traded company releases yearly. This annual report provides a comprehensive overview of the company's business and financial condition and includes audited financial statements.

Once the csv file has been downloaded to your computer, the following code can be used to read the data:

```
# specify TICKER as index column
df = pd.read_csv('2014_Financial_Data.csv', index_col=0)
```

The following function **df.info()** gives us the dataset's identity card, giving its size, the type of data, and column labels:

```
df.info()
Index: 3808 entries, PG to WTT
Columns: 224 entries, Revenue to Class
dtypes: float64(222), int64(1), object(1)
memory usage: 6.5+ MB
```

This means that there are 3808 rows and 224 columns. Among these columns, one is a text column (**object type**), and the rest of the data are numeric columns. For details of the type of each column, we use **df.dtypes**:

```
df.dtypes
Revenue                    float64
Revenue Growth             float64
Cost of Revenue            float64
Gross Profit               float64
```

---

11 https://internationalbanker.com/brokerage/what-is-quantamental-investing
12 https://www.kaggle.com/datasets/cnic92/200-financial-indicators-of-us-stocks-20142018

```
R&D Expenses                 float64
                               ...
R&D Expense Growth           float64
SG&A Expenses Growth         float64
Sector                        object
2015 PRICE VAR [%]           float64
Class                          int64
Length: 224
```

The last two columns are the stock market performance data we hope to predict using the machine learning model.

The second-to-last column, **PRICE VAR [%]**, represents the variation in the share price between 1 January and 31 December 2015 following the publication of the fundamental accounting data.

The **Class** column is a binary indicator derived from the previous column. The value of this indicator is 0 (negative class) or 1 (positive class), depending on whether the variation indicated in the previous column (**PRICE VAR [%]**) is positive or negative.

This column will be used as a target to learn to predict by the classification algorithm, which seeks to predict a class or category.

Each row in the dataset represents a company. These are grouped by sector (**Sector** column) as follows:

```
print(df[['Sector','2015 PRICE VAR [%]']])
```

```
                    Sector   2015 PRICE VAR [%]
PG      Consumer Defensive           -9.323276
VIPS    Consumer Defensive          -25.512193
KR      Consumer Defensive           33.118297
RAD     Consumer Defensive            2.752291
GIS     Consumer Defensive           12.897715
...                    ...                  ...
TSRI            Technology           29.362884
TZOO            Technology          -31.167763
USATP           Technology          -23.558900
WSTG            Technology            7.779579
WTT             Technology          -34.099613
[3808 rows x 2 columns]
```

Here is the distribution of companies in terms of sector:

```
df['Sector'].value_counts()
```

```
Financial Services      660
Healthcare              582
Technology              576
Industrials             501
Consumer Cyclical       457
Basic Materials         242
Real Estate             224
Energy                  221
Consumer Defensive      165
Utilities                97
Communication Services   83
```

We are now starting the data preparation phase as follows:

This phase will involve the following steps:

1. Removing outliers
2. Imputing missing data
3. Remove column
4. Label encoding
5. Prepare the target column
6. Split dataset

Let us start by removing outliers as follows:

1. **Removing outliers**: We will identify the extreme values for each column and then replace them with the quantile value **(0.95)**.

   Let us start by calculating the quantile as follows:

   ```
   # Cut outliers (extrem HIGH values)
   top_q = df.quantile(numeric_only =True, q = 0.95)
   top_q
   ```

   ```
   Revenue             2.137668e+10
   Revenue Growth      8.804800e-01
   Cost of Revenue     1.212385e+10
   Gross Profit        8.570324e+09
   R&D Expenses        1.760486e+08
   ```

```
                    . . .
Debt Growth                 1.876595e+00
R&D Expense Growth          7.013900e-01
SG&A Expenses Growth        9.633700e-01
2015 PRICE VAR [%]          5.701303e+01
Class                       1.000000e+00
Name: 0.95, Length: 223, dtype: float64
```

The rest of the method is in the following code. We use the missing data (**type np.nan: not a number**) as a marker to identify them unambiguously and then replace (**df.fillna**) them with the accepted value.

```
# identify outliers -> replace outlier values by Nan -> replace Nan
by top_q values
outliers = df > top_q
df[outliers] = np.nan
df.fillna(top_q , inplace = True)


We proceed in the same way for the extrem low values :
# Cut outliers (extrem LOW values)
top_q = df.quantile(numeric_only =True, q = 0.05)
# identify outliers -> replace values by Nan -> replace Nan by top_q
values
outliers = df < top_q
df[outliers] = np.nan
df.fillna(top_q , inplace = True)
```

2. **Imputing missing values**: In the next step, for each column, we replace (**fillna** function) the missing values with the median (**transform('median')**) for the sector (**groupby**).

   This is the method recommended and followed by accountants and financial analysts:

   ```
   df.fillna(df.groupby('Sector').transform('median') , inplace = True)
   ```

3. **Remove column**: Column labeled **2015 PRICE VAR [%]** is not known in advance.

   Care must be taken not to introduce a data leak. In other words, information that is not available when the model is run. Consequently, this column must not be shown to the algorithm and must not be part of the model input. We remove the column from the list of model inputs and store it for future use:

   ```
   y_price_var = df.pop('2015 PRICE VAR [%]' )
   ```

   The next step is label encoding.

4. **Label encoding**: Label encoding consists of replacing each alphanumeric (text) categorical data value with a numeric code. In other words, a number. The reason for this is that most machine learning algorithms only accept numbers as input data and produce an error message for alphanumeric (text) data. The encoding to be performed concerns the '**Sector**' column. Label encoding consists of replacing each alphanumeric (text) categorical data value with a numeric code. In other words, a number. The reason for this is that most machine learning algorithms only accept numbers as input data and produce an error message for alphanumeric (text) data. The encoding to be performed concerns the '**Sector**' column.

The following is a list of the values found in this column:

```
lst_sector = list(np.unique(df['Sector']))
lst_sector
['Basic Materials',
 'Communication Services',
 'Consumer Cyclical',
 'Consumer Defensive',
 'Energy',
 'Financial Services',
 'Healthcare',
 'Industrials',
 'Real Estate',
 'Technology',
 'Utilities']
```

This list is encoded using a **LabelEncoder** object from the Scikit-Learn machine learning API, which we used in the previous chapter:

```
from sklearn.preprocessing import LabelEncoder
lbl = LabelEncoder()
# learn the encoding
lbl.fit(lst_sector)
# apply this encoding (transform)
df['Sector'] = lbl.transform(df['Sector'])
```

The result of the encoding can be seen in the following code:

```
dict(zip(lst_sector , lbl.transform(lst_sector) ))
{'Basic Materials': 0,
 'Communication Services': 1,
 'Consumer Cyclical': 2,
 'Consumer Defensive': 3,
```

```
      'Energy': 4,
      'Financial Services': 5,
      'Healthcare': 6,
      'Industrials': 7,
      'Real Estate': 8,
      'Technology': 9,
      'Utilities': 10}
```

5. **Prepare target column:** The penultimate step is to prepare the target column (y) that the algorithm will learn to map from the inputs to this target. This target column is the sign of the return (the class to which it belongs: positive or negative):

```
y = df.pop('Class')
```

6. **Split data**: All that remains is to separate the data into two sets: learning and test. As we mentioned in the previous chapter[13], only the training data (subset **X_train**) is used during the learning phase:

```
from sklearn.model_selection import train_test_split
X_train , X_test , y_train , y_test = train_test_split(df , y ,
shuffle = False)
```

Training phase

We chose **Random Forest**[14], a high-performance algorithm likely to yield accurate predictions without any particular calibration effort. The principle of this algorithm is to automatically construct a set of decision trees. Picture a **decision tree** as a series of yes-or-no questions guiding a choice (optimal questionnaire). Each tree learns from data to classify items, like whether to invest in this stock based on accounting data.

The following is an example of a decision tree built from the training set:

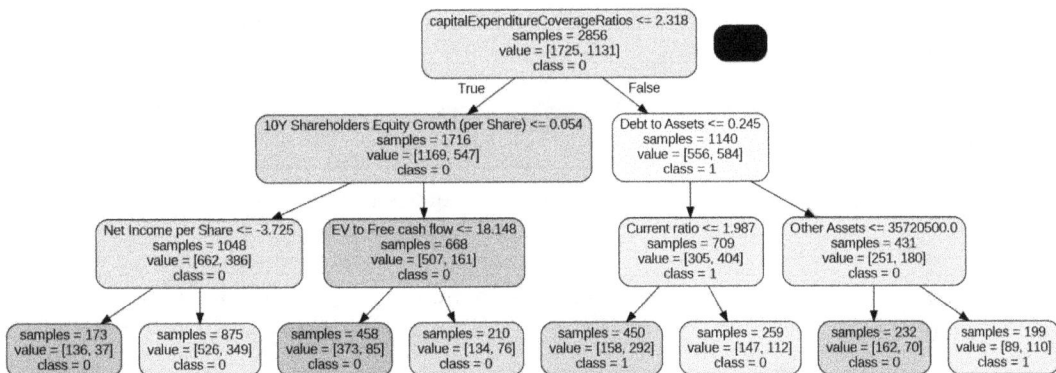

Figure 2.3: Decision tree classification model

---

13 We will come back to all these points in Chapter 5, which will be devoted to supervised learning.
14 https://en.wikipedia.org/wiki/Random_forest

The **optimal** sequence of questions and answers constructed by the learning algorithm can be seen. Here is the first question-answer: "**Is the CapitalExpenditureRatio < -2.318?**". If **False**, then the next question is, **Is the Debt to Asset ratio < 0.245...**

This automated expertise produces a questionnaire optimized to lead to the most accurate answers.

Now, envision a Random Forest as a group of these trees, a diverse crowd of decision-makers. They all learn from the data in their unique ways. When we need a decision, each tree votes on the answer. The outcome with the most votes wins, ensuring a balanced and accurate result. It is a committee of experts.

The novelty of machine learning is that each decision tree is learned, constructed, and optimized without any expert human intervention. Using the training data (**X_train**) containing the accounting and financial information for each company, the Random Forest algorithm learns to deduce the class (**y_train**) to which it belongs:

```
from sklearn.ensemble import RandomForestClassifier
# define classifier
clf = RandomForestClassifier()
# fit classifier on training data
clf.fit( X_train , y_train)
```

Once the learning process has been completed, an accuracy score[15] is calculated, counting the number of correct predictions in relation to the total number of predictions made. This score is always calculated on the test set (**X_test**). In other words, the data not seen during model training:

```
clf.score(X_test , y_test)
0.63
```

To get a more precise idea of the distribution of predictions according to each of the two classes (positive and negative), we calculate the following two metrics: **classification_report** and **confusion_matrix**.

The **classification_report** function in Scikit-Learn is used to assess the performance of a classification model.

It provides a comprehensive summary of various metrics for each class, including:

- **precision**: Accuracy of positive predictions
- **recall (or Sensitivity)**: Recall checks if the model catches the most real positives, avoiding misses
- **F1-score**: Balance between precision and recall
- **Support**: The number of samples in each class

---

15 https://scikit-learn.org/stable/modules/model_evaluation.html#accuracy-score

```
from sklearn.metrics import classification_report , confusion_matrix
```

After importing the two metric calculation functions, we use the trained model (**clf**, as classifier) to calculate (**clf.predict**) a set of predictions (**pred**) for the entire test set aforementioned:

```
pred = clf.predict(X_test)
```

The classification report will compare these predictions with the actual values (**y_test**) of the returns (positive or negative class):

```
print(classification_report(y_test , pred))
```

	precision	recall	f1-score	support
0	0.58	0.84	0.68	449
1	0.76	0.46	0.56	503
accuracy			0.63	952

As far as interpretation is concerned, the scores should be read as 'the higher, the better.' The values obtained are encouraging. The metrics are well above the random prediction (0.5: coin toss).

The negative class (negative returns) is detected less precisely than the positive. In fact, its Precision score is lower (0.58 compared with 0.76 for the positive class). On the other hand, there are a few negative returns falsely detected as positive returns. In fact, the Recall score of the negative class is high.

Positive returns are detected very precisely. There are very few false positives. In concrete terms, this would mean very few long-losing trades (expected to be positive but, in reality, is negative). 76% of the positive returns are correctly predicted.

This is what we corroborate with the confusion matrix (**confusion_matrix**). This metric takes the previous concepts and organizes them in a table called the confusion matrix:

```
# tp : true positive , fp : false positive ,tn : true negative ,fn : false
negative
tn, fp, fn, tp = confusion_matrix(y_test , pred).ravel()
print(f"FALSE PREDICTIONS : {fp} negative returns wrongly detected as
positive return and {fn} positive returns not detected")
print(f"CORRECT PREDICTIONS : {tp} positive returns correctly detected as
positive return and {tn} negative returns detected")


FALSE PREDICTIONS : 72 negative returns wrongly detected as positive return
and 277 positive returns not detected
CORRECT PREDICTIONS : 226 positive returns correctly detected as positive
```

```
return and 377 negative returns detected
```

```
confusion_matrix(y_test , pred)
array([[377,  72],
       [277, 226]])
```

Optimize hyperparameters

Although the performance of this algorithm is quite satisfactory, we are going to try to improve it. To achieve this, we will optimize a specific type of parameter known as **hyperparameters**. The algorithm parameters were optimized during the learning phase. Parameters that are not automatically optimized during this phase are called hyperparameters. Hyperparameters are settings of a machine learning algorithm that we choose before training. These hyperparameters adjust the algorithm's structure and influence how the model learns from the data. Picking good hyperparameters is crucial for the model's performance.

Examples include the number of trees in a random forest. However, we will leave it unchanged. On the other hand, we are going to optimize the hyperparameter called **max_depth** in the Scikit-Learn API. It represents the depth of each expert's knowledge:

```
from sklearn.model_selection import GridSearchCV , ParameterGrid
grid = {'max_depth' : [None , 5 , 15 , 30],
        'min_samples_split': [ 5, 10 , 15],
        'min_samples_leaf': [1, 2, 4]}
```

Here again, we are using the fantastic tools of the Scikit-Learn API. **GridSearchCV**, as its name suggests, allows you to conduct an exhaustive search, within a given range (grid), for the best possible parameter:

```
clf = GridSearchCV(estimator= RandomForestClassifier(),
                   cv = 2,
                   param_grid = grid,
                   n_jobs = -1,
                   scoring = 'f1',
                   verbose = 2)
```

clf.best_params_ and clf.best_estimator_ contains the search results:

```
clf.best_params_
{'max_depth': 30, 'min_samples_leaf': 1, 'min_samples_split': 10}
```

```
clf.best_estimator_
RandomForestClassifier
```

All that remains is to make a series of predictions on the Test data to get an idea of the model's performance on fresh data.

We buy the stocks (long position) whose returns are predicted to be positive, and we sell (short position) those whose returns are predicted to be negative.

The graph shows the result of an investment (long position) in all the stocks on the panel as follows:

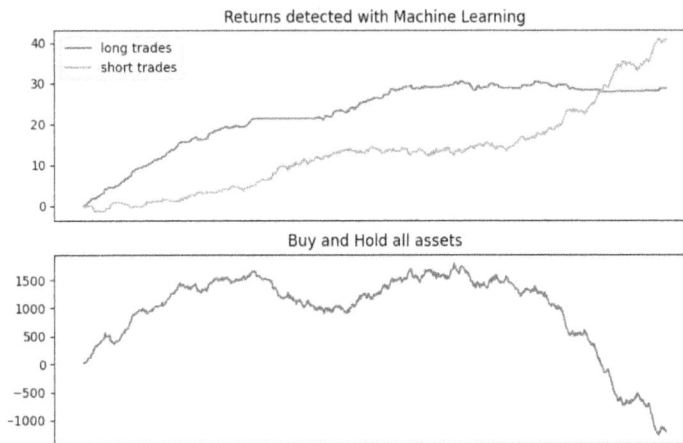

Figure 2.4: Machine learning vs Buy-and-Hold trading strategy

This exhaustive study of machine learning on accounting data gives us some promising results. This completes the demonstration devoted to machine learning on fundamental accounting and financial data.

Another prevalent form of data utilized as input for machine learning algorithms involves the asset's trading price (both opening and closing) in the financial market, along with statistics like the highest and lowest recorded prices.

Open-High-Low-Close price

These OHLC data, which you are no doubt familiar with, are the most widely used and are a natural ingredient for machine learning algorithms. We have already started to experiment with this data in the previous chapter. As before, we are using the Yahoo Finance API, which stands out for its ease of use:

```
import pandas as pd
import numpy as np
import yfinance as yf
yf.pdr_override()

symbol = 'NVDA'
```

```
ticker = yf.Ticker(symbol)
#Valid intervals: [1m, 2m, 5m, 15m, 30m, 60m, 90m, 1h, 1d, 5d, 1wk, 1mo,
3mo]
df = ticker.history(period='1000d', interval='1d')
```

The following are the daily opening and closing prices for NVIDIA's NYSE-listed shares, plotted in the graph as shown:

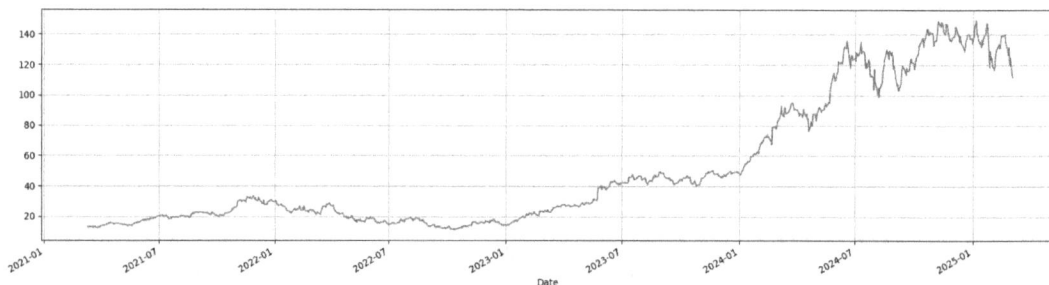

Figure 2.5: Close price NVDA

The API provides us with the highest and lowest data for each interval.

```
df.info()
DatetimeIndex: 1000 entries, 2019-09-04 00:00:00-04:00 to 2023-08-23
00:00:00-04:00
Data columns (total 7 columns):
 #   Column         Non-Null Count   Dtype
---  ------         --------------   -----
 0   Open           1000 non-null    float64
 1   High           1000 non-null    float64
 2   Low            1000 non-null    float64
 3   Close          1000 non-null    float64
 4   Volume         1000 non-null    int64
 5   Dividends      1000 non-null    float64
 6   Stock Splits   1000 non-null    float64
```

Introduce variable bars

Relying solely on OHLC price data can be limiting. To gain a deeper understanding of market dynamics, traders are turning to variable bar constructions. Unlike traditional time-based bars, variable bars adapt to market conditions. They dynamically adjust their size and frequency based on factors like volume, volatility, or other indicators. This allows for a more nuanced representation of price movements and patterns, enabling traders to capture insights that might be missed with fixed-time intervals. Variable bars open the door to more sophisticated trading strategies and enhanced decision-making.

Traditional data sources can also be extended. Readers are encouraged to expand their perspectives beyond conventional data sources and explore unconventional ones, like social media sentiment and geopolitical events. These sources could offer distinctive and anticipatory insights into market trends.

Report, studies, and unstructured data

We live through a period characterized by an explosion in the volume of data captured in all our daily activities.

Naturally, this data can be used as an input ingredient for predictive machine learning algorithms. This data, which is far more original than OHLC, includes:

- App Usage
- Credit / Debit Card
- Data Aggregator
- Data Broker
- Email / Consumer Receipts
- Geo-location
- Other
- Point of Sale
- Mobile phone traffic data
- Public Data
- Satellite
- Sell-side
- Social / Sentiment
- Survey
- Weather
- Web Data
- Web Traffic

Of course, this data is more challenging to acquire than the very abundant OHLC data. However, the additional difficulty will be offset by the originality and wealth of information contained in these data, which are off the beaten track.

A very interesting entry point (aggregator) is alternativedata.org[16].

This site lists a whole host of suppliers of this new type of data, such as:

16 https://alternativedata.org/data-providers/

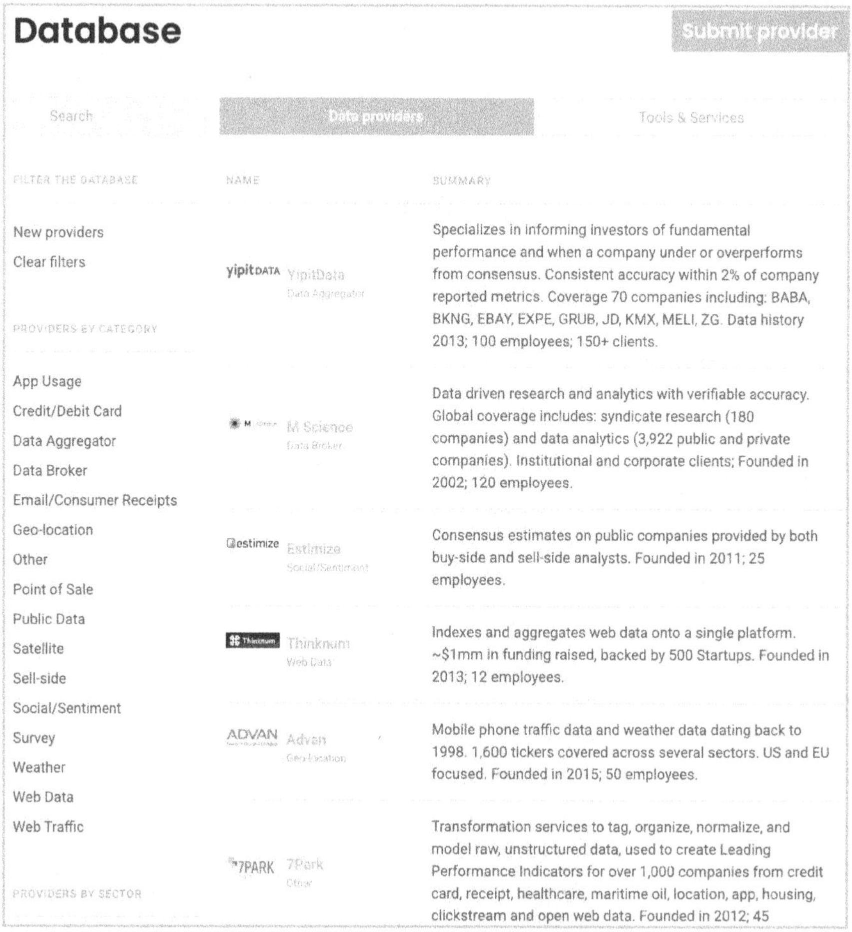

Figure 2.6: Alternativedata.org

Conclusion

In this chapter, we covered the basics of data management for algorithmic trading. We explored key data sources, such as economic and fundamental, and financial market data using APIs. Pre-processing techniques were discussed to ensure clean data sets. We provided a detailed example of quantamental investing, which blends financial analysis with machine learning. Finally, we touched on alternative data sources, such as social media sentiment and unstructured data, for unique predictive opportunities and set the stage for back and forward testing.

In the next chapter, we will understand the specifics of backtesting and forward testing and how they play a vital role in algorithmic trading. As we progress, we will understand more about how to select, process, and use different types of data effectively, enabling you to build more robust and potentially profitable trading strategies.

## CHAPTER 3

Optimizing Trading Systems, Metrics, and Automated Reporting

Introduction

This chapter focuses on optimizing trading systems for maximum performance. By leveraging advanced tools like Hyperopt, traders can enhance their strategies, experiment with new approaches, and uncover valuable insights to improve their models.

The selection of metrics plays a critical role, guiding traders in making well-informed decisions. Effective risk management and thoughtful metric selection are essential for evaluating models thoroughly and achieving long-term success.

Additionally, automated reporting, made efficient through Python libraries, enables the transformation of trading data into actionable insights.

Structure

In this chapter, we will cover the following topics:

- Designing a trading system
- Improving trading systems
- Selecting metrics for trading systems
- Automated trading reports

Objectives

Our primary focus is on designing and refining an algorithmic trading strategy. Our journey starts with selecting a classifier responsible for adeptly predicting future returns.

This chapter aims to establish a solid foundation for the trading system by leveraging the classifier's capabilities, optimizing hyperparameters to enhance the strategy's robustness, analyzing the strategy's performance using detailed risk and performance metrics, and presenting the findings through industry-standard reporting tools.

Designing a trading system

This chapter will focus on the algorithm tailored to classify future bars. Our journey will encapsulate the entire process, from data inception to the final reporting of a learned and evaluated model characterized by its performance and risk metrics.

The roadmap includes the following:

- Preparing data
- Undertaking feature engineering
- Training with an ensemble of competitive models
- Gauging the model through performance and risk metrics
- Comprehensive reporting

Preparing data

A word on the analysis data. We have chosen to ground our investigations using the Microsoft (MSFT ticker) data, recorded at 5-day intervals, amassing a total of 5000 days. The 5-day interval separating the quotes allows us to explore a weekly time horizon. The feed comes from the Yahoo! Finance library, which we have used many times.

The following graph shows this data:

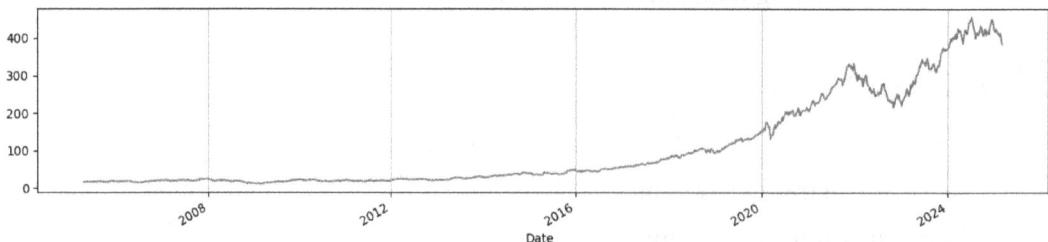

Figure 3.1: *Weekly closing prices of Microsoft Share (in the log)*

Undertaking feature engineering

In this process, we execute two key operations sequentially:

- **create_lag_past_values():** This function augments the dataframe with lagged price values from preceding periods. For every price column (OHLC), a new column with these lagged values is added. The naming convention for these new columns involves appending a suffix, indicating the lag period, to the original column name. For instance, **_1** indicates a lag of one period, **_2** denotes two periods, and so on[1]:

- **return_past_values():** This function transforms all price data into consecutive returns. For each of the price columns, a corresponding return column is introduced. These new columns are aptly named by appending the suffix **_ret** to the original column name as follows:

Together, these operations, incorporating lagged values and calculating returns, constitute our **feature engineering** step. This prepares the patterns that our analysis algorithms will utilize to predict future returns. We will learn more about this crucial stage in *Chapter 6, Improving Model Capability with Features,* which is entirely devoted to feature engineering.

Feature correlation

In the field of algorithmic trading, understanding feature correlation is essential. Correlated features can introduce redundancy into the data, leading to overfitting and reducing the ability of the model to **generalize**.

When algorithms encounter features that echo similar information, they can assign excessive importance to those intertwined features, skewing results. This is particularly vital for linear models like linear regression and tree-based algorithms like decision trees and random forests, where correlated features can result in biased or inflated feature importance. To ensure robustness and maintain the integrity of the model's predictive power, it's essential to identify and eliminate highly correlated features, thereby streamlining the input and enhancing model efficiency.

Detecting and eliminating correlated features

Traditional Pearson correlation provides insight into linear relationships but may miss non-linear associations. Enter **Spearman's rank** correlation, which identifies monotonic relationships, and **mutual information**, capturing both linear and non-linear dependencies. These alternatives are critical because real-world financial data often exhibits non-linear behavior. Scikit-learn offers tools like `VarianceThreshold` and `SelectKBest` for feature selection, and the `correlation_matrix` for visual examination. Additionally, libraries like **feature-engine**[2] provide advanced techniques for handling correlated variables.

---

1 We arbitrarily set the number of delays at 5 (without looking for any optimum)

2 https://feature-engine.trainindata.com

Embracing these strategies and diversifying correlation metrics ensures that your model is receiving the most informative, non-redundant inputs, optimizing its predictive potential.

The following code displays the correlation matrix before the phase of eliminating correlated features:

```
import seaborn as sns
# Calculate the correlation matrix for the features
correlation_matrix = df_lag.corr()
# Create a mask for the upper triangle of the correlation matrix
mask = np.triu(np.ones_like(correlation_matrix, dtype=bool))
# Plot the correlation matrix
plt.figure(figsize=(15, 10))
sns.heatmap(correlation_matrix, mask=mask, cmap='coolwarm', vmax=1, vmin=-
1, center=0, annot=False, fmt=".2f")
plt.title('Correlation Matrix of Features')
plt.show()
```

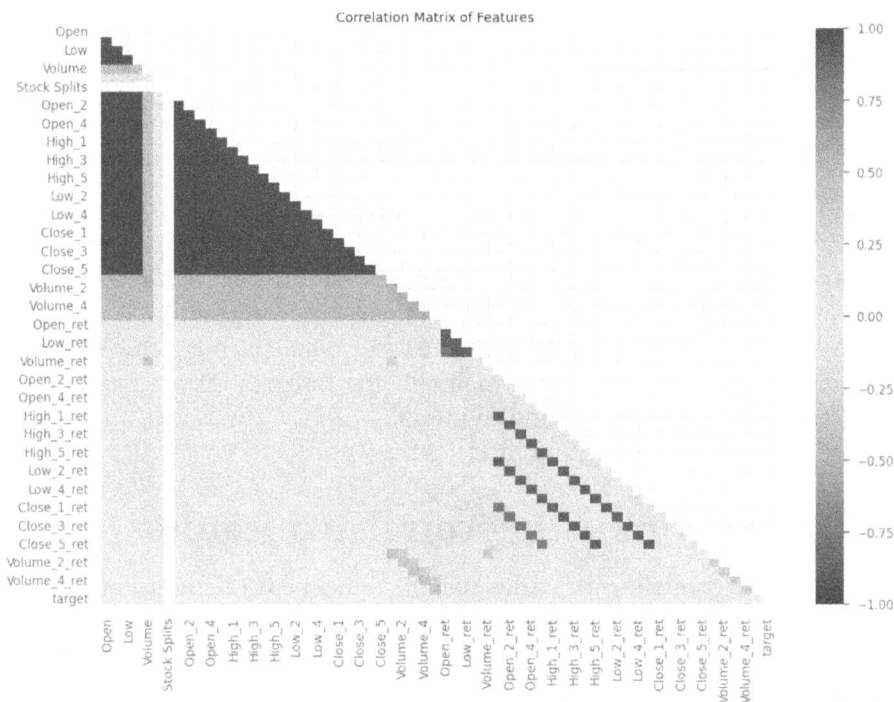

Figure 3.2: Correlation matrix of features before prunning

The correlation matrix highlights relationships between features in the dataset, with a red gradient indicating strong positive correlations. Features that are highly correlated, as indicated by the red regions, provide redundant information. These highly correlated variables are removed to reduce multicollinearity and improve the interpretability and efficiency of the model.

Let us continue with the prunning algorithm, which consists of eliminating features whose correlation exceeds the admissible value (threshold of `0.9`):

```
# Identify features that are highly correlated
to_drop = []
for i in range(len(correlation_matrix.columns)):
    for j in range(i):
        if abs(correlation_matrix.iloc[i, j]) > 0.9:
            colname = correlation_matrix.columns[i]
            if colname not in to_drop and not colname.endswith('_ret') :
                to_drop.append(colname)
# Drop the highly correlated features
df_lag.drop(columns=to_drop , inplace =True)
```

The effect of pruning is checked using the matrix of correlated features as previously discussed. Even if there are still traces of correlation, we can see in the following graph that the remaining correlations are much more acceptable than those observed previously:

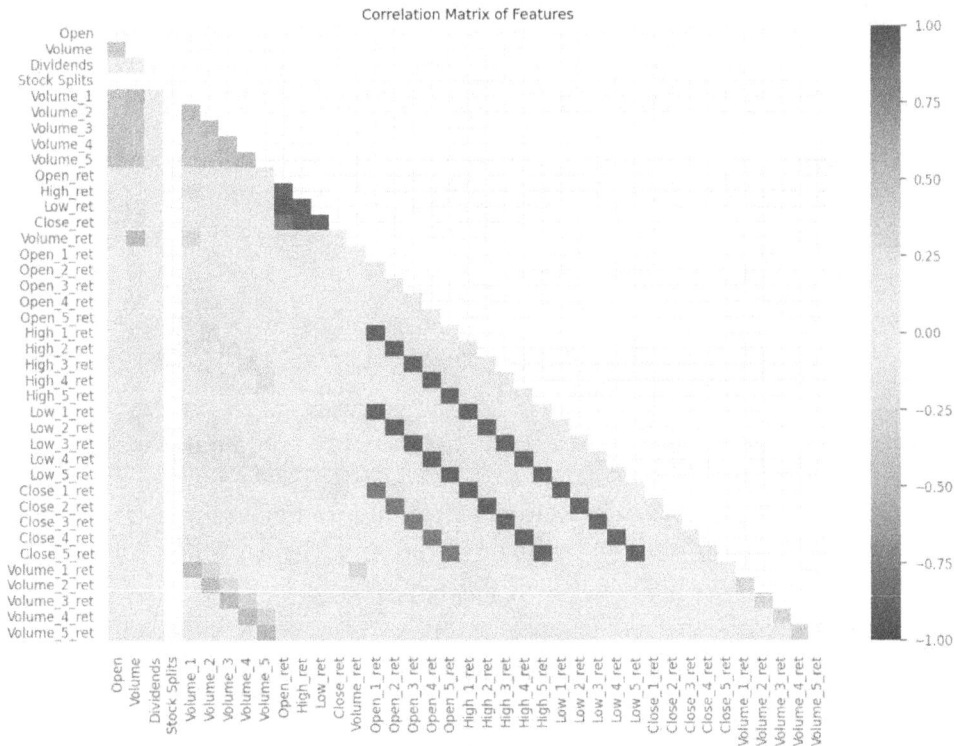

Figure 3.3: Correlation matrix of features after prunning

Missing values and target column

With a modern, powerful library such as **Pandas**, dealing with missing values becomes a quick and easy formality.

We then go on to define the column that we are going to define as the target to learn to predict:

```
# predict 'lag_predict' ahead in advance
lag_predict = 1
# predict 'lag_predict' ahead in advance
df_lag.dropna(inplace = True)
# classify returns next day (shift = -1) : negative->-1 ; positive-> +1
df_lag['target'] = np.where(df_lag['Close_ret'].shift(-lag_predict) >= 0 ,
1 , -1)
```

The previous line of code is probably one of the most important. It defines the class of problem we are dealing with (i.e., classification problem, the states of the world are **+1** or **-1** depending on the sign of the return) and designates the target column (**target**) to be learned to predict.

This column contains the next day's returns (**shift(-1)** function), which we will predict using today's information. This is the classic "one step ahead" prediction.

Splitting and scaling

We put the target variable in the 'y' (input) variable and the remaining in the 'X' (output) variable:

```
from sklearn.model_selection import train_test_split
y = df_lag.pop('target')
X = df_lag.copy()
X_train , X_test , y_train , y_test = train_test_split(X , y , shuffle =
False)
```

Once this has been done, we can rescale the data. For those unfamiliar with the concept, rescaling ensures that all columns of data are on a consistent scale, simplifying the analysis process for algorithms. In particular, columns detailing trading volumes can vary widely in scale compared to return columns, which typically vary by a few percentage points:

```
from sklearn.preprocessing import StandardScaler
sclr = StandardScaler()
X_train_tr = sclr.fit_transform(X_train)
X_test_tr = sclr.transform(X_test)
```

We are now ready to train a classifier to discriminate between positive and negative returns. For our initial approach, we opt for classifiers that are reasonable to train, aiming to minimize the development time. Our goal is to have one or more good classifiers that we can refine.

In the field of algorithmic classifiers, several stand out as foundational pillars, each with its own unique strengths and underlying principles:

- **Linear discriminant analysis (LDA)**: LDA projects data points onto a line, aiming to maximize the separation between categories. It's robust and often used.

- **Quadratic discriminant analysis (QDA)**: QDA, a sibling of LDA, allows for quadratic boundaries between categories, providing flexibility when classes have distinct covariance structures.

- **Logistic regression**: Despite its name, it's a classification algorithm. It models the probability that a given instance belongs to a particular category, making it particularly effective for binary classification tasks.

- **Decision trees (DT)**: As the name suggests, DTs make decisions based on asking a series of questions. They are intuitive and visual and can capture non-linear relationships. We have already tried out this algorithm in *Chapter 2, Data Feed, Backtests, and Forward Testing*.

- **Random forest (RF)**: An ensemble of decision trees, RF aggregates their outputs. This often results in increased accuracy and reduced overfitting compared to a single decision tree.

- **Naive Bayes**: Based on Bayes' theorem, it assumes feature independence, making it especially efficient for large datasets.

These algorithms are excellent starting points due to their interpretability, ease of implementation, and historical effectiveness. The import and algorithm definition code:

```
from sklearn.discriminant_analysis import (LinearDiscriminantAnalysis as
LDA,QuadraticDiscriminantAnalysis as QDA)
from sklearn.tree import DecisionTreeClassifier
from sklearn.linear_model import LogisticRegression
from sklearn.naive_bayes import GaussianNB
from sklearn.ensemble import RandomForestClassifier, VotingClassifier


clf1 = LDA()
clf2 = QDA()
clf3 = RandomForestClassifier()
clf4 = GaussianNB()
clf5 = LogisticRegression()
clf7 = DecisionTreeClassifier()
lst_clf= [('lda',clf1), ('qda',clf2),  ('nb',clf4),('lr',clf5) ,
('rf',clf3) , ('dt',clf7)]
```

We run the training (**fit**) for all the algorithms in the list **lst_clf**:

```
for tpl in lst_clf:
  clf_base = tpl[1]
  clf_name = tpl[0]
  clf_base.fit(X_train , y_train)
  clf_sc = np.round(clf_base.score(X_test , y_test) , 2)
  print(f"classifier {clf_name} -> accuracy score = {clf_sc}")
```

Here are the global accuracy scores (**clf_base.score**) measured on all the algorithms in the test set:

```
classifier lda -> accuracy score = 0.51
classifier qda -> accuracy score = 0.43
classifier nb -> accuracy score = 0.59
classifier lr -> accuracy score = 0.49
classifier rf -> accuracy score = 0.55
classifier dt -> accuracy score = 0.49
```

Features selection

Following our initial iteration, we aim to enhance the prediction accuracy through **feature selection**. This phase identifies (**sorted** variable) and retains only the most influential features (**k_best**). In a conservative approach, the goal is to achieve similar prediction capabilities with fewer features, while a more ambitious approach seeks to improve performance using a **trimmed feature** set.

Why prioritize feature reduction? A streamlined feature set simplifies the model's task, leading to both enhanced accuracy and more straightforward subsequent implementation:

This selection is based on a score (**clf_base.feature_importances_**) calculated during the development of the **decision tree** algorithm:

```
sorted = np.argsort(clf_base.feature_importances_)
k_besk = int(40/100 * len(sorted))
X_train.iloc[: , sorted[-k_besk:]].columns


columns_to_drop = X_train.columns[sorted[:-k_besk]]
# retain only k_best features
X_train = X_train.drop(columns=columns_to_drop)
X_test = X_test.drop(columns=columns_to_drop)
```

Here are the global accuracy scores measured on all the algorithms in the test set with the selected **k_best** features:

```
classifier lda -> accuracy score = 0.58
classifier qda -> accuracy score = 0.55
classifier nb -> accuracy score = 0.56
classifier lr -> accuracy score = 0.58
classifier rf -> accuracy score = 0.57
classifier dt -> accuracy score = 0.53
```

The results from the two steps provide valuable insights into the importance of feature selection in model performance:

- Initial performance with all features:

  o **Naive Bayes (NB)** stands out with the highest accuracy of **0.59**, suggesting that the underlying assumptions of this model might be a good fit for the original feature set.

  o **LDA and logistic regression (LR)**, both linear classifiers, show similar performance around the **0.50** mark.

  o QDA notably underperforms with an accuracy of **0.43**, indicating potential overfitting or that the data doesn't suit a quadratic boundary.

  o RF demonstrates decent performance at **0.55**, while its simpler counterpart, DT, scores **0.49**.

- Performance post feature selection:

  o Every classifier sees an improvement in accuracy, underscoring the value of selecting relevant features.

  o **LDA** and **LR** see significant jumps to **0.58**, reinforcing the idea that reducing dimensionality can help linear models. Their similar performance isn't surprising given that both algorithms aim to linearly separate data, albeit with different methodologies.

  o **QDA** also improves notably, suggesting that some of the originally included features might have been introducing noise.

  o **RF** and **DT** both benefit from the feature selection, with RF still outperforming DT, highlighting the value of the ensemble method.

  o **NB**, despite an initial high performance, sees a slight drop. This could be due to the reduction of some features that the model initially found valuable.

Feature selection has proven to be critical. The improved performance of all models after retaining only the top 40% of features demonstrates the importance of using relevant predictors.

Improving trading systems

Let us move on to the next phase. We will refine our chosen models through hyperparameter optimization using HyperOpt and then merge these models into an ensemble.

Boosting models with adaptive parameters search

In our prior discussions, we touched upon the use of **SKlearn's GridSearchCV** to hone in on optimal hyper-parameters for the Random Forest in our quantamental strategy (in *Chapter 2, Data Feed, Backtests, and Forward Testing*). We stressed the importance of this stage in developing a trading strategy based on machine learning. We propose to go further and explore adaptive methods.

While **GridSearchCV** offers a systematic exploration of hyper-parameter combinations, it may not be the most time-efficient or even the most effective solution. Enter HyperOpt[3], a more nuanced tool designed for hyper-parameter tuning.

HyperOpt's true strength lies in its adaptive search process. Instead of exhaustively searching through a pre-defined list of hyper-parameters, HyperOpt deploys a probabilistic approach. It employs a technique known as the **sequential model-based optimization**. This method models the objective function, in our case, the model's performance using a probabilistic model[4], and then selects new hyper-parameters to test based on this model. The idea is to focus on hyper-parameter regions that seem promising rather than randomly scattered or predefined grids (as exposed in the following figure):

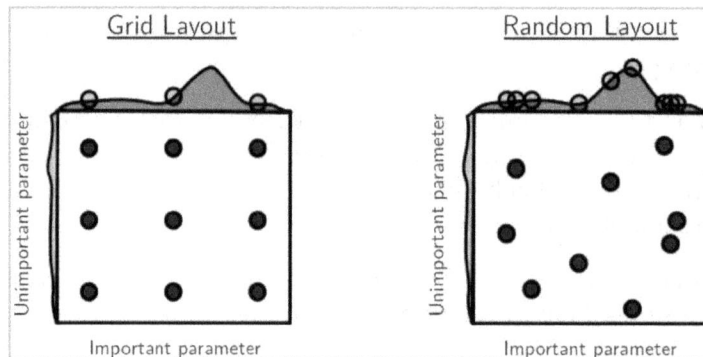

Figure 3.4: Grid and random layout for hyperparameter search

- **Difference between search methods**: Several benchmark studies have highlighted the efficiencies of HyperOpt. One key observation is its ability to converge on optimal hyper-parameters faster than traditional grid search or even random search. While RandomSearch introduces an element of randomness, potentially

3 https://hyperopt.github.io/hyperopt

4 *How to automate model tuning with HyperOpt*, M. Berk

https://towardsdatascience.com/hyperopt-demystified-3e14006eb6fa

helping explore the hyper-parameter space more diversely, HyperOpt brings a strategic approach by intelligently and adaptively navigating this space. In essence, HyperOpt offers a blend of exploration (trying new hyper-parameter regions) and exploitation (refining around the best hyper-parameters found). This balance, informed by its underlying probabilistic model, often leads to more accurate results in fewer iterations compared to other techniques.

- **Search framework with HyperOpt**: To streamline our approach, we will concurrently assess all the algorithms within a unified framework. This unified method not only simplifies the codebase but also enhances its clarity and maintainability.

The procedure can be distilled into the following steps:

1. Begin by importing the requisite libraries and methods.

2. Construct the objective function that requires optimization. This function will accept a classifier as its parameter. Our strategy involves iterating through our chosen classifiers, feeding them individually to this function. It is worth noting that we are minimizing a specific metric (refer to *Chapter 2, Data Feed, Backtests, and Forward Testing,* for an in-depth discussion on the *recall* performance metric), hence the negative sign in the objective function.

3. Chart out the search space using a dictionary in Python. This step offers ample room for creativity. One can either opt for a controlled search confined to a set of predefined values or venture into a broader exploration.

4. Initiate the search process.

5. Consolidate and present the results.

6. Finally, integrate these optimal hyper-parameters back into the classifiers

The code is as follows:

- **Step 1:** Import libraries.

```
from hyperopt import fmin, tpe, hp, STATUS_OK, Trials
from sklearn.model_selection import cross_val_score
```

- **Step 2**: Define the objective.

```
# Define the objective function that takes the classifier type as
an argument
def objective(params):
    classifier_type = params['classifier']
    if classifier_type == 'lr':
        clf = LogisticRegression(**params['lr'])
    elif classifier_type == 'dt':
```

```
        clf = DecisionTreeClassifier(**params['dt'])
    elif classifier_type == 'rf':
        clf = RandomForestClassifier(**params['rf'])
    # Add more elif conditions for other classifiers
    score = -np.mean(cross_val_score(clf, X_train, y_train,
cv=5, n_jobs=-1, scoring='recall'))
    return {'loss': score, 'status': STATUS_OK}
```

- **Step 3:** Define the space search.

```
# Define the search space for hyperparameters
space = {
    'classifier': hp.choice('classifier', ['lr', 'rf' , 'dt']),
    'lr': {# hyperparameter for Logistic Regression
            'penalty':hp.choice('penalty',['l2']),
        'C': hp.loguniform('C', -5, 5),
    },
    'rf': {
        'n_estimators': hp.choice('n_estimators', range(100,
1000, 50))
    },
    'dt':{'max_depth' : hp.choice('max_depth', [5 , 10])}
    # Add more hyperparameters for different classifiers
}
```

Unlike other classifiers in our analysis, LDA and QDA have no hyper-parameters to tune.

- **Step 4:** Perform optimization.

```
# Create a Trials object to keep track of the optimization
process
trials = Trials()
# Run the optimization using fmin
best = fmin(fn=objective, space=space, algo=tpe.suggest, max_
evals=5, trials=trials)
```

- **Step 5**: Report results.

```
from hyperopt import space_eval
print(best)  # The best hyperparameters found
100%|████████| 5/5 [00:25<00:00,  5.16s/trial, best loss:
-0.6352158390133074]
{'C': 20.908013685132712, 'classifier': 1, 'max_depth': 0, 'n_
```

```
estimators': 1, 'penalty': 0}

print(space_eval(space, best)['classifier'])
print(space_eval(space, best)['lr'])
print(space_eval(space, best)['lr']['C'])
print(space_eval(space, best)['rf'])
print(space_eval(space, best)['dt'])


lr
{'C': 109.96023525188563, 'penalty': '12'}
109.96023525188563
{'n_estimators': 100}
{'max_depth': 10}
```

- **Step 6:** Inject the best parameters in classifiers.

```
# optimized parameters (best) in each classifiers
lst_clf_opt = []
for tpl in lst_clf:
  tpl0 = tpl[0]
  tpl1 = tpl[1]
  if tpl0 == 'rf':
    tpl1 = RandomForestClassifier(space_eval(space, best)['rf']
['n_estimators'])
  elif tpl0 == 'lr':
    C = space_eval(space, best)['lr']['C']
    penalty = space_eval(space, best)['lr']['penalty']
    tpl1 = LogisticRegression(C = C , penalty = penalty)
  elif tpl0 == 'dt':
    m_depth = space_eval(space , best)['dt']['max_depth']
    tpl1 = DecisionTreeClassifier(max_depth = m_depth)
  lst_clf_opt.append((tpl0 , tpl1))
```

We will then merge these models to create an ensemble.

Ensembling modeling

Individual classifiers, no matter how finely tuned, often have their limits. They each bring a unique perspective, but can they do better together? The idea of ensemble modeling is akin to building a symphony orchestra from individual musicians. While a violin or a trumpet can make beautiful music on its own, their collective performance can offer a much richer and more harmonious experience.

The code snippet aforementioned embodies this philosophy. It starts by optimizing individual classifiers. We have explored the hyper-parameters of various classifiers, like RF, LR, and DT, and have identified their best configurations. This optimization process ensures that each model is at its peak performance before being incorporated into the ensemble.

Once optimized, these classifiers are harmonized into a cohesive ensemble using the **VotingClassifier** from **ScikitLearn**. The term *voting* here is apt; each model in the ensemble gets a **vote** on the outcome, and the final decision is a democratic one based on the majority.

The ensemble method[5], especially the **hard** voting technique used here, capitalizes on the strengths of each individual model, mitigating their individual weaknesses and often resulting in a more robust and accurate forecasting system.

Notice, in the following code, how easy this method is with scikit-learn; we pass a list of classifiers (**lst_clf_opt**), and everything else is taken care of by the API:

```
# blended algorithm: voting classifier
clf_blend = VotingClassifier( voting='hard' , estimators= lst_clf_opt)
clf_blend.fit(X_train, y_train)
clf_blend.score(X_test , y_test)
```

We have now completed the second phase, where we fine-tuned each predictor and harmonized their collective operation. Let us take a look at the following results:

	precision	recall	f1-score	support
-1	0.44	0.15	0.22	103
1	0.59	0.87	0.70	146
accuracy			0.57	249
macro avg	0.52	0.51	0.46	249
weighted avg	0.53	0.57	0.50	249

In summary, with a precision of 59% vs. 44%, the model performs much better at identifying the **1** class (positive returns) than the **-1** class (negative ones), with a notably high recall of 87% for the **1** class. However, its precision for the **-1** class needs improvement. Additionally, our system is not continuously updated with fresh data. Consider that we are assessing 2023 data using a system trained on data from four years prior. This method aids in gauging the system's resilience.

---

5 Ensemble methods can significantly reduce overfitting (variance), especially when the correlation among individual models is low. Statistically, as the number of weakly correlated components increases, the overfitting (variance) diminishes proportionally.

Equity curve

To visualize the strategy's equity curve, we merely need to incorporate some additional elements. Specifically, we must account for brokerage charges (typically about three basis points per transaction) and the gains from both long and short trades:

```
# broker fee in basis point
fee = 3 /100 /100
stop_loss = -4/100

target_ret = df_lag.loc[y_test.index , 'Close_ret'].shift(-lag_predict)
# Calculate cumulative returns for long trades (+1 predictions)
long_returns = np.where(pred_blend == 1, target_ret , 0)
# apply stop loss
long_returns = np.where(long_returns < stop_loss, stop_loss , long_returns)
cumulative_long_returns = np.cumsum(long_returns)

# Calculate cumulative returns for short trades (-1 predictions)
short_returns = np.where(pred_blend == -1, -target_ret, 0)  # We inverse
the returns for short trades
# apply stop loss
short_returns = np.where(short_returns < stop_loss, stop_loss , short_
returns)
cumulative_short_returns = np.cumsum(short_returns)

# pay fee each time position change (detect with np.diff)
brk_fee = np.where(np.diff(pred_blend) != 0 , fee , 0)
# adjust dimension with pad (add one element (zero), at the beginning)
brk_fee = np.pad(brk_fee , pad_width=(1,0))
```

Figure 3.5: Long short machine learning ensemble strategy

The strategy seems very interesting. The green line is our strategy, and the dash line is the **buy-and-hold (B&H)** strategy[6]. Moreover, we could easily apply a more conservative stop-loss policy to smooth out the inevitable drawdowns on low-frequency strategies such as this one (weekly frequency).

As a final assessment, we implement the same strategy as Microsoft's daily shares, incorporating a meta-strategy[7], as elaborated in chapter one. The results reveal the following:

The **machine learning strategy**, which employs stacked classifiers, seems to outperform the B&H strategy for a significant portion of the timeline. This indicates that the ML model was successful in capturing and predicting price movements.

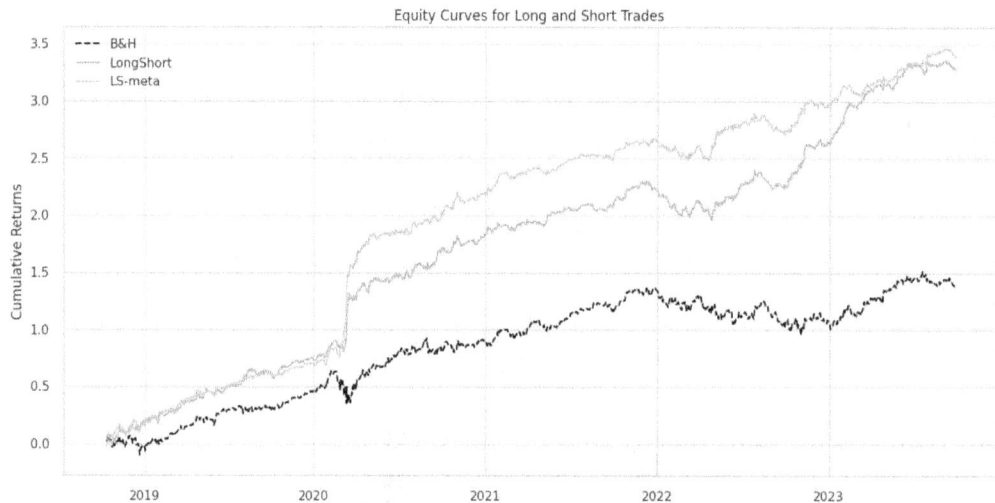

Figure 3.6: Microsoft daily strategies

The **meta strategy** shows significant outperformance compared to both the B&H and the ML strategies. This suggests that the meta strategy could be using additional information or employing a more dynamic approach to trading, allowing it to capitalize on more trading opportunities and manage risk more effectively. This strategy stands out as the most effective, indicating that a combination of strategies can lead to superior performance in this context.

We are satisfied with what we've achieved. In fact, the strategy poses no difficulty in transitioning from a weekly to a daily frequency.

---

6 This strategy represents a passive investment approach where Microsoft shares are bought and held throughout the entire period. This is typically used as a **benchmark**.

7 The meta-strategy is an advanced trading approach that employs a secondary model to predict the effectiveness of a primary classifier in specific market conditions. Instead of solely relying on a single classifier's predictions, it gauges when and how to best utilize the classifier based on the prevailing context, enhancing overall strategy robustness and adaptability.

We will now check this rigorously with the appropriate tools of modern risk management.

Selecting metrics for trading systems

A strategy's success is not just about higher returns. It is about understanding the risk undertaken, the consistency of those returns, and various other facets that together paint a comprehensive picture of performance.

This section explores the essence of evaluating trading strategies, transitioning from basic metrics like annualized return to professional gauges such as CAGR, VaR, and Sharpe ratio. By the end, you will grasp the significance of each metric, its ideal benchmarks, and how they interplay.

Ordering criteria for strategy evaluation metrics

Trading strategy evaluation demands systematic analysis to yield valuable insights and meaningful comparisons. Performance metrics span from fundamental measures to sophisticated institutional indicators, each serving specific analytical needs.

Understanding the following metrics by category helps investors select evaluation methods that match their goals and risk preferences:

- **Basics**: Metrics that give an overall sense of the performance of the strategy, suitable for all levels of investors

- **Risk-adjusted returns**: Metrics that account for the risk taken to achieve returns. This differentiates strategies that might have the same return but take vastly different amounts of risk

- **Drawdowns**: These metrics revolve around understanding the magnitude and duration of losses

- **Statistical significance**: Metrics that assess whether the strategy's performance could be due to chance

- **Risk metrics**: These metrics provide insights into the tail risks and **extreme events** the strategy might face

- **Consistency and stability**: Metrics that analyze the consistency and stability of strategy returns over time

- **Professional**: Advanced metrics are often used by institutional investors to deeply analyze and dissect strategy performance

List of statistics for evaluating a trading strategy

The following statistics represent key quantitative tools for strategy evaluation, organized by complexity and purpose. Each metric reveals distinct aspects of trading performance, starting with fundamental metrics, progressing through risk-adjusted measures, and ending with institutional-grade analytics.

- **Basics statistics**
  - **Total return**: The overall return of the strategy
  - **Annualized return**: The average yearly return
  - **Volatility (standard deviation)**: The dispersion of returns
- **Risk-adjusted returns**
  - **Sharpe ratio**: Return achieved for each unit of total risk
  - **Sortino ratio**: Return achieved for each unit of downside risk
  - **Calmar ratio**: Annualized return to maximum drawdown
- **Drawdowns:**
  - **Maximum drawdown**: Largest drop from peak to trough
  - **Average drawdown**: Average of all drawdowns
  - **Drawdown duration**: The length of time it takes to recover from a drawdown
- **Statistical significance:**
  - **T-Stat**: Assess if the strategy's returns are statistically different from zero
  - **P-value**: Probability that the observed returns are due to chance
- **Risk metrics:**
  - **Value at Risk (VaR)**: The maximum loss not exceeded with a given probability
  - **Conditional Value at Risk (CVaR)**: Expected loss given that the loss is beyond the VaR
  - **Skewness**: Measures the asymmetry of returns
  - **Kurtosis**: Measures the tail risk or extreme returns
- **Consistency and stability:**
  - **Win rate**: Percentage of trades that were profitable
  - **Average win to average loss ratio**: Average profit of winning trades to average loss of losing trades
  - **Profit factor**: Gross profit to gross loss
- **Professional:**
  - **Omega Ratio**: Return to downside risk
  - **Information Ratio**: Active return to active risk
  - **Beta**: Strategy's sensitivity to market moves

- o **Alpha**: Excess return after adjusting for beta
- o **R-squared**: How closely the strategy follows the market
- o **Treynor Ratio**: Excess return to beta
- o **Compound Annual Growth Rate (CAGR)**: Geometric progression ratio that provides a constant rate of return
- o **Downside deviation**: Volatility of negative returns
- o **Upside potential**: Measures the upside of the returns distribution
- o **Active share**: Degree of the strategy's deviation from a benchmark
- o **Tracking error**: Dispersion from the benchmark
- o **Leverage**: The amount of debt used to finance the strategy's assets

Now, we gauge the acceptable benchmarks for each metric.

The following is the acceptable order of magnitude:

- **Total Return**: Positive is good, but it depends on the duration and risk taken
- **Annualized Return**: >10% good, 5%-10% acceptable, <5% needs review
- **Volatility**: Depends on the strategy, but generally lower is better
- **Sharpe Ratio**: >1.5 very good, 1-1.5 good, <1 review
- **Sortino, Calmar Ratios**: >2 very good, 1-2 good, <1 review
- **Maximum Drawdown**: <10% very good, 10%-20% acceptable, >20% bad
- **T-Stat**: >2 indicates statistical significance
- **P-value**: <0.05 indicates statistical significance
- **VaR, CVaR**: Lower is better
- **Skewness**: Closer to 0 is normal. Positive is preferred as negative indicates tail risks on the downside
- **Kurtosis**: <3 is preferred, >3 indicates fat tails
- **Win Rate**: >60% good, 50%-60% average, <50% bad
- **Average Win to Average Loss Ratio**: >2 very good, 1-2 good, <1 bad
- **Profit Factor**: >2 very good, 1.5-2 good, <1.5 average
- **Omega, Information, Treynor Ratios**: Higher

Having taken a comprehensive look at the risk management metrics, we will now put them into practice. By computing these metrics for our system, we can ensure a thorough evaluation.

Automated trading reports

We will utilize the following libraries (ranked in ascending order of difficulty in use) to achieve this:

- **Ffn**: Financial functions for Python offers a straightforward and quick approach for visualizing returns and statistical metrics.

- **Empirical**: Common financial risk metric developed by Quantopian, builds upon pyfolio to provide in-depth risk, return, and analytical metrics.

- **QuantStats**: Portfolio analytics for Quants delivers a comprehensive suite for analyzing performance, visualizing results, and benchmarking against various statistics.

Financial functions for Python

ffn[8] is a library that contains many useful functions for those who work in quantitative finance. It stands on the shoulders of giants (Pandas, Numpy, Scipy, etc.) and provides a vast array of utilities, from performance measurement and evaluation to graphing and common data transformations.

Let us begin by installing and importing the library as follows:

```
!pip install -q ffn
import ffn
```

```
# download price data from Yahoo! Finance. By default,
# the Adj. Close will be used.
symbol = 'MSFT'
prices = ffn.get(symbol, start='2010-01-01')
```

Then, calculate statistics as follows:

```
stats = ffn.calc_stats(pd.Series(np.cumprod(1+long_returns - brk_fee) ,
index = X_test.index))
print(stats.display())
```

This instruction first gives us the basic statistics as described in the previous section. From yield to drawdown as follows:

```
Stats for None from 2018-10-11 00:00:00-04:00 - 2023-09-28 00:00:00-04:00
Annual risk-free rate considered: 0.00%
Summary:
Total Return      Sharpe  CAGR    Max Drawdown
```

---

8 https://pmorissette.github.io/ffn

```
-------------- -------- ------ --------------
-                    2.28  59.89%  -14.65%
```

```
Annualized Returns:
mtd     3m      6m      ytd     1y      3y      5y      10y     incep.
------  -----   ------  ------  ------  ------  ------  -----   --------
-5.07%  0.45%   24.40%  46.23%  62.54%  43.79%  59.89%  -       59.89%
```

Then, risk metrics and detailed drawdown statistics as follows:

```
Periodic:
        daily   monthly   yearly
------  ------- --------- --------
sharpe  2.28    2.44      1.65
mean    49.40%  48.66%    59.46%
vol     21.68%  19.98%    36.11%
skew    2.03    0.82      0.77
kurt    12.43   1.62      1.66
best    14.19%  23.82%    115.00%
worst   -2.03%  -6.07%    15.96%
```

```
Drawdowns:
max       avg       # days
-------   ------    --------
-14.65%   -1.93%    10.35
```

Then, consistency and stability as follows:

```
Misc:
--------------- -------
avg. up month   5.77%
avg. down month -3.43%
up year %       100.00%
12m up %        100.00%
--------------- -------
```

The following drawdown visualization maps the cumulative decline from peak equity, revealing the strategy's capital preservation characteristics during adverse periods. The temporal distribution and depth of drawdowns provide critical insights into risk exposure patterns and recovery dynamics that may not be apparent from aggregate performance metrics alone.

```
ax=stats.prices.to_drawdown_series().plot(grid=True,title='maxDrawDown')
```

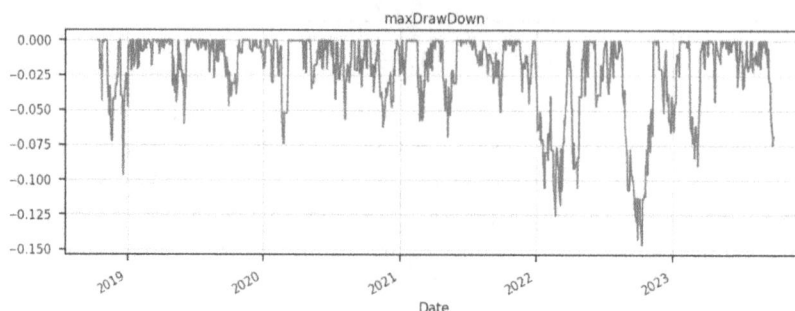

Figure 3.7: Maxdrawdown visualization

We will use the benchmarks detailed in the previous section to drill down into these metrics. This step is critical in determining our next course of action.

The following is the analysis of the trading strategy:

- **Total return**: A positive CAGR indicates the return is positive.

- **Annualized return**: At 59.89%, this is good, well above the >10% benchmark.

- **Volatility**: The strategy exhibits a volatility of 21.68% on a daily basis and 19.98% on a monthly basis. This is moderate, but generally, lower volatility is preferred.

- **Sharpe ratio**: A value of 2.28 is good, indicating the strategy has strong risk-adjusted returns.

- **Maximum drawdown**: At -14.65%, this is acceptable but approaching the upper end of the acceptable range. It means the strategy has experienced a 14.65% drop from peak to trough in its worst period.

- **Skewness**: A positive skewness of 2.03 daily and 0.82 monthly suggests that the strategy has a higher probability of large positive returns than large negative ones.

- **Kurtosis**: Values above 3 (12.43 daily and 1.62 monthly) suggest the strategy may exhibit **fat tails** or a higher likelihood of extreme events, indicating additional risk.

- **Drawdowns**: The average drawdown is -1.93 % over 10.35 days, which is quite good. This means that the average dip from a peak before a new peak is achieved is less than 2%.

- **Consistency and stability**: The average up month is at 5.77% and the average down month is at -3.43%, showing decent consistency. The 100% up year and 12m up percentages are excellent, indicating the strategy has consistently delivered positive returns over the years.

In conclusion, this strategy exhibits strong risk-adjusted returns with a high Sharpe ratio and annualized returns. While there is some risk evident in the kurtosis and max drawdown, the consistently positive yearly returns and a high Sharpe ratio suggest that the strategy is robust.

Let us move on to the next library.

Common financial risk metric

Empyrical[9] is developed by Quantopian, builds upon **Pyfolio** to provide in-depth risk, return, and analytical metrics.

As usual, install and import it as follows:

```
!pip install -q empyrical
```

Then, compute various statistics as follows:

```
from empyrical import max_drawdown, annual_return, sharpe_ratio, sortino_
ratio

# calculate the max drawdown
max_drawdown(long_returns - brk_fee)
-0.1428624776295528

drawdown = max_drawdown(long_returns - brk_fee)
ann_return = annual_return(long_returns - brk_fee)
sharpe = sharpe_ratio(long_returns - brk_fee)
sortino = sortino_ratio(long_returns - brk_fee)

print(f"Maximum Drawdown: {drawdown:.2%}")
print(f"Annual Return: {ann_return:.2%}")
print(f"Sharpe Ratio: {sharpe:.2f}")
print(f"Sortino Ratio: {sortino:.2f}")

Maximum Drawdown: -14.65%
Annual Return: 59.96%
Sharpe Ratio: 2.28
Sortino Ratio: 4.52
```

As with the previous library, ease of use presents no particular difficulties. This will also be the case for the last of our exploration of risk management libraries.

QuantStat analytical library

QuantStats[10] is a Python library that performs portfolio profiling, allowing quantitative analysts and portfolio managers to understand their performance better by providing them with in-depth analytics and risk metrics. Built on top of industry standard libraries

9 **https://github.com/quantopian/empyrical**

10 Portfolio anaytics for quantitative analysts, **https://github.com/ranaroussi/quantstats**

like pandas and numpy, **QuantStats** streamlines post-trade analysis with institutional-grade metrics. It is a Swiss Army knife for performance analysis, eliminating the need for multiple disconnected tools.

QuantStats is comprised of 3 main modules:

- **quantstats.stats** for calculating various performance metrics, like Sharpe ratio, win rate, volatility, etc.

- **quantstats.plots** for visualizing performance, drawdowns, rolling statistics, monthly returns, etc.

- **quantstats.reports** for generating metrics reports, batch plotting, and creating tear sheets that can be saved as an HTML file.

```
!pip  install -q quantstats
import quantstats as qs


# Input : Pandas Series with an equity curve compounded
serie_long_trades = pd.Series(np.cumprod(1+long_returns - brk_fee) ,
index = X_test.index)
serie_long_trades.head(3)
serie_long_trades.index = serie_long_trades.index.tz_
convert('America/New_York')
```

quantstats.stats

This computational engine calculates over 70 essential metrics, from basic ratios to complex risk-adjusted measures. The module handles time-series manipulations internally, requiring only your raw returns as input, as shown:

```
print('sharpe : ' , qs.stats.sharpe(serie_long_trades))
print('sortino : ',qs.stats.sortino(serie_long_trades))
print('mdd : ',qs.stats.max_drawdown(serie_long_trades))


sharpe :   2.2766106559178523
sortino :   4.521295932898164
mdd :   -1.0
```

Quantstats.plot

This module generates publication-quality visualizations focusing on crucial performance aspects and risk metrics. Each plot is designed for immediate pattern recognition, which is particularly useful for strategy comparison and risk monitoring as follows:

```
import warnings
import logging
```

```
# ignore matplotlib warnings (concerning fonts)
warnings.simplefilter(action='ignore', category=FutureWarning)
warnings.simplefilter(action='ignore', category=UserWarning)
logging.getLogger('matplotlib.font_manager').disabled = True


qs.plots.snapshot(serie_long_trades , benchmark = symbol , title='Machine
Learning Strategy' , show=True)
```

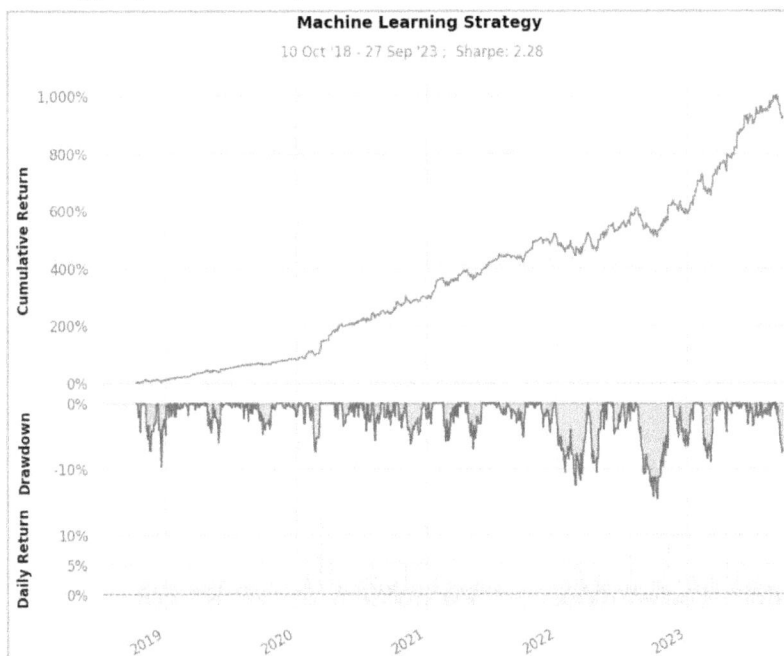

Figure 3.8: Strategy reporting with QuantStats

The high returns stem from the capitalization employed by the tool.

We will save the best for last. If you are not familiar with **QuantStats**, we recommend that you give this command a try. The reporting (HTML file) is sumptuous. All in all, these three risk management libraries provide us with free access to professional tools.

Quantstats.report

This module automates the generation of professional tear sheets similar to those used by hedge funds, combining both metrics and plots. The HTML output enables easy sharing with stakeholders while maintaining interactivity.

```
qs.reports.html(serie_long_trades , output=symbol +'-rapport.html')
```

You then need to browse your hard disk to find the HTML file at the location of the notebook. The following figure is a fragment of the file:

Cumulative Returns

Cumulative Returns (Log Scaled)

EOY Returns

Key Performance Metrics

Metric	Strategy
Risk-Free Rate	0.0%
Time in Market	86.0%
Cumulative Return	593.36%
CAGR%	30.9%
Sharpe	1.89
Prob. Sharpe Ratio	100.0%
Smart Sharpe	1.77
Sortino	3.88
Smart Sortino	3.45
Sortino/√2	2.6
Smart Sortino/√2	2.44
Omega	1.48
Max Drawdown	-23.69%
Longest DD Days	274
Volatility (ann.)	21.99%
Calmar	1.3
Skew	2.1
Kurtosis	12.67
Expected Daily	0.16%
Expected Monthly	3.28%
Expected Yearly	36.09%
Kelly Criterion	14.06%
Risk of Ruin	0.0%
Daily Value-at-Risk	-2.11%
Expected Shortfall (cVaR)	-2.11%
Max Consecutive Wins	6
Max Consecutive Losses	6
Gain/Pain Ratio	0.48
Gain/Pain (1M)	4.79
Payoff Ratio	1.93
Profit Factor	1.48
Common Sense Ratio	1.83
CPC Index	1.24

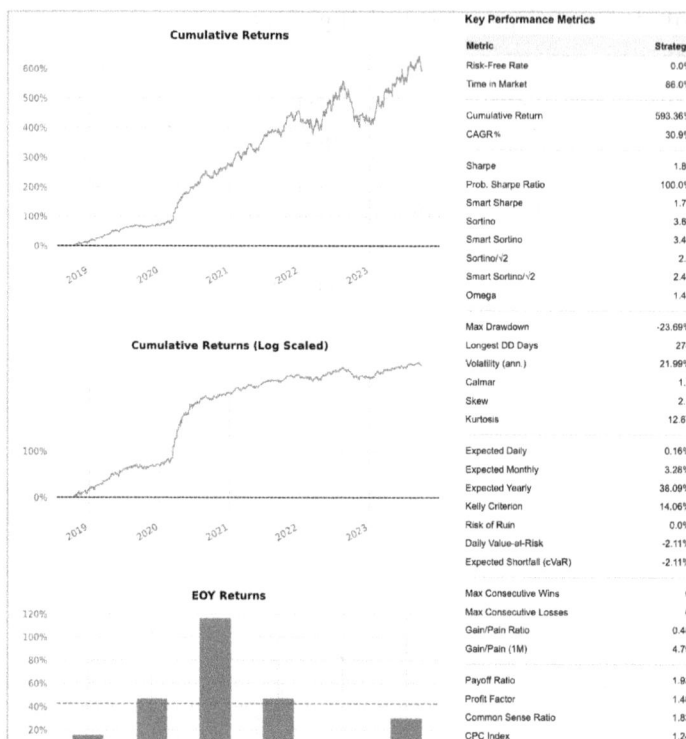

***Figure 3.9** Reporting with QuantStats*

Conclusion

This chapter provided a practical look at advanced tools, guided metric selection and risk management, facilitated insightful reporting, and provided strategies for maintaining model performance.

In the next chapter, we will demystify production-grade backtesting, covering both high-level frameworks and granular implementation details using the BackTrader library. We will also navigate through the critical aspects of strategy validation, from efficient execution to comprehensive performance evaluation, to ensure that your backtests accurately reflect live trading conditions.

References

1. *Benchmarking Hyper-parameters search methods:*

    "The Overlooked Limitations of Grid and Random Search ...and what to try instead with", Avi Chawla

    https://www.blog.dailydoseofds.com/p/the-overlooked-limitations-of-grid

2. *Ensemble modeling: "Bagging predictors", Machine Learning, Breiman, L. (1996)., 24(2), 123-140.*

CHAPTER 4

Implement Trading Strategies

Introduction

In this chapter, we will explore the wide range of algorithmic trading libraries, examine their features, and understand how to choose the best one. The focus then shifts to practical implementation, using the event-driven BackTrader library to design and test trading strategies.

We will cover the entire process, including developing a trading strategy, setting up and running backtests, and incorporating risk management. As we progress, we will enhance our strategies with advanced features such as multi-asset support and execution logic, providing traders with a well-rounded toolkit for algorithmic trading.

Structure

In this chapter, we will cover the following topics:

- Backtesting and trading libraries
- Implementing a strategy with BackTrader
- Risk management

Objectives

This chapter focuses on Python-based platforms and their key role in running advanced trading strategies. We start by introducing the most effective algorithmic trading libraries for backtesting and execution, highlighting their features and advantages. Along the way, we will outline the critical factors to consider when choosing the library and API that best fit your trading requirements.

Having laid this foundation, we will move on to practical applications with BackTrader. The chapter will then cover the basics of managing algorithmic orders, followed by a closer look at how to run a backtest with this engine. Risk management will also be a major focus. Next, we will look at evaluating performance and improving strategies. Finally, we will extend the discussion to multi-asset strategies.

Backtesting and trading libraries

Python platforms for algorithmic trading and backtesting provide traders with a wide range of libraries, each offering different tools and features. **BackTrader**[1] stands out for its versatility and ease of use, making it a go-to choice for both novice and seasoned traders.

It includes all key elements for a robust algorithmic strategy, including order types, management, monitoring, risk controls, stopping losses, and taking profits. Additionally, BackTrader supports live trading.

Zipline[2], the open-source backtesting engine powering Quantopian's IDE, operates locally and can be adapted for virtual environments and Docker containers. It inherits Quantopian's extensive functions but allows for the integration of custom data sets for more personalized backtesting scenarios. Zipline furnishes detailed backtest data, facilitating diverse visualization applications. Although Zipline ceased offering live trading features in 2017, the Zipline-live project continues to support live trading through **InteractiveBrokers**, maintaining a feature set comparable to the original Zipline.

On the other hand, **PyAlgoTrade**[3] distinguishes itself with robust support for multi-asset trading. It allows the addition of multiple data feeds and variable timeframes, catering to traders who deal with a diverse portfolio. For those seeking real-time data feeds, PyAlgoTrade offers solutions that align with the demands of high-frequency trading.

Furthermore, **Alpaca**[4], with its modern approach, provides a seamless interface with brokerages, bridging the gap between strategy development and live execution. This makes it an attractive option for traders who prioritize direct market access and real-time trading capabilities.

---

1 https://backtrader.com
2 https://zipline-trader.readthedocs.io/en/latest/index.html
3 https://gbeced.github.io/pyalgotrade
4 https://alpaca.markets

Without forgetting **QuantRocket**[5], a platform tailored for **InteractiveBrokers**[6] users, enabling both backtesting and live trading for forex and US equities. It distinguishes itself with its adaptability, supporting its proprietary Moonshot engine along with user-selected third-party engines. Instead of a conventional interface (IDE), QuantRocket leverages Jupyter notebooks to create a comparable environment. This service is subscription-based.

Criteria for choosing the right library and API

To identify the best library for your algorithmic trading needs, it is important to assess them based on specific criteria that address the diverse requirements of backtesting and live trading:

- **Ease of implementation**: Evaluate how straightforward and user-friendly the library is, considering the quality of its documentation and the level of community support. Also, take into account your familiarity with the library's programming language.

- **Adaptability**: Determine the library's flexibility in allowing customization and scaling. Can it easily adapt to the unique demands of your trading strategies?

- **Broker integration**: Evaluate the library's compatibility with various brokers, particularly if you have a preference or existing relationship with a specific broker.

- **Multi-asset trading**: Analyze the library's capability to handle diverse asset classes (stocks, forex, commodities, crypto currencies, ETF, bonds).

- **Execution speed**: Consider the computational efficiency of the library, as a higher speed can be a significant advantage for high-frequency trading strategies, but is not a concern for low-frequency strategies (hourly, daily, or weekly).

- **Community and developer support**: The presence of a robust community and developer support can be invaluable for troubleshooting and evolving the library's capabilities.

- **Cost**: Factor in any associated costs with using the library, as some may require a subscription or have hidden fees.

- **Data handling and storage**: Look at how the library manages data feeds, historical data access, and data storage, which are critical for both backtesting and live trading.

- **Risk management tools**: Ensure that the library includes or supports the integration of advanced risk management tools and metrics.

- **Performance metrics and reporting**: The ability to generate detailed reports and access comprehensive performance metrics is essential for analyzing the effectiveness of your strategies.

---

5 https://www.quantrocket.com
6 https://www.interactivebrokers.com/en/trading/ib-api.php

Using these criteria, we can rank these libraries accordingly:

1. **BackTrader**: Highly adaptable, great for beginners and experienced traders, supports multiple brokers and data feeds, but can be slower in execution for complex strategies.

2. **Zipline**: Offers robust data handling and is well-suited for equity markets, though it has less broker integration and primarily focuses on backtesting rather than live trading.

3. **QuantConnect**: Excellent for multi-asset trading, offering high-speed execution and extensive broker integration, but may have a steeper learning curve.

4. **PyAlgoTrade**: Good for educational purposes and straightforward, simple strategies due to its minimal complexity, less overhead, but lacks advanced features for complex strategy development.

5. **Alpaca**: Noteworthy for its commission-free brokerage services that cater to algorithmic trading, providing a modern and developer-friendly platform that integrates seamlessly with many of these tools for streamlined live trading capabilities.

By comparing these libraries against the specified criteria, traders can make informed decisions tailored to their specific requirements for backtesting and live execution, ensuring a strategic fit with their algorithmic trading system.

Implementing a strategy with BackTrader

As detailed in the previous section, BackTrader is a prime candidate for implementing and backtesting algorithmic strategies. This is why this library will enable us to discover together the essential points that make up the execution of systematic strategies.

BackTrader is a robust **event-driven** backtesting framework that enables traders to build and test strategies with precision. It is designed to react to market events in the trade lifecycle, from order submission to execution and settlement. This setup mimics live-trading environments, providing a robust platform for strategy development and validation. By handling a wide array of market data and events, BackTrader facilitates a realistic simulation of trading strategies, essential for identifying potential issues and optimizing performance before deployment in real-world scenarios.

Let us start by looking at the roadmap for implementing a strategy with BackTrader.

Guide to backtesting with BackTrader

In this section, we explore a structured roadmap for implementing a strategy with BackTrader, breaking the process into actionable steps. Implementing a trading strategy in BackTrader is a structured process that involves the following steps:

1. **Import libraries**: Begin by importing necessary Python libraries, including BackTrader and any data libraries you may need.

2. **Define strategy**: Create a subclass of **bt.Strategy** within BackTrader. This is where you define parameters, initialize indicators, and set up the trading logic.

3. **Initialize indicators (Optional)**: Within the strategy subclass, initialize any indicators you will use, like moving averages.

4. **Set up trading logic**: Use methods like **__init__** for setting up the strategy and **next** for defining the logic to be executed with each incoming data point.

5. **Create Cerebro engine**: Instantiate a **Cerebro** object, which is the core engine of BackTrader that handles the backtesting workflow.

6. **Add data feed**: Add market data to the Cerebro engine. This could be live or historical data from various sources (csv file, Pandas data frame, etc.).

7. **Add strategy to Cerebro**: Attach your defined strategy to the Cerebro engine with **addstrategy.**

8. **Set initial cash and broker parameters (Optional)**: Define the initial capital and broker parameters like commission, slippage, etc.

9. **Run backtest**: Execute the backtest using the **run** method on your Cerebro instance.

10. **Analyze Results (optional)**: After running the backtest, you can analyze the results, extract performance metrics, or plot the performance chart using **cerebro. plot()**.

11. **Optimize (optional)**: You can optimize your strategy by adjusting parameters and running the strategy through the Cerebro engine to see how these changes affect performance.

Following this structured approach, even beginners with some programming experience can successfully backtest their trading strategies using BackTrader. We will discuss concrete examples of all these stages in further sections.

As a preamble, let us look at what differentiates a strategy based on a machine learning algorithm from systematic strategies that do not make use of it.

Coding a machine learning strategy with BackTrader

We have opted to employ a strategy driven by machine learning, diverging from reliance on technical indicators or similar methods. Those keen on exploring such an approach will find ample resources[7] on BackTrader's official website. Our focus within the BackTrader

---

7 https://backtrader.com/home/helloalgotrading

environment is to utilize the output of a machine learning model and its predictions and simulate the subsequent events, essentially translating these forecasts into tangible profit and loss outcomes.

The coding approach for a machine learning-based strategy differs from traditional methods such as *Moving Average Crossover*. Instead of encoding specific trading rules, we are provided with a vector of predictions, ranging from simple **buy** or **sell** signals to more complex schemes, which must be interpreted and translated into actionable orders within the BackTrader simulation environment. This shift emphasizes the algorithm's predictive output as the driving force behind trade decisions.

The elements relating to this point (from predictions to orders) belong to *phase 2 (Define Strategy)* of the step-by-step guide we gave at the beginning of this section. We will go into more detail about this and write the corresponding code when the time comes.

Import libraries and set-up

Let us start with the first step of importing and installing the essential libraries. Firstly, BackTrader:

```
pip install -q backtrader[plotting]
```

```
import numpy as np
import pandas as pd
import yfinance as yf
import matplotlib.pyplot as plt
```

We are initializing the **data feed (df)** with ten days of daily **Procter & Gamble (PG)**. To illustrate the backtesting of a machine learning-based trading strategy, we **simulate** predictions using a random number generator (**np.random.choice**). While these dummy predictions serve to demonstrate the backtest process, they can be replaced with predictions from a machine learning model:

```
symbol = 'PG'
ticker = yf.Ticker(symbol)
df = ticker.history(period='10d', interval='1d')
# Simulate predictions, favoring a 70% chance of '1' ('buy') and 30% chance
of '-1' ('sell')
pred_dumb = np.random.choice( [-1 , 1], size = df.shape[0] , p = [0.3 , 0.7])
# insert new column in the dataframe to keep track predictions
df['custom'] = pred_dumb
```

At this stage, we have prices and the buy/sell decisions that go with them.

Define strategy in an event-driven environment

Create a subclass of **bt.Strategy** within BackTrader. This is where you define parameters, initialize indicators, and set up the trading logic.

The following is an example named **CustomSignalStrategy**, with the essential methods that will enable you to manage order flow when the time comes (sending and receiving subsequent notifications):

```
# Define Custom Strategy
class CustomSignalStrategy(bt.Strategy):
    def __init__(self):
        # method called once at the beginning of the strategy to declare
indicators and variables
        pass
    def log(self, txt, dt=None):
        # utility method logs the given text with an optional date-time (dt)
stamp
        pass
    def next(self):
        # method called for every data point (bar) in the dataset. This is
where the main strategy logic is executed.
        pass
    def notify_order(self, order):
# method called whenever there is a change in order status. Useful for order
confirmation, cancellation, or rejection.
        pass
```

All that remains is to fill in and complete the code for each of these methods (**init, log, notify_order**, and **next**) with the logic specific to the trading system we want to backtest. This is what we do for each of the methods.

The **__init__** method is tasked with handling the predictions provided by the machine learning algorithm, serving as a preliminary setup. It accesses the strategy's (buy/sell) signals located within **self.datas[0].custom**. The variable **custom_signal** is then set to reference the latest signal (at the forefront of the queue):

```
    def __init__(self):
        # 'custom' signal <- predictions
        self.custom_signal = self.datas[0].custom
```

The log function is responsible for displaying a date (**dt**) and a text (**txt** argument) each time it is executed:

```
def log(self, txt, dt=None):
    ''' Logging function'''
    dt = dt or self.datas[0].datetime.date(0)
    print('%s, %s' % (dt.isoformat(), txt))
```

Set-up trading logic

Within the event-driven programming framework, we craft methods that are triggered by specific events. The operational flow is steered by the sequence of these events. For the next method, the event in question is the advent of a new bar or price update.

The following method is invoked for each data point within the data set, and it's at this juncture that the core logic of the strategy unfolds. Here, we manage and dispatch our trade orders, discerning between buy and sell types based on the signal received from **self.custom_signal**.

The provided code snippet exemplifies how to execute buy or sell orders in response to incoming signals:

```
def next(self):
    # logic : pyramid positions
    if self.custom_signal[0] == 1:
        self.buy()
    elif self.custom_signal[0] == -1:
        self.sell()
```

There is a wide range of trading strategies. One example is a flipping strategy, where the position alternates between long and short with each signal change, while maintaining a constant target quantity of a financial instrument.

BackTrader simplifies this process with the **order_target_size** method, which allows traders to easily set a fixed position size. This method is part of the versatile **order_target_xxx** family, which allows traders to define their desired portfolio target in a variety of ways:

- **order_target_size**: The number of shares or contracts of a particular asset.
- **order_target_value**: The monetary value of the asset in the portfolio.
- **order_target_percentage**: A percentage of the current portfolio value allocated to the asset.

```
def next(self):
    if self.custom_signal[0] == 1:
        self.order = self.order_target_size(target = 1)
    elif self.custom_signal[0] == -1:
        self.order = self.order_target_size(target = -1)
```

To conclude on the implementation of the strategy, we should mention the **notify_order** method. In BackTrader, the **notify_order()** method is used to **intercept messages** regarding the status of orders. When an order is placed, it goes through several states in its lifecycle (such as **Created**, **Submitted**, **Accepted**), and **notify_order()** provides updates at each state change.

notify_order() is used to take appropriate action when an order changes state, for example, to log the event, update strategy state, or handle order completion or failure. It is an essential part of the strategy logic in BackTrader, enabling the developer to manage the order flow and respond to the events as needed:

```
def notify_order(self, order):
    if order.status in [order.Submitted, order.Accepted]:
        # Buy/Sell order submitted/accepted to/by broker - Nothing to do
        return
    # Check if an order has been completed
    if order.status in [order.Completed]:
        if order.isbuy():
            self.log('BUY EXECUTED, Price: %.2f, Size: %d' % (order.
executed.price, self.getposition().size))
        elif order.issell():
            self.log('SELL EXECUTED, Price: %.2f, Size: %d' % (order.
executed.price, self.getposition().size))
        self.bar_executed = len(self)
    # Attention: broker could reject order if not enough cash
    elif order.status in [order.Canceled, order.Margin, order.Rejected]:
        self.log('Order Canceled/Margin/Rejected')
    # Write down: no pending order
    self.order = None
```

Create Cerebro engine

The following code (**init_cerebro_before_run**) serves as a **checklist** for setting up a BackTrader 'Cerebro' engine, ensuring that all necessary components, from data integration to execution specifics, are properly configured.

This preparation is critical for the subsequent addition of data and strategy (**CustomSignalStrategy**) to the engine, preceding the execution phase:

```
# Subclass the PandasData feed to include 'custom' as an additional line
class CustomPandasData(bt.feeds.PandasData):
    lines = ('custom',)
    params = (('custom', -1),)
```

```python
cash = 100000

def init_cerebro_before_run():
  # Load data into BackTrader using the custom data feed
  data = CustomPandasData(dataname=df)
  # Create a new Cerebro engine
  cerebro = bt.Cerebro()
  # Open / Close position on Open (next bar after signal)
  cerebro.cheat_on_close = False
  # Add data feed to the engine
  cerebro.adddata(data)
  # Add the strategy to the engine
  cerebro.addstrategy(CustomSignalStrategy)
  # Set our desired initial cash
  cerebro.broker.set_cash(cash)
  # Print out the starting cash
  print('Starting Portfolio Value: %.2f' % cerebro.broker.getvalue())
  return cerebro
```

```python
cerebro = init_cerebro_before_run()
```

The result of this initialization code is:

```
Starting Portfolio Value: 100000.00
```

Run backtest

All that remains is to activate Cerebro's backtest engine and let it manage the sequence of operations:

```python
# Run the backtest
results = cerebro.run()
```

This gives us the following sequence of orders:

```
2023-10-23, SELL EXECUTED, Price: 147.86, Size: -1
2023-10-24, BUY EXECUTED, Price: 148.12, Size: 1
2023-11-02, SELL EXECUTED, Price: 149.54, Size: -1
```

```python
# Print out the final cash
print('Ending Portfolio Value: %.2f' % cerebro.broker.getvalue())
```

```
Ending Portfolio Value: 99999.74
```

The following table lists the prices and signals during this period, providing a transparent view of how the strategy would react to market changes and prediction signals:

Date	Open	Close	custom
2023-10-20	149.050003	148.050003	-1
2023-10-23	147.860001	148.149994	1
2023-10-24	148.119995	149.899994	1
...	...	...	...
2023-11-01	150.679993	149.610001	-1
2023-11-02	149.539993	150.960007	-1

Table 4.1: Opening, closing price, and prediction

To gain a solid understanding and trust in our backtesting code, it is essential to manually trace the sequence of events as they unfold in real-time trading. This process involves closely following the asset's price movements, specifically the opening and closing prices on given dates, and aligning them with the predictions (column **custom**) from our machine learning algorithm.

The following is a breakdown of the backtesting engine's actions, aligned with our expectations:

- On October 20, 2023, a sell signal (-1) is indicated at the close of the trading day

- Consequently, a short position is initiated at the opening price of the next trading day, which is October 23, 2023, at the price of $147.86:

- 2023-10-23, SELL EXECUTED, Price: 147.86, Size: -1

- On October 23, 2023, the signal shifts to a buy (+1)

- A long position is established at the market opening on October 24, 2023:

- 2023-10-24, BUY EXECUTED, Price: 148.12, Size: 1

- This position is held until the next signal reversal, which occurs on November 1, 2023

- On November 1, 2023, the signal reverts to a sell (-1), indicating a shift back to a short position:

- 2023-11-02, SELL EXECUTED, Price: 149.54, Size: -1

Having meticulously dissected and verified each result produced by the engine, we are now ready to progress to the subsequent phase, risk management.

Risk management

In this section, we will guide you through setting up both a stop loss and take profit for each trade to ensure your strategy includes protective and profit-targeting measures.

Adding stop-loss

In algorithmic trading, safeguarding automated systems is imperative. This essential safeguard involves pre-setting a stop-loss level for every **market order**.

Specifically, in the **notify_order** method, we define a stop loss at 5% below the execution price for long positions as soon as an order is completed. Subsequently, with **each new** price tick, the engine evaluates it against the set stop loss level to determine if the stop loss should be activated.

The check and execution of the stop-loss are coded in the next method, where if the current close price dips below the stop-loss price for a long position, the system triggers a sell at the stop loss level, thereby executing a protective exit from the position.

In this example, we will set the stop-loss level at 5% below the executed buy price for long positions. You can adjust these percentages as you see fit:

```python
class CustomSignalStrategy(bt.Strategy):
    # 5% below the buy price
    params = (('stop_loss_multiplier', 0.95))

    def __init__(self):
        # Initialize any indicators, signals, and variables
        self.order = None
        self.buyprice = None
        self.stop_loss_price = None

    def notify_order(self, order):
        if order.status in [order.Completed]:
            if order.isbuy():
                self.buyprice = order.executed.price
                    # Set-up stop loss price based on the buy price and the
multiplier
                self.stop_loss_price = self.buyprice * self.params.stop_loss_
multiplier

    def next(self):
```

```
    # Check if there is a position in the market
    if self.position:
        # Check if the current price has fallen to the stop loss level
        if self.data.close[0] <= self.stop_loss_price:
            # If so, sell with a stop order at the stop loss price
            self.sell(exectype=bt.Order.Stop, price=self.stop_loss_price)
```

To enhance your trading strategy with a take-profit mechanism, you can implement a predefined profit target that, once reached, will trigger an automatic sale of the position, securing your earnings.

Adding take-profit with limit order

In your trading script, you would add logic to monitor the price levels relative to your entry point and define a specific threshold for taking profits. When the current market price crosses this threshold, a sell **limit order** would be executed, closing the position and capturing the gains. Let us examine how to implement a take-profit mechanism using limit orders. This strategy automatically places a sell limit order at a predefined price level (here set to 5% above entry) whenever a new long position is initiated.

We can do it in BackTrader as follows:

```
class CustomSignalStrategy(bt.Strategy):
    params = (
        ('take_profit_multiplier', 1.05),   # 5% above the buy price
    )

    def __init__(self):
        # Initialize any indicators, signals, and variables
        self.order = None
        self.buyprice = None
        self.take_profit_price = None

    def notify_order(self, order):
        if order.status in [order.Completed]:
            if order.isbuy():
                self.buyprice = order.executed.price
                # Set the take profit price based on the buy price and the
multiplier
                self.take_profit_price = self.buyprice * self.params.take_
profit_multiplier
```

```
def next(self):
    # Check if there is a position in the market
    if self.position:
        # Check if the current price has reached the take profit level
        if self.data.close[0] >= self.take_profit_price:
            # If so, sell with a limit order at the take profit price
            self.sell(exectype=bt.Order.Limit, price=self.take_profit_price)
```

In BackTrader, to account for slippage and commission, you could make use of the **Cerebro** instance to set up the broker simulation parameters.

Set broker commission and slippage

This section shows how to configure both broker commission and slippage settings. Slippage, the difference between the expected price of a trade and the actual executed price, is a common factor in trading. The following examples show how you can set these parameters to reflect realistic trading conditions in your backtesting environment:

```
# Set broker parameters for slippage and commission
# 0.5% slippage
slippage = 0.005
commission = 5 / 100 / 100 # 5 basis point
# Set up slippage
cerebro.broker.set_slippage_fixed(fixed = 0.01)   # Fixed slippage per trade
# or :
cerebro.broker.set_slippage_perc(prec = slippage)
cerebro.broker.setcommission(commission = commission)
```

The following is an explanation of the parameters used in the preceding code:

- Slippage:

  o **set_slippage_fixed(fixed=0.01)** applies a fixed amount of slippage to each trade, meaning every order will be executed with an additional cost of 0.01 in the asset's price units

  o **set_slippage_perc(perc=0.005)** applies a percentage of slippage based on the asset's price at the time of order execution, with 0.005 representing five basis points (0.5% of the price)

- **Commission: setcommission(commission=0.001)** sets the commission fee as a percentage of the trade value. Here, 0.1% of the trade value will be deducted as commission costs

You can add these configurations to your Cerebro setup before running the backtest. This ensures that the backtesting environment realistically simulates slippage and commission, significantly affecting any trading strategy's performance!

In the next section, we incorporate a suite of performance indicators, including the Sharpe ratio, drawdown analysis, and annualized returns, to enhance the evaluation of your trading strategy's effectiveness.

Analyze results

Prior to initiating the backtest, it is important to set up your Cerebro engine with performance metrics to assess strategy viability. Include **analyzers** for trade details and drawdowns to gain insights into trade efficiency and risk exposure.

The following is an enhanced script snippet to embed in the Cerebro configuration (at the beginning of the program):

```
# Import the analyzers from Backtrader
import backtrader.analyzers as btanalyzers
# Add a TradeAnalyzer to the Cerebro engine
cerebro.addanalyzer(btanalyzers.TradeAnalyzer, _name="trade_analyzer")
# Add analyzers
cerebro.addanalyzer(btanalyzers.DrawDown, _name='drawdown')
```

The launch code is unchanged:

```
# Run the backtest
results = cerebro.run()
# Print out the final cash
print('Ending Portfolio Value: %.2f' % cerebro.broker.getvalue())
```

To access specific risk statistics from the results of your backtest, you will utilize a dictionary structure provided by the **analyzers**. This enables you to query and retrieve detailed risk metrics:

```
# Extract the first strategy from the list of results
strat = results[0]
# Access Maximum Drawdown from the strategy's drawdown analyzer
print('Max    Drawdown:',    strat.analyzers.drawdown.get_analysis()['max']
['drawdown'])
```

In this code, **strat.analyzers.drawdown.get_analysis()** retrieves a comprehensive dictionary of drawdown statistics. By keying into **['max']['drawdown']**, we extract the maximum drawdown experienced by the strategy during the backtest period. This metric is essential for understanding potential losses the strategy may incur and evaluating its risk tolerance. For a detailed discussion of risk management metrics, refer to *Chapter 3, Optimizing Trading Systems, Metrics, and Automated Reporting*.

Trade statistics

For individuals interested in obtaining a detailed analysis of trade performance, the following code snippet provides comprehensive statistics. It calculates the hit rate, average profit for winning trades, average loss for losing trades, and the distribution of wins and losses across long and short positions:

```
try:

    trades = strat.analyzers.trade_analyzer.get_analysis()
    hit_rate = trades['won']['total'] / trades['total']['closed']
    avg_win = trades['won']['pnl']['average']
    avg_loss = trades['lost']['pnl']['average']
    long_win = trades['long']['won']
    long_lost = trades['long']['lost']
    short_win = trades['short']['won']
    short_lost = trades['short']['lost']

    print('Total trades :', trades['total']['closed'])
    print('Wins :', trades['won']['total'])
    print('Losses :', trades['lost']['total'])
    print(f'Hit Rate : {(100*hit_rate):.0f}%')
    print(f'Avg Win : {avg_win:.1f}')
    print(f'Avg Loss : {avg_loss : .1f}')
    if avg_loss != 0:
      print(f'Avg win on Lost : {(-avg_win / avg_loss):.1f}')
    print()

    print('LONG TRADES:')
    print('trades long (win)',trades['long']['won'])
    print('trades long (lost)',trades['long']['lost'])
    print(f'pct : {(100*long_win / (long_win + long_lost)):.0f}%')
    print()

    print('SHRT TRADES:')
    print('trades short (win)',trades['short']['won'])
    print('trades short (lost)',trades['short']['lost'])
    if short_win or short_lost != 0:
      print(f'pct : {(100*short_win / (short_win + short_lost)):.0f}%')
except Exception as e:
  print(e)
```

It prints out the following output:

```
Total trades : 2
Wins : 1
Losses : 1
Hit Rate : 50%
Avg Win : 1.4
Avg Loss : -0.3
Avg win on Lost : 5.5


LONG TRADES:
trades long (win) 1
trades long (lost) 0
pct : 100%


SHRT TRADES:
trades short (win) 0
trades short (lost) 1
pct : 0%
```

Incorporating this code into your trading strategy evaluation provides valuable insights into its potential effectiveness.

The following are a few more details about the structure containing all the statistics:

```
trades = strat.analyzers.trade_analyzer.get_analysis()
trades.keys()
```

This is the output for the preceding code:

```
odict_keys(['total', 'streak', 'pnl', 'won', 'lost', 'long', 'short', 'len'])
```

This output represents the keys of a dictionary returned by the trade analyzer. Each key gives access to a specific set of trade statistics:

- **total**: Information about the total number of trades
- **streak**: Statistics on consecutive wins and losses
- **pnl**: Profit and loss statistics
- **won**: Details of winning trades
- **lost**: Details of losing trades
- **long**: Statistics specifically for long positions
- **short**: Statistics specifically for short positions
- **len**: The duration of trades

We now turn our attention to the final section of this chapter, which is focused on **multi-asset support**. This will be particularly relevant for traders engaged in multi-asset strategies such as arbitrage and portfolio management.

Multi-asset support and advanced features

In this section, we will go into detail to guide you through the following processes:

- Incorporating multiple data sources into your strategy

- Executing trading strategies that involve several assets.

We will develop a trading system that automatically executes a buy order for one asset and **simultaneously** places a sell order for another, akin to a **hedging strategy** where assets are inversely traded.

The following shows how you can modify your existing code to include multi-asset support:

```
# Download data for two assets: PG (Procter & Gamble) and KO (Coca-Cola Cie)
data1 = yf.download('PG', period='10d', interval='1d')
data2 = yf.download('KO', period='10d', interval='1d')
```

Add (**custom**) column containing signals:

```
# insert new column to keep track predictions
data1['custom'] = pred_dumb
data2['custom'] = pred_dumb
```

Adding multiple data feeds

Adding more than one data feed to Cerebro, each representing a different asset. This is done in the **init_cerebro_before_run()** function:

```
def init_cerebro_before_run(data1 , data2):
  # Add multiple data feeds to Cerebro
  data1 = CustomPandasData(dataname =  data1)
  data2 = CustomPandasData(dataname = data2)
  cerebro = bt.Cerebro()

  # Add data feed to the engine
  cerebro.adddata(data1, name='PG')
  cerebro.adddata(data2, name='KO')

  # rest of code unchanged
```

To handle multiple assets in your strategy, you need to modify the **__init__** method to initialize variables for each asset. This step ensures that your strategy can process data and signals for multiple assets simultaneously, enabling more robust and flexible trading logic.

```
def __init__(self):
    self.custom_signal1 = self.datas[0].custom
    self.custom_signal2 = self.datas[1].custom
    # ... (other initializations)
```

To implement trading logic for multiple assets, you need to modify the next method to include logic for each asset. This ensures that your strategy evaluates and executes trades **independently** for each asset, allowing for tailored decision-making based on their respective custom signals (**custom_signal1** and **custom_signal2**). If **custom_signal1** triggers a buy for **Asset1**, it does not affect the trading behavior of **Asset2**. Similarly, a signal for **Asset2** does not influence trading decisions for **Asset1**. This logic is suitable when each asset is managed separately, and their trades are not interdependent.

```
def next(self):
    # Trading logic for Asset1
    if self.custom_signal1[0] == 1:
        self.buy(data=self.datas[0])
    elif self.custom_signal1[0] == -1:
        self.sell(data=self.datas[0])

    # Trading logic for Asset2
    if self.custom_signal2[0] == 1:
        self.buy(data=self.datas[1])
    elif self.custom_signal2[0] == -1:
        self.sell(data=self.datas[1])
```

If we are implementing a **flipping trading system,** where the purchase of an asset **automatically** triggers the selling of another, you can modify the trading logic in the next method as follows. Now, the **next** function implements a **flipping trading system,** where buying one asset automatically triggers selling the other. Here, the strategy uses **order_target_size** to manage the position sizes of both assets explicitly.

```
def next(self):
  # buy signal
  if self.custom_signal1[0] == 1:
      self.order_target_size(data=self.datas[0], target=1)   # Buy Asset1 : PG
      self.order_target_size(data=self.datas[1], target=-1)  # Sell Asset2 : KO

  # sell signal
  if self.custom_signal1[0] == -1:
```

```
self.order_target_size(data=self.datas[0], target=-1)  # Sell Asset1
self.order_target_size(data=self.datas[1], target=1)  # Buy Asset2
```

In this modified code, buying or selling one asset automatically triggers the opposite action for the other asset. This is done by using **order_target_size** to set the target size to 1 share for a buy and -1 share for a sell. If **custom_signal1** signals a buy for **Asset1**, the strategy will not only buy **Asset1** but also sell **Asset2**, conversely, for a sell signal. This logic is ideal when the two assets are inversely correlated or when the strategy aims to maintain a balanced exposure (e.g., a pair trading strategy).

Next, update the order notifications to account for multiple assets. This involves modifying the **notify_order** method to identify which asset each order is associated with, ensuring that notifications are correctly handled for all assets in your strategy:

```
def notify_order(self, order):
    data_name = order.data._name
    # ... (existing logic, now aware of which asset the order is for)


# initialize Cerebro engine and Run the backtest
cerebro = init_cerebro_before_run(data1 , data2)
results = cerebro.run()
print('Ending Portfolio Value: %.2f' % cerebro.broker.getvalue())


2023-10-23, PG : SELL EXECUTED, Price: 147.12, Size: -1
2023-10-23, KO : BUY EXECUTED, Price: 54.65, Size: -1
2023-10-24, PG : BUY EXECUTED, Price: 148.86, Size: 1
2023-10-24, KO : SELL EXECUTED, Price: 55.37, Size: 1
2023-11-02, PG : SELL EXECUTED, Price: 148.79, Size: -1
2023-11-02, KO : BUY EXECUTED, Price: 56.78, Size: -1
Ending Portfolio Value: 99995.12
```

The following is the price history of the **Procter&Gamble** (**PG**) share contained in the **data1** structure to trace and reconstitute the sequences:

Date	Open	Close	custom
2023-10-20	149.050003	148.050003	-1
2023-10-23	147.860001	148.149994	1
2023-10-24	148.119995	149.899994	1
...	...	...	...
2023-11-01	150.679993	149.610001	-1
2023-11-02	149.539993	150.865005	-1

Table 4.2: Price History of the 'PG' share

We can see the sequence of trades in line with the desired logic: intervention on one asset (PG), which triggers an opposite trade on the other asset (KO) in a hedging logic.

Conclusion

In this chapter, we explored the basics of backtesting and trading libraries. We introduced key libraries and criteria for selecting the right tool and then provided a practical, step-by-step guide to implementing a strategy using BackTrader. Along the way, we explored key concepts such as managing algorithmic orders, incorporating risk management techniques (e.g., setting stop-loss limits or position sizing rules). With this solid understanding of backtesting using a state-of-the-art, event-driven library, you are now equipped to design and test sophisticated trading strategies.

In the next chapter, we will look at supervised learning and its applications in trading. You will learn how these algorithms analyze historical data to identify patterns and predict market movements. By focusing on key algorithms and evaluation metrics, this chapter lays the ground for the practical strategies and implementations that follow.

Multiple choice questions

1. **Which of the following is a key feature of the BackTrader library?**
    a. Exclusively supports live trading
    b. Versatility and ease of use for backtesting and live trading
    c. Limited to basic order types
    d. Requires a subscription fee

2. **What is the primary function of the 'Cerebro' object in BackTrader?**
    a. To manage risk parameters
    b. To define trading strategies
    c. To handle the backtesting workflow
    d. To visualize performance metrics

3. **Which method in a BackTrader strategy is called for every data point (bar) in the dataset?**
    a. __init__
    b. log
    c. notify_order
    d. next

4. **What does the order_target_size method in BackTrader allow traders to do?**
   a. Set a percentage of the current portfolio value allocated to the asset.
   b. Set the monetary value of the asset in the portfolio.
   c. Set the number of shares or contracts of a particular asset
   d. Set a stop loss price

5. **In BackTrader, what is the purpose of the notify_order method?**
   a. To define trading logic
   b. To log trade executions
   c. To intercept messages regarding the status of orders
   d. To set the initial cash

6. **What does slippage refer to in trading?**
   a. The commission charged by the broker
   b. The difference between the expected price of a trade and the actual executed price
   c. The profit made on a trade
   d. The initial capital required for a trade

7. **Which of the following is NOT a criterion for choosing a trading library?**
   a. Ease of implementation
   b. Adaptability
   c. Broker integration
   d. The color of the library's logo

8. **What is a key advantage of using a machine learning-based strategy in BackTrader?**
   a. It is simpler than using traditional methods
   b. It relies on technical indicators
   c. It uses predictive outputs to drive trade decisions
   d. It does not need historical data

9. **What is the function of a stop-loss order?**
   a. To automatically sell a position to secure earnings
   b. To limit potential losses by selling an asset when the price drops below a predefined level
   c. To buy an asset at a lower price
   d. To monitor market trends

10. **In a multi-asset strategy, how can you manage trades for different assets in BackTrader?**

    a. By combining all data into one feed

    b. By using the same trading logic for all assets

    c. By initializing variables and trading logic specific to each asset

    d. By only trading one asset at a time

Answers

1.	b
2.	c
3.	d
4.	c
5.	c
6.	b
7.	d
8.	c
9.	b
10.	c

References

1. The official website for BackTrader, a versatile Python library for algorithmic trading

    https://backtrader.com

2. The documentation for Zipline, a backtesting engine that was originally part of Quantopian

    https://zipline-trader.readthedocs.io/en/latest/index.html

3. The Github page for PyAlgoTrade, which offers robust support for multi-asset trading

    https://gbeced.github.io/pyalgotrade

4. The website for Alpaca, a platform for direct market access and real-time trading

    https://alpaca.markets

5. The website for QuantRocket, which is tailored for InteractiveBrokers users

    https://www.quantrocket.com

6. The InteractiveBrokers API page

    https://www.interactivebrokers.com/en/trading/ib-api.php

Join our book's Discord space

Join the book's Discord Workspace for Latest updates, Offers, Tech happenings around the world, New Release and Sessions with the Authors:

https://discord.bpbonline.com

CHAPTER 5

Supervised Learning for Trading Systems

Introduction

This chapter covers the principles of supervised **machine learning** (ML) with a focus on trading applications. We will examine how algorithms analyze historical data to identify patterns and predict market movements, breaking down their structure into key components such as data input, functional representation, and optimization. The chapter also reviews essential classification and regression algorithms, as well as key evaluation metrics. Unlike other chapters, the focus here is on building a solid conceptual framework for supervised learning in trading rather than on specific implementation examples.

Structure

In this chapter, we will cover the following topics:

- Role of supervised learning
- Supervised learning for predictive trading
- Advantages of supervised learning
- Supervised learning landscape
- Core principle of supervised learning
- Main supervised learning algorithms
- Selection criteria for trading applications

Objectives

This chapter introduces supervised learning and its role in creating advanced algorithmic trading strategies. You will learn how to use historical data and labeled outcomes to build predictive models for forecasting market behavior. We will cover key classification algorithms such as logistic regression and **Support Vector Machines (SVMs)**, as well as essential regression methods such as decision tree regressors, gradient boosting, and k-nearest neighbors, with a focus on their practical applications in trading. We will also explore how to choose the right algorithm based on your data, prediction goals, and evaluation metrics, such as accuracy and precision, enabling you to refine and optimize your trading systems effectively.

Role of supervised learning in trading

This section examines trading from a technological perspective, highlighting how supervised learning plays a key role in building predictive trading systems by using historical data and labeled outcomes to anticipate future market trends.

Before we continue, let us briefly review the main points from the first chapter.

Note: This section focuses only on reviewing these key ideas; new information is introduced in the following section.

Rise of ML in trading

ML, a key branch of artificial intelligence, enables computer systems to learn from data and improve themselves without explicit programming. Introduced by *Arthur Samuel* in 1959, this approach is unique in that it derives rules directly from data rather than relying on predefined instructions. Unlike traditional programming, where rules are set manually, ML algorithms analyze data to uncover patterns and correlations that guide decision-making. In trading, ML demonstrates its value by processing vast amounts of financial data to predict market trends.

Supervised learning for predictive trading's foundation

In algorithmic trading, supervised learning, a branch of ML, introduces an important step forward in strategy development. It works with labeled data, where the training set includes both the input features and their corresponding outputs. This method is like guided learning in that the model learns from specific examples of what it should predict.

In the context of trading, these labeled datasets typically consist of various market indicators as inputs (like fundamental data[1], historical prices, volumes, and technical indicators) and specific outcomes as outputs (such as future price movements or trend classifications), as depicted in the following graph:

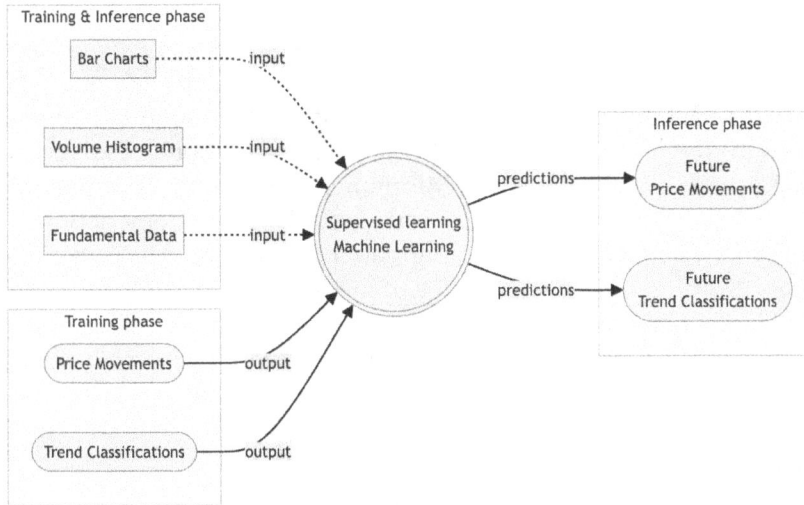

Figure 5.1: *Supervised learning in trading*

This sketch illustrates the workflow of supervised learning within the context of financial trading, where the model is trained using various types of market data, bar charts, volume histograms, and fundamental data, as inputs. During the training phase, the algorithm learns to correlate these inputs with known outputs, specifically historical price movements and trend classifications.

Once trained, the model enters the inference phase, applying its learned rules to new data to make predictions about future price movements and market trends, thereby informing trading decisions.

Building on the basics of supervised learning with traditional market data, the field is expanding into more sophisticated areas. Techniques such as graph learning, image-based ML, and the analysis of textual and auditory data are increasingly shaping and transforming trading strategies.

Graph learning, for instance, is used to analyze market networks, where stocks are nodes, and correlations are edges, offering insights into market dynamics. ML from images, such as Deep Convolutional Neural Networks, is applied to interpret candlestick charts, identifying patterns that predict price movements. Natural language processing techniques analyze news, social media chatter, and earnings call transcripts for sentiment analysis, influencing trading decisions. Similarly, analyzing auditory data, like fluctuations in

---

1 In *Chapter 2, Data Feed, Backtests, and Forward Testing*, we discussed in detail an example of a strategy based on accounting data as published in the profit and loss account.

tone during earnings calls, provides subtle cues about company performance, aiding in predictive analysis. These innovative approaches leverage diverse data forms, going far beyond traditional numerical data, offering traders a more holistic view of the market and an edge in decision-making.

Advantages of supervised learning in trading

The quintessence of ML lies in its unparalleled ability to **autonomously** derive decision-making rules directly from data, a stark contrast to traditional statistical techniques that often rely on pre-established rules. ML models can identify complex patterns and relationships in data, allowing them to make reliable predictions about new, unseen information. Rather than simply recognizing patterns, these models undergo a thorough training process, learning from a wide range of market data and outcomes to understand market behavior. This ability makes them well-suited for developing trading systems that use historical data to predict future market trends more accurately than traditional methods. Furthermore, ML's capability to extract structured insights, such as those gleaned from decision tree analysis, provides clear, interpretable models - an advantage in understanding complex market behaviors.

The following figure is a concrete example[2] of structured knowledge extracted by an ML algorithm (decision tree):

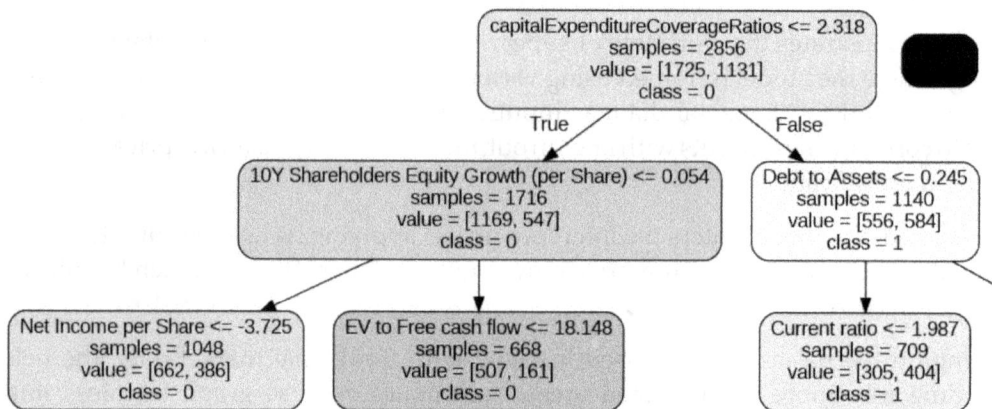

Figure 5.2: Structured knowledge

ML surpasses traditional statistical methods with its inherent capability to autonomously distill structured knowledge from complex datasets, a feat typically unattainable with conventional techniques. Unlike traditional approaches that often rely on static business rules, which can quickly become outdated due to ever-evolving market conditions, ML stands out with its dynamic adaptability. It continuously updates and refines its predictive rules in response to new data, ensuring that the insights and strategies remain relevant and effective. Furthermore, ML excels in handling **high-dimensional data** spaces and

---

2 See Chapter 2, Data Feed, Backtests, and Forward Testing for details of this example

uncovering *non-linear relationships*, which are often encountered in financial markets but are challenging for traditional models to capture.

After examining the advantages of supervised learning in trading, we now shift to the mechanics behind it. The next section explores the core principles, such as labeled data, training algorithms, and prediction generation, to understand how these models operate effectively.

Supervised learning landscape

Supervised learning is a key part of ML with growing importance in finance. Learning from labeled datasets enables algorithms to predict outcomes based on historical data, making it essential for advanced trading strategies. Unlike unsupervised learning, which finds hidden patterns without labels, or reinforcement learning, which learns through interaction with an environment, supervised learning relies on known outcomes, making it well-suited for predictive analytics in trading.

Core principles of supervised learning

In trading, supervised learning is useful for predicting market trends, price movements, and investment opportunities using historical data. Its structured input-output approach helps traders and analysts build models that process large amounts of data and make accurate predictions. This improves decision-making and strategy development.

Role of labeled data in supervised learning

A deeper understanding of supervised learning reveals the fundamental importance of labeled data.

In supervised learning for trading, labeled data is the foundation for building predictive models. This data consists of **inputs**, including stock prices, trading volumes, and other relevant market signals, **paired** with their corresponding **outputs**. These outputs are the **labels** that guide the learning process, hence the term **supervised** learning. In regression tasks, the goal is to predict a continuous outcome, and labels might be future prices. In classification tasks, where the objective is to categorize data, labels could be trend indicators, such as **buy**, **sell**, or **hold**.

The labels teach the algorithm how to interpret the data and, consequently, how to make accurate predictions. For instance, a classification model might learn from labeled data to identify whether a market trend is bullish or bearish. Conversely, in a regression setting, the model could use labeled data to predict the specific future price of an asset.

In supervised learning for trading, algorithms are essentially trained to answer two key questions. For regression problems, it is *How much?*, seeking a precise numerical prediction, such as a future stock price. For classification tasks, the question is *Is that?*, determining the category a data point belongs to, such as whether a trading signal indicates a buy, sell, or hold situation.

Let us take a moment to analyze a few examples of these two types of prediction. First, we will examine some immediate applications, followed by examples that extend beyond them.

For regression, a typical example involves training a model to predict the future price of a stock. See the following figure for an illustration:

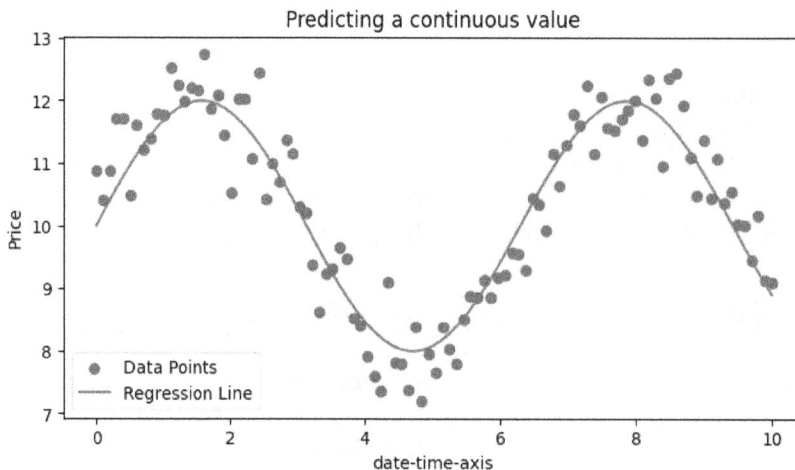

Figure 5.3: Regression task

Let us discuss beyond simple price forecasting.

A more complex regression problem could involve estimating the probability of a market crash based on economic indicators, a task that entails quantifying risk in probabilistic terms.

Another advanced example is estimating the impact of earnings announcements on sector indices. The focus is on predicting the impact of quarterly earnings announcements on specific sector indices. By analyzing a combination of pre-announcement financial metrics, market sentiment, and historical performance data of companies, the model aims to estimate the **percentage change** in the index following the earnings release. This approach provides an understanding of how corporate performance metrics influence broader market segments, aiding in sector-specific investment strategies.

In the context of classification, a basic instance is determining whether a stock will go up or down, classifying the movement into binary categories based on financial feature values. The following figure illustrates this point and introduces an additional **Hold** category:

Classification with Decision Boundaries

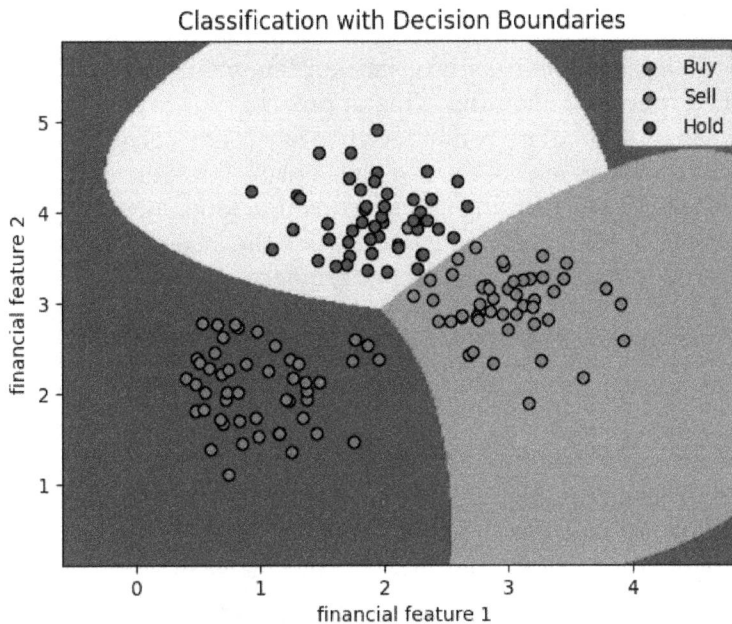

Figure 5.4: *Learn to predict a category*

An original example that extends beyond this binary scope might involve classifying the **type of market regime**, ranging from bullish or bearish to more specific states like **volatile uptrend or quiet consolidation**, based on a combination of price patterns, trading volume, and macroeconomic signals.

To conclude this series of application examples, let us look at the prediction of rare events such as mergers and acquisitions. Here is how supervised learning algorithms can help. Predicting corporate mergers is an application of ML, blending elements of both classification and regression.

In a classification context, the model could assess the likelihood of a merger between specific companies, classifying potential mergers as probable or improbable based on financial health, market conditions, and historical merger patterns in the industry.

Alternatively, as a regression task, the model might predict the financial impact of a potential merger, estimating metrics like post-merger stock price changes or market share shifts. Such predictions require analyzing complex datasets, including financial statements, market trends, and even text data from news and corporate communications, to capture the multifaceted nature of merger activities.

As these examples show, supervised learning offers a powerful advantage in finance. Models can learn to understand complex market dynamics, providing traders with nuanced insights for better decision-making. By using labeled data, professionals can build models that outperform traditional trading strategies in both accuracy and sophistication.

Let us look at beyond supervised learning.

While supervised learning relies heavily on labeled datasets, it is important to acknowledge the role of **semi-supervised learning**. This approach, which utilizes both labeled and unlabeled data, can be particularly valuable when labels are scarce or expensive to obtain. We will not deal with this approach in detail, but it is important to be aware of this possibility. Semi-supervised learning can leverage the large amounts of unlabeled data available in financial markets, using them alongside the labeled instances to enhance the learning process and improve the model's performance.

Having explored the role of labeled data and diverse methodologies of supervised learning in financial contexts, we will now go on to understand the learning process.

Learning process

The primary objective of the learning process is to minimize the discrepancies between the results predicted by an ML algorithm and the data that accurately represent the market reality. The following figure illustrates this:

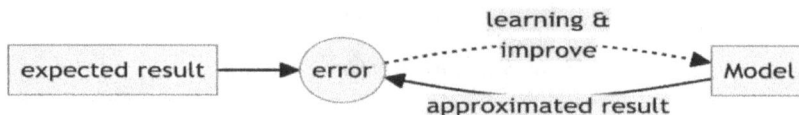

Figure 5.5: Learning process

To achieve this, an optimization process is used to iteratively refine the parameters of the ML algorithm. This iterative refinement seeks to minimize the discrepancy between predicted and observed values in the historical data.

For this reason, all ML algorithms include an error function[3], which the optimizer explores as efficiently as possible to find its minimum.

The loss function quantifies the difference between predicted values and actual values. During training, the algorithm iteratively processes each data point, predicting an output and comparing it to the actual observed value. The error function calculates the magnitude of the deviation between these values.

In the update phase, the algorithm adjusts its parameters to reduce this error. This adjustment is represented as **new_param = old_param - update**. A larger error leads to a more significant update, gradually steering the parameters towards values that minimize the error function.

We will not go deeper into the mathematical aspects of the learning process, since contemporary ML libraries (**Scikit-learn, Tensorflow, pyTorch**, …) fully abstract the underlying algorithmic complexities. The practical implementation of the learning process is typically encapsulated within a single command: **fit**.

---

3 The value of which depends on the parameters of the ML algorithm

To summarize this section, all ML algorithms can be broken down into the following key components:

- **Data**: The foundation of any ML model.
- **Optimizer**: The engine that drives ML models to refine their parameters, thus improving predictive performance.
- **Model representation**: This defines how the algorithm captures relationships within the data. In trading, it determines how market trends and behaviors are modeled.
- **Loss function**: A critical tool for measuring the model's accuracy, quantifying the cost of errors in predictions, and guiding the model to make more accurate future predictions.

These components are essential for performant ML algorithms. Now, let's explore the main supervised learning algorithms.

Main supervised learning algorithms

Our goal is to provide a practical overview of **essential** ML algorithms from introductory to advanced levels. Rather than an exhaustive catalog, we'll distill the core concepts and highlight the defining features of each algorithm. This will give you an intuitive understanding of how each algorithm works and where it fits into the field of ML. We will start with classification algorithms and then move on to regression algorithms.

Classification algorithms

The purpose of a classifier is to position a boundary to separate the two classes. We will demonstrate the range of classification algorithms by testing them on three datasets of varying complexity and difficulty. As you can see in the following graph, the **2 moons dataset**, featuring distinctly non-linear data, is likely to challenge the more basic classifiers. A similar observation is made for the dataset representing intertwined **circles**. However, data from the **linear separation** dataset will probably be easier to separate, even for linear class algorithms:

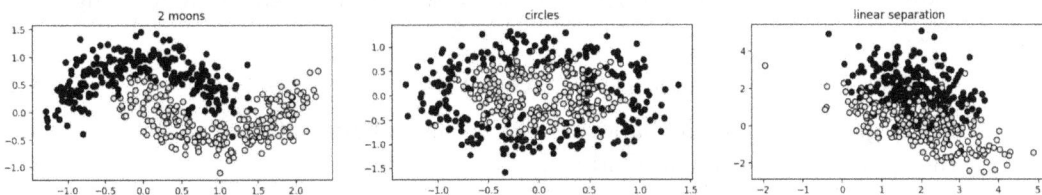

Figure 5.6: Datasets for Classification Algorithms

The aim is not to find the best settings for the algorithms but simply to show how they behave on the datasets proposed to draw general conclusions.

Logistic regression

Logistic regression is employed for relatively straightforward binary classification problems due to its linear nature. It can be a valid choice when relationships between variables are expected to be linear or close to linear. For example, logistic regression could be used to predict whether a stock's price will close above or below a certain threshold based on a set of technical indicators.

The following are some of its strengths and weaknesses:

- **Advantages**: Simple, interpretable, and efficient for small to medium datasets (up to ~100k rows)

- **Limitations**: Limited to linear relationships and can overfit small datasets. Less effective for complex relationships and high-dimensional data

- **Important parameter and range**[4]: Regularization strength (C) often in the range [0.01, 100]

Here is the result of applying the logistic regression algorithm to the three datasets mentioned in the introduction. You can see from the following graph that the logistic regression algorithm is a linear separator. In fact, it draws a linear boundary between the two different classes of data (yellow vs. black dots), as follows:

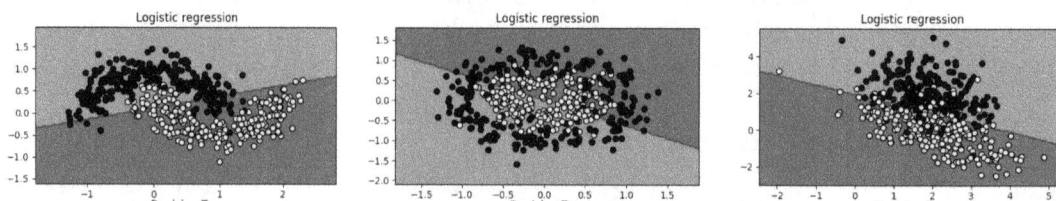

Figure 5.7: *Logistic regression algorithm*

Decision trees

Decision trees can be employed to model market behavior and make predictions. The algorithm **automatically** learns a series of if-then-else rules from the data, forming a tree-like structure.

Let us look at the following strengths and weaknesses:

- **Advantages**: Interpretable, handles both numerical and categorical data. Robust to outliers, handles non-linear relationships

- **Limitations:** Prone to overfitting, less effective for large datasets (>100k rows)

- **Important parameter and range**: Tree depth (**max_depth**) is often in the range [3, 15]

---

4 Please note that these rough dataset size estimates and parameter ranges are general guidelines and can vary based on the specific characteristics of the data and the computational resources available.

The following graph illustrates the points highlighted in the description sheet:

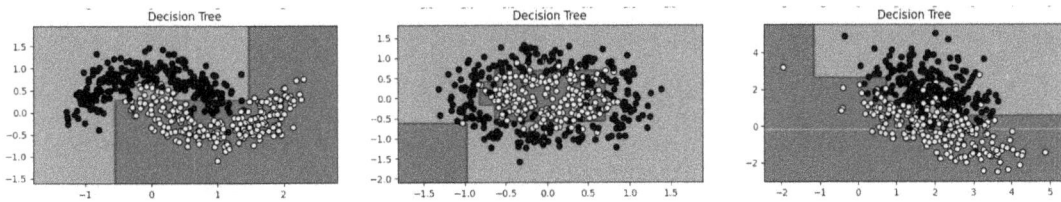

Figure 5.8: Decision tree algorithm

Particularly, the central graph shows the algorithm's effort to include the isolated point in the bottom left in its model, suggesting a tendency to consider it in its predictions. This situation presents a pronounced risk of overfitting. It is not certain that the label associated with this region will apply to future, unseen data. Instead, it appears as a statistical anomaly caused by an aberrant point.

Random forest

The random forest algorithm, a composite of multiple decision trees, serves to mitigate the effects observed in the earlier single decision tree algorithm. Consequently, it not only smoothens the outcomes but also markedly enhances the predictive performance when compared to the initial decision tree approach.

Let us examine the following pros and cons:

- **Advantages**: Combines multiple decision trees to reduce overfitting and handles non-linear relationships. Robust to overfitting, works well with medium datasets (up to ~1M rows).

- **Limitations**: Less interpretable and can be slow for large datasets (computationally expensive).

- **Important parameter and range**: Number of trees (**n_estimators**) in the range [10, 200], **max_depth** often in the range [5, 30].

The random forest algorithm, a composite of **multiple** decision trees, serves to mitigate the effects observed in the earlier single decision tree algorithm. Consequently, it not only smoothens the outcomes but also markedly enhances the predictive performance when compared to the initial decision tree approach. The points highlighted in the description sheet are illustrated in the following figure:

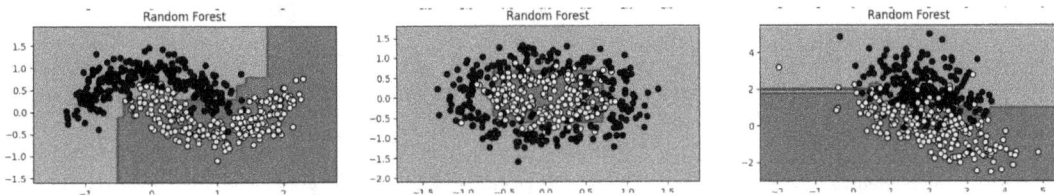

Figure 5.9: Random forest algorithm

Support Vector Machines

SVMs is a valuable tool for classification, particularly when dealing with complex, non-linear relationships in data. The following is an overview:

- **Advantages**: Effective in high-dimensional spaces, versatile

- **Limitations**: Not ideal for datasets larger than 100k rows, requires tuning

- **Important parameter and range**: Regularization parameter (C) is often in the range [0.1, 100]

The SVM algorithm is adept at modeling highly non-linear decision boundaries, a capability clearly demonstrated in the following graph:

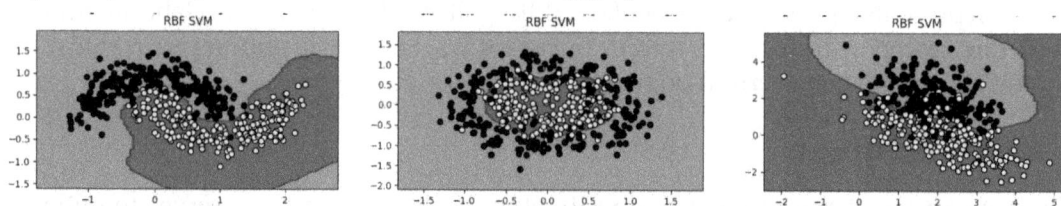

Figure 5.10: SVM algorithm

This makes it an exceptionally efficient tool for handling complex non-linear data, particularly in scenarios involving large-dimensional spaces (a high number of features or columns).

k-nearest neighbors

In a trading context, **k-nearest neighbors** (**k-NN**) can be used to identify similar market conditions and predict future price movements based on historical data. The algorithm classifies new data points by considering the k most similar historical examples.

Consider its strengths and limitations:

- **Advantages**: Simple and effective for small datasets (up to 50k rows)

- **Limitations**: Computationally intensive, not suitable for large datasets or high-dimensional data. Its effectiveness diminishes in high-dimensional spaces due to its fundamental reliance on the distance between data points for classification. In such complex, multidimensional environments, the conventional concept of distance becomes less discerning, leading to the *curse of dimensionality*[5] where kNN struggles to accurately classify instances.

- **Important parameter and range**: Number of neighbors (k) typically in range [3, 20]

---

5 *Curse of dimensionality* referred to an increased computational complexity and distance distortion that arise when analyzing and organizing data in high-dimensional spaces (often with many features). It is a term coined by Richard Bellman when considering problems in dynamic optimization

The **kNN** algorithm provides an excellent balance between simplicity and efficiency. These graphs show how a kNN can effectively create non-linear decision boundaries for classification:

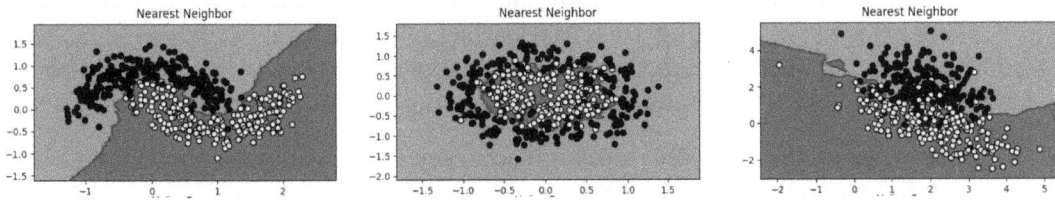

Figure 5.11: kNN algorithm

Naïve Bayes

Naive Bayes classifiers use Bayes' theorem to predict the probability that a data point belongs to a particular class. They assume that all input features are independent of each other, which simplifies the computation but may not always reflect reality. It is a good algorithm to start your learning path with.

The following are its key advantages and limitations:

- **Advantages**: Fast and efficient for high-dimensional datasets
- **Limitations**: Assumes feature independence
- Works well with text data and smaller datasets (up to 100k rows)

The following figure provides a visual representation of the key points outlined in the description sheet:

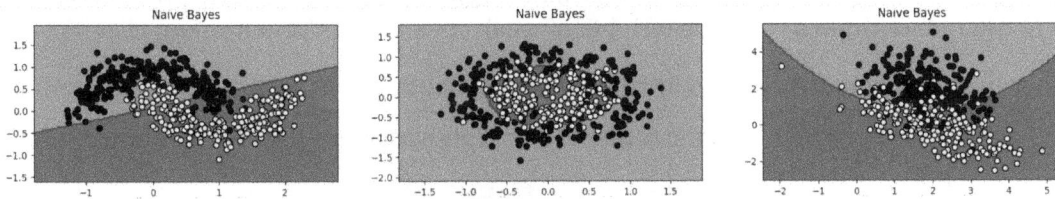

Figure 5.12: Naïve Bayes algorithm

For the final classification algorithms (Gradient Boosting, AdaBoost, XG Boost, and lightGBM), we will explore rank among the most effective in ML, stemming from ensemble methods like bagging and boosting. These techniques, which we will examine in depth in *Chapter 7, Advanced Machine Learning Models for Trading*, essentially enhance performance by integrating multiple models. This combination leverages the strengths of each component, resulting in a more robust and accurate predictive capability.

Gradient Boosting Machines

Imagine a team working together to solve a complex problem. **Gradient Boosting Machines (GBMs)** work similarly, building an ensemble of decision trees step by step. Based on the principle of **boosting**, each tree learns from the mistakes of its predecessors, gradually improving overall prediction accuracy like a team refining its strategy through collaboration. The following are its advantages and disadvantages:

- **Advantages**: Highly flexible and high accuracy. Can handle complex relationships and different data types

- **Limitations**: Can overfit, computationally intensive for large datasets (>500k rows)

- **Important parameter and range**: `learning_rate` often in the range [0.01, 0.3], number of trees in the range [100, 500]

As shown in the following figure, it is adept at modeling nonlinear decision boundaries:

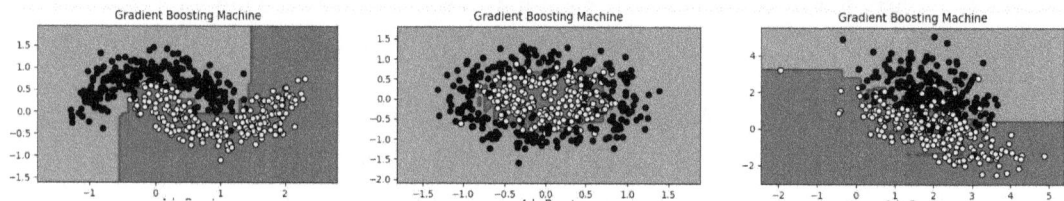

Figure 5.13: GBM algorithm

AdaBoost (adaptive boosting)

This algorithm sequentially builds an ensemble of classifiers and adapts to previous errors. A boosting technique adjusts the weights of weak classifiers to form a strong classifier.

We will now examine its advantages and disadvantages:

- **Advantages**: Increases the accuracy of simple classifiers, handles medium datasets (up to 500k rows)

- **Limitations**: It can be computationally expensive and prone to overfitting. Sensitive to noisy data and outliers

- **Important parameter and range**: Number of estimators (**n_estimators**) often in the range [30, 100]

The following graphs illustrate how AdaBoost uses sequential weak learners to create complex decision boundaries:

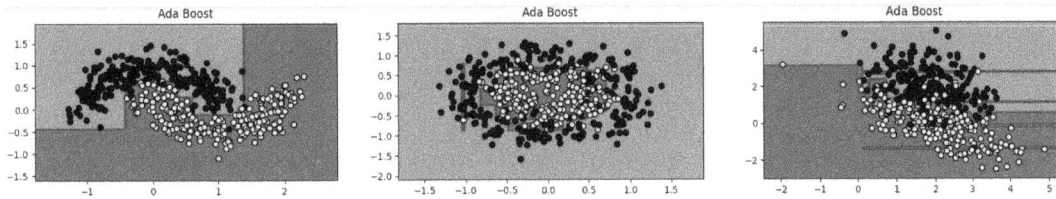

Figure 5.14: AdaBoost algorithm

XGBoost

Building upon the principles of GBM, **Extreme Gradient Boosting** (**XGBoost**) offers a highly optimized and efficient implementation. It is widely regarded as one of the **most powerful** ML algorithms. XGBoost is an advanced implementation of GBM that has gained immense popularity. XGBoost takes the concept of GBMs to the next level, introducing several enhancements for improved performance and efficiency.

Consider the following key features:

- **Advantages**: High performance, efficiency, and flexibility. Handles missing values
- **Limitations:** Can overfit if not tuned properly, suitable for datasets up to ~1M rows. Computationally expensive
- Important parameter and range: `max_depth` in range [3, 10], `learning_rate` in range [0.01, 0.3]

As a powerful implementation of GBM, XGBoost effectively classifies complex datasets, as shown in the following graph:

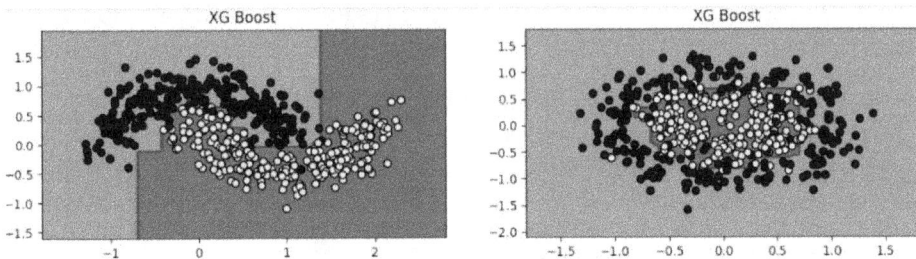

Figure 5.15: XGBoost algorithm

LightGBM

Developed by Microsoft Research and designed for speed and efficiency, LightGBM is a gradient boosting framework that excels at handling large datasets.

The following are its key features:

- **Advantages**: Fast, efficient, and great for handling large datasets (up to several million rows)

- **Limitations**: Can be overfitting on small datasets, requires careful tuning

- **Important parameter and range**: Number of leaves often in the range [20, 40], `learning_rate` in the range [0.01, 0.1]

The following is a visual representation of how LightGBM creates decision boundaries for classification across different datasets:

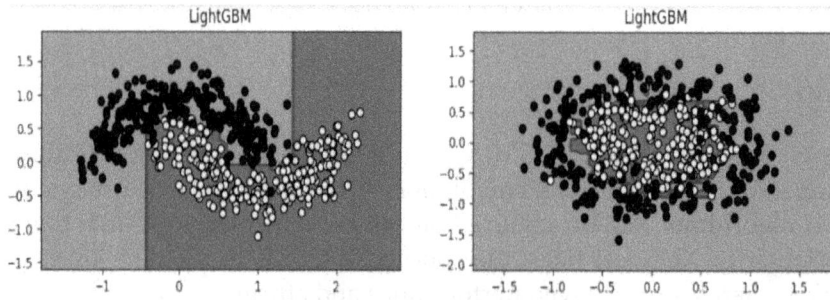

Figure 5.16: LightGBM algorithm

These graphs demonstrate LightGBM's ability to model both linear and non-linear relationships in data. In the first two graphs, we see it successfully separating two classes that are not linearly separable. The rightmost graph shows LightGBM creating simpler linear boundaries.

It is important to interpret all the preceding findings cautiously, as the insights gained here may not directly apply to real-world datasets.

Especially in high-dimensional spaces, where data often becomes more separable in a linear fashion, the straightforward nature of classifiers like **Naive Bayes** and **linear SVMs** could result in more effective generalization compared to more complex classifiers.

To conclude, **random forest, GBMs, AdaBoost, XGBoost**, and **LightGBM** are well-suited for handling complex relationships and non-linear patterns in financial data. However, they may require careful parameter tuning and can be computationally expensive.

While simpler models like **logistic regression, decision trees**, kNNs, and **Naive Bayes** may not always achieve the highest signal-to-noise ratios (as measured by the Sharpe ratio), they offer simplicity, interpretability, and robustness to outliers, making them suitable for specific scenarios.

After exploring algorithms that predict categorical labels, we turn to regression algorithms designed to predict numerical quantities.

Regression algorithms

Regression algorithms are used to predict a continuous numerical value based on one or more input features. In this section, we will explore several regression algorithms, starting with simpler linear models and progressing to more complex nonlinear models.

Understanding the distinction between linear and nonlinear models is essential: linear models assume a straight-line relationship between the input features and the target variable, while nonlinear models can capture more complicated, curved relationships.

To illustrate these concepts and the capabilities of different regression algorithms, we will use a **toy example**. This will allow us to visually observe how each algorithm attempts to model the underlying pattern in the data. Our primary goal is not to achieve optimal prediction accuracy on this specific dataset but rather to gain an intuitive understanding of each algorithm's behavior, strengths, and limitations.

By observing how these models perform on this controlled example, we can gain broader insights into their applicability to real-world regression problems, as follows:

Linear regression

As a basic algorithm in statistical modeling, linear regression models the relationship between a dependent variable and one or more independent variables using a linear equation. Now, let us consider the following strengths and weaknesses:

- **Advantages**: Simple, interpretable, and efficient for small to medium datasets
- **Limitations**: Assumes a linear relationship, not suited for complex patterns
- **Dataset limit:** Efficient for small to medium datasets (up to ~100k rows)
- **Import syntax:** `from sklearn.linear_model import LinearRegression`

As a first step, we apply linear regression to our noisy periodic wave dataset, keeping in mind its inherent limitation in modeling non-linear patterns, illustrated as follows:

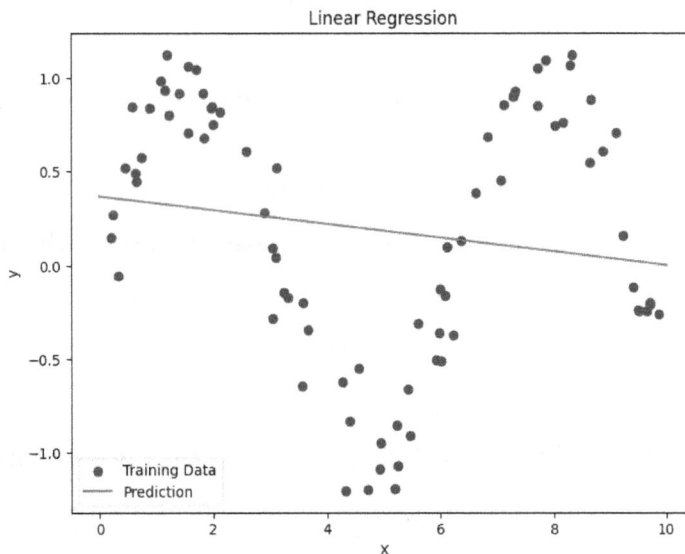

Figure 5.17: Linear regression

The graph depicts a linear regression model (red line) attempting to fit a noisy, periodic dataset, resulting in a straight line that poorly captures the underlying wave pattern. This highlights linear regression's fundamental limitation: its inability to model non-linear relationships, as it can only produce a linear approximation of the data.

Ridge regression

Ridge regression is a variation of linear regression designed to prevent overfitting, especially when input features are correlated. It does this by adding a penalty to the model's equation that discourages overly complex models.

Consider the following pros and cons:

- **Advantages**: Reduces overfitting, good for correlated features

- **Limitations**: Still assumes linear relationships, not ideal for non-linear data

- **Key parameter**: `alpha` (regularization strength)

- **Plausible value**: Typically, in the range [0.1, 100]

- **Dataset limit**: Good for small to medium datasets (up to ~100k rows)

- **Import syntax**: `From sklearn.linear_model import Ridge`

The results of Ridge regression are often very similar to those obtained using Lasso regression, as illustrated in the Lasso regression graph (*Figure 5.18*).

Lasso regression

Another approach to regularized linear regression is Lasso, which stands for Least Absolute Shrinkage and Selection Operator. Its key feature is the use of a penalty, which not only prevents overfitting but also performs automatic feature selection by driving some coefficients to zero.

The following are its key advantages and limitations:

- **Advantages**: Feature selection is inherent, good for models with high interpretability

- **Limitations**: Can struggle with complex non-linear data

- **Key parameter**: `alpha` (regularization strength)

- **Plausible value**: Usually in the range [0.001, 1]

- **Dataset limit**: Suitable for small to medium datasets (up to ~100k rows)

- **Import syntax**: `from sklearn.linear_model import Lasso`

Despite the added penalty, the Lasso regression model applied to this non-linear dataset still produces a linear fit, as illustrated as follows:

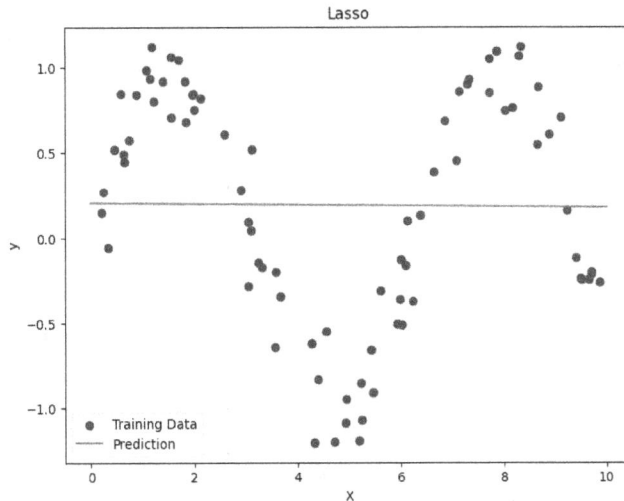

Figure 5.18: *Lasso regression*

ElasticNet

ElasticNet regression combines the penalty approaches of both Ridge and Lasso, resulting in a more flexible linear model that can handle a wider range of data scenarios, especially when dealing with correlated features.

The following are its advantages and disadvantages:

- **Advantages**: Balances feature selection and regularization, good for multicollinear data

- **Limitations**: Requires tuning of parameters, more complex than simple linear models

- Key parameters: **alpha** and **l1_ratio**

- **Plausible value**: **alpha** in [0.1, 100], **l1_ratio** in [0.1, 0.9]

- **Dataset limit**: Good for medium datasets (up to ~500k rows)

- **Import syntax**: `from sklearn.linear_model import ElasticNet`

Given the simplicity of our dataset, an ElasticNet graph would appear nearly identical to the Lasso graph, so we will omit it here.

Decision tree regressor

Unlike the previous linear methods, decision tree regressors use a tree-like structure to model the data, making them capable of capturing non-linear relationships.

The following is a summary of their key features:

- **Advantages**: No assumptions about data distribution, handles non-linear data well

- **Limitations**: Can overfit easily, sensitive to data changes

- **Key parameter**: `max_depth`

- **Plausible value**: Commonly in range [3, 10]

- **Dataset limit**: Works well with small to medium datasets (up to ~100k rows)

- **Import syntax**: `from sklearn.tree import DecisionTreeRegressor`

The following graph shows the characteristic step-like prediction curve of a decision tree regressor, resulting from its branching structure and how it partitions the data space:

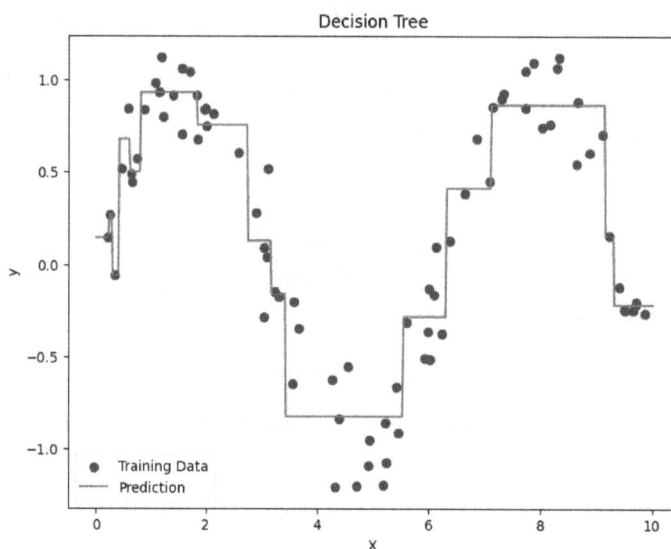

Figure 5.19: Decision tree regression

Random forest regressor

A highly efficient ensemble method, the random forest regressor combines multiple decision trees to improve prediction accuracy and reduce the risk of overfitting.

The following are the pros and cons:

- **Advantages**: Robust to overfitting, good performance on many problems

- **Limitations**: Less interpretable, can be slow with large datasets

- **Key parameter**: `n_estimators` (number of trees)

- **Plausible value**: Typically, in the range [10, 200]

- **Dataset limit**: Suitable for medium to large datasets (up to 1M rows)
- **Import syntax**: `from sklearn.ensemble import RandomForestRegressor`

The following graph shows the smoother, more generalized, and refined predictions of a random forest regressor on our noisy dataset:

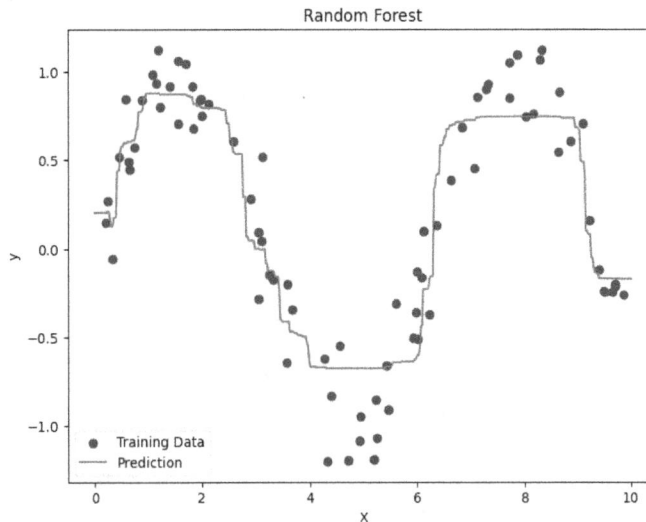

Figure 5.20: *Random forest regression*

Gradient boosting regressor

Known for their high predictive accuracy, gradient boosting regressors achieve this by iteratively building trees. Each new tree is specifically trained to correct the errors of the previously built ones, giving more weight to misclassified instances.

The following are its strengths and weaknesses:

- **Advantages**: Often high performing, handles various data types
- **Limitations**: Prone to overfitting, computationally intensive
- **Key parameters**: `n_estimators` and `learning_rate`
- **Plausible value**: `n_estimators` in [100, 500], `learning_rate` in [0.01, 0.3]
- **Dataset limit**: Good for medium datasets (up to ~500k rows)
- **Import syntax**: `From sklearn.ensemble import GradientBoostingRegressor`

As you can see, the Gradient Boosting regressor, similar to random forest, is able to capture non-linear relationships but creates a smoother, less step-like prediction curve than a single decision tree, as follows:

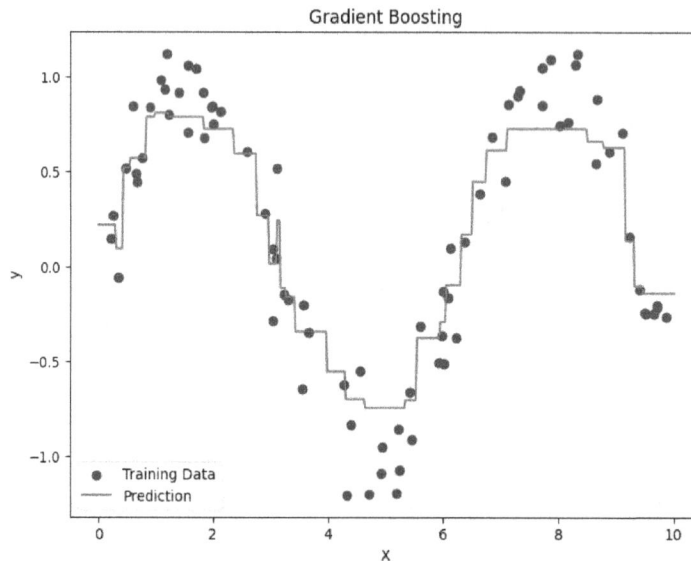

Figure 5.21: *Gradient Boosting Regression*

K-nearest neighbors regressor

This algorithm predicts the value of a data point based on the average of its k-nearest neighbors. To make a prediction, it identifies the **k** training data points most similar to the new input point and averages their target values. Let us explore the advantages and disadvantages of using the k-NN algorithm for regression tasks in a trading context, as follows:

- **Advantages**: Simple and effective for small datasets

- **Limitations**: Computationally intensive, not suitable for high-dimensional or large datasets

- **Key parameter**: `n_neighbors`

- **Plausible value**: Typically, in the range [3, 20]

- **Dataset limit**: Effective for small datasets (up to ~50k rows)

- **Import**: `From sklearn.neighbors import KNeighborsRegressor`

The following graph illustrates how the k-NN regressor, which predicts based on the average of the k-nearest neighbors, produces a step-like prediction curve when applied to our noisy periodic dataset:

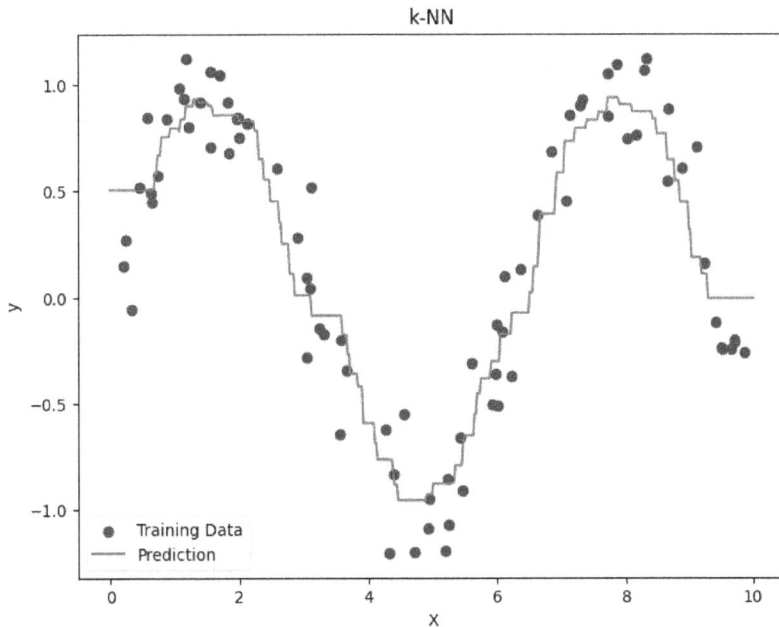

Figure 5.22: k-NN regression

Bayesian ridge regression

Bayesian ridge regression extends standard linear regression by providing a probabilistic framework for estimating model parameters. This allows us to quantify the uncertainty associated with our predictions, resulting in not just a single prediction value but also a prediction interval.

The following are its main characteristics:

- **Key parameters**: alpha and lambda (precision of the weight and noise)

- **Plausible value**: Typically fine-tuned via cross-validation; often starts with default values

- **Dataset limit**: Suitable for small to medium datasets (up to 50k-100k rows), depending on feature complexity

- **Import syntax**: `from sklearn.linear_model import BayesianRidge`

Bayesian ridge regression can provide robust predictions with an estimation of the uncertainty, as depicted in the following graph, where we apply a sliding window approach with Bayesian ridge to our dataset. In this visualization, each segment of the red prediction line represents the model fitted to a different window of the data, while the shaded area around it indicates the prediction interval, reflecting the model's uncertainty about its predictions:

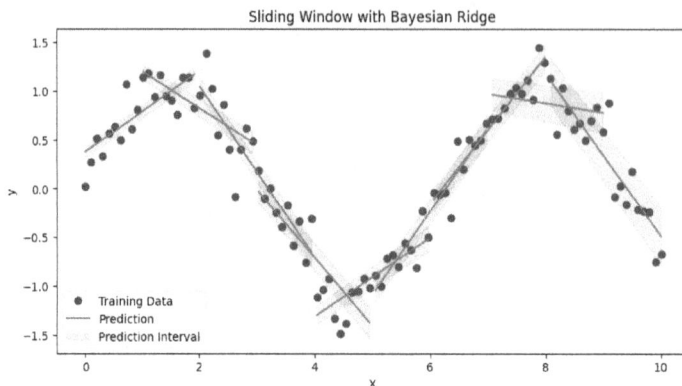

Figure 5.23: Bayesian ridge regression

Having explored the key supervised learning algorithms, we now shift our focus to the selection criteria and metrics essential for choosing the most suitable algorithm for specific trading applications, considering factors like data characteristics, prediction types, and performance metrics, including accuracy, precision, and recall.

Selection criteria for trading applications

In this section, we address the critical task of evaluating and selecting ML algorithms, with a particular focus on distinguishing between classification and regression models due to their different applicable metrics.

For classification algorithms, key metrics such as accuracy, precision, recall, and F1 score play a central role in evaluating performance.

Conversely, for regression models, we focus on metrics such as **Mean Squared Error (MSE)**, **Root Mean Squared Error (RMSE)** and **Mean Absolute Error (MAE)**. This distinction is critical to accurately gauge the effectiveness of each algorithm in its respective domain, ensuring that the right models are selected for the right tasks in trading applications.

Classification metrics

Classification metrics primarily focus on the quantity of accurately classified instances, diverging from regression, where distance measures are key. Instead of assessing the degree of error, classification metrics count the instances misclassified by the algorithm. This principle holds true regardless of the number of classes involved. In other words, these metrics are equally applicable whether we are dealing with binary classification (two classes) or multi-class problems (more than two classes).

Confusion matrix

The table that contains all instances, whether correctly classified or not, is known as the **confusion matrix**. We will look at its definition and explore how this matrix serves as a tool for calculating and understanding key metrics such as precision, accuracy, and recall.

The confusion matrix is a structured array that captures the performance of classification models by categorizing all instances based on their predicted and actual classifications. Structurally, the matrix has columns representing the instances predicted by the model to be positive or negative and, therefore, labeled as **positive** or **negative**:

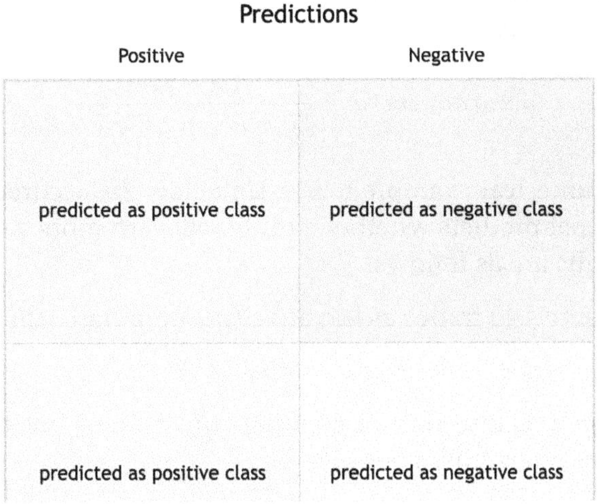

Predictions

Positive	Negative
predicted as positive class	predicted as negative class
predicted as positive class	predicted as negative class

Figure 5.24: Confusion matrix

Think of the confusion matrix as a detailed report card for a classification model. In supervised learning, we have the answer key (the true labels). The confusion matrix compares the model's answers (predictions) to the answer key, giving us a detailed breakdown of its performance. It categorizes each prediction into four groups: **True Positives (TP)**, **False Positives (FP)**, **True Negatives (TN)**, and **False Negatives (FN)**, providing a comprehensive view of the model's accuracy:

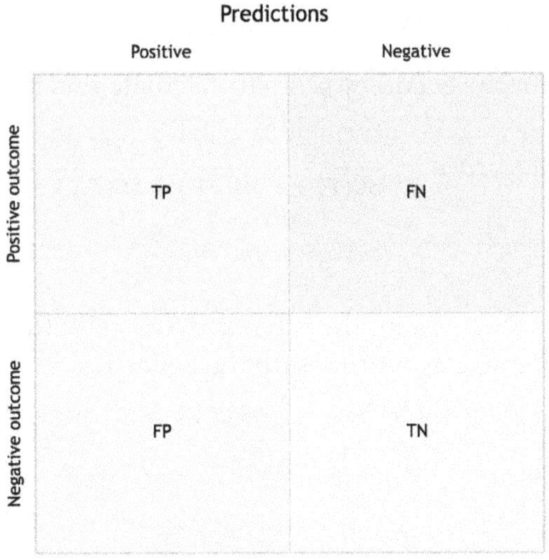

Predictions

	Positive	Negative
Positive outcome	TP	FN
Negative outcome	FP	TN

Figure 5.25: A complete confusion matrix

Accuracy score

Within the confusion matrix, the instances that fall along the diagonal (top-left to bottom-right) represent correctly classified cases[6]. These instances where the predicted class aligns perfectly with the actual class indicate the model's successful predictions. This is the essence of the accuracy score:

$$accuracy\ score = \frac{TP + TN}{TP + TN + FP + FN}$$

Let us use a simple, **numerical example** to illustrate how the accuracy score is calculated. Imagine a ML model that predicts whether a trade will earn money or not. After testing it on 100 trades, the results are as follows:

- The model predicts 40 trades as lucrative (positive class label).
- Out of these 40 trades, only 30 are profitable TP.
- The remaining 10 trades do not generate any money, but the model incorrectly labeled them as interesting ones, FP.
- Out of these 60 trades, 25 do not generate any money for TN.
- The remaining 35 are, in fact, profitable but were incorrectly labeled as not profitable FN.

This gives us:

- **True Positives (TP): 30** (Model correctly predicted profitable trades)
- **False Positives (FP): 10** (Model incorrectly predicted profitable trades)
- **True Negatives (TN): 25** (Model correctly predicted unprofitable trades)
- **False Negatives (FN): 35** (Model incorrectly predicted unprofitable trades)

Let us use the equation for the accuracy score to calculate this metric:

$$Accuracy\ score = \frac{30(TP) + 25(TN)}{30(TP) + 10(FP) + 25(TN) + 35(FN)}$$

$$accuracy\ score = \frac{55}{100}$$

The following is the code that enables the fill in a matrix with the data from the numerical example and then calculating the metrics with the Scikit-Learn API:

```
from sklearn.metrics import confusion_matrix , accuracy_score
import numpy as np

# Classification predictions and actual labels:
```

6 All the instances on the main diagonal are correctly classified, which is why they are labelled 'True', either 'Positive' or 'Negative' (TP or TN).

```
y_true = [1]*30 + [0]*10 + [1]*40 + [0]*25  # 30 TP, 40 FN, 10 FP, 25 TN
y_pred = [1]*30 + [1]*10 + [0]*40 + [0]*25  # Predicted labels
# Create the confusion matrix
conf_matrix = confusion_matrix(y_true, y_pred)

accuracy = accuracy_score(y_true, y_pred)
print("Accuracy:", np.round(accuracy,2))
```

Accuracy: 0.55

Precision score

The precision score metric is driven by the intuition of how accurately the model predicts positive instances. It specifically focuses on the proportion of TP among all the instances that the model predicted as positive. In essence, precision tells us how reliable the model's positive predictions are, disregarding how it performs in negative instances.

The formula is as follows:

$$precision\ score\ = \frac{TP}{TP + FP}$$

Let us use the **numerical example** to illustrate how precision is calculated:

The ML model predicts whether a trade will earn money or not. After testing it on 100 trades, the results are as follows:

- The model predicts 40 trades as lucrative (positive class label).
- Out of these 40 trades, only 30 are profitable TP.
- The remaining 10 trades do not generate any money, but the model incorrectly labeled them as interesting ones, FP.

The following figure shows how to organize these elements in the confusion matrix:

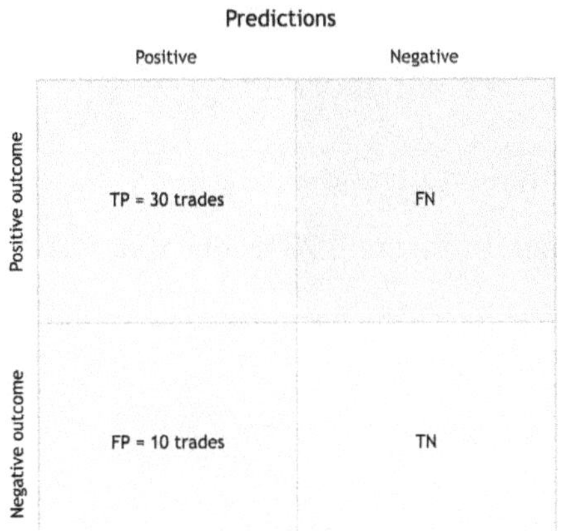

Figure 5.26: The precision score

Now, let us calculate the precision score:

- **TP**: 30 (trades correctly identified as lucrative)
- **FP**: 10 (trades incorrectly identified as profitable)

Use the formula for precision, as follows:

$$precision\ score\ = \frac{TP}{TP + FP}$$

$$precision\ score\ = \frac{30}{30 + 10}$$

This means that 75% of the trades that the model identified as worthwhile were worthwhile. In this context, precision tells us how reliable the model's predictions are.

To calculate precision programmatically, we can use the **precision_score** function from the **sklearn.metrics** module in Python, as demonstrated:

```
# Calculate Precision:
from sklearn.metrics import precision_score
precision = precision_score(y_true, y_pred)
print("Precision:", np.round(precision,2))


Precision: 0.75
```

Recall score

Recall focuses on the model's ability to identify all actual positives correctly. It measures the proportion of **true positive predictions** relative to the total number of actual positive instances.

Unlike precision, recall considers **both** correctly identified positives and missed positives (FN), providing a measure of how well the model is capturing all **relevant** instances:

$$recall\ score\ = \frac{TP}{TP + FN}$$

Continuing with the trade prediction model example:

- As already mentioned, there were 70 trades that were profitable.
- Out of these 70 profitable trades, the model only identified 30 (TP), while it missed 40 (FN):

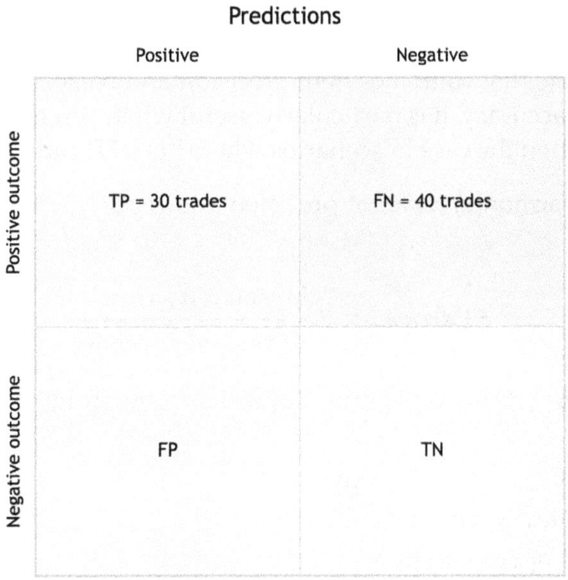

Predictions

Figure 5.27: Recall Score in confusion matrix

Now, let us calculate the recall:

- **TP**: 30 (trades correctly identified as profitable)
- **FN**: 40 (profitable trades that the model missed)

Using the formula for recall:

$$recall\ score\ =\ \frac{TP}{TP + FN}$$

$$recall\ score\ =\ \frac{30}{30 + 40}$$

recall score = 30/70 or 43%

Applying the **recall_score** function from scikit-learn to our trading example, we get:

```
from sklearn.metrics import recall_score
recall = recall_score(y_true, y_pred)
print("Recall:", np.round(recall,2))
```

```
Recall: 0.43
```

This means that the model correctly identified 43% of all the profitable trades. Recall reflects the model's capacity to **find all potentially profitable trades**, regardless of how many it incorrectly labeled as unprofitable.

F1-score

The F1-score is a metric that combines both precision and recall, providing a single score to measure a model's accuracy. It is particularly useful when you need to balance precision and recall, which is often the case in scenarios where both FP and FN are costly.

The F1-score is the (harmonic) mean of precision and recall, giving equal weight to both metrics, as follows:

$$F1\ score\ =\ 2.\frac{precision\ .\ recall}{precision\ +\ recall}$$

Applying the **f1_score** function from scikit-learn to our trading example, we get the following:

```
from sklearn.metrics import f1_score
f1 = f1_score(y_true, y_pred)
print("F1-Score:", np.round(f1,2))
```

```
F1-Score: 0.55
```

The F1-score metric is a good choice when you seek a balance between identifying all relevant instances (recall) and ensuring those identified are indeed relevant (precision).

Now that we understand the key metrics for evaluating classification models, we turn our attention to the metrics tailored for regression tasks, where the focus shifts from categorical accuracy to measuring the precision of continuous value predictions.

Regression metrics

Evaluating regression models requires metrics that quantify the difference between predicted and actual values. Let us explore some common regression metrics, starting with MSE.

Mean Squared Error

MSE measures the average squared difference between the estimated values and the actual value. It is a common measure of the accuracy of a regression model. The following graph visualizes the prediction errors of a linear regression model by plotting the actual values against the predicted values, with vertical lines representing the error for each point.

These errors are then squared and averaged to calculate the MSE, as follows:

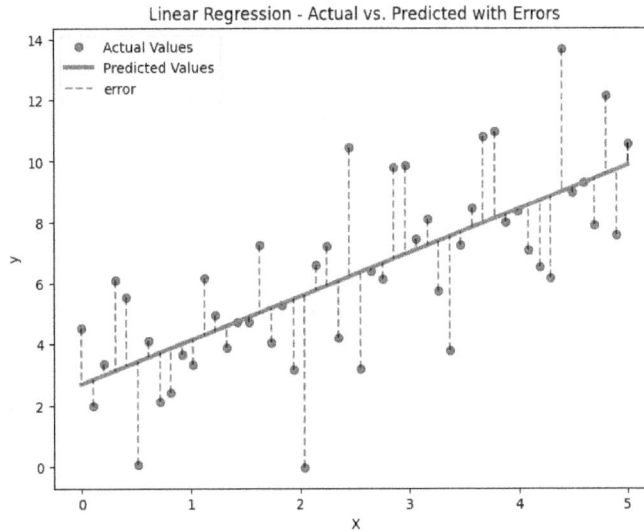

Figure 5.28: Prediction errors

MSE penalizes larger errors more severely than smaller ones due to the squaring of each error term. This makes it sensitive to outliers and amplifies the impact of larger errors compared to other metrics, as shown:

$$MSE = \frac{1}{n}\sum_i (real_i - prediction_i)^2$$

Calculate the MSE using the **mean_squared_error** function from scikit-learn, as follows:

```
from sklearn.metrics import mean_squared_error, mean_absolute_error
# Example: MSE can be calculated using
mean_squared_error(y_true, y_pred)
```

Root Mean Squared Error

RMSE is the square root of the MSE. It is also a measure of the accuracy of a regression model.

By taking the square root of MSE, RMSE converts the error metric back to the same unit as the target variable, making it more interpretable as follows:

$$RMSE = \sqrt{MSE}$$

The following is the implementation code with Scikit-Learn:

```
from sklearn.metrics import mean_squared_error
# Example: RMSE can be calculated using:
sqrt(mean_squared_error(y_true, y_pred))
```

Mean Absolute Error

MAE measures the average magnitude of the errors in a set of predictions without considering their direction. It is the average of the absolute differences between the prediction and the actual observation:

$$MAE = \frac{1}{n}\sum_i |real_i - prediction_i|$$

Unlike MSE or RMSE, MAE gives a linear score, which means all the individual differences are weighted equally. It is not sensitive to outliers, as shown:

```
from sklearn.metrics import mean_absolute_error
mean_absolute_error(y_true, y_pred)
```

Conclusion

By the end of this chapter, we were introduced to supervised learning as a powerful tool for data-driven trading. The core principle was to train algorithms on labeled historical data to predict future market behavior, the direction of movements with classification, and the magnitude of movements with regression.

Choosing the right algorithm and evaluation metrics (accuracy, precision, recall for classification; MSE, RMSE, MAE for regression) is critical. Supervised learning provides a framework for developing sophisticated and potentially profitable trading strategies, but requires careful consideration of model complexity, interpretability, and the specifics of financial data.

In the next chapter, we will explore feature engineering for trading, starting with basic features derived from price data. We will then incorporate technical indicators before moving on to more advanced feature engineering, including memory-based features, information-based features (such as Hurst exponent and entropy), and even features derived from the ML models themselves. Finally, we will cover dimensionality reduction techniques such as PCA and UMAP and discuss strategies for effective feature selection to improve model performance and interpretability.

Join our book's Discord space

Join the book's Discord Workspace for Latest updates, Offers, Tech happenings around the world, New Release and Sessions with the Authors:

https://discord.bpbonline.com

CHAPTER 6

Improving Model Capability with Features

Introduction

Improving model performance depends heavily on effective feature engineering. In this chapter, we examine different approaches to **feature engineering** and selection, covering a wide range of techniques. We start with basic methods based on **Open, High, Low, Close (OHLC)** features and progress to more advanced machine learning-based techniques such as PCA and UMAP. We also discuss **feature selection** methods and their critical role in model optimization. This chapter introduces a variety of methods for feature engineering, starting with statistical and information-based features such as the Hurst exponent and entropy. It then explores more advanced techniques, including features derived from decision trees. By presenting these approaches, the chapter provides readers with the tools necessary to transform raw data into meaningful inputs, thereby improving model performance and interpretability.

Structure

In this chapter, we will cover the following topics:

- Basic features based on OHLC
- Technical features
- Volatility and dollar-based features

- Memory-preserved features
- Statistical and information-based features
- Machine learning-based features
- Feature selection

Objectives

By the end of this chapter, readers will have a clear, practical understanding of feature engineering and its impact on model performance. They will learn how to apply a variety of techniques, from basic transformations to advanced machine learning-based methods.

A key takeaway is the ability to select and engineer features that improve predictive accuracy while mitigating the risk of overfitting. The chapter emphasizes the importance of balancing informative features with model complexity to ensure more robust and generalizable results.

In addition, readers will develop analytical thinking skills and gain insight into the decision-making process behind feature engineering and selection. Through hands-on practice, they will learn to turn raw data into useful features that improve model performance.

Basic features based on OHLC

When discussing machine learning for algorithmic trading, understanding basic features, such as OHLC data, is essential. OHLC data represents the primary structure of time series financial data, providing important information about price movements.

Lag values as features

Including lagged values as features introduces a **memory** of past observations into the analysis. This approach recognizes that past values can have a significant impact on future trends, capturing the temporal dependencies that are critical to accurate forecasting. By using lagged features, models can better understand and predict patterns based on historical data, leading to more robust and informed decisions.

For example, the following is a table showing a simple 1D time series with values from 1 to 7 and the results of adding lagged features with a lag of 2:

Time-Index	Value	Lag_1	Lag_2
0	1		
1	2	1	
2	3	2	1
3	4	3	2

Time-Index	Value	Lag_1	Lag_2
4	5	4	3
5	6	5	4
6	7	6	5

Table 6.1: Time series to lagged features

Having explored the benefits of incorporating memory into our models through lag features, let us now use simple arithmetic operations on OHLC data to extract insightful features to further enhance our time series analysis.

Arithmetic-based features

In the context of quantitative finance, various features can be created using basic arithmetic operations[1] on OHLC data. These features involve combinations and transformations of OHLC values to capture different aspects of market behavior:

- **Volatility-based feature:**

   Formula: *((high - low) / open)*

   It measures the relative volatility of the price within a single trading period.

- **Price momentum feature:**

   Formula: *(close / close.shift(5)) - 1*

   It represents the percentage change in the closing price over the past five periods.

- **Intraday price range feature:**

   Formula: *(high - low) / (high.shift(1) - low.shift(1))*

   It compares today's price range with the previous day's range.

- **Closing position relative to range:**

   Formula: *(close - low) / (high - low)*

   It indicates where the closing price is situated within the day's range.

- **Gap from previous close feature:**

   Formula: *(open - close.shift(1)) / close.shift(1)*

   It measures the gap in price from the previous close to today's open.

- **Normalized high feature:**

   Formula: *(high - mean(OHLC)) / std(OHLC)*

   It normalizes the high price relative to the mean and standard deviation of the OHLC values.

---

1 The arithmetic transformations that follow can be seen as precursors to the technical indicators (RSI, MACD, ...) that will be discussed in the next section.

- **Relative close-to-open change:**

  Formula: *(close - open) / open*

  It measures the percentage price movement within the same trading session, comparing the closing price to the opening price as a proportion of the opening price.

- **Weighted OHLC average:**

  Formula: *(open + high + 2*close + low) / 5*

  It represents a weighted average of OHLC, giving more weight to the closing price.

- **Normalized volume-weighted close:**

  Formula : *(close * volume) / mean(volume)*

  It represents the closing price adjusted by its trading volume, normalized by the average volume.

- **High-low clustering:**

  Formula: *(high - high.shift(1)) * (low - low.shift(1))*

  It examines the clustering effect of highs and lows compared to the previous period and provides a quantitative measure of the relationship between consecutive periods' highs and lows.

The following chart visualizes the high-low clustering effect for SPY ETF prices, an **exchange-traded fund (ETF)** that tracks the S&P 500. It shows how these fluctuations are consistent with the calculations described:

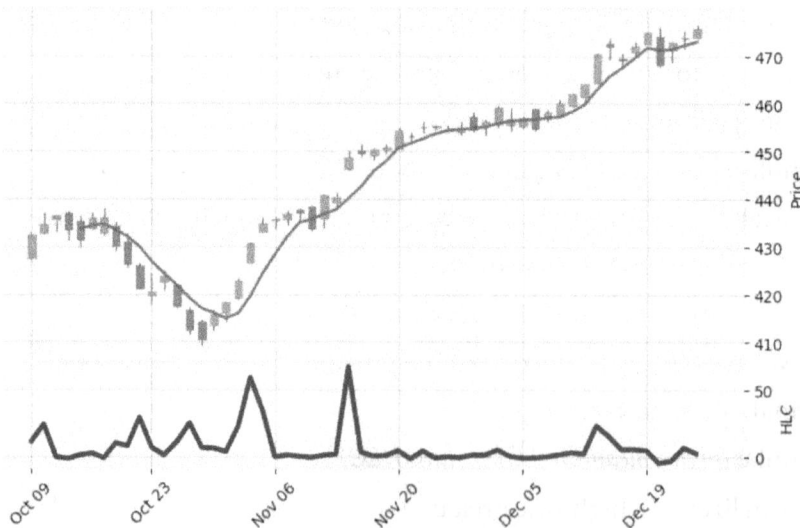

Figure 6.1: *High-low clustering for SPY ETF*

The bottom line represents the HL clustering measure, where noticeable spikes indicate significant deviations between consecutive highs and lows, reflecting periods of increased price volatility.

These features, created using simple arithmetic operations, can be useful when used in algorithmic trading models. They capture various aspects of market behavior, from volatility and momentum to relative positioning and price movement trends. Let us continue to explore the creation of simple features that do not require intensive operations.

Feature discretization

Feature discretization can be a valuable transformation. Financial time series data is often continuous and highly variable, making it challenging for machine learning algorithms to process. By converting continuous features into a finite set of discrete intervals or categories, feature discretization simplifies the data and enhances model interpretability. Scikit-learn offers an implementation of this principle. As explained in the documentation[2], feature discretization involves the following steps:

1. Breaking down each feature into a series of bins, with each bin having an equal width.

2. These discrete values are encoded.

3. Feed these features into an ML algorithm.

The following is the code needed for these steps:

```
from sklearn.preprocessing import KBinsDiscretizer
# transform the dataset with KBinsDiscretizer
enc = KBinsDiscretizer(n_bins=8, encode="onehot")
X = enc.fit_transform(df)
```

This procedure allows the model to exhibit **non-linear behavior** (even in the case of a linear classifier!). Appropriately applied feature discretization can therefore improve the model's performance, enabling more effective strategies to be devised.

All these features, along with the percentage change across all columns and lagged values, form a comprehensive set of initial features for a machine learning algorithm. This feature set is applied to the SPY ETF with daily frequency using a Random Forest classifier. For an understanding of supervised learning concepts used here, refer to *Chapter 5, Supervised Learning for Trading Systems.* The resulting classification is used to generate an equity curve, providing a visual representation of the model's performance over time:

---

2 https://scikit-learn.org/stable/auto_examples/preprocessing/plot_discretization_classification.html

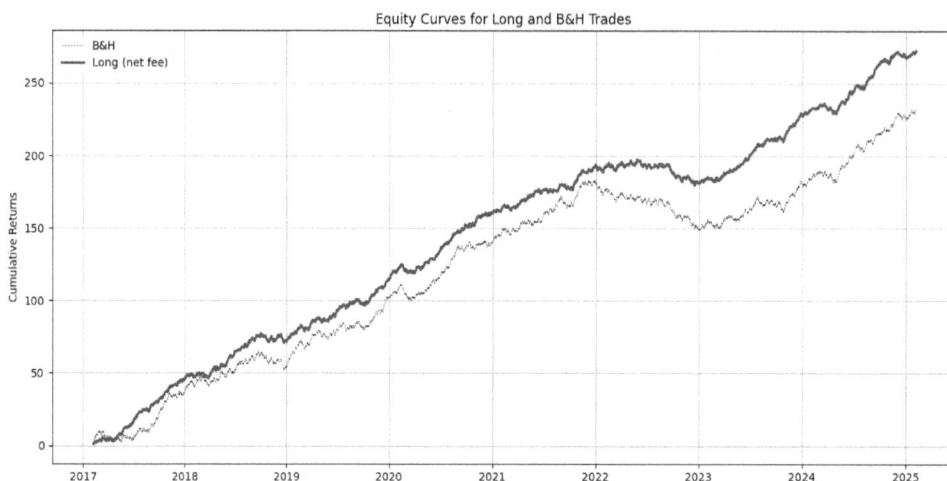

Figure 6.2: *Classification with OHLC based features*

Thew following is the confusion matrix for this system:

	precision	recall	f1-score	support
-1.0	0.11	0.51	0.18	143
1.0	0.92	0.55	0.69	1364
accuracy			0.55	1507
macro avg	0.51	0.53	0.43	1507
weighted avg	0.84	0.55	0.64	1507

This example serves as an initial promising exploration, and the detailed analysis of this specific algorithm is not the focus here[3], as the subsequent sections of this chapter present further experiments.

Building on the foundation of basic features, we now move on to explore features based on technical trading indicators that provide more profound insights into market trends and trader behavior.

Technical features

Technical indicators, rooted in market price and volume data, are essential tools for traders to detect trends, identify market regimes, and gauge momentum and volatility. These indicators reflect trading expertise and market psychology, bridging the gap between raw financial data and actionable insights. They provide a critical foundation for feature engineering in machine learning, where they are transformed into measurable attributes to improve predictive models.

3 For those interested in more details, the accompanying notebook provides in-depth insights

For those interested in evidence on the profitability of technical analysis in financial markets, the study[4] conducted by Park and Irwin offers a comprehensive review. It covers survey, theoretical, and empirical studies to assess the effectiveness of technical trading strategies. The paper notes that while early studies indicated profitability in foreign exchange and futures markets, later research showed consistent profits across various markets.

These indicators are often basic components in the feature sets of machine learning models used in algorithmic trading. We will explore a range of key technical indicators, categorizing them based on their primary functionalities, such as trend detection, momentum indicators, money flow, and volatility analysis.

Let us briefly introduce the **Pandas_ta** library that will help us implement these indicators.

Implementing technical indicators with Python

When it comes to implementing technical indicators as features for machine learning in Python, two popular libraries are **TA-Lib**[5] and **pandas_ta**[6].

Choosing between them depends on your specific needs:

- **TA-Lib** is widely used, comprehensive, efficient, and has bindings for various programming languages. However, its installation can be complex on some systems, and it is less integrated with the **Pandas** library.

- **pandas_ta** is super easy to use with pandas DataFrames, more Pythonic, and has a straightforward installation. However, it might be slower for large datasets.

In our case, for these reasons of ease of use and nesting with the **Pandas** library, we are going to use **pandas_ta**.

In the following sections, let us look at the main indicators (with their implementations) to build features for trading systems.

Trend detection

To effectively analyze and interpret market trends, the following indicators are commonly used:

- **Moving Average (MA)**: Identifies underlying trends by smoothing out price fluctuations

- **Exponential Moving Average (EMA)**: More responsive to recent price changes, aiding in detecting short-term trends

- **Moving Average Convergence Divergence (MACD)**: Highlights trend direction and momentum, as well as potential reversals

---

4 "The Profitability of Technical Analysis: A Review" by Cheol-Ho Park and Scott H. Irwin in AgMAS Project Research Report 2004-04
5 https://ta-lib.org
6 https://github.com/twopirllc/pandas-ta

To implement these indicators, install and import **pandas_ta**:

```
pip install -q pandas_ta
import pandas_ta as ta
```

The use of this library consists of calling the appropriate function and then adding the result of the calculation to a **Pandas** DataFrame:

```
# Moving Average (SMA) with a window of 5 periods
df['SMA_5'] = df.ta.sma(close='Close', length=5)
# Exponential Moving Average (EMA)
df['EMA_5'] = df.ta.ema(close='Close', length=5)
```

The following code represents the **MACD line**, which is the difference between the 12-period EMA (short-term) and the 26-period EMA (long-term):

```
# Calculating MACD using pandas_ta
df['MACD'] = df.ta.macd(close='Close')['MACD_12_26_9']
```

Additionally, a 9-day EMA of the MACD is often used as a trigger to generate buy and sell signals, indicating potential entry or exit points when it crosses above or below the MACD line. This smoothed line (**MACD_signal**) helps to generate buy and sell signals by identifying crossovers with the MACD line.

It is calculated by the following code:

```
df['MACD_Signal'] = df.ta.macd(close='Close')['MACDs_12_26_9']
```

Momentum indicators

Momentum indicators help traders assess the strength and speed of price movements and identify potential overbought, oversold, or trend reversal conditions.

The following indicators are commonly used in technical analysis, with corresponding code snippets demonstrating their implementation:

- **Relative Strength Index** (RSI): Measures the velocity of price movements, indicating overbought or oversold conditions[7] as shown:

  ```
  # RSI
  df['RSI'] = df.ta.rsi(close='Close', length=14)
  ```

- **Stochastic Oscillator**[8]: Shows the position of the closing price relative to the high-low range, identifying potential turning points, as shown:

---

7 RSI oscillates between zero and 100 and is typically used to identify overbought or oversold conditions in trading assets. An asset is usually considered overbought when the RSI is above 70 and oversold when it is below 30.

8 Stochastic Oscillator consists of two lines: the %K line (which measures the current price relative to the low/high range) and the %D line (which is a moving average of the %K line).

```
# Stochastic indicator
stoch = df.ta.stoch(high='High', low='Low', close='Close')
df = pd.concat([df, stoch], axis=1)
```

- **Commodity Channel Index** (**CCI**): Identifies new trends or cyclical conditions, useful in diverse market environments. CCI measures the difference between a security's current price change and its average price change, helping traders identify cyclical trends in commodities and other securities, as shown:

```
# CCI
df['CCI'] = df.ta.cci(high='High', low='Low', close='Close')
```

Volatility measurement

Volatility measurement indicators help assess the intensity of price fluctuations, providing insights into market conditions and potential breakouts. These indicators are particularly useful for identifying periods of high or low volatility, which can influence trading strategies.

The following are key volatility indicators along with their implementation in code:

- **Bollinger Bands**[9]: Adapt to market volatility, providing insights into market conditions and potential breakouts.

```
# Calculating Bollinger Bands using pandas_ta
bollinger = df.ta.bbands(close='Close', length=20, std=2)
df = pd.concat([df, bollinger], axis=1)
```

- **Average True Range** (**ATR**): Measures market volatility by decomposing the entire range of an asset for that period.

Volume and money flow

Volume and money flow indicators help assess market participation and liquidity, providing insights into trend strength and potential reversals, as follows:

- **Volume**: Essential for confirming the strength and sustainability of a trend

- **Money Flow Index** (**MFI**): Combines price and volume to measure the inflow and outflow of money, often signaling potential reversals

Up to this point, we have maintained the original time structure of the OHLC bars, which serves as the basis for all subsequent steps in the development of the trading algorithm.

---

9 Bollinger Bands consists of three lines: the middle line is a moving average of the closing prices, and the upper and lower bands are typically two standard deviations away from this moving average. Bollinger Bands expand and contract based on market volatility, with wider bands indicating more volatility and narrower bands indicating less. Bollinger Bands give insights into the volatility and potential price breakout points. When the price touches the upper band, it is often considered overbought, and when it touches the lower band, it is considered oversold.

In the following sections, we will discuss research that challenges this rigid structure of dividing OHLC bars into consistent time intervals.

Volatility and dollar bars-based features

The basic idea behind **dollar bars** is to aggregate the data into bars rather than time intervals or trade counts, where the cumulative dollar value (price multiplied by volume) reaches a specified threshold. This approach is useful in various contexts where capturing the impact of trading volume and price movements is more informative than just looking at time-based slices.

The applicability of dollar bars is particularly relevant in intraday data or in high-frequency trading environments where traditional time-based bars may not adequately capture market dynamics. They are particularly effective in managing the noise and variability in intraday data.

Dollar bars can also be adapted in markets with irregular trading volumes or high volatility, dollar bars can help normalize the data by focusing on the value traded rather than time intervals, which might be sparse or inconsistent.

Here is an example of a typical time-based dataset for **Microsoft** (**MSFT**) stock, showing prices recorded at 60-minute intervals during the trading day:

Datetime	Open	High	Low	Close	Adj Close	Volume	Dollar
2021-02-08 09:30:00	243.149994	243.679993	241.860001	242.350006	242.350006	4039211	9.789028e+08
2021-02-08 10:30:00	242.330002	242.770004	241.550003	241.669998	241.669998	2237594	5.407593e+08
2021-02-08 11:30:00	241.660004	241.897903	240.809998	241.675003	241.675003	1876452	4.534915e+08
2021-02-08 12:30:00	241.666504	241.949997	241.341705	241.794998	241.794998	1241859	3.002753e+08
2021-02-08 13:30:00	241.789993	242.199997	241.360001	241.460007	241.460007	1159471	2.799659e+08
...	...	...	...	...	...	...	...
2024-01-02 11:30:00	369.959991	371.359985	369.899994	370.476990	370.476990	1957295	7.251328e+08
2024-01-02 12:30:00	370.474609	371.019989	369.140015	369.630005	369.630005	1609221	5.948164e+08
2024-01-02 13:30:00	369.635010	370.200012	368.890015	369.549988	369.549988	1243301	4.594619e+08
2024-01-02 14:30:00	369.540009	369.760010	368.285004	369.320007	369.320007	1743397	6.438714e+08
2024-01-02 15:30:00	369.320007	371.200012	369.225800	370.869995	370.869995	3235802	1.200062e+09

5094 rows × 7 columns

Figure 6.3: Time bar dataset

Now, we can observe the distinct differences that emerge when applying a dollar bar slicing approach to this dataset.

We set-up a threshold based on the history of the dollar value exchanged for this share (mean of the dollar value augmented by one standard deviation):

```
# Dollar value of each trade
df['Dollar'] = df['Close'] * df['Volume']
# Set your dollar bar threshold
threshold = df['Dollar'].mean() + df['Dollar'].std()
print(threshold / 1e8)
15.612632865944716
```

In the following, we observe that each time the market exchange surpasses the set threshold, a new bar is formed. This is achieved by calculating the standard statistics (OHLC) for the corresponding time slice:

```
for index, row in df.iterrows():
    if open_price is None:
        open_price = row['Open']
        index_bar = index

    high_price = max(high_price, row['High'])
    low_price = min(low_price, row['Low'])
    volume += row['Volume']
    cum_dollar += row['Dollar']
```

This process ensures that bars are created dynamically based on market activity rather than at fixed time intervals. The following code snippet demonstrates how standard price statistics OHLC are calculated for each new bar as soon as the exchange crosses the predefined threshold, effectively capturing meaningful price movements.

We obtained the following dataset. As you can see in the following figure, the number of bars is reduced to half (5094 vs 2145) by computing bars based on the value exchanged:

Datetime	Open	High	Low	Close	Volume
2021-02-08 09:30:00	243.149994	243.679993	240.809998	241.675003	8153257.0
2021-02-08 12:30:00	241.666504	244.759995	240.990005	244.014801	15598840.0
2021-02-09 10:30:00	244.009995	244.500000	242.559998	243.959198	6500595.0
2021-02-09 14:30:00	243.969803	245.880005	242.250000	242.524994	8621235.0
2021-02-10 10:30:00	242.559998	243.291901	240.889999	241.380005	6480030.0
...	...	...	...	...	...
2023-12-29 10:30:00	377.089996	377.109985	373.480011	375.255005	4940932.0
2023-12-29 13:30:00	375.230011	376.859985	375.200012	375.980011	5866861.0
2024-01-02 09:30:00	373.859985	375.899994	366.770996	368.299988	6438914.0
2024-01-02 10:30:00	368.250000	371.359985	367.000000	370.476990	4683864.0
2024-01-02 12:30:00	370.474609	371.019989	368.285004	369.320007	4595919.0

2145 rows × 5 columns

Figure 6.4: Dollar bar dataset

For **volatility bars**, the principle is as follows: the bars are formed based on the level of price volatility rather than time or volume. This means that a new bar is created only when a certain threshold of price movement or volatility is reached. The purpose of volatility bars is to capture significant market movements and to filter out noise, making them particularly useful in choppy or highly volatile markets. By focusing on volatility, these bars provide a clearer view of market trends and potential reversals based on the actual market behavior rather than arbitrary time frames.

In the next section, we will continue our exploration of strategies to improve OHLC bars. Our next focus is not on altering the division of the bars, as previously examined, but rather on ensuring the retention of information within the price bars while maintaining stable statistical characteristics.

Memory-preserved features

One of the major challenges in computational finance is to achieve stationarity[10] in the input series. Why do we care about this nasty statistical detail? The answer is simple.

Machine learning algorithms perform better when the input features are stationary.

So, the question is, "How do we make sure that the inputs to the model are stationary?" *Fractional differentiation.*[11] This may help in achieving stationarity while still retaining some **memory** of the series. Fractional differentiation is valuable because it transforms time series data while preserving some memory, making it more informative for forecasting than fully differenced series that lose all past dependencies.

In simple terms, a **differentiated series** is often used to compute returns () in financial data:

$$r_t = \frac{price_t - price_{t-1}}{price_{t-1}}$$

A simpler way to illustrate fractional differentiation is to modify the standard differentiation formula to allow for partial differentiation. Instead of simply subtracting the previous price (as in standard differentiation,), we introduce a fractional weighting:

---

10 *Stationarity* is a statistical concept where a time series exhibits consistent properties over time, such as a constant mean and variance. In a stationary series, the way data fluctuates or varies around its mean is uniform throughout its length, making it predictable and analyzable.

1. 11 *Fractional differentiation* is a concept popularized by Dr. Marcos López de Prado. For a comprehensive understanding of fractional differentiation, the following article is a valuable resource: **"Fractional Differentiation and Its Use in Machine Learning"**, S. Uddin, M. A. Hossain, *Journal of Risk and Financial Management*, 2021. This article explores fractional differentiation on stock index data to achieve stationarity while preserving predictive power. It compares fractional and classical differentiation using artificial neural networks, showing that fractional differentiation significantly improves accuracy based on RMSE and MAE metrics.

$$P_t - dP_{t-1} + \frac{d(d-1)}{2}P_{t-2} - \frac{d(d-1)(d-2)}{6}P_{t-3} + \cdots$$

There is a trade-off when choosing the differentiation order **d**, as shown:

- **Lower d, closer to 0**: More memory is preserved, meaning valuable historical patterns and dependencies remain, but the series may still exhibit non-stationary behavior.

- **Higher d, closer to 1:** More stationarity is achieved, making the data better suited for machine learning algorithms, but at the cost of losing some past information that might hold predictive value. When $0 < d < 1$, Past prices still contribute, but their influence gradually decreases. This means fractional differentiation smoothly reduces memory rather than completely removing it, helping traders retain useful historical patterns while making the data more stable for modeling when $d = 1$, it simplifies to standard differentiation (returns).

Furthermore, by transforming the series, you may also be **filtering out noise**, which can lead to clearer patterns for the machine learning model to learn from.

In the following graph, we implement the method we have discussed on the CAC40 index (Yahoo ticker '^FCHI'), representing the French equity market.

The result aligns with our expectations:

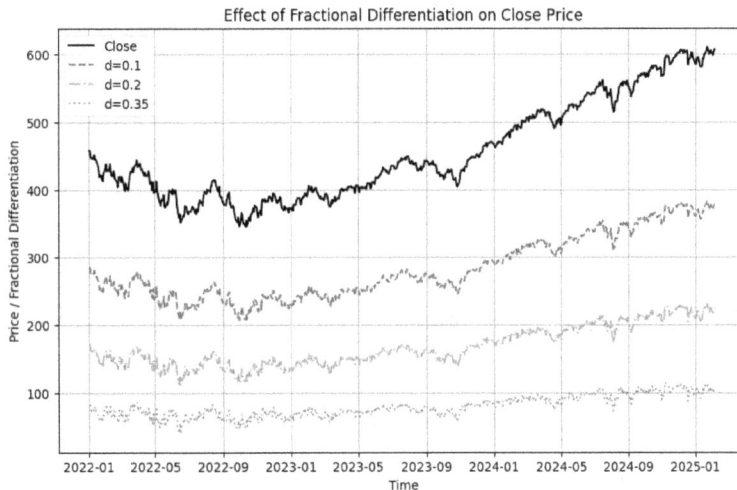

Figure 6.5: Effect of fractional differentiation

In the graph, we can see how different levels of fractional differentiation (d=0.1, 0.2, 0.35) progressively smooth the data while keeping the overall patterns intact. This means that the series becomes more stable and less noisy, which helps machine learning models perform better by focusing on the essential trends rather than being distracted by random noise.

To test[12] the stationarity of a series, a common method is to use the **Augmented Dickey-Fuller** (**ADF**) test, which evaluates whether a time series is non-stationary. For those unfamiliar, the test essentially tests whether the series has consistent properties over time, which is essential for many statistical and machine learning models.

The following is an example of its implementation:

```python
from statsmodels.tsa.stattools import adfuller
# Performing Augmented Dickey-Fuller test
for item in lst:
    print(item)
    adf_result = adfuller(df_lag[item].dropna())
    # Extracting the test statistic and the p-value
    adf_statistic, p_value = adf_result[0], adf_result[1]
    # Displaying the results
    print(np.round(p_value , 4))
    print(f'this series is stationary ? -> {p_value < 0.05}')
```

```
^FCHI_Close
0.3037
this series is stationary ? -> False


^FCHI_Close_diff_frac_0.1
0.0563
this series is stationary ? -> False


^FCHI_Close_diff_frac_0.2
0.0092
this series is stationary ? -> True


^FCHI_Close_diff_frac_0.3
0.0007
this series is stationary ? -> True
```

We conclude that the effects are as expected: a small degree of fractional differentiation is sufficient to bring the series in line with statistical requirements. By applying fractional differentiation, one can maintain a balance between removing enough noise to prevent overfitting while keeping sufficient memory in the series to allow for meaningful predictions. This is critical for financial time series, where complete differencing can sometimes remove the very signal, one is trying to model.

---

12 A low p-value (typically < 0.05) suggests that the series is stationary.

Fractional differentiation is not without its challenges. One issue is that it requires a careful choice of the differentiation order[13], which is not straightforward and typically requires some empirical or statistical justification. Additionally, the computational complexity[14] is higher than that of a traditional method.

To conclude on this method, we need to integrate this transformation into the sequence of operations within a machine learning framework. At first, we apply **fractional differentiation to a series and then we use the transformed series for machine learning.** Once the series has been transformed, it can be used as a feature in machine learning algorithms. The machine learning model is trained to classify or predict outcomes based on this transformed series, along with any other relevant features.

We next turn our attention to **statistical and information-based features** to enhance our data analysis.

Statistical and information-based features

In this section, our focus will be on examining two key indicators: entropy and the Hurst exponent. Let us start with the Hurst exponent.

Hurst exponent

The history of the Hurst exponent is a fascinating one, beginning in the mid-20th century with efforts to harness the power of the *Nile River* in *Egypt*, particularly through monumental projects such as the construction of dams. The British Empire accomplished this colossal feat largely due to the contributions of the eminent hydrologist *Harold Edwin Hurst*, who discovered a remarkable statistical method that captures memory effects within a time series. Hurst was tasked with understanding the long-term variability of the river to optimize the storage capacity of reservoirs in Egypt. He observed a persistence, a phenomenon of long-term memory, in the river's flow and levels. This led to the development of the Hurst exponent, a statistical measure that has since been widely used in various fields, particularly in science and engineering, to analyze time series data.

This method, which provided significant knowledge about the Nile's flood patterns, is the same one we plan to use as a feature in our machine learning algorithm.

Computing the Hurst exponent (denoted H value in honor of E. Hurst) is a way to quantify the extent to which a time series is **trending** or **mean-reverting**. The H value indicates the presence of a trend or mean-reversion and quantifies the persistence.

---

13 We can see the effects of the degree chosen in the previous graph.

14 Implementing fractional differentiation typically involves calculating weights that apply to past values of the time series. These weights decrease in magnitude as the lag increases and are applied in a manner that is dependent on the chosen order of differentiation. The resulting series is then constructed by applying these weights to the original series, which adjusts the series in a way that can be thought of as a "fractional" differencing process.

To grasp the functionality of the Hurst exponent, we will create three time series, each exhibiting distinct behaviors, one with a strong mean-reverting tendency, another representing a random walk, and the third displaying persistent behavior.

We will then compute the Hurst exponent for each series to verify if this statistical measure accurately discerns the specific nature and regime of each process:

- $H < 0.5$ indicates **mean-reverting behavior**.

  In the following graph, the upper subplot illustrates a mean-reverting process, while the lower subplot displays the corresponding rolling Hurst exponent for this process:

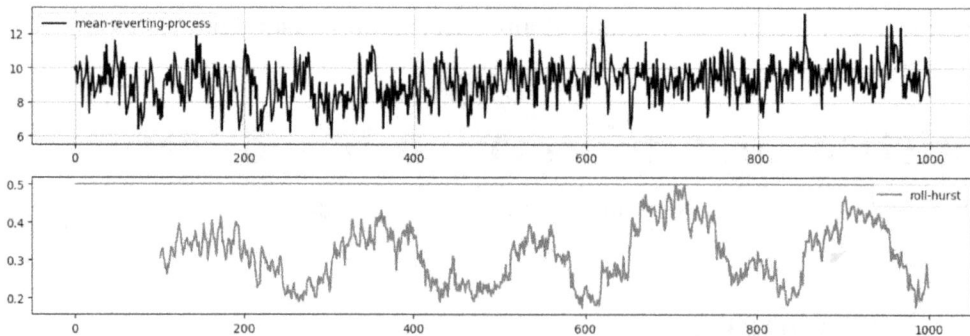

Figure 6.6: *A mean reverting process and Hurst exponent*

We observe that, consistent with theoretical expectations, the Hurst exponent remains under the 0.5 threshold during its entire trajectory. This threshold signifies the attributes of a mean-reverting process, which regularly oscillates around a central value. Thus, the Hurst exponent effectively identifies the regime of this time series as mean-reverting and anti-persistent. In a trading scenario, this insight enables us to implement strategies tailored to this specific dynamic.

- H around 0.5 suggests a pure random walk. This means **unpredictable noise**.

  In the following graph, the upper subplot illustrates a pure random noise process, while the lower subplot displays the corresponding rolling Hurst exponent for this process:

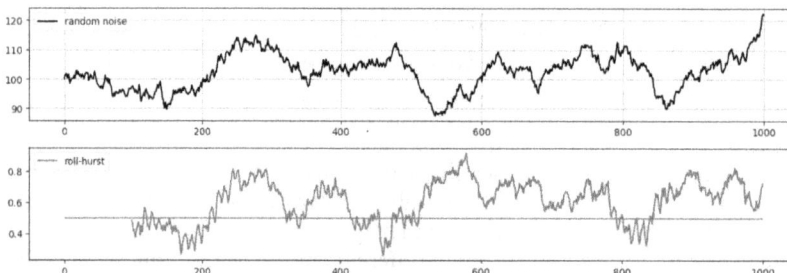

Figure 6.7: *A random noise process and Hurst exponent*

What we see aligns with theoretical expectations. In a random walk, the Hurst exponent typically hovers around the central value (0.5) as seen in the following histogram of the Hurst exponent:

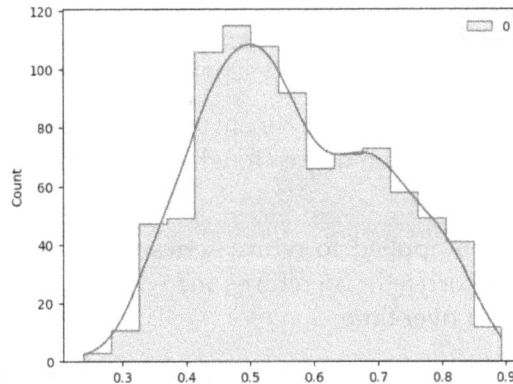

Figure 6.8: Histogram of Hurst Exponent

However, we also notice distinct transient phases where the process intermittently exhibits characteristics of mean reversion (H < 0.5) and persistent trends (H > 0.5). Consequently, in this case, if we look only at the Hurst exponent, the conclusion is not as clear-cut and easy as in the previous case. The random walk can be seen as an intermediate process between mean reversion (the previous case) and persistence (the case discussed next).

- H > 0.5 indicates a **trending behavior**.

For a series to be classified as persistent, indicating that memory effects are consistently present and the increments are positively correlated, the values of the exponent should remain above 0.5 over an extended period. Thus, we can swiftly conclude that the Hurst exponent has accurately pinpointed the **persistent** characteristic of the series.

This can be seen in the following graph:

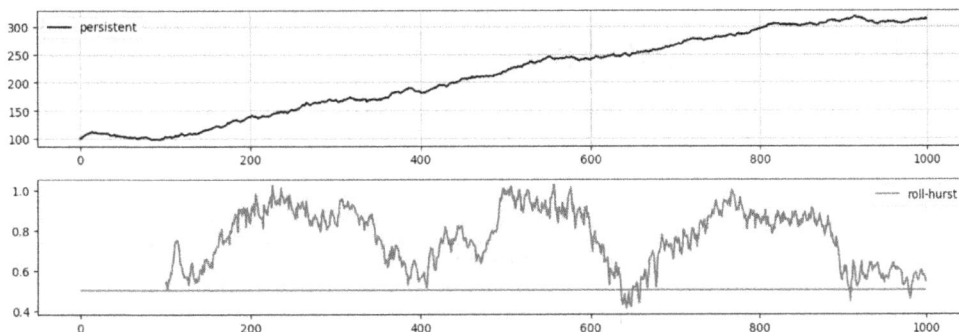

Figure 6.9: Hurst exponent for persistent trend

The graph illustrates that during long periods, the Hurst exponent significantly exceeds the 0.5 threshold, indicating a strong trending behavior. These higher Hurst values suggest a persistent, directional momentum in the price movements, meaning that upward or downward trends are more likely to continue over these intervals. This persistence could be leveraged by trend-following trading strategies during such phases. Hurst exponent can be applied to both price series and return series. The interpretation may vary slightly:

- **Price series**: Applying the Hurst exponent to a price series can help you understand the long-term trends and the degree to which the series deviates from a random walk

- **Return series**: When applied to return series, the Hurst exponent can provide insight into the autocorrelation of returns and whether they exhibit mean-reverting or trending behavior over time

To estimate[15] the Hurst exponent on a sliding window basis through a historical series, we can create a loop that moves through our time series data, computing the Hurst exponent on a subset of the data at each iteration:

```
from hurst import compute_Hc
def rolling_hurst(series):
    try:
        H, c, data_reg = compute_Hc(series.dropna(),
kind='price',simplified=True)
        return H
    except FloatingPointError:
        return np.nan  # Or return a specific value that indicates a failure


# And then apply as rolling:
df['hurst'] = df['Close'].rolling(window=window_size).apply(rolling_hurst,
raw=False)
```

This will give a time-varying estimate of the Hurst exponent, which can be particularly insightful for analyzing changes in market behavior over time.

Introduction to Entropy

Entropy (H) is a measure[16] of randomness or uncertainty in a dataset.

To better understand entropy, we create a simulated time-series.

---

15 https://pypi.org/project/hurst
16 Here is the mathematical expression for the entropy :
Where:
- is the entropy of the random variable
- is the probability of occurrence of the -th outcome
- The summation runs over all n possible outcomes of

The following graph displays a visualization of entropy (red dotted line, right-hand side axis across the four distinct segments of this time series data (blue line, left-hand side axis):

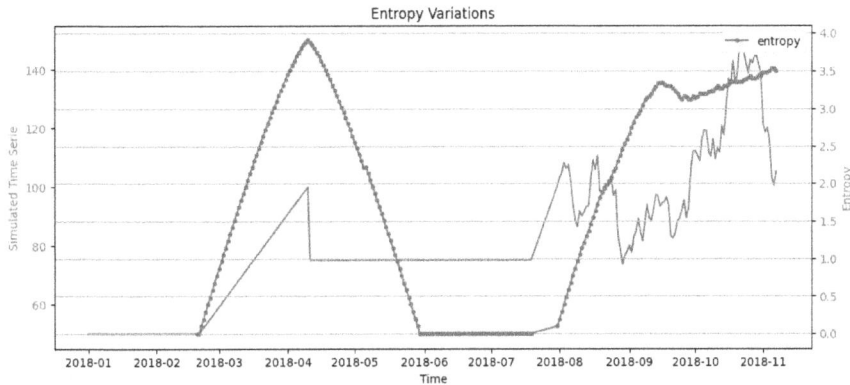

Figure 6.10: Entropy of a time-series

In the constant segment (2018-01 to 2018-03), the entropy is very low, indicating no uncertainty or variability. As the series progresses into the linear trend, there is a slight increase in entropy, suggesting a bit more complexity but still a predictable pattern.

The flat segment following the linear trend exhibits a drop in entropy, returning to low values due to the absence of variability.

The entropy for the random segment is not as high as one might expect for a completely stochastic process, which suggest that the randomness is constrained.

This behavior of entropy in different data regimes can be leveraged to understand the underlying patterns and inform predictive modeling in machine learning.

To estimate[17] the entropy, we proceed in the same way as for Hurst exponent. We use a sliding window basis through a historical series. Then, we can create a loop[18] that moves through our time series data. The following code block generates the entropy values displayed in the previous graph. It computes entropy using the **PyInform** library, which provides tools for information-theoretic calculations. Specifically, it applies the Shannon entropy function to a rolling window of size 30 over the 'Close' column in the dataset, creating a new feature, "Entropy," that quantifies the uncertainty or variability within each window:

```
from pyinform.dist import Dist
from pyinform.shannon import entropy


def compute_entropy(df1:pd.DataFrame):
```

17 https://elife-asu.github.io/PyInform
18 The rolling mechanism in Pandas efficiently manages the complex task of invoking the entropy computation function (compute_entropy) and repeatedly applies it across each sliding window. More details here: https://pandas.pydata.org/docs/reference/api/pandas.DataFrame.rolling.html

```
d = Dist(500)
for x in df1:
  d.tick(int(x))
return(entropy(d))#, b=10))
```

```
window_size = 30
# Calculate entropy for the combined dataset
df_combined['Entropy'] = df_combined['Close'].rolling(window=window_size).
apply(compute_entropy, raw=False)
```

Next, we incorporate entropy values as a feature for a machine learning algorithm.

Using entropy as a feature

Using entropy as a feature in machine learning involves quantifying the uncertainty or disorder within a dataset and leveraging this information to improve the model's predictive capabilities.

The following is a general approach to using entropy as a feature:

- **Calculate entropy**: Compute the entropy of different segments of your data. For instance, in time series data, you might calculate the entropy of price changes over fixed intervals. The preceding code served as a basis in this way.

- **Feature creation**: Treat the calculated entropy values as features. These features can provide insights into the level of predictability or randomness in different parts of the data.

- **Incorporate into machine learning models**: Include these entropy-based features alongside other features in your machine learning model.

- **Analysis of subgroups**: In datasets with various subgroups (like different stocks in a market), compare entropy across these groups. Higher entropy in a subgroup might indicate more unpredictability.

- **Temporal analysis**: For time-dependent data, analyze how entropy changes over time. Sudden changes in entropy might indicate important events or shifts in the underlying data generation process.

- **Combining with other statistical features**: Entropy can be combined with other statistical features like variance, skewness, or kurtosis to provide a comprehensive view of the data's characteristics. For a detailed introduction to these statistical measures, refer to *Chapter 3, Optimizing Trading Systems, Metrics, and Automated Reporting*.

Having examined the concepts of statistical and information-based features to understand data behavior, we now transition to the exploration of features derived from supervised and unsupervised machine learning techniques.

Machine learning-based features

Machine learning-based features are a powerful addition to traditional analytics. Unlike statistical measures such as Hurst and entropy, or technical indicators (such as MACD and RSI), machine learning-based features can capture more complex, non-linear interactions within the data that may be invisible to traditional methods.

The advantage of using these features lies in their ability to reveal the intrinsic structure of the data, improve model interpretability, and potentially improve predictive performance. They enable the development of more sophisticated, data-driven trading strategies that can adapt to complex market dynamics.

In this section, we will introduce some of these features, starting with PCA, then UMAP, and finally decision tree leaf-based features.

PCA-based features

Principal Component Analysis (PCA) can condense information from numerous variables into a smaller set of components that best explain the variability of the data, thereby reducing dimensionality while retaining essential information.

PCA is used in feature engineering to transform a high-dimensional dataset into a lower-dimensional one while retaining as much information (variance) as possible. In the following graph, the entire dataset[19] is compressed and projected into two dimensions as a result of the PCA transformation[20] :

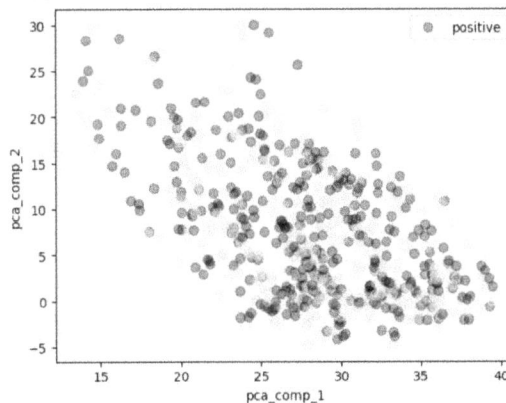

Figure 6.11: *PCA representation of the data*

---

19 OHLC, technical indicators and all the features presented so far.
20 Sckit-Learn implementation:
n_components_pca = 2

```
from sklearn.decomposition import PCA
pca = PCA(n_components = n_components_pca)
pca.fit(X_train)
vct = pca.transform(X_train)
plt.scatter(vct[:,0] , vct[:,1] , c=y_test ,s=50 , cmap = 'viridis' , alpha = 0.4)
plt.show()
```

In the graph, the two categories shown (yellow and purple dots) correspond to the positive and negative return classes (up and down). While there are certain regions that are predominantly occupied by a single class, indicating homogeneity, the classes are still largely interspersed and mixed.

This finding does not question the usefulness of the features generated by PCA. To be clear, the goal is not to completely solve the classification problem with this new representation of features alone. Instead, our goal is to assist the classification algorithm by introducing information that was not evident in the original dataset.

These new **PCA features** can then be used as **inputs** for machine learning models, providing a reduced, yet informative representation of the original data. This is particularly useful when dealing with multicollinearity[21] or when trying to improve algorithm performance due to high dimensionality.

PCA finds simple (linear) combinations of your original features, so if the classes are not linearly separable in the original feature space, PCA may not result in clear separation. This is usually the case with complex financial data. In this case, the points of each class are not grouped together in separate zones, but methods such as UMAP can be beneficial.

UMAP-based features

In contrast to PCA, which captures the global data structure through simple transformations, **Uniform Manifold Approximation and Projection (UMAP)** excels at preserving both local and global data structures, making it particularly useful for detecting the underlying structure of the data, as shown in the following figure:

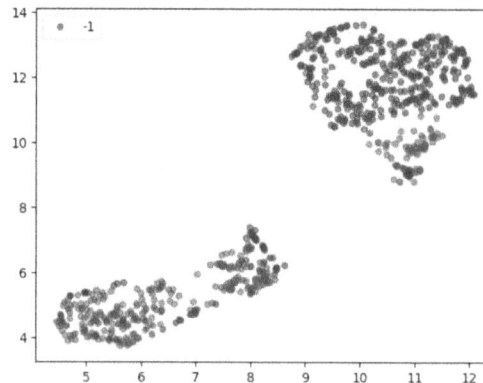

Figure 6.12: UMAP transformation for the dataset

As seen in the graph, UMAP allows for the identification of distinct zones where one class predominates in the absence of the other. This pronounced separation is consistent

21 Multicollinearity refers to the occurrence of high correlations among variables, which lead to unreliable and unstable predictive power. For example, if a model includes both **trading volume** and **dollar volume** (price × volume), the strong correlation between them can distort feature importance, leading to unreliable signals and overfitting.

with UMAP's explicit goal of showing clear distinctions between classes. Consequently, a classification algorithm armed with this representation of the data will find the task of separation easier. Such enhancement of data for easier algorithmic processing is the core role of feature engineering.

UMAP is a complex technique, but we can rely on an elegant and simple API[22] that implements this algorithm:

```
from umap import umap_ as UMAP
clusterable_embedding = UMAP.UMAP(n_neighbors=30,min_dist=0.0,n_
components=8).fit_transform(vct_bin)
plt.scatter(clusterable_embedding[:, 0], clusterable_embedding[:, 1], c=y_
test, s=20 , cmap = 'viridis' , alpha = 0.4)
plt.legend(['-1','1'])
```

All you need are these lines to perform and represent the result of the calculation. To integrate UMAP features, we simply need to adhere to the process previously outlined for entropy and PCA features.

Let us continue to explore the creation of machine learning based-features.

Decision tree leaf based features

Decision tree **leaf indices** provide a unique way to extract features by exploiting the paths a model takes to make decisions. This method captures how a decision tree processes the data, transforming its internal decision-making process into useful numerical representations.

The following graph represents a decision tree trained[23] to classify the SPY daily return:

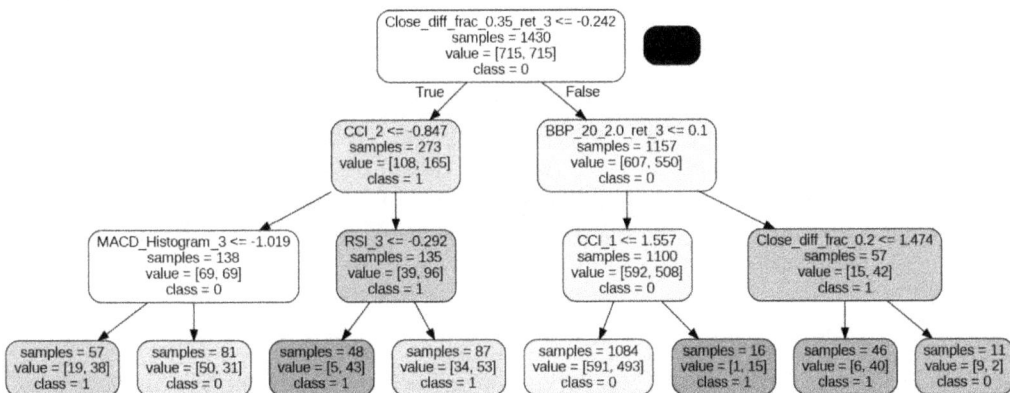

Figure 6.13: Decision tree for returns classification

---

22 https://umap-learn.readthedocs.io
23 The corresponding dataset comprised the OHLC columns augmented with all the feature engineering methods discussed so far.

The idea is simple, we first train a decision tree on the data set. Once trained, each data point is classified by moving from the root of the tree to a leaf node, following decision rules at each step. The key insight is that the specific **leaf node** where a data point lands contains valuable information about its characteristics.

To convert this into features, we assign a unique index to each leaf node. A new feature is then created for each data point, indicating which leaf node it belongs to. This method effectively converts the tree structure into a format that can be used as input for other machine learning models, adding a new layer of predictive information beyond traditional features.

Sklearn API offers a practical approach for implementing this feature engineering method. After training the tree, we simply need to use the `apply` method, which conveniently provides us with the desired output: the sequence of leaf indexes that guides us from the root to the decision leaf:

```
# Get the leaf indices for each sample
leaf_indices_train = clf.apply(X_train)
leaf_indices_test = clf.apply(X_test)


# merge leaf indexes with other features
X_train = pd.DataFrame(np.hstack([X_train , pd.DataFrame(leaf_indices_
train) ]))
X_test = pd.DataFrame(np.hstack([X_test , pd.DataFrame(leaf_indices_test)
]))


# Train a new model on the combined dataset
clf = RandomForestClassifier(max_depth = 15)
clf.fit(X_train, y_train)
```

We have now completed our in-depth exploration of feature engineering, presenting cutting-edge methods that push the boundaries of feature analysis and processing (UMAP, fractional differentiation, etc.). After constructing and computing thousands of new features, the next step is to reduce the number of features. The various techniques used to achieve this **reduction** are the subject of the last section of this chapter.

Feature selection

Feature selection is the process of identifying and selecting the most relevant features for a model. This helps reduce the number of input variables to those that are most useful for making predictions, thereby increasing model efficiency.

The importance of reducing the number of features cannot be overstated. In high-dimensional datasets, where the number of features significantly exceeds the number of observations, the model may suffer from overfitting and the *curse of dimensionality*. This term describes the phenomenon where the feature space becomes so large that the available data becomes sparse. This sparsity makes it difficult for the model to learn effectively. As a result, the model becomes overly tuned to the training data and performs poorly on unseen data.

Conversely, having too few features might lead to **underfitting**, where the model fails to learn the underlying patterns in the data effectively.

Finding the right balance is key. A common heuristic is that the number of features should be significantly less than the number of observations.

While there is no hard and fast rule, a guideline like having 5-10 times as many observations as features can be a starting point.

Now, let us look at how to reduce the number of features.

Mutual information as a feature selection method

Mutual information statistic can capture any kind of statistical dependency between the variables. It is equal to zero if and only if two random variables are independent, and higher values mean higher dependency.

This mutual information statistic is calculated[24] between each feature and the target variable to determine if the feature has sufficient information to predict the outcome. If it does, the feature is retained; otherwise, it is discarded.

Using the following code, for this classification problem, we select the **pct%** (5%) best features using the mutual information criterion:

```
from sklearn.feature_selection import mutual_info_classif , RFE,
SelectKBest

pct = 5
# Assuming you want to select pct% best features
k_best = int(pct/100 * len(X_train.columns))

# Initialize SelectKBest with mutual information
sel2 = SelectKBest(mutual_info_classif, k = k_best)
sel2.fit(X_train, y_train)

# Get the boolean mask of selected features
selected_features_mask = sel2.get_support()
# Get the column labels of selected features
X_train.columns[selected_features_mask]
```

---

24 https://scikit-learn.org/stable/modules/generated/sklearn.feature_selection.mutual_info_classif.html

In return we obtain the list of features selected:

```
['Adj Close_ret', 'Low_ret' , 'Relative_Change_Open_Close_ret' ,
'BBB_20_2.0_ret', 'High_1',   … ]
```

Recursive feature elimination

Given an external estimator (**clf**) that assigns importance[25] (weights) to features, the goal of **recursive feature elimination** (**RFE**) is to select features by recursively considering smaller and smaller sets of features. First, the estimator is trained on the initial set of features and the importance of each feature is obtained. Then, the least important features are pruned from the current set of features. That procedure is recursively repeated on the pruned set until the desired number of features to select is reached.

```
from sklearn.feature_selection import RFE
sel3 = RFE(clf, n_features_to_select = k_best , step = 0.3)
sel3.fit(X_train, y_train)
sel3.get_feature_names_out()[:100]
```

The following is a small extract of the features selected:

```
['Gap_Previous_Close', 'CCI', 'GOOG_Adj Close_ret', 'AMZN_Open_ret',
      'TSLA_Low_ret', 'NVDA_Low_ret', 'IBM_Low_ret', 'IBM_Adj Close_ret',
      'Close_diff_frac_0.2_ret', 'Price_Momentum_ret', 'BBB_20_2.0_ret',
      'MSFT_Volume_5', 'IBM_Open_4', 'IBM_Low_3', 'IBM_Volume_3',
      'IBM_Volume_5', 'Price_Momentum_3', 'Intraday_Price_Range_1',
      'Intraday_Price_Range_4', 'Intraday_Price_Range_5','Closing_
Position_1',        'Gap_Previous_Close_5','Relative_Change_Open_Close_3'
'Normalized_Volume_Weighted_Close_1', 'MACD_Histogram_3',
      'Open_ret_5', 'Adj Close_ret_3', …]
```

RFE iteratively removes the least important features until only the most relevant ones remain. The code above demonstrates how RFE is applied using a classifier (**clf**) to rank feature importance and select the top **k_best** features.

After fitting the model, the **get_feature_names_out()** function retrieves the most informative features that contribute to predictions. Below is a sample of the selected features, which include technical indicators (e.g., **CCI**, **MACD_Histogram**), price-based transformations (e.g., **Gap_Previous_Close**, **Intraday_Price_Range**), and fractional differentiations (**Close_diff_frac_0.2_ret**). These selected features enhance the model's predictive power by reducing noise and focusing on the most impactful variables.

---

25 We can access these weights, which denote the importance attributed to each feature, using the attribute (feature_importance) calculated when the model was trained. The code for displaying weights of the most discriminating k_best features:
sorted = np.argsort(clf.feature_importances_)
sorted[-k_best:]
clf.feature_importances_[sorted[-k_best:]]

With RFE identifying the most relevant features, we now explore feature selection using dimensionality reduction techniques like PCA and UMAP.

Feature selection with PCA and UMAP

Previously, we discussed PCA and UMAP as methods for feature engineering. These techniques are often used in the feature selection phase. In such scenarios, the original features are **substituted** with the new features derived from PCA or UMAP.

Rather than simply selecting the **right** features for input into the model, the focus shifts to using **all** the features and merging them using PCA or UMAP techniques. This approach creates a new set of features with **reduced dimensions**. For the implementation, we have already exposed the code in the previous section dedicated to UMAP.

Now that we know how to select significant features let us look at how to proceed when you want to benefit from the virtues of each of these propositions.

Combine best features with set operators

The **set** operators are an appropriate answer for combining all these feature proposals. In this example, we combine the proposals of the three competing feature selection methods (**sel1**, **sel2,** and **sel3**) exposed in the previous sections:

```
sel1 = SelectPercentile(mutual_info_classif, percentile = pct , n_neighbors = 10)
# Initialize SelectKBest with mutual information
sel2 = SelectKBest(mutual_info_classif, k = k_best)
sel3 = RFE(clf, n_features_to_select = k_best , step = 0.3)
```

The **set** methods encapsulate the selected features in sets:

```
set1 = set(sel1.get_feature_names_out())
set2 = set(sel2.get_feature_names_out())
set3 = set(sel3.get_feature_names_out())
```

Sets are combined using the set operators **union**[26] and **intersection**[27]:

```
set1or2 = set1.intersection(set2)
print(len(set1or2))
set1or2or3 = set1or2.union(set3)
```

Choosing between the **union** and **intersection** of feature sets from competitive feature selection methods depends on the context:

- For datasets with a limited number of observations (compared to the number of features), the **intersection** is the safer choice to avoid **overfitting**.

---

26 "Union": In set theory, the union of two sets is a set containing all elements that are in either set.
27 "Intersection": The intersection of two sets is the set of elements that are common to both sets.

- If the feature selection methods are fundamentally different and complementary (e.g., one is statistically based, as `mutual_info_classif`, and the other is model-based, as `RFE`), their union could result in a more comprehensive feature set. `union` is beneficial when the methods are complementary, and there is sufficient data to support a larger feature set. Otherwise, `union` could result in a larger feature set, which could increase the complexity of the model and possibly lead to overfitting.

Conclusion

By the end of this chapter, we understood how to master the feature engineering and feature selection techniques that are essential for optimizing the performance of machine learning models.

This applies not only to predictive performance but also, and equally importantly, to the aspects of post-production, deployment, and maintenance of machine learning models. These facets are collectively referred to as **Machine Learning Operations (ML-Ops)**. We should also mention that feature selection has practical benefits in a production environment. Models with fewer features are generally faster to run, easier to interpret, and more cost-effective, particularly when handling large datasets.

Now that we have a solid foundation in machine learning, we are ready to explore advanced algorithms.

In the next chapter, we will focus on sophisticated machine learning methods, ranging from ensemble techniques to continuous online learning approaches.

Join our book's Discord space

Join the book's Discord Workspace for Latest updates, Offers, Tech happenings around the world, New Release and Sessions with the Authors:

https://discord.bpbonline.com

CHAPTER 7

Advanced Machine Learning Models for Trading

Introduction

This chapter explores advanced machine learning techniques for algorithmic trading, examining methods that go beyond traditional supervised learning. We will look at state-of-the-art ensemble methods and online learning approaches to improve trading strategies.

The chapter begins with an in-depth look at ensemble methods, which combine multiple models to improve predictive accuracy and reduce overfitting. We then discuss boosting, bagging, and specific algorithms such as *XGBoost* and *LightGBM*, highlighting their applications in algorithmic trading.

The chapter also explores advanced regression methods, including **Least Absolute Shrinkage and Selection Operator (LASSO)** and **ridge regression,** and provides insight into their effectiveness in financial forecasting. In addition, we will explore online learning, examining tools such as **Scikit-multi flow** to show their role in real-time financial signal tracking. The goal of this chapter is to provide a comprehensive understanding of these advanced methods so that readers can apply them effectively.

Structure

In this chapter, we will cover the following topics:

- Understanding advanced machine learning

- Introduction to ensembling methods
- Advanced ensembling method for classification
- Advanced regression methods

Objectives

This chapter introduces advanced machine learning techniques for algorithmic trading, with a focus on improving predictive accuracy and preventing overfitting. Readers will explore ensemble methods such as bagging and boosting and understand how they reduce variance and bias. They will implement random forests for volatility prediction, fine-tune XGBoost using Scikit-Optimize, and evaluate models using classification reports. In addition, the chapter covers LASSO and ridge regression, showing how to use LASSO for feature selection to reduce overfitting and improve model interpretability. Readers will also explore kernel methods for nonlinear relationships and online learning with Scikit-multiflow for real-time model adaptation. These techniques, including XGBoost and online learning, represent the state of the art in machine learning and provide readers with the tools to build adaptive and robust trading models for dynamic market conditions.

A case study on spread prediction demonstrates these advanced methods. First, we classify normal vs. abnormal price dynamics; then, we predict the spread's value within a volatility range.

Understanding advanced machine learning

Modern machine learning for trading requires both predictive accuracy and adaptability. Traditional models that are trained once and applied indefinitely often fail in financial markets due to constant changes in trends, volatility, and market structure. To stay competitive, traders must use machine learning techniques that incorporate the latest advances in model ensembling, optimization, and real-time adaptation.

Ensemble methods, including **bagging** and **boosting** techniques like *XGBoost*, represent the cutting edge of predictive modeling. They improve accuracy by combining multiple models, iteratively correcting errors, and optimizing decision boundaries. These methods have become the industry standards for structured data tasks, including financial forecasting. *LASSO* and *ridge* regression introduce regularization, refining models by penalizing over-complexity and preventing over-fitting. **Kernel methods** extend traditional regression by capturing nonlinear relationships, allowing models to better reflect complex financial dependencies.

A key limitation of standard ML is its static nature: once trained, models remain **fixed** until retrained. **Online learning** overcomes this limitation by allowing models to be continuously updated with fresh data, making them highly effective for fast-moving markets. This real-time adaptation is critical for high-frequency trading, streaming data environments, and algorithmic strategies that must instantly adapt to new patterns.

Understanding these methods provides traders with the tools to build robust, adaptive, and high-performance models that go beyond traditional approaches. The following sections break down these techniques and their real-world applications in trading. To achieve greater predictive stability and accuracy, we turn to ensemble methods, which combine multiple models to improve performance and reduce errors.

Introduction to ensembling methods

Ensemble methods are a powerful approach to improving model performance by combining multiple weak learners into a stronger, more reliable predictor. This technique leverages the principle that aggregated models generally outperform individual models in stability and accuracy. We introduced ensemble learning in *Chapter 5, Supervised Learning for Trading Systems,* and earlier chapters; now, we will explore it in greater depth and apply it to trading strategies.

The core advantage of ensembling[1] is its ability to reduce errors and lower noise in predictions. By pooling the strengths and insights of different models, ensemble methods can effectively iron out the particularities and biases of individual predictors. This process of averaging or voting among models helps mitigate overfitting.

However, ensemble methods are not without their limitations. One key challenge is the potential correlation between predictors. If the individual models are too similar or correlated, the ensemble loses its diversity and, thus, some of its power. Another consideration is the number of predictors; too few may not provide sufficient diversity, while too many may lead to increased complexity and diminishing returns. We will discuss these points in detail in the following section, *Statistical foundations of ensembling.*

In the following sections, *fight overfitting with bagging methods* and *Achieving high accuracy with boosting,* we will explore two primary forms of ensembling, boosting and bagging, each with its unique approach to model combination and its strengths in the context of trading algorithms.

Advanced ensembling method for classification

In this section, we look at the two cornerstone techniques of ensemble learning, **bagging** and **boosting**. We will explore the basic principles of these methods[2], highlighting their distinct advantages and how they differ from each other. As we unpack these methods,

1 Historically, the concept of ensembling can be traced back to the work of pioneers like Leo Breiman and Thomas Dietterich, who recognized the potential of combining multiple weak learners to form a stronger collective learner. Their insights laid the groundwork for modern ensemble techniques that are now integral in predictive modeling across various domains, including finance.
2 Bagging and boosting are versatile techniques, applicable to a wide range of machine learning tasks, including both classification and regression.

we will gain an understanding of their role in improving predictive accuracy and model robustness in various scenarios.

In the next section, we will explain the statistical foundations and motivations behind ensembling. This segment is optional and can be skipped if preferred.

Statistical foundations of ensembling

In the context of ensemble learning, the theoretical motivation for error reduction when combining models can be understood through the bias-variance trade-off[3]. The overall error of an ensemble can be decomposed into the following three components:

$$Total\ Error = Bias^2 + Variance + Irreducible\ Error$$

Let us define these three components:

- **Bias** is the tendency of a model to **consistently** make incorrect predictions due to overly simplistic assumptions in the learning algorithm. The simplicity of the model will lead to a high bias, which manifests itself as a **systematic** deviation from the true relationship in the data. The following graphs illustrate this:

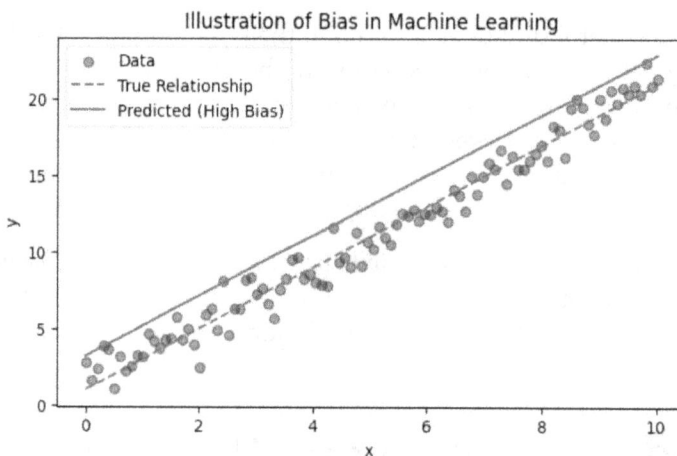

Figure 7.1: Bias error component in regression

The predictions illustrated in the linear relationship consistently deviate from accuracy (dotted line). Similarly, we demonstrate how bias impacts a machine learning classification algorithm.

In the following graph, the algorithm's overly simplistic boundary (frontier) between classes consistently results in poor classification outcomes:

---

3 The bias-variance trade-off highlights a fundamental challenge in machine learning: minimizing both bias (error from erroneous assumptions) and variance (error from sensitivity to data fluctuations) simultaneously is not typically possible. Reducing bias often increases variance and vice versa, necessitating a compromise for optimal model performance.

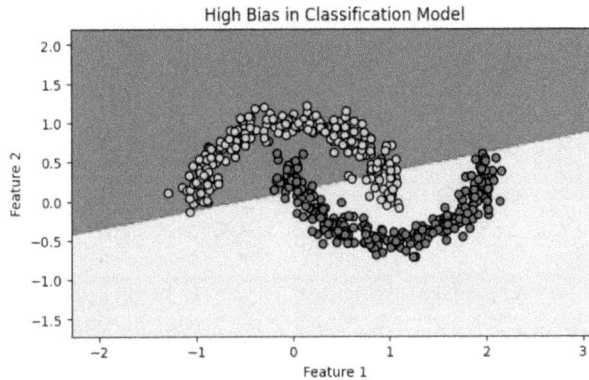

Figure 7.2: *Bias error component in classification*

- **Variance** describes how much the model's prediction errors **fluctuate** when applied to different sets of training data, highlighting the inconsistency of the model under varying data conditions.

- **Irreducible error** is the unavoidable error inherent in any model, caused by factors like unknown variables or inherent randomness in the data.

Now that we have grasped the fundamental terms let us explore how they interact and contribute to the overall error in a model.

Consider an ensemble of N independent models, each with a variance of and a bias of b. When these models are averaged, the bias of the ensemble remains b but the variance is reduced to $\frac{\sigma^2}{N}$, assuming the models are independent and have equal variance.

This reduction in variance contributes significantly to the decrease in the total error of the ensemble, as the total error is a combination of bias squared, variance, and irreducible error.

Ensemble variance for an ensemble of models can be determined as follows:

$$Ensemble\ Variance = \frac{\sigma^2}{N}$$

This demonstrates how ensembling leads to a significant reduction in error by decreasing the variance component of the error.

To provide a more accurate explanation of how ensembling reduces error by reducing variance, it is essential to include a discussion of the correlation between models. Indeed, correlation can be a double-edged sword; it can help if the models are sufficiently different, or it can hurt if the models are too similar.

This correlation significantly influences the overall effectiveness of the ensemble, as depicted in the following graph:

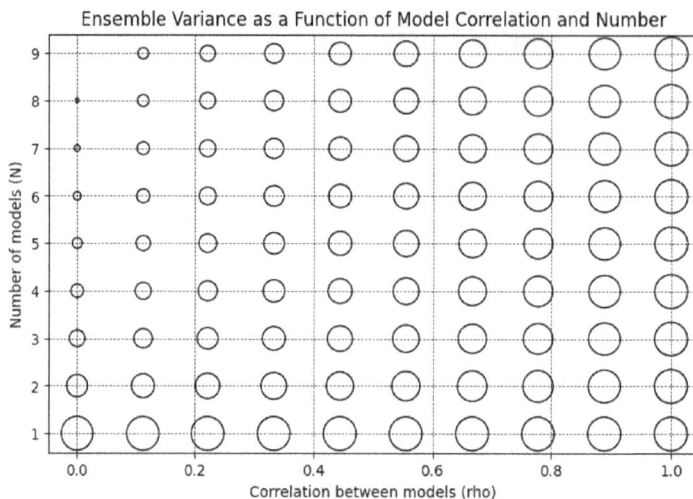

Figure 7.3: Ensemble variance

Large dots indicate higher variance, while small dots indicate lower variance. This representation illustrates the relationship between correlation ϱ and the number of models N, clearly depicting the impact of model correlation and the size of the ensemble on variance reduction. In conclusion, if the models are not fully independent and exhibit some degree of correlation, the reduction in variance achieved through ensembling[4] is adjusted by the extent of this correlation. In other words, the more correlated the models are, the less variance reduction is achieved by combining them.

Building on the statistical foundations of ensembling, we will now focus on bagging as a practical illustration of these principles.

Fight overfitting with bagging methods

Bootstrap aggregating (Bagging, in short) with any machine learning algorithm involves training multiple instances of the **same algorithm** on different subsets of the training data and then combining their predictions.

Each model is trained on a randomly sampled subset of the data, allowing the ensemble to capture diverse patterns and **reduce the risk of overfitting** that a single model might encounter. The final output harnesses the collective power of multiple models[5] to achieve more accurate and robust results.

Now, we will proceed to illustrate an application of bagging involving an ensemble of decision trees.

---

4 The mathematical representation taking into account the correlation between models is as follows:
It illustrates how the ensemble's variance is a function of both the average pairwise correlation and the number of models in the ensemble.
5 Averaging the predictions in regression tasks or using majority voting in classification tasks.

Predict volatility patterns with the bagging algorithm

The most known application of bagging is the random forest[6], which is an ensemble of decision trees, each trained on a different sample of the data set.

Given that we have previously utilized this algorithm with real market data in earlier chapters and have detailed its characteristics in *Chapter 5, Supervised Learning for Trading System*, which was devoted to the main principles of supervised learning, we can proceed with a clear understanding of the concepts of the random forest classifier. This familiarity allows us to focus more on the application of the algorithm in this specific context, leveraging our prior knowledge of its workings and strengths in supervised learning scenarios.

In this application, we will explore the ability of this bagging algorithm to predict instances where the closing price deviates significantly from a median line in relation to the [7] **(ATR)**. This research aims to leverage the robustness of random forest [8] that signify notable price movements against a backdrop of market volatility.

The following dataset is the *Nifty50 India Market index* (ticker ^NSEI on Yahoo Finance), a major stock market index representing the Indian stock market, with data at a 1-minute frequency ::

Datetime	Open	High	Low	Close	Adj Close	Volume
2024-01-19 09:15:00+05:30	21615.199219	21620.849609	21606.650391	21614.949219	21614.949219	0
2024-01-19 09:16:00+05:30	21614.849609	21631.599609	21614.849609	21627.650391	21627.650391	0
2024-01-19 09:17:00+05:30	21628.000000	21644.550781	21620.699219	21644.550781	21644.550781	0
2024-01-19 09:18:00+05:30	21643.550781	21649.449219	21627.500000	21627.800781	21627.800781	0
2024-01-19 09:19:00+05:30	21628.550781	21647.599609	21627.650391	21646.349609	21646.349609	0

Table 7.1: Nifty50 Index Intra-day dataset

---

6 Random Forest gained significant popularity in the early 2000s to 2010s, particularly for winning kaggle.com data science competitions, due to its robustness and ease of use. Although newer algorithms have since emerged as the state-of-the-art in machine learning, random forest remains a highly effective and versatile algorithm, widely used across various fields beyond just finance for its strong performance in a diverse range of applications.

7 The Average True Range (ATR) is a technical analysis indicator used to measure market volatility. The ATR is a 14-period moving average of the True Range (TR) calculated as follow,

$TR = \max\{(\text{High}-\text{Low}), |\text{High}-\text{Previous Close}|, |\text{Low}-\text{Previous Close}|\}$. We have discussed technical indicators in the previous chapter.

8 The ATR is employed as a volatility indicator, and this approach aligns closely with the concept of the Z-score discussed in Chapter 1, *Algorithmic Trading and Machine Learning in a Nutshell*, where we examined mean-reversion strategies.

The outcome we aim to predict is structured as a **classification** problem. In the next section, *Advanced Regression Methods*, we will reframe this classification problem as a regression task, predicting the exact spread.

For now, the specific condition we are modeling can be expressed as follows:

$$\texttt{Class} = 1, \ \text{if} \ \frac{Close_t - Average(Close.period=20)}{ATR(period=14)} > mult, \text{ or}$$

$$\texttt{Class} = 1, \text{if} \ \frac{Close_t - Average(Close.period=20)}{ATR(period=14)} > mult, \text{ or}$$

$$\texttt{Class} = -1, \text{otherwise}$$

In typical classification problems, the **positive** class denotes the event of interest we seek to predict. Accordingly, in this scenario, the target is assigned a value of 1 when there is a significant deviation of the closing price () from its established **volatility range** . Conversely, if there is not a notable deviation, the target is set to -1:

In simple financial terms, this model predicts whether the **closing price is about to experience a significant rise or drop beyond the expected volatility range**. A classification of **1** signals that the price is likely to break out of its normal range, while **-1** indicates that no such breakout is expected.

The following code computes the volatility range:

```
mult = 2
df['target'] = \
np.where((np.abs(df['Close'] - df['BBM_20_2.0'])/ df['ATR']) > mult , 1 ,
-1)
```

In our analysis, we will utilize the **Pandas_ta** library, as introduced in the previous chapter, to compute key technical indicators (**Average** and **ATR**) essential for our model. These include the Bollinger Bands middle line (**'BBM_20_2.0'**) as the simple **moving average**.

We represent the previous expression in the following graph:

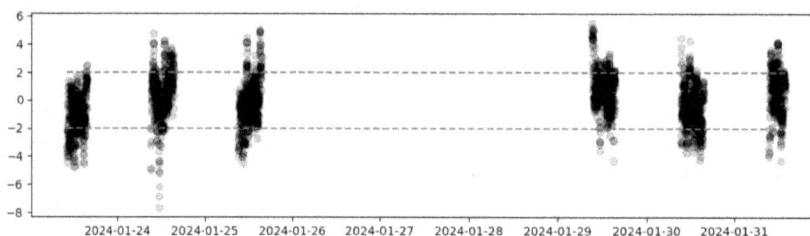

Figure 7.4: Volatility patterns

The negative class (**no detection**) in this context is associated with the price pattern staying **within the volatility channel** ([-2 , +2]), which is considered **normal** behavior. Inversely, for positive class.

In our current analysis, we are not engaging in parameter optimization[9]. This means we are using default hard-coded values for the periods in our calculations: a 14-period setting for the **ATR** and a 20-period setting for the average middle line. The volatility channel set to a range of [-2, +2] is indeed an arbitrary choice. A more in-depth statistical analysis (computing quantiles) could refine this approach.

Additionally, we are not conducting a search for optimal hyperparameters for the random forest algorithm. This approach simplifies our model and focuses on the inherent predictive power of the algorithm with standard settings rather than fine-tuning for potentially improved performance.

In the same manner, the feature engineering is intentionally kept to a bare minimum, focusing solely on the **ATR** and Bollinger Bands (specifically, the average line):

```
# Calculating Bollinger Bands using pandas_ta
bollinger = df.ta.bbands(close='Close', length=20, std=2)
df = pd.concat([df, bollinger], axis=1)
#ATR
df['ATR'] = df.ta.atr()
df['TR'] = df.ta.true_range()
```

As we have already defined the outcome (**df['target']**), the next step involves instantiating a bagging classifier and training it with the prepared dataset:

```
y = df.pop('target')
X = df.copy()
```

This process entails creating an instance of the random forest model from scikit-learn, configuring its parameters (**max_depth = 4**), and then fitting the model to our training data:

```
clf = RandomForestClassifier(max_depth = 4)
X_train , X_test , y_train , y_test = train_test_split(X , y)
clf.fit(X_train , y_train)

pred = clf.predict(X_test)
clf.score(X_test , y_test)
0.73

from sklearn.metrics import confusion_matrix , classification_report
print(confusion_matrix(y_test , pred))
print()
print(classification_report(y_test, pred ))
```

9 See Chapter 3, *Optimizing Trading Systems, Metrics and Automated Reporting*, for details and implementations of parameter optimization.

```
[[312 115]
 [ 32  96]]
```

We can analyze this confusion matrix as follows:

- **True negatives**: 312 instances correctly predicted as negative.

- **False positives**: 115 instances incorrectly predicted as positive.

- **False negatives**: 32 instances incorrectly predicted as negative.

- **True positives**: 96 instances correctly predicted as positive.

The following is a detailed report given by **classification_report**:

```
              precision    recall  f1-score   support

        -1.0       0.91      0.73      0.81       427
         1.0       0.45      0.75      0.57       128

    accuracy                           0.74       555
   macro avg       0.68      0.74      0.69       555
weighted avg       0.80      0.74      0.75       555
```

As we already said, the negative class in this context is associated with the price pattern staying within the volatility channel, which is considered **normal** behavior.

The report above highlights a high accuracy in predicting the **negative class**; when the model predicts a negative class, it is correct **91%** of the time. The **recall** metric[10] is also high (**73%**) suggesting that the model is quite good at detecting the **normal** behavior (price pattern inside the volatility channel).

Conversely, a lower precision for the **positive class**, suggesting that when the model predicts the positive class, it is correct less than half of the time (**45%**).

In the following graph, we can see that the model is effective in identifying the normal behavior (negative class) and has an average ability to detect significant deviations (positive class):

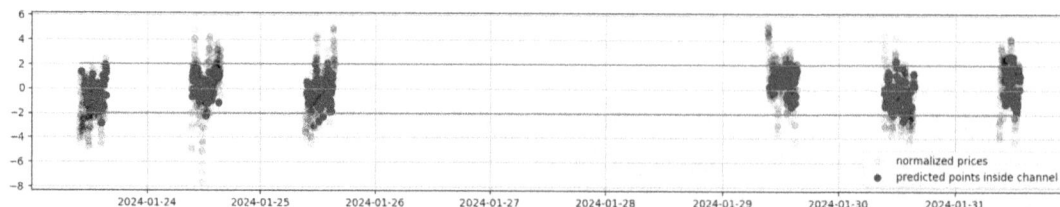

Figure 7.5: Predictions of 'normal' behavior

---

10 Refer to Chapter 5, *Supervised Learning for Trading Systems*, for an in-depth discussion on the 'recall' performance metric.

In the preceding figure, the points, which represent the model's prediction of **normal** behavior, are predominantly within the channel, indicating that the model is largely successful in identifying periods of standard volatility. There are only a few excursions beyond the channel, suggesting that the model has a good grasp of the price pattern relative to the volatility range established.

Transitioning from **bagging** to **boosting**, both powerful ensembling techniques that share a common goal of model improvement, we will now investigate what differentiates these methods and how each of them uniquely contributes to the predictive strength of a model.

Achieving high accuracy with boosting methods

Boosting is a **sequential process** where each subsequent model attempts to correct the errors of its predecessors, effectively combining weak learners to create a strong overall model. Unlike **bagging**, which builds models independently, **boosting focuses on raising the accuracy** of the ensemble by paying more attention to the training instances that previous models misclassified.

The primary strength of boosting lies in its ability to continually improve by concentrating on the harder-to-classify examples.

Popular boosting algorithms include AdaBoost (Adaptive Boosting), **Gradient Boosting Machines (GBM)**, **eXtreme Gradient Boosting (XGBoost)**, and **Light Gradient Boosting Machine (LightGBM)**:

- **AdaBoost** is often considered one of the simpler boosting methods and can serve as a good starting point.

- **GBM** is more flexible but requires careful tuning.

- **XGBoost**[11] is known for its performance and speed, often winning machine learning competitions due to its efficiency and scalability.

- **LightGBM**[12] is designed to be faster and efficient, particularly with large datasets, making it a powerful tool for trading where large volumes of data are processed and quick decision-making is crucial.

However, these latter algorithms can be more challenging to tune due to their complexity and the sheer number of hyperparameters[13], which also implies a higher computational demand. You can refer to *Chapter 5, Supervised Learning for Trading Systems*, for details of these algorithms.

---

11 **https://xgboost.readthedocs.io**
12 **https://lightgbm.readthedocs.io**
13 As a reminder, hyperparameters are structural choices. Unlike model parameters, which are learned during the training phase, hyperparameters are set **before** training begins and **remain constant** throughout the process. This distinction underscores their designation as "hyperparameters" and emphasizes their role as external configurations that influence the behavior and performance of the algorithm.

XG-Boost

For tabular data, which is common in trading scenarios such as OHLC datasets, XGBoost was hailed as a state-of-the-art algorithm upon its release. Since then, however, newer algorithms such as LightGBM have emerged, offering superior performance in some cases.

Unfortunately, maximizing the efficiency of these algorithms often requires careful hyperparameter tuning, a process that can be both challenging and time-consuming.

Leveraging insights from *Chapter 3, Optimizing Trading Systems, Metrics and Automated Reporting*, which focused on enhancing trading strategies with tools like HyperOpt[14], we will now apply a similar approach using **Scikit-Optimize**[15]. This toolbox enables us to conduct an intelligent Bayesian search within the hyperparameter space. Our objective is to fine-tune these hyperparameters and achieve optimal performance.

First, install the required tool using the following code:

```
!pip install -q scikit-optimize
from skopt import BayesSearchCV
import xgboost as xgb
from xgboost import XGBClassifier


# Hyperparameter search space
space = {
    'learning_rate': Real(0.01, 0.3, prior='uniform'),
    'n_estimators': Integer(100, 1000, prior='uniform'),
    'max_depth': Integer(3, 25, prior='uniform'),
    'gamma': Real(0, 1, prior='uniform'),
    'min_child_weight': Integer(1, 10, prior='uniform'),
    'subsample': Real(0.5, 1, prior='uniform'),
    'colsample_bytree': Real(0.5, 1, prior='uniform'),}
```

To set up XGBoost and utilize GPU acceleration (if available) for faster computations, you can define an XGBoost classifier and specify the use of a GPU (**device ='cuda:0'**).

Here is how you can do it:

```
opt = BayesSearchCV(
    xgb.XGBClassifier(booster = 'gbtree' , device ='cuda:0'),
    space,
    n_iter=10,
    cv=3,
    scoring="accuracy",
```

14 https://hyperopt.github.io
15 https://scikit-optimize.github.io

```
      n_jobs=-1,
      verbose=0
)
```

Replace coding of negative class (**-1** becomes **0**) and run the hyper-parameter search:

```
opt.fit(X_train, np.where(y_train == -1 , 0 , 1))
```

Print the best hyper-parameters:

```
from pprint import pprint
print("best params: ")
pprint(opt.best_params_)


best params:
OrderedDict([('booster', 'gbtree'),
            ('colsample_bytree', 0.56732736545028),
            ('gamma', 0.15926453431310586),
            ('learning_rate', 0.14141716914255373),
            ('max_depth', 25),
            ('min_child_weight', 5),
            ('n_estimators', 824),
            ('subsample', 0.7342246091928176)])
```

We also retrieve the **best model** for use in the rest of the analysis, as shown:

```
best_model = opt.best_estimator_
accuracy = best_model.score(X_test, np.where(y_test == -1 , 0 , 1))
print(f"Accuracy: {accuracy * 100.0}%")
Accuracy: 81.52350081037277%
```

We also print the confusion matrix and classification report, as follows:

```
print(confusion_matrix(y_test , pred))
print()
print(classification_report(y_test, pred ))


[[404  62]
 [ 41 110]]
```

	precision	recall	f1-score	support
0	0.91	0.87	0.89	466
1	0.64	0.73	0.68	151

accuracy			0.82	617
macro avg	0.77	0.80	0.78	617
weighted avg	0.84	0.83	0.82	617

The classification report indicates a model with a good level of accuracy in identifying the normal volatility behavior of assets, with an overall accuracy of approximately 81.5%. The model demonstrates a strong ability to predict the negative class (normal volatility behavior), as evidenced by a high precision (0.91) and a solid recall (0.87) for this class. This suggests that the model is effective at identifying instances where the closing price remains within a typical volatility range.

For the positive class (instances where the closing price is outside the normal volatility range), the model shows a decent performance with a precision of 0.64 and a recall of 0.73. This indicates that the model is reasonably good at detecting significant deviations from normal volatility, albeit with a higher likelihood of false positives (as suggested by the lower precision) compared to its ability to detect normal behavior.

The confusion matrix further supports these observations:

- The model correctly identified 404 instances of normal volatility behavior (true negatives) and correctly flagged 110 instances of significant deviation (true positives).

- However, it incorrectly predicted 62 instances as significant deviations when they were not (false positives) and failed to identify 41 instances of significant deviation (false negatives).

Overall, the model demonstrates a strong capability to identify normal volatility behavior and a respectable ability to detect significant deviations, making it a valuable tool for monitoring asset price movements. The balance between sensitivity to deviations (recall) and accuracy in predictions (precision), especially for the positive class, suggests a thoughtful consideration of the model's application in trading strategies, where both avoiding false signals and capturing significant movements are important.

In addition, the detection of the positive class (prices above the volatility range) has improved significantly compared to the previous random forest model. The accuracy for this class has increased from 0.45 to 0.64, a substantial gain of 40%. With the XGBoost algorithm optimized through hyperparameter tuning, we now have a well-balanced detector that is effective for both classes of events - whether the price is inside or outside the volatility range.

Having explored the application of boosting algorithms, we now compare the complementary ensemble methods of bagging and boosting.

Comparing bagging and boosting

While bagging and boosting are both ensemble methods that combine multiple models to improve performance, they differ in their underlying approach. As you may have noticed, a key difference between bagging and boosting is that **bagging** builds models independently and combines them through averaging or voting, which helps **reduce overfitting** (variance prediction) by averaging the predictions of multiple models. **Boosting**, on the other hand, builds models sequentially to **reduce bias**. It focuses on the most difficult or error-prone data points, resulting in improved overall performance, and can sometimes increase overfitting (variance) if not carefully managed.

The performance of boosting models needs to be carefully monitored in production because they are prone to overfitting if not properly tuned, a process we outlined in the previous section. This vulnerability stems from their focus on achieving accurate predictions (low bias). Therefore, if the overall architecture cannot be fine-tuned, bagging may be a more manageable alternative to implement, as it typically requires less intensive monitoring due to its inherent robustness against overfitting, primarily due to its focus on variance reduction.

In the next section, we will invoke another ensemble method beyond bagging and boosting. This method provides a different approach to combining models and can be used to further improve performance on complex tasks.

Voting methods

In *Chapter 3, Optimizing Trading Systems, Metrics and Automated Reporting,* we successfully trained a voting ensemble to classify the returns of MSFT stock. As a recap, voting ensembles combine predictions from diverse machine learning models to provide a robust outcome. This approach proves valuable by leveraging their strengths and minimizing individual weaknesses. While the underlying concept shares similarities with bagging and boosting, a key distinction lies in the model selection. Voting ensembles intentionally incorporate *diverse* algorithms, whereas bagging and boosting utilize variations of the same algorithm.

Next, we transition to advanced regression methods, where we will explore Lasso, ridge, online learning, and kernel methods, focusing on enhancing our understanding and application of these sophisticated regression techniques.

Advanced regression methods

In this section, we will provide an overview of several advanced machine learning techniques. Initially, we will explore quantitative methods, specifically LASSO, and ridge, which are employed to combat overfitting. Following this, we will discuss Kernel methods, recognized among the most effective strategies in machine learning. Lastly, we address the challenge of applying machine learning in scenarios where it is impractical to store extensive training data for repeated iterations. Instead, we focus on leveraging only the most recent data to continually refine our models, a practice known as online machine learning.

Defeating overfitting

LASSO and ridge regression are both techniques used to enhance the performance of linear regression models, particularly when dealing with overfitting or when the dataset features are strongly correlated.

At their core, both methods introduce a regularization[16] term to the linear regression objective function. This regularization helps reduce the model's complexity by penalizing large coefficients. A key aspect they share is their ability to shrink coefficients to lower values, thereby **reducing overfitting** and **improving model generalization**. However, a unique feature of LASSO is its capacity to reduce some coefficients to zero, effectively performing **feature selection** by excluding irrelevant features from the model. Both methods require the selection of a regularization parameter, which controls the strength of the penalty applied.

Step-by-step guide for advanced regressions

Building on our analysis of asset price behavior within a volatility range, we now take a deeper approach. Previously, we classified closing prices based on whether they stayed within or broke out of a normal volatility channel. Now, we want to quantify the exact extent of these deviations. This transition from classification to precise measurement naturally leads us to regression algorithms, which allow for a more detailed assessment of price movements.

Regression algorithms differ from their classification counterparts by predicting continuous outcomes rather than discrete categories. In the context of our study, while classification helped us identify whether closing prices fell into a normal range, regression will enable us to predict the normalized value of a closing price.

To begin this advanced exploration, we would typically follow these steps:

1. **Data preparation**: First, ensure your dataset is well-prepared, with closing prices and any relevant features that might influence these prices. Then, **scaling** is important for training LASSO and ridge regression models. Both LASSO and ridge add a penalty to the size of the coefficients in linear regression models. The **scale** of the features directly influences the magnitude of these coefficients and, consequently, the penalty applied during regularization. Especially in LASSO regression, which can zero out coefficients for **feature selection**, scaling ensures

---

16 LASSO adds a second term which is a penalty equal to the absolute value of the magnitude of coefficients :

Ridge adds a penalty proportional to the square of the magnitude of coefficients:

In both cases, is a regularisation parameter.

that the decision to eliminate a feature is not unduly influenced by the feature's scale. This makes the model more interpretable.

2. **Feature selection**: Identify which features are most predictive of your target variable. This could involve statistical analysis and the use of feature selection techniques as we seen in the previous *Chapter 6, Improving Model Capability with Features*, devoted to these techniques.

3. **Model selection**: Choose a regression model. Linear models, such as LASSO and ridge regression, are excellent starting points due to their simplicity and effectiveness. For more complex, non-linear relationships, consider models like kernel ridge regression or ensemble methods like GBM or random forest regressors.

4. **Model training**: Split your dataset into training and testing subsets to validate the model's performance. Train your selected model on the training set, carefully tuning any hyperparameters to optimize performance.

5. **Evaluation**: Assess the model's accuracy using appropriate metrics for regression, such as **Mean Squared Error (MSE)**.

6. **Iteration**: Refine your model based on performance metrics and domain knowledge. Adjusting features, experimenting with different models, or further tuning hyperparameters can lead to improved accuracy.

7. **Application**: You can now apply this trained and validated model to predict normalized closing prices on new, unseen data. This capability can be a powerful tool in forecasting future price movements and making strategic decisions.

By shifting from classification to regression, we move beyond identifying whether prices fall within a normal range to **predicting the magnitude of their deviation**. This approach provides a detailed and actionable understanding of price movements in relation to market volatility, enabling more precise trading decisions.

LASSO method

Since we have already done steps 1 to 4 for classification in the previous section on *Achieving high accuracy with boosting*, these steps will be significantly abbreviated.

We start by scaling the features as follows:

```
from sklearn.preprocessing import StandardScaler
scl = StandardScaler().set_output(transform="pandas")
X_train = scl.fit_transform(X_train)
X_test = scl.transform(X_test)
```

Next, invoke Sklearn to import the required models:

```
from sklearn.linear_model import Lasso , Ridge
```

In the following code, we fine-tune the regression model to achieve our objective of quantifying price deviations within the volatility range:

```
#  hyperparameter search space
space = {
    'alpha': Real(0.001, 10, prior='log-uniform'),
        # log scale for regularization
}

opt = BayesSearchCV(
    Lasso(),
    space,
    n_iter=30,
    cv=5,
    scoring="neg_mean_squared_error",
    n_jobs=-1,
    verbose=0)

# optimize hyper parameters
opt.fit(X_train, y_train)

print("best params: ")
pprint( opt.best_params_)

best params:
OrderedDict([('alpha', 0.001)])
```

Let us keep track of the best model to use it as of now:

```
rgr = opt.best_estimator_
```

The following graph represents the predictions made by the optimized model on the test set, alongside realizations of the spread values (normalized closing price):

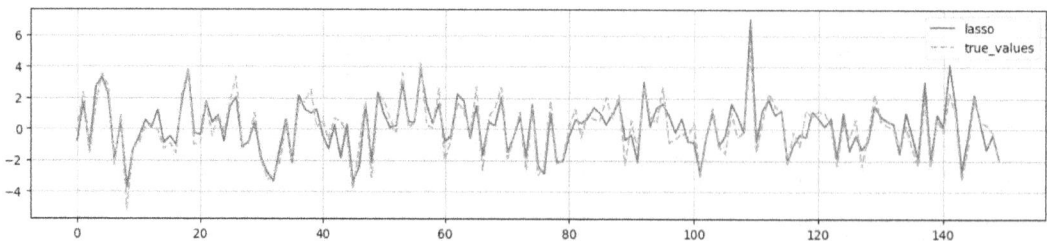

Figure 7.6: Normalized price predictions and realizations

We check the goodness of fit with a scatterplot of predictions versus actuals. The proximity of the data points to the diagonal dashed line measures the accuracy of the model. The closer the points are to this line, the more accurate the model is:

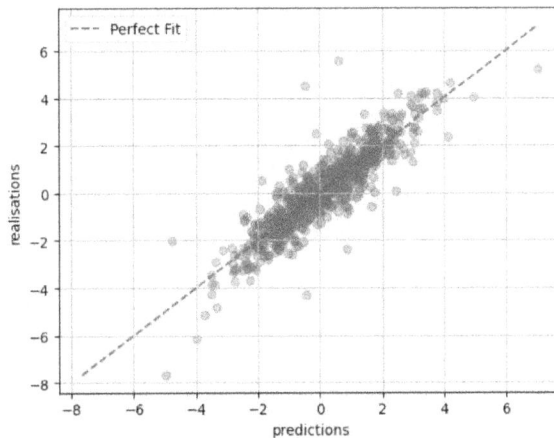

Figure 7.7: *Predictions and realizations*

In this case, the points cluster near the diagonal, suggesting that the optimized model provides a good fit. To quantify this observation, in the following code, we compute the regression score, which is normalized between [-1, 1], and obtain a score of 0.8.

This score, being closer to maximum value **1**, indicates a **strong** predictive performance by the mode as follows:

```
print(rgr.score(X_test , y_test))
0.8
```

As mentioned in the introduction, LASSO has a strong **feature selection** capability by setting the coefficients of less relevant features to zero. To identify which features LASSO considers significant for our model, we can inspect (through the variable **regr.coef_**) the non-zero coefficients assigned after model training:

```
lst_coef = np.argwhere(rgr.coef_ !=0).reshape(1 , -1)[0]
print("columns of interest :",list(X_test.iloc[: , lst_coef ].columns))
```

Out of the hundreds of features given to the LASSO model, it selects only this list of relevant features:

```
columns of interest : ['Close_diff_frac_0.2_4', 'Close_diff_frac_0.25_4',
'Close_diff_frac_0.3_4', 'Close_diff_frac_0.35_1', 'Close_diff_
frac_0.35_2', 'Close_diff_frac_0.35_3', 'Close_diff_frac_0.35_4', 'Close_
diff_frac_0.35_5', 'Volatility', 'Closing_Position', 'Gap_Previous_Close',
'Normalized_High', 'Relative_Change_Open_Close', 'High_Low_Clustering',
'SMA_30', 'SMA_35', 'MACD', 'MACD_Histogram', 'RSI', 'STOCHk_14_3_3',
'STOCHd_14_3_3', 'CCI', 'BBB_20_2.0', 'BBP_20_2.0', 'ATR', 'TR']
```

The coefficient assigned to each of these features gives us information about the influence of this feature on the prediction.

This is very important information, as shown:

```
print("coef values :")
dict(zip(list(X_test.iloc[: , lst_coef ].columns) , rgr.coef_[lst_coef]))
coef values :
{'Close_diff_frac_0.2_4': 0.0017052507726205356,
 'Close_diff_frac_0.25_4': 0.03357515414777998,
 'Close_diff_frac_0.3_4': 0.013239358125294583,
 'Close_diff_frac_0.35_1': 0.08641385813114096,

 ....

'CCI': -0.055638867385273676,
 'BBB_20_2.0': 0.06799642558179593,
 'BBP_20_2.0': 0.34890179044959546,
 'ATR': -0.008401739981565862,
 'TR': -0.1300218401488396}
```

The application of the ridge method gives us a close result. As a good exercise, you can verify this statement without any difficulties with ridge implementation in the Scikit-Learn API:

```
from sklearn.linear_model import Ridge
```

With this ridge regression method, we obtain a regression score of 0.7, which is not as good as the previous LASSO method but still correct.

Now, transition to the kernel method to discover if this non-linear method improves the result given by LASSO.

Kernel methods

Kernel methods allow us to find patterns in data that is not linearly separable—that is, when you cannot draw a straight line to separate different classes. It relies on a trick[17] that transforms the data into a higher-dimensional space where these classes can be separated by a hyperplane. It is like viewing the data through a set of new lenses that reveal structures not visible in the original dimensions, allowing for accurate classifications.

Having already addressed the labor-intensive tasks of data preparation and feature engineering, we can now proceed directly to the task at hand, optimizing the hyperparameters of our model to fine-tune its performance:

---

17 The kernel trick is a mathematical technique that transforms the data into a higher-dimensional space where these classes can be separated by a hyperplane, without the need to compute the coordinates in this new space explicitly. it's this kernel trick that makes this technique applicable and gives it its name.

```python
from sklearn.kernel_ridge import KernelRidge

#  hyperparameter search space
space = {
      # log scale for regularization strength
    'alpha': Real(0.001, 10, prior='log-uniform'),
    'kernel': Categorical(['linear', 'rbf', 'polynomial', 'sigmoid']),
        #kernel coefficient
    'gamma': Real(0.001, 10, prior='log-uniform'),
        # Extended range for 'polynomial' kernel degree
    'degree': Integer(2, 10),
        # 'coef0', a parameter for 'polynomial' and 'sigmoid' kernels
    'coef0': Real(0, 10, prior='uniform'), }
```

Next, we print the result of the optimization (characteristics of the model, choice of the kernel, and coefficients):

```python
print("best params: ")
pprint( opt.best_params_)


best params:
OrderedDict([('alpha', 1.3324499412363422),
            ('coef0', 10.0),
            ('degree', 2),
            ('gamma', 0.0016201598106302523),
            ('kernel', 'polynomial')])


best_model = opt.best_estimator_
accuracy = best_model.score(X_test,y_test)
print(f"score:", accuracy * 100.0)
score: 80.30608312013042
```

The fact that both non-linear kernel methods and LASSO yield similar results after hyperparameter optimization suggests that computing the normalized spread may fundamentally be a linear problem. This implies that the underlying relationship between the features and the target variable can be effectively captured through linear models, which LASSO is specifically designed to optimize.

The final section of this chapter explores online learning, a method specifically developed to apply machine learning techniques to **streaming** data. This approach updates the model incrementally as new data arrives, making it ideal for situations where it is impractical to store or reprocess large volumes of data.

Online learning methods

Online machine learning is an adaptive strategy where the model is trained incrementally, processing individual samples or small batches of data sequentially as they become available. This method is particularly useful in environments where data is **continuously** generated, making it infeasible to retrain a model from scratch with every new piece of information.

The utility of online learning is evident in its ability to instantly **adapt to new patterns** and changes[18] in the data, maintaining the relevance and accuracy of the model over time. It is especially beneficial in situations where the computational **cost of training** a model on the **entire** dataset is prohibitive, or when the dataset is too large to fit into memory.

However, online learning presents its own set of challenges. The primary difficulty lies in the need for careful algorithm design to prevent **overfitting**, as the model is constantly exposed to new data, which may not be representative of the overall distribution. For similar reasons, it is critical to minimize the influence of **outliers** in online learning to prevent the model from learning in the incorrect direction. Outliers can disproportionately affect the incremental learning process, leading to skewed predictions if not appropriately managed. Furthermore, the algorithm must be efficient enough to update the model in real time without significant **latency**.

Online learning indeed confronts many of the most complex challenges found in machine learning, from managing non-stationary environments and concept drift to dealing with outliers and ensuring the model remains robust and relevant over time.

In the trading domain, online learning has several compelling applications. For instance, in **high-frequency trading** (**HFT**), models can quickly adapt to sudden market movements.

In terms of implementation, there are two notable libraries in online learning: Scikit-multiflow and Vowpal Wabbit:

- *Scikit-multiflow*[19] offers a wide range of tools for stream learning, allowing for the evaluation and training of models on streaming data. It keeps an ease-of-use philosophy like Scikit-learn, making it approachable for a broad audience. It is the recommended tool I recommend if you begin in this space.

- *Vowpal Wabbit*[20], on the other hand, is designed for high-speed (due to its implementation in C++), large-scale learning, and streaming data. It supports advanced features such as online learning, feature hashing, and out-of-core learning, making it suitable for advanced experts looking for high efficiency and scalability in their machine learning solutions.

---

18 This is called *concept drift*. It refers to the phenomenon where the statistical properties of the target variable, which the model is trying to predict, change over time in unforeseen ways, causing the model to lose accuracy.
19 https://scikit-multiflow.readthedocs.io
20 https://vowpalwabbit.org

Implement an online regression with Scikit-multiflow

We continue with data from the Indian index (NIFTY50) at a 1-minute frequency. This intraday frequency is not HFT. However, it is fast enough to consider an online learning approach. We predict the value of the spread on the intraday data stream.

First, install Scikit-multiflow and import the required tools:

```
!pip install -q scikit-multiflow
from skmultiflow.data import DataStream
from skmultiflow.meta import AdaptiveRandomForestRegressor
from skmultiflow.evaluation import EvaluatePrequential


# Initialize the AdaptiveRandomForestRegressor
regressor = AdaptiveRandomForestRegressor(n_estimators = 20)
pred_stream =[]
```

We will process (**function DataStream(data=…)**) the dataset iteratively to mimic a data stream, simulating the influx of high-speed data typical to production environments. This approach allows us to predict the next outcome and promptly update (**partial_fit function**) the model with the latest data, ensuring the model remains as accurate as possible:

```
# Convert the DataFrame to a DataStream object for skmultiflow
stream = DataStream(data=np.column_stack((X_test, y_test)))


# Training the model with the streaming data
while stream.has_more_samples():
    # acquire new data
    X_stream, y_stream = stream.next_sample()
    y_pred = regressor.predict(X_stream)
    # keep track predictions
    pred_stream.append(y_pred[0])
    # refit model
    regressor = regressor.partial_fit(X_stream, y_stream)


from sklearn.metrics import mean_squared_error
mean_squared_error(pred_stream , y_test)
1.1329364818706054
```

The stream, alongside its predictions, is represented in the following graph:

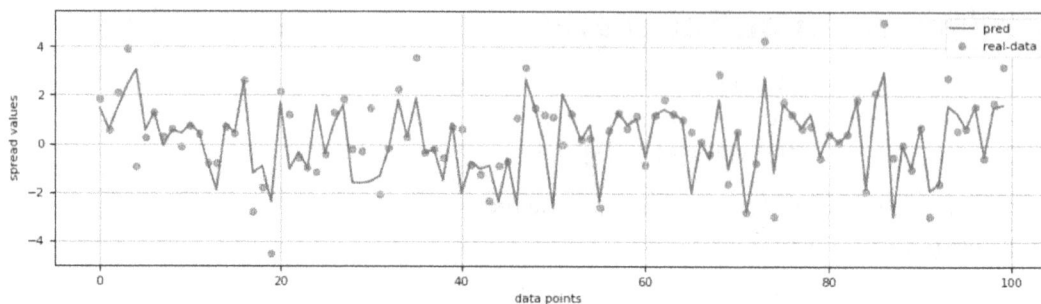

Figure 7.8: On-line predictions with Scikit-multiflow

The graph visualizes the performance of our online regression model in predicting spread values over a stream of incoming data points. The red dots represent the actual observed spread values, while the green line corresponds to the model's real-time predictions.

We can see that the model effectively captures the overall trend and fluctuations in the spread and dynamically adapts as new data arrives. However, some deviations remain, especially at extreme values, indicating potential areas for further refinement, such as improved feature selection, hyperparameter tuning, or alternative online learning approaches.

Conclusion

By the end of this chapter, we gained the ability to apply advanced machine learning techniques to algorithmic trading. We can now implement ensemble methods such as bagging and boosting to improve predictive accuracy and mitigate overfitting. We can also apply advanced regression techniques such as LASSO and kernel methods for more accurate financial forecasting. In addition, we understood how to use online learning to adapt models to real-time market conditions and to fine-tune hyper-parameters with Scikit-Optimize for optimal performance.

A key achievement in this chapter is the development of a highly accurate model for predicting volatility range dynamics, enabling better risk assessment and trade execution. Readers can also now perform feature selection with LASSO, which improves model interpretability and efficiency. Armed with these skills, they will be ready to build sophisticated, data-driven trading strategies that dynamically adapt to complex market behavior and go beyond traditional supervised learning approaches.

In the next chapter, we will explore how autoML and low-code platforms are revolutionizing machine learning for trading strategies, making advanced models more accessible and automating key steps such as feature selection, model tuning, and strategy optimization. We will also examine their application in global macro modeling, forecasting interest rates using macroeconomic features, and compare their performance to traditional hand-crafted algorithms.

## CHAPTER 8

AutoML and Low-Code for Trading Strategies

Introduction

Developing trading algorithms based on machine learning requires extensive domain knowledge, not only in finance but also in statistical and machine learning techniques. This dual requirement is a significant barrier to entry for many professionals in the field. However, the advent of **Automated Machine Learning** (**AutoML**) and **low-code** platforms has begun to revolutionize the field, providing powerful tools that **democratize** the development of sophisticated trading strategies.

Low-code and AutoML platforms significantly lower the barrier to entry for developing machine learning models, making them accessible to a broader audience, including those without a deep programming background. This aligns well with the theme of democratizing access to advanced data analysis and model development tools, especially in the context of financial trading strategies where the user base can range from highly technical data scientists to financial analysts with limited coding expertise.

Structure

In this chapter, we will cover the following topics:

- Introduction to AutoML and low-code
- Global macro modelling

- Hand-crafted algorithm as a benchmark
- Core components of AutoML
- Results compared to manual

Objectives

AutoML and low-code platforms do not introduce new methods; rather, they streamline and automate key components of the machine learning process.

This chapter will explore how these tools can efficiently optimize techniques covered in *Chapter 6, Improving Model Capability with Features*, model selection and ensemble methods from *Chapter 7, Advanced Machine Learning Models for Trading*, and hyperparameter optimization from *Chapter 3, Optimizing Trading Systems, Metrics, and Automated Reporting*.

By the end of this chapter, readers will be able to use AutoML and low-code platforms to develop efficient and automated trading strategies. They will gain a solid understanding of global macro modeling, as well as the ability to incorporate macroeconomic features into predictive models. In addition, they will learn to automate key machine learning processes such as feature engineering, model selection, hyperparameter tuning, and evaluation using AutoML tools. Finally, they will be able to implement and compare trading strategies developed using traditional methods with those using state-of-the-art AutoML and low-code frameworks, giving them a more adaptable and scalable approach to algorithmic trading.

Introduction to AutoML and low-code

AutoML completely automates the tedious and complex processes of model selection, training, and optimization. This process includes everything from data preprocessing and feature selection to hyperparameter tuning and model validation.

Low-code platforms streamline the development process by minimizing the need for extensive coding. Unlike **no-code**[1] platforms that rely entirely on graphical user interfaces for application development, low-code platforms require some coding but **significantly** reduce the complexity and amount of code needed to build models. Hence the term "Low-Code". They make model development faster and more accessible to those with limited programming skills.

When discussing the distinction between low-code and AutoML tools, a common source of confusion is the overlap between the two. While it may seem that they require different levels of coding, the distinction can become blurred. When you start customizing options with an AutoML library, you are essentially moving toward low-code development. On

1 Here are some valuable no-Code tools :
https://altair.com/altair-rapidminer
https://www.knime.com
https://bigml.com

the other hand, if you use a low-code library without specifying any options and let the tool make the decisions, you are approaching the functionality of AutoML. Therefore, it is better to think of low-code and AutoML tools as a spectrum of complementary and overlapping solutions, rather than getting caught up in the labels. The focus should be on understanding how to use these tools effectively, not on the labels used to describe them.

Global macro modelling

We present the dataset: the **CBOE Interest Rate 10 Year T Note**, identified by the ticker symbol ^TNX. This future contract represents the 10-year debt of the United States and is widely traded around the world, serving as a benchmark for all types of bond trading, from government to corporate debt.

The following graph visually represents this contract, highlighting its historical movements and trends:

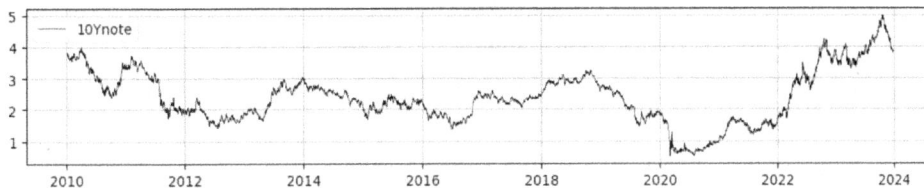

Figure 8.1: *10 Years Treasury Bond Yield*

We begin by collecting historical data for this contract, followed by executing a simple modeling exercise using Scikit-learn. The results of this initial modeling will serve as a benchmark for subsequent analysis using AutoML and low-code platforms.

Our goal is to use machine learning to replicate a strategy used by hedge fund managers, known as the **global macro strategy**. This strategy involves analyzing and forecasting the movements of financial assets considering their fundamental macroeconomic drivers, such as inflation, commodity cycles, GDP growth, and other relevant factors.

The primary concern of macro strategists is to understand the impact of macroeconomic variables on asset prices to make informed investment decisions. Machine learning can assist in this endeavor by using macroeconomic variables as features to predict the yield of the US 10-year bond.

Macroeconomic features

Predicting the 10-year treasury yield[2] as a regression task involves selecting input variables that are believed to affect interest rates. These variables include a mix of economic indicators, financial market data, and other macroeconomic factors.

2 Our focus is on the yield, or return, of the underlying bond that is associated with the future contract, rather than the price. There is a direct relationship between the yield and the price of the bond. When the price of the bond increases, the yield decreases, and vice versa.

List of the variables used to predict 10-year treasury yield. We make a note of the Yahoo ticker symbol for each of these features, along with a brief explanation of their relevance to bond yields:

- **S&P 500 index (ticker : SPY)**: Reflects overall stock market performance

- **Dow Jones Industrial Average (DJI)**: Gauge of economic outlook

- **Russell 2000 Index (IWM)**: Measures the performance of small-cap stocks

- **Gold prices (GC=F)**: Gold price can inversely relate to confidence in the economy

- **Crude oil prices (CL=F)**: Oil prices can indicate inflation expectations.

- **prices (HG=F)**: Ability to predict economic trends due to its wide range of industrial uses

- **Silver prices (SI=F)**: Similar to gold, but with more industrial uses

- **U.S. Dollar index (DX-Y.NYB)**: The strength of the USD against a basket of currencies can impact treasury yields

- **Euro to USD exchange rate (EURUSD=X)**: Reflects the strength of the Euro against the USD, influencing international investment flows

- **Japanese Yen (JPY=X)**: The Yen is another safe-haven currency; its exchange rate affect U.S. bond yields

- **VIX - CBOE Volatility Index (VIX)**: The **fear gauge** of the market; higher volatility leads to lower yields as investors seek safety in bonds

- **High Yield Corporate Bonds (HYG)**: High-yield bonds indicate risk tolerance and influence treasury yields

- **Investment grade corporate bonds (LQD)**: Shows the performance of safer corporate debt, a direct competitor to treasuries

- **Real Estate Investment Trusts Index (VNQ)**: REIT performance indicate real estate market health and inflation expectations

- **Consumer Price Index (CPI) Proxy via ETFs like: Treasury Inflation-Protected (TIP)** securities serve as a proxy for inflation expectations

- **Federal funds rate (via proxies like ^IRX)**: Short-term interest rate set by the Federal Reserve directly influences treasury yields

First, we use the Yahoo API to get the features we need. Next, we calculate the percentage variation for each of these features using the Pandas library. Finally, we construct a correlation matrix to visualize the economic relationships between these key macroeconomic drivers and our primary outcome, the 10-year treasury yield.

This process allows us to gain a better understanding of the factors that influence the yield on the 10-year treasury note, as shown in the following chart:

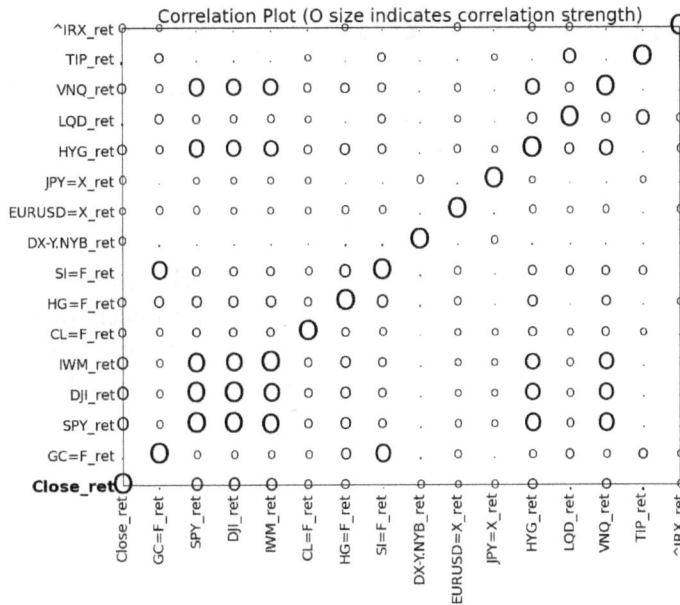

Figure 8.2: Correlation plot

The correlation plot provides insights into how different asset classes move in relation to the yields of the 10-year US treasury note indicated by **Close_ret** in the first column.

- **Negative correlation** (small '.' in the plot): Metals like gold (**GC=F_Close**) fall into this category. Gold is considered a safe-haven asset that does not yield interest. When bond yields rise, the **opportunity cost** of holding gold increases, as investors earn more from yields without the risk of holding a non-yielding asset. Silver and copper follow similar patterns, but copper (**"HG=F_Close"**) is also influenced by industrial demand, affecting its correlation with bond yields.

  Negative correlations with **HYG** (high-yield bonds) and **LQD** (investment-grade bonds) reflect market risk sentiment, as rising yields often drive corporate bond prices lower. This widening **spread between corporate bonds and treasuries** materializes credit risk, highlighting the difference between government borrowing costs and those of private companies.

- **Positive correlation** (larger 'O' in the plot): In the context of currencies, a higher bond yield strengthens the domestic currency as it attracts foreign investments seeking higher returns, impacting currency pairs like EURUSD (**EURUSD=X_Close**) and JPY (**JPY=X_Close**).

Our goal is to use these macroeconomic variables to predict returns **two days ahead** (**ahead = 2**), and to develop trading strategies that can take advantage of these predictions:

```
ahead = 2
df['target'] = df['Close'].shift(-ahead)
```

Hand-crafted algorithm as a benchmark

In this section, we aim to carry out a fundamental and robust benchmark to compare all the results from both the AutoML and low-code API. Our objective is not to explore complex methods to achieve exceptional results, but rather to establish a reliable point of comparison. This will allow us to evaluate the performance of each approach (AutoML and low-code) and make informed decisions based on their relative strengths and weaknesses.

A key principle in this comparison is Occam's Razor, which emphasizes that simpler models should be preferred unless a more complex approach demonstrates a clear advantage. If sophisticated AutoML or low-code solutions do not outperform a fast benchmark regression, they are not considered because their added complexity does not justify their use. This ensures that model selection balances both **performance** metrics and **computational efficiency**, maintaining a practical and effective approach to algorithmic trading.

LASSO

The **Least Absolute Shrinkage and Selection Operator (LASSO)** algorithm is an excellent choice for a benchmark, due to its inherent regularization capabilities. By incorporating regularization, L[3] allows for the selection of a concise list of significant features, which is beneficial for achieving solid results in the initial stages of regression analysis with linear algorithms:

```
from sklearn.linear_model import LassoCV
```

X contains the macroeconomics features, and **y** contains the target values we aim to learn to predict:

```
y = df.pop('target')
X = df.copy()
```

```
X_train , X_test , y_train , y_test = train_test_split(X , y , shuffle = True)
rgr = LassoCV()
rgr.fit(X_train , y_train)
```

The results are as follows:

```
from sklearn.metrics import mean_squared_error
```

```
print('RMSE = ',np.sqrt(mean_squared_error(pred , y_test)))
```

3 We import LassoCV which helps in tuning the optimal hyperparameters of the Lasso model (specifically the alpha parameter) using cross-validation. This can improve the model's performance (at no cost) by finding the optimal alpha value that minimizes the cross-validation error. We have presented this technique in the section of the previous chapter devoted to "Advanced Regressions" in the context of "Over-fitting".

```
print(np.round(rgr.score(X_test , y_test),3))
```

```
RMSE =   0.54
0.397
```

As anticipated, the results are satisfactory yet not exceptional. The metric loss, **Root Mean Square Error (RMSE)**, indicates that the standard deviation of prediction errors for the yield is approximately 0.54, which implies that, for instance, if the actual yield is 2.0, the predicted values could range from 1.54 to 2.54.

Regarding the R2 score, which ranges from -1 to +1, with +1 indicating perfect prediction, a higher score is better. Our score is around 0.4, which, while not disastrous, is **significantly below** the best possible outcomes.

The following graph reports the predictions alongside realized values:

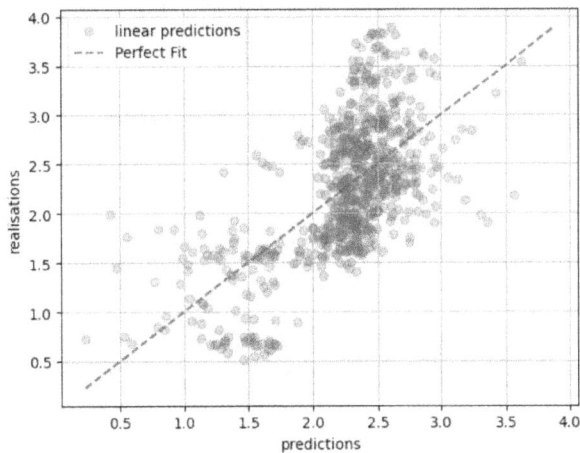

Figure 8.3: Predictions vs realizations

Predictions that closely align with actual values are typically found near the diagonal line of perfect fit. However, in this case, this ideal alignment is **not** observed.

The following graph confirms this:

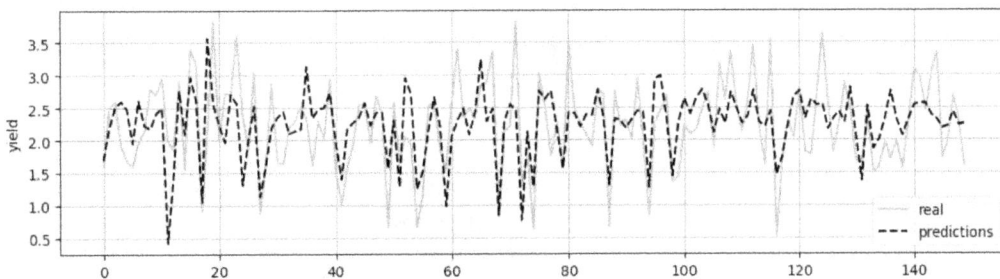

Figure 8.4: Predictions vs realizations

The predictions follow the general trend of the real values suggesting the model has captured the underlying pattern in the data. In the next sections, we will see if automatic methods (autoML and low-Code) improve the precision of these predictions and manage to do better than our brief analysis.

Core components of AutoML

Let us explore how to handle the complex tasks (feature engineering and selection, algorithm selection, hyperparameter optimization, and model evaluation) of a machine learning project **automatically**, the methods employed, their computational requirements, and how the results compare to our manual approach.

Feature engineering and selection

Feature engineering involves creating new input variables from raw data to improve a model's predictive power. In contrast, feature selection focuses on choosing the most relevant features to improve efficiency and reduce overfitting. These processes are critical to building high-performing models because they determine what information is fed into the algorithm.

For a detailed exploration of feature engineering and selection techniques, *Chapter 6, Improving Model Capability with Features*, is entirely devoted to this topic. Here, we will use automated tools to streamline the process and compare them to traditional manual approaches.

We can streamline the creation of relevant features using libraries designed specifically for automated feature engineering.

Feature engineering with Feature-engine

We start with *Feature-engine*[4] a Python library with multiple transformers to engineer and select features to use in machine learning models.

The following command installs the library:

```
!pip install -q feature-engine
```

The rest of the code is straightforward, it essentially involves selecting a subset of features (**variables=[...]**) and applying specific transformations (**func = [...]**) to them. These transformations are designed to **improve predictive power** by creating new features that capture relationships and patterns in the data. **MathFeatures** apply mathematical operations (e.g., sum, product, average) to selected variables, while **RelativeFeatures** and **CyclicalFeatures** help capture relative changes and seasonal patterns in data.

---

4 https://feature-engine.trainindata.com

The following code demonstrates how to apply these transformations:

```
from feature_engine.creation import MathFeatures , RelativeFeatures ,
CyclicalFeatures
mf = MathFeatures(variables=['Open_ret', 'High_ret', 'Low_ret', 'Close_
ret'] , func = ["sum","prod","mean"])
```

Once the transformer (**mf**) has been defined, it is applied to the DataFrame (**df**) containing the specified set of features (**['Open_ret','High_ret','Low_ret','Close_ret']**) provided during the initialization phase:

```
df_feat = mf.fit_transform(df)
```

The specified transformation columns (last three, **df_feat.iloc[:,-3:]**) are integrated (**pd.concat()**) with the rest of the features:

```
df = pd.concat([df , df_feat.iloc[:,-3:]] , axis = 1)
```

Subsequently, additional transformations[5] are applied to a fresh set of features, leading to the creation of **thousands** of automatically engineered features, precisely 1332 in this case:

```
df.info()
```

```
<class 'pandas.core.frame.DataFrame'>
DatetimeIndex: 2668 entries, 2010-01-05 to 2022-03-01
Columns: 1332 entries, Open to High_ret_add_High_ret
```

In this section, we used Feature-engine to automate feature engineering, creating new features from existing ones using mathematical transformations. These transformations expanded our data set to capture more complex relationships that can improve predictive performance. By applying these methods, we generated a large set of engineered features, laying the groundwork for more advanced model development.

Next, we explore **autofeat**, another powerful library designed for **automated feature engineering and selection**. While Feature-engine focuses on structured transformations, autofeat integrates **feature selection** alongside engineering, helping to refine and optimize the dataset by automatically identifying the most relevant variables.

Feature engineering and selection with autofeat

We now use **autofeat**[6], a similar library dedicated to automated feature engineering, and selection. We install the autofeat library and initialize it in the following code:

```
!pip3 install -q autofeat
```

We initialize the autofeat model with the number (**feateng_steps**) of feature engineering steps to perform:

---

5 'add', 'mul','sub', 'div', 'truediv', 'floordiv', 'mod', 'pow'
6 https://pypi.org/project/autofeat

```
auto_feat = AutoFeatRegressor(verbose=1, feateng_steps = 1)
```

Then, we fit the model on the selected set of the data. This step will generate new features and **select** the best ones for our model:

```
X_train_feat = auto_feat.fit_transform(X_train[['Open_ret','High_ret','Low_
ret','Close_ret']] , y_train)
[featsel] Scaling data...done.
```

Then, transform the test set (**X_test**) with the same transformations and feature engineering steps applied to the training set:

```
X_test_feat = auto_feat.transform(X_test[['Open_ret','High_ret','Low_
ret','Close_ret']])
```

We inspect the columns that are generated and selected automatically:

```
# columns from AUTO features engineering :
lst = list(set(X_train_feat.columns) - set(X_train.columns))
lst
['Abs(High_ret)', 'High_ret**2', 'Open_ret**3', 'Close_ret**2',
 '1/High_ret', 'Abs(Close_ret)', 'Abs(Open_ret)','Abs(Low_ret)', 'Open_
ret**2']
```

The selected columns have been subjected to the application of various mathematical functions, resulting in many potential features. library autofeat then narrows down this extensive collection of newly created features, retaining only those with predictive power and the ability to predict the outcome.

Algorithm selection

AutoML platforms automate algorithm selection, the process of choosing the best machine learning algorithm for a given dataset and problem. This is typically achieved through a combination of search strategies, such as grid search, random search, or more sophisticated methods like Bayesian optimization for **auto-SkLearn**[7] tool or genetic programming in the case of **TPOT**[8].

AutoML platforms evaluate multiple algorithms, from linear models to complex ensemble methods, against the dataset to determine which algorithm yields the most promising results based on predefined metrics.

This step-by-step progression from simple to more complex models is a fundamental principle of machine learning development. We followed the same approach in *Chapter 5, Supervised Learning for Trading Systems,* and *Chapter 7, Advanced Machine Learning Models for Trading,* where we first introduced simple and linear models, such as logistic regression, before increasing the sophistication in subsequent chapters. This iterative process continues until we reach the desired level of performance.

7 https://automl.github.io/auto-sklearn
8 https://epistasislab.github.io/tpot

Machine learning practitioners widely use this methodology and is consistent with Occam's Razor, as discussed earlier. AutoML platforms encapsulate this approach by systematically automating the search process, starting with simpler models and increasing complexity only when necessary. In this way, they streamline model development while maintaining the balance between interpretability, computational efficiency, and predictive performance.

AutoML and sophisticated low-code platforms[9] provide users with simplified interfaces to initiate algorithm selection processes. Users can specify their problem type (e.g., classification, regression, etc.) and let the platform recommend or automatically choose the best algorithms to try, reducing the need for in-depth programming and machine learning knowledge to almost zero.

AutoML with FLAML

A perfect example of such an advanced AutoML API is **Fast Library for AutoML and Tuning** ([10]) by **Microsoft Research**.

On Microsoft Research's website, FLAML is presented as a lightweight Python library for efficient automation of machine learning and AI operations. It automates workflow based on large language models, machine learning models, etc., optimizes their performance.

(https://microsoft.github.io/FLAML)

In the following code, we install the library and then define the type of problem (**task= "regression"**) we are addressing, supply the data, and specify the **allowable time budget** (**time_budget** in seconds) for the process. The time budget sets a limit on how long AutoML can search for the best model, ensuring a balance between **computational efficiency** and **model performance** within a predefined timeframe:

```
!pip install -q flaml
```

```
from flaml import AutoML
automl = AutoML()
automl.fit(X_train, y_train, task="regression", time_budget=60)
```

Executing this code enables the AutoML engine to explore and evaluate a variety of sophisticated algorithms (such as **XGBoost, LightGBM, extra_tree,** and **RandomForestRegressor**) to identify the most effective solution for our challenge, adhering to the specified time constraints (one minute in this example).

The output produced is as follows:

```
[flaml.automl.logger: 02-27 23:51:27] {1679} INFO - task = regression
[flaml.automl.logger: 02-27 23:51:27] {1690} INFO - Evaluation method:
```

---

9 a highly recommended low-code API is pyCaret, it balanced efficiency and easy to use, https://pycaret.org

10 https://microsoft.github.io/FLAML

```
holdout
[flaml.automl.logger: 02-27 23:51:27] {1788} INFO - Minimizing error metric:
1-r2
[flaml.automl.logger: 02-27 23:51:27] {1900} INFO - List of ML learners in
AutoML Run: ['lgbm', 'rf', 'xgboost', 'extra_tree', 'xgb_limitdepth']
[flaml.automl.logger: 02-27 23:51:27] {2218} INFO - iteration 0,current
learner lgbm
[flaml.automl.logger: 02-27 23:51:27] {2344} INFO - Estimated sufficient time
budget=1033s. Estimated necessary time budget=7s.
[flaml.automl.logger: 02-27 23:51:27] {2391} INFO -  at 0.4s,      estimator
lgbm's best error=0.4972, best estimator lgbm's best error=0.4972
[flaml.automl.logger: 02-27 23:51:27] {2218} INFO - iteration 1, current
learner lgbm
[flaml.automl.logger: 02-27 23:51:27] {2391} INFO -  at 0.5s,      estimator
lgbm's best error=0.4972, best estimator lgbm's best error=0.4972
[flaml.automl.logger: 02-27 23:51:27] {2218} INFO - iteration 2, current
learner lgbm
[flaml.automl.logger: 02-27 23:51:28] {2391} INFO -  at 0.6s,      estimator
lgbm's best error=0.1415, best estimator lgbm's best error=0.1415
...


[flaml.automl.logger: 02-27 23:52:27] {2630} INFO - retrained model:
ExtraTreesRegressor(max_features=0.7552682732533821, max_leaf_nodes=108,
                    n_estimators=6, n_jobs=-1, random_state=12032022)
[flaml.automl.logger: 02-27 23:52:27] {1930} INFO - fit succeeded
[flaml.automl.logger: 02-27 23:52:27] {1931} INFO - Time taken to find the
best model: 6.1406309604644775
```

This output provides a detailed log of the AutoML process, tracking the steps taken to find the best-performing model within the specified time budget, as follows:

- **Task**: The log confirms that the problem is set as regression.

- **Error metric**: AutoML informs us about the measure of how well the model explains the target variable.

- **List of ML learners in AutoML run:** It is a list of candidate models, including LightGBM, Random Forest (**rf**), XGBoost, etc

- **Iteration process**: The model selection process runs iteratively, starting by refining hyperparameters to improve performance. Each iteration records the best error achieved so far.

- **Time estimations**: AutoML **estimates** the sufficient and necessary time budgets to optimize performance, ensuring efficient resource allocation.

- **Final model selection**: After testing various learners, AutoML selects the best.

- **Completion**: The log confirms a successful fit, indicating that the best model was found in 6 seconds, highlighting AutoML's ability to efficiently search for optimal configurations.

This output demonstrates how AutoML systematically tests models, tunes hyperparameters, and selects the best-performing approach, streamlining the process of model selection and optimization.

Then, calculating prediction errors and R2 score, we obtain:

```
# Evaluate the classifier on the test data
print('RMSE = ',np.sqrt(mean_squared_error(pred , y_test)))
print(automl.score(X_test , y_test))
```

```
RMSE =   0.071
0.989
```

This represents a **huge enhancement** compared to our manually engineered benchmark using the **Lasso** algorithm, which reported an average error of around 0.54 in terms of **RMSE** and an R2 score of 0.4:

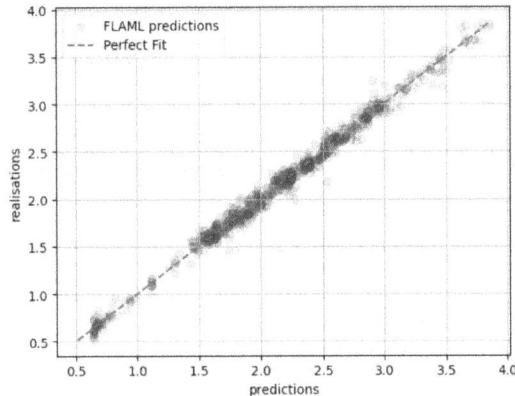

Figure 8.5: AutoML predictions vs realized values

As we can see in the previous graph, predictions are closely aligned with real values. They are almost confused with the diagonal marking the perfect prediction.

AutoML with H2O

We persist in our examination of sophisticated AutoML frameworks. Like FLAML, H2O ranks as one of the top options for powerful open-source platforms. H2O[11] offers a comparable interface to FLAML, allowing the testing of various cutting-edge algorithms within specified limits such as time budget or a fixed number of iterations.

---

11 https://docs.h2o.ai/h2o/latest-stable/h2o-docs/automl.html

The description is provided on the H2O website, **https://docs.h2o.ai/h2o/latest-stable/h2o-docs/automl.html**, as follows:

Although H2O has made it easy for non-experts to experiment with machine learning, there is still a fair bit of knowledge and background in data science that is required to produce high-performing machine learning models. For machine learning software is truly accessible to non-experts, we have designed an easy-to-use interface that automates the process of training a large selection of candidate models. H2O's autoML can also be a helpful tool for the advanced user by providing a **simple wrapper function** that performs a large number of modeling-related tasks that would typically require many lines of code, and by freeing up their time to focus on other aspects of the data science pipeline tasks such as data-preprocessing, feature engineering and model deployment.

Let us evaluate this framework to verify the accuracy of these claims. After installation, we start with the initialization phase:

```
!pip3 install -q h2o
import h2o
from h2o.automl import H2OAutoML
```

The code initializes an H2O instance locally and prepares the data for modeling:

```
h2o.init()
```

H2O starts a (local) server to run the experiments. This is because H2O needs to set up this local server before running any machine learning experiments, which is done automatically when H2O is initialized:

```
Checking whether there is an H2O instance running at http://
localhost:54321..... not found.
Attempting to start a local H2O server...
Starting server
Server is running at http://127.0.0.1:54321
Connecting to H2O server at http://127.0.0.1:54321 ... successful.
```

This step ensures that an H2O server instance is running to efficiently distribute computations across available system resources.

The sole prerequisite involves formatting the data by labeling the predictive target as **target** and converting the Pandas DataFrame into an H2O container:

```
df['target'] = df['Close'].shift(-ahead)
df.dropna(inplace = True)
# 'df' : pandas DataFrame with the target variable named 'target'
h2o_df = h2o.H2OFrame(df)
```

```
Parse progress: |███████████████████████████████████████
████████| (done) 100%
```

This H2O container is then divided into training and test sets by **h2o_df.split_frame()** function. This task requires **minimal effort** compared to the subsequent extensive processes carried out by the AutoML engine:

```
# Split the data into train and test sets
train, test = h2o_df.split_frame(ratios=[.8], seed=42)


# Identify predictors and response
x = train.columns
y = "target"
x.remove(y)


# Run AutoML for x base models (limited here for speed)
aml = H2OAutoML(max_models = 5, seed = 1)
```

This **H2OAutoML()** command executes H2O's engine with the following specifications:

- **max_models=5**: Limits the number of base models to 5, ensuring a quick execution time. Of course, this number can be increased to explore a broader range of models.

- **seed=1**: Sets a random seed for reproducibility, ensuring that the results remain consistent across multiple runs.

The following code **aml.train()** starts the training process using:

- **x**: The feature columns (independent variables).

- **y**: The target column (dependent variable).

- **training_frame=train**: The dataset used for training.

    ```
    aml.train(x = x, y = y, training_frame = train)
    ```

The process begins with **feature selection** by eliminating constant columns that are not useful for predictions:

```
06:24:28.549: _train param, Dropping unused columns: [DX-Y.NYB_Volume]
███████████████████████████████████| (done) 100%
```

After a few trials, the random forest regressor, **H2ORandomForestEstimator**, emerges as the best candidate:

```
Model Details
=============
H2ORandomForestEstimator : Distributed Random Forest
Model Key: DRF_1_AutoML_1_20240226_62057
```

Then, the engine evaluates the best model:

```
ModelMetricsRegression: drf
** Reported on cross-validation data. **
```

```
MSE: 0.002954176243244988
RMSE: 0.05435233429435196
MAE: 0.04027944498639655
```

This error magnitude (**RMSE: 0.05**) represents a step forward compared to our earlier trials with the **FLAML** AutoML engine (**RMSE: 0.07**).

Furthermore, the H2O reports highlight the significance of each feature. Notably, following OHLC, the most important features are those initially identified as highly correlated during our preliminary exploration with the correlation plot, specifically TIP Inflation Protected and LQD Corporate Bonds:

Variable importance:

variable	relative_importance	scaled_importance	percentage
Close	10857.5126953	1.0	0.2762052
Low	5061.9379883	0.4662152	0.1287711
High	4167.9204102	0.3838743	0.1060281
Open	3686.7221680	0.3395549	0.0937868
TIP_Open	1184.7832031	0.1091211	0.0301398
TIP_High	1182.2382812	0.1088867	0.0300751
LQD_Open	725.5785522	0.0668273	0.0184581
TIP_Close	583.2502441	0.0537186	0.0148374
LQD_Close	552.1102905	0.0508505	0.0140452

Table 8.1: Feature importances

Additionally, examining the **leaderboard** allows us to identify the top-performing models from the trials:

```
# View the AutoML Leaderboard
aml.leaderboard
```

One very interesting option is to use the top candidates from the leaderboard to create an ensemble algorithm (**metalearner**) that combines these leading algorithms, potentially improving accuracy even further:

```
# Get model ids for all models in the AutoML Leaderboard
model_ids = list(aml.leaderboard['model_id'].as_data_frame().iloc[:,0])
# Get the "All Models" Stacked Ensemble model
se = h2o.get_model([mid for mid in model_ids if "StackedEnsemble_AllModels"
in mid][0])
# Get the Stacked Ensemble metalearner model
metalearner = se.metalearner()
```

Investigating the variable importance within the ensemble's metalearner (or combiner) algorithm reveals the contribution level of each base learner to the overall ensemble. Essentially, H2O intelligently blends the models based on their performance capabilities. Subsequently, we evaluate the ensemble's error magnitude using the RMSE metric:

```
# Evaluate the classifier on the test data
print('RMSE = ',np.sqrt(mean_squared_error(pred_df.values,test_
df['target'].values)))
RMSE =  0.0496
```

This score surpasses that of the leaderboard's top model, aligning with the expectation that ensemble strategies typically outperform the pursuit of a single best candidate, as seen in *Chapter 7, Advanced Machine Learning Models for Trading*. The combination results in an RMSE loss of approximately 0.04, marking a 20% improvement (from an RMSE of 0.05 to 0.04) compared to the best individual model and an even greater enhancement relative to FLAML's performance (with an RMSE of around 0.07), which was already considered a significant achievement.

Although we did not mention it explicitly, AutoML platforms perform hyperparameter optimization during training, fine-tuning models in the background to improve their performance. Since this step plays a critical role in achieving optimal results, we will now recapitulate its importance, and the different techniques used to systematically explore the hyperparameter space.

Hyperparameters optimization

Hyperparameter optimization is critical for fine-tuning models to achieve the best performance. AutoML platforms employ techniques like grid search, random search, or Bayesian optimization to systematically explore the hyperparameter space. These methods aim to find the optimal set of hyperparameters that result in the best model performance, as seen in *Chapter 3, Optimizing Trading Systems, Metrics, and Automated Reporting*.

In AutoML and low-code platforms, hyperparameter optimization is abstracted behind user-friendly interfaces, allowing users to either select levels of optimization intensity or trust the platform to manage the optimization process automatically. This significantly reduces the complexity involved in manually tuning hyperparameters, though it may still offer the option for more advanced users to customize their optimization strategies.

While AutoML simplifies hyperparameter tuning, selecting the best model requires a rigorous evaluation process. AutoML platforms automate model evaluation, comparing different architectures and hyperparameter configurations to ensure optimal performance.

Model evaluation

Model evaluation in AutoML involves automatically applying evaluation techniques to assess the performance of different models and hyperparameter configurations. This process includes generating metrics such as accuracy, precision, recall, F1 score, or Mean Squared Error, depending on the problem type, to identify the most effective model.

Low-code platforms provide simplified mechanisms for model evaluation, often presenting users with a dashboard or report summarizing the performance of various models. This allows users to easily compare models based on key metrics.

With automated model evaluation, AutoML and low-code platforms streamline the process of selecting the best-performing model based on predefined metrics. But a key question remains: how do these automated approaches compare to traditional manual model development?

Results compared to manual approaches

AutoML and low-code platforms can often achieve results that are comparable to or even surpass manual model development, especially for users with limited machine learning expertise. These platforms are designed to explore a vast space of possibilities more systematically and efficiently than a human might, increasing the chances of identifying high-performing models. However, expert data scientists might still outperform AutoML in certain complex scenarios where deep domain knowledge, custom feature engineering, and nuanced model tuning are critical. Nonetheless, AutoML and low-code platforms offer a compelling advantage in terms of speed, resource efficiency, and accessibility, making them invaluable tools in the modern data scientist's toolkit.

Conclusion

By the end of this chapter, we discussed how AutoML and low-code platforms streamline the development of trading strategies by automating key processes such as feature engineering, model selection, hyperparameter tuning, and evaluation. State-of-the-art tools such as *H2O* and FLAML optimize model selection, while Feature-engine and autofeat provide reliable automatic feature engineering and selection.

Using these tools, we outperformed our handcrafted benchmark in our global macro modelling, demonstrating the power of automation in identifying high-performing models. While manual modeling still has value in complex, domain-specific cases, AutoML significantly improves efficiency and lowers the barrier to entry for the machine learning area.

A key takeaway is how different tools can be strategically combined to maximize model performance. A practical approach, we follow includes an accurate feature generation using AutoFeat and Feature-engine to create and refine predictive inputs. Then, model selection and optimization with FLAML and H2O to ensure the most effective algorithms are identified. Finally, ensemble methods are used to blend models for even greater predictive accuracy.

Readers have now gained practical skills in applying AutoML and low-code frameworks to trading, from global macro modeling to strategy optimization. These tools not only speed up the development process but also increase predictive power, making them indispensable in modern algorithmic trading.

In the next chapter, we will focus on unsupervised learning methods and their application to trading strategy development. Unlike supervised learning, which relies on labeled data, unsupervised techniques help uncover hidden structures, market regimes, and key transition points in financial data without predefined outcomes. We will explore detection methods to identify sudden shifts in market dynamics, and clustering algorithms to segment financial time series into meaningful groups. These techniques will provide traders with new ways to analyze price action, detect market shifts, and classify different trading environments.

Join our book's Discord space

Join the book's Discord Workspace for Latest updates, Offers, Tech happenings around the world, New Release and Sessions with the Authors:

https://discord.bpbonline.com

CHAPTER 9

Unsupervised Learning Methods for Trading

Introduction

Trading relies on identifying patterns and trends in financial data to guide investment decisions. While supervised learning predicts specific outcomes, unsupervised learning excels at revealing hidden structures and relationships. This chapter explores how unsupervised learning applies to trading, focusing on two key techniques, **change point detection (CPD)** and clustering.

CPD involves the identification of sudden changes or shifts in the underlying dynamics of a time series, while clustering enables the grouping of similar sequences or patterns in data. This chapter aims to provide a comprehensive and original introduction to unsupervised learning methods for trading through a combination of theoretical explanations, practical examples, and real-world applications.

Structure

In this chapter, we will cover the following topics:

- Introduction to change point detection
- Challenges, limitations, and applications of CPD
- Online CPD with ChangeFinder library

- Offline CPD with ruptures library
- Clustering sequences

Objectives

By the end of this chapter, you will have gained practical skills in unsupervised analytical methods, giving you the ability to uncover hidden patterns and statistical structures in financial data. You will learn to think like a market analyst, analyzing the underlying dynamics of an asset to build a data-driven trading strategy.

Through hands-on techniques, you will identify key moments of market reversals and significant shifts, apply statistical filtering to separate critical events from noise and construct meaningful event sequences.

You will also develop expertise in clustering algorithms to categorize market behavior and segment financial data into distinct phases. These insights will improve your trading decisions and strategy development.

Introduction to change point detection

Identifying changes in market trends, volatility and underlying dynamics is critical. One of the most effective ways to do this is through CPD, a statistical technique designed to detect abrupt changes or anomalies in time series data. CPD is an essential tool for uncovering hidden patterns, optimizing trading strategies, and improving risk management.

In the following sections of this introduction, we will introduce CPD, discuss its types, methods, algorithms, and examine its challenges and limitations.

Defining change points

CPD identifies moments in a time series when the statistical properties of the data change significantly. In financial markets, these **change points** signal regime shifts driven by investor sentiment, regulation, or unexpected events. Detecting them allows traders to adjust strategies, manage risk, and take advantage of opportunities.

The **key challenge** is to distinguish true shifts from noise. How do we distinguish a permanent market shift from a temporary blip? Financial data is noisy, making it easy to overfit models to irrelevant patterns. News events and high-frequency trading can trigger short-lived movements that do not reflect structural shifts. The goal is to identify real changes quickly, ideally in real time, before the market has fully adjusted. The ability to identify true shifts early allows traders to position themselves advantageously and take advantage of opportunities as they arise.

A critical step in achieving this is choosing the right approach to CPD, depending on whether the goal is real-time adaptation or retrospective analysis.

Types of CPD

There are two primary categories of CPD: online and offline detection. **Online** CPD involves real-time monitoring of data streams to detect changes as they occur, whereas **offline**[1] CPD focuses on analyzing historical data to identify change points retrospectively. Offline CPD is for backtesting trading strategies, evaluating the performance of algorithms, and identifying recurring patterns in historical data.

Methods and algorithms

CPD includes several methods and algorithms, each with its own strengths and weaknesses. **Parametric methods** assume a specific distribution for the data and use statistical tests to detect changes in the distribution's parameters. **Non-parametric methods** do not rely on a predefined distribution and instead use empirical measures, such as density estimates or clustering algorithms. **Machine learning approaches** apply advanced techniques to identify complex patterns and shifts in the data, which is the primary focus of this book. **Hybrid methods** integrate multiple approaches to maximize their advantages while mitigating their limitations.

Challenges, limitations, and applications of CPD

While CPD is a powerful tool, it comes with challenges and limitations. **Data quality** is a critical factor, as CPD is highly sensitive to missing values and noise, with outliers needing to be carefully managed to avoid false change points. **Model selection** is another challenge, as choosing the wrong CPD method or algorithm can produce misleading results. **Interpretation** also plays a key role, requiring a solid understanding of the underlying data and market dynamics to accurately analyze detected changes.

CPD has numerous applications in finance, including:

- **Trend detection**: Identifying changes in market trends to optimize trading strategies and position sizing

- **Volatility modeling**: Detecting changes in volatility to improve risk management and option pricing

- **Anomaly detection**: Identifying unusual patterns or outliers in financial data to detect potential fraud or errors

- **Portfolio optimization**: Using CPD to identify changes in asset correlations and optimize portfolio construction

As previously mentioned, there are two main types of CPD algorithms: online and offline methods. We will begin with online CPD.

1 We will come back to this point in the section devoted to the limits of CPD algorithms.

Online CPD with ChangeFinder library

ChangeFinder is a statistical algorithm designed to detect change points and anomalies online. In the context of CPD, *online* refers to methods that detect changes as the data is being received in real-time.

ChangeFinder utilizes the following two-stage approaches:

- **Smoothing and probability density estimation**: The algorithm begins by applying a smoothing process to the data to reduce noise and estimate the underlying probability distribution of the data. This is typically achieved using a statistical model (**AutoRegressive Integrated Moving Average (ARIMA)**), which helps in understanding the data's normal behavior over time.

- **Change point score calculation**: After the probability density estimation, ChangeFinder calculates a score for each point in the time series, which measures how much the data at each point deviates from the model's prediction. This score is derived from the likelihood ratio between the current model and a newly estimated model that includes more recent data points.

As the time series progresses, ChangeFinder **continuously** updates the model based on new data and recalculates scores. When the score exceeds a predetermined threshold, a change point is detected, indicating a potentially significant change in the underlying process generating the time series.

Here is an example using a simulated time series, in which the location of the change points is already known, to test if the algorithm can accurately detect it.

Let us simulate two change points (**change_point_1** and **change_point_2**) positioned at 250 and 300. After each of these points, we abruptly increase the variability (standard-dev) of the series to clearly indicate a change in regime:

```
n = 500
change_point_1 = 250
change_point_2 = 300
stdev = 1
mult = 3
data = np.concatenate([np.random.normal(0, stdev, change_point_1),
                    np.random.normal(0, mult * stdev , change_point_2 -
change_point_1),
                    np.random.normal(0, 3 * mult * stdev , n - change_
point_2 )])
```

The following graph clearly illustrates the three distinct phases, with predefined change points at 250 and 300 (dashed vertical line). The sudden spikes in variability are apparent to the eye, and we want to test whether the algorithm can accurately detect these changes:

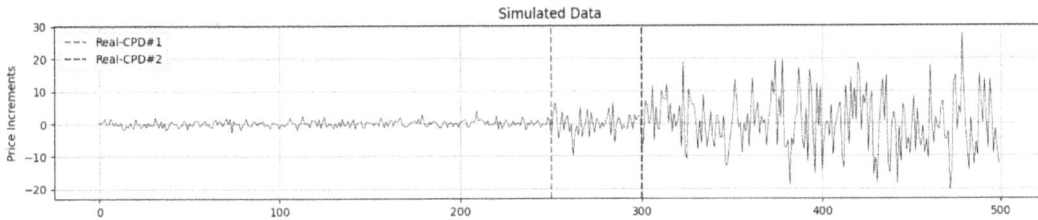

Figure 9.1: *Simulated data with two change points*

We feed these increments (data) into the CPD algorithm to calculate the anomaly score for each point in the series, as described previously. The highest scores provide a definitive signal for CPD:

```
import changefinder
#Initiate changefinder function
cf = changefinder.ChangeFinder(r = 0.2)
# compute scores to detect Change Points
scores = [cf.update(p) for p in data]
```

In the set-up instruction above, **r** is the forgetting factor for the stochastic model, typically ranging between 0 and 1. Smaller values make the model more sensitive to recent changes. The other parameters[2] are set to default values.

The anomaly scores are updated **in real-time** using the **cf.update()** function, as demonstrated in the code, where each new data point is processed by the algorithm to evaluate its **normality** in comparison to previous data.

We can now verify whether the CPD algorithm accurately identifies the correct change points. In the ChangeFinder library, change points are identified by peaks in the anomaly scores. Therefore, our task is to locate the position (**np.argsort(scores)**) of the extrema in the data:

```
print('True Change Point at position :',change_point_1)
cpd = np.argsort(scores)[-1]
print('CPD detected at position:',cpd)


True Change Point at position : 250
CPD detected at position:  255
```

The CPD algorithm successfully detects the two consecutive change points (**CPD#1** and **CPD#2** in the graph below), although there is a slight delay before detection.

This lag is expected due to the windowed slicing of the data as follows:

---

2 order: the order of the AR model used for modeling the time series data.
smooth: the number of past scores to consider when smoothing the detection score, which helps in reducing noise in the detection results.

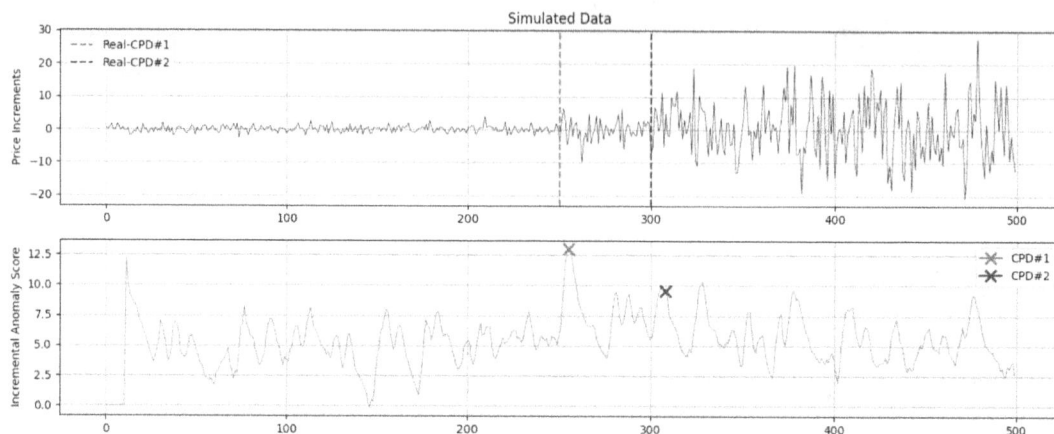

Figure 9.2: *Change points detected with CPD algorithm*

The ChangeFinder algorithm is particularly useful in any **real-time monitoring** system where identifying sudden changes is critical for prompt decision-making. Now, let us continue exploring CPD methods with an offline library.

Offline CPD with ruptures library

Ruptures is a Python library for offline CPD. Despite this limitation due to its resolutely offline nature, **ruptures** is the library of choice for taking your first steps in discovering CPD algorithms.

This package provides methods for the analysis and segmentation of non-stationary signals. "Non-stationary" refers to data whose statistical properties such as mean and variance change over time. Detecting these changes is precisely the goal of our analysis. Implemented algorithms include exact and approximate detection for various parametric and non-parametric models. For our purpose of CPD, we will focus on non-parametric[3] kernel methods.

The core idea of CPD is to find the change points that minimize a certain cost function, which measures how well the segmented signal fits the data.

When the number of change points is known, you can solve a specific optimization problem to find the best segmentation. If you do not know the number of change points, you can use a penalty term to balance the goodness of fit against the complexity of the segmentation.

---

3 In change point detection, the use of a kernel method can be considered a **non-parametric** approach. This is because kernel methods do not assume a specific parametric form for the underlying data distribution; instead, they rely on data-driven techniques to estimate changes based on similarities (distances) calculated using kernels.

Introduction to kernel CPD methods

In the context of CPD and machine learning, a kernel is a function used to measure the similarity or relationship between two data points in a transformed feature space. Kernels allow algorithms to operate in a higher-dimensional space without explicitly computing the coordinates of the data in that space, thanks to the kernel trick. This may sound fancy, but it is just a way to make CPD more powerful and versatile by analyzing the signal from a different perspective. This approach is particularly useful for identifying patterns or structures in data that are not linearly separable in the original space.

Kernel methods can be used to detect change points by evaluating how the relationship between data points changes over time. By applying a kernel function, one can measure the similarity between segments of the time series. A significant change in the similarity metric can indicate a **structural break** or change point in the data. In practice, algorithms like Kernel CPD leverage this concept, comparing segments of data before and after potential change points to identify where significant changes occur.

Detecting change points

The process of identifying where change points occur in a time series involves analyzing the data to pinpoint the locations where significant changes in its properties (like mean, variance, trend, or pattern) happen. Comparing segments of data before and after potential change points is a key strategy in this analysis.

It is typically done as follows:

- **Segmentation**: The time series is divided into segments, either based on fixed intervals, sliding windows, or using an algorithm that proposes potential segmentation points. These segments are chosen so that each segment is hypothesized to be statistically homogeneous within itself but different from adjacent segments.

- **Comparison**: For each potential change point, the data segments immediately before and after the point are compared. This comparison can be based on **distance** metrics.

A kernel function calculates the similarity (or distance) between segments in kernel-based methods. A significant change in similarity indicates a potential change point.

Comparing kernel CPD to traditional methods

A comparison of kernel-based CPD with traditional methods reveals several advantages. Kernel methods are adept at capturing complex, **nonlinear relationships** within data that traditional linear methods often miss, enhancing their ability to analyze complicated time series. In addition, the **flexibility** of kernel CPD is enhanced by the variety of kernel functions available, such as linear, polynomial, or radial basis functions, which allow analysts to tailor the detection process to the specific characteristics of their data. Some kernel methods also offer **computational efficiency**, allowing them to handle large data sets more effectively than exhaustive search methods.

Overall, kernel methods provide a powerful and flexible approach to CPD, capable of uncovering complex patterns in time series data that traditional linear techniques may miss.

Despite their advantages, kernelized methods for CPD have a notable drawback: in their standard form, they rely on data from both before and after a potential change point to assess the similarity or dissimilarity between segments.

Drawback of kernelized methods

Kernelized methods for CPD, in their standard form, indeed rely on information both before and **after** a potential change point to evaluate the similarity or dissimilarity between segments. This approach typically requires a **retrospective** analysis of the entire time series to identify where significant shifts occur, making it challenging to apply directly in a real-time context where future data points are not yet available.

However, it is possible to adapt these methods for online or real-time analysis with certain adjustments.

Application of kernel CPD

In this section, we will explore the application of CPD techniques. This analysis aims to demonstrate how CPD can uncover significant shifts in market dynamics over time. Specifically, we will analyze the monthly closing prices of copper futures contracts.

The Yahoo Finance ticker is **'HG=F'**:

```
asset = 'HG=F'
start_date = '2000-01-01'
end_date = '2024-04-25'
```

We start by downloading the data:

```
# monthly frequency
df = yf.download(asset, start=start_date, end=end_date , interval='1mo')
```

Next, we calculate the price increments () along with the closing prices and present them in the subsequent sub-plots:

```
import matplotlib.pyplot as plt
plt.plot(df['Close'])
plt.plot(df['Close'].diff())
```

The following are the closing prices and their successive price increments:

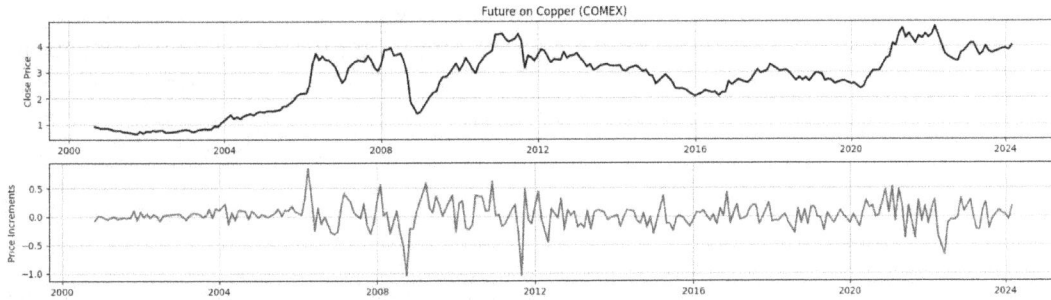

Figure 9.3: *Prices and increments for copper prices*

Next, we will display a snippet of the copper price dataset, showing the 10 most recent entries, as follows:

```
df.tail(10)
```

Date	Open	High	Low	Close	Adj Close	Volume
2023-06-01	3.6835	3.9500	3.6625	3.7410	3.7410	34713
2023-07-01	3.7475	4.0010	3.7120	3.9945	3.9945	14797
2023-08-01	4.0025	4.0025	3.6515	3.7725	3.7725	51432
2023-09-01	3.7920	3.8620	3.6100	3.7260	3.7260	16135
2023-11-01	3.6485	3.8400	3.5835	3.8290	3.8290	50776
2023-12-01	3.8375	3.9490	3.7130	3.8805	3.8805	15971
2024-01-01	3.8825	3.9360	3.7200	3.9025	3.9025	9910
2024-02-01	3.8955	3.8975	3.6860	3.8345	3.8345	39340
2024-03-01	3.8380	4.1460	3.8090	4.0035	4.0035	18033
2024-04-01	4.0740	4.6245	4.0445	4.5690	4.5690	8073

Table 9.1: *Copper prices*

When using **ruptures** for financial time series analysis, such as CPD in stock prices, you have two main options for how to format your data before analysis. You can inject a raw series (of closing prices, for example) or **increments** of the raw series to analyze variations in the series. The following are some tips for choosing the best option:

- **Choosing between prices and increments**:
  - **Using price increments (P(t) - P(t-1))**: This approach involves feeding the model with the differences between consecutive prices. It is particularly useful when you are interested in changes in the **volatility** or when you are looking for changes in the **return** rate rather than the absolute price levels. This method is sensitive to periods where the change in price becomes significantly different from the norm, which could indicate a change in market regime or volatility.

- o **Using direct prices (P(t))**: Alternatively, you can feed the model directly with the stock prices. This approach might be more suitable when you are interested in **detecting shifts in the level of prices**, such as long-term trends or sudden jumps in prices. Direct prices can highlight different types of **structural breaks**, such as those related to the underlying value of the asset rather than its volatility.

- **Choosing an approach**:

  - o **For volatility changes**: If your primary interest lies in detecting changes in volatility or trading volume, using increments is more appropriate. This format can more directly reveal periods where the price movement's intensity changes, which is a common indicator of volatility shifts.

  - o **For price level changes**: If you are more concerned with identifying shifts in the asset's price levels (for example, detecting a sudden jump in stock prices due to an external event or a gradual shift indicating a new trend), using direct prices is preferable.

For our part, we are exploring the library's ability to detect changes in volatility. For this reason, we calculate the price increments as follows. This line of code extracts the values of the cleaned price increments after removing any missing values:

```
data = df['Close'].diff().dropna().values
```

Then, we input these increments (**data**) into the CPD algorithm. The three kernel functions are available are **linear**, **rbf**, and **cosine**.

Each kernel provides a unique method for analyzing the signal, offering the flexibility to select the approach that best fits your data. We can initiate a loop to test various kernel values and visually review the outcomes[4] to determine the most effective option:

```
import ruptures as rpt
for i, kernel in enumerate(['linear', 'rbf', 'cosine']):
    algo = rpt.KernelCPD(kernel = kernel, min_size = 10)
    algo.fit(data)
    result = algo.predict(pen = 1e-3)
```

Here are the results of applying the different kernel models to the data: the top plot shows the result using a linear kernel, the middle plot uses a radial basis function (**rbf**) kernel, and the bottom plot uses a **cosine** kernel.

Each plot shows the identified change points with vertical dashed lines, allowing a comparison of how each kernel type affects the accuracy and sensitivity of CPD, as follows:

---

4 Setting min_size = 10 specifies that the minimum number of observations between any two detected change points must be at least 10.
In the graphic, the dotted vertical bars are positioned on turning points (Change Points).

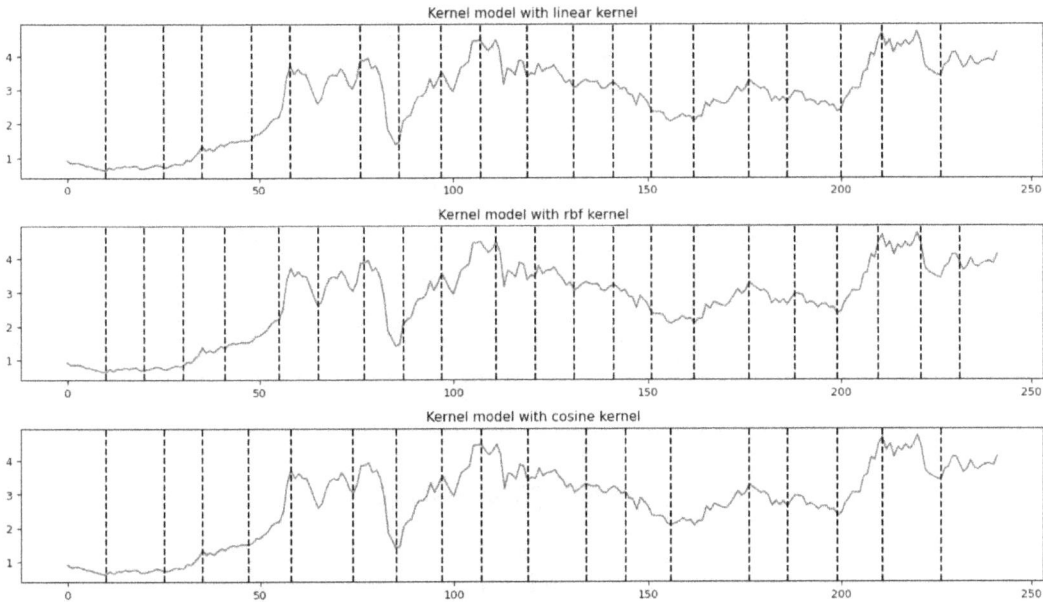

Figure 9.4: *Kernel CPD methods on copper prices*

Based on the graphic, the following points can be analyzed to ascertain the optimal choices:

- **Clarity of detection**: All three kernel models appear to successfully identify significant change points. However, the linear and cosine kernels show change points with sharper transitions, which could imply a more definitive detection of CPD events.

- **Frequency of signals**: The RBF kernel presents a slightly noisier signal with more frequent peaks, which might lead to a higher rate of **false positives**[5] **detections** or may detect minor changes that are not as relevant for some applications.

- **Precision of change points**: The linear and cosine kernels seem to offer a clearer distinction between regular fluctuations and true change points, suggesting a better precision which is crucial for accurate CPD in breakout modeling.

- **Simplicity and interpretability**: The linear kernel, due to its simplicity, tends to have fewer parameters to tune and can be more interpretable, which is often advantageous in practical applications.

5 To test for false positive detection in CPD, you can set up a framework that includes the following steps:
   1.**Ground Truth Establishment**: Identify or simulate a dataset with known change points to serve as the ground truth.
   2 **Algorithm Application**: Apply the CPD algorithm to the dataset to detect change points.
   3. **Comparison**: Compare the algorithm's detected change points against the ground truth to identify matches and discrepancies.
   4. **Metrics Calculation**: Calculate performance metrics such as precision, recall, and the false positive rate (see Chapter 5 for a detailed explanation of these metrics) to quantify the algorithm's accuracy and its propensity for false positive detection.

In conclusion, each of the employed techniques consistently identifies key transition points as CPD events. While all techniques are effective, the linear and cosine kernels demonstrate a marginally higher precision and accuracy in pinpointing CPD. They might be preferable for their clear and precise CPD, potentially making them the better choice for CPD in **breakout modeling**.

To further analyze the detected change points, we need to perform a detailed assessment to understand the significance of each change. This involves a statistical test - a somewhat technical process - to distinguish true changes in market behavior from false positives (noise mistaken for signal). While this step requires some statistical understanding, it is critical to evaluate the reliability of the turning points identified by the CPD algorithm. Although it is useful for a thorough understanding, readers can skip this section without losing the overall context.

Assessing the quality of segmentation

Utilizing the Ljung-Box statistic, a measure of residual autocorrelation, allows us to validate each change point using established statistical testing methods.

After the model identifies potential change points, we segment the signal based on these detected breakpoints[6]. For each segment, the statistical test is applied to the residuals —the differences between the observed values and the model's predictions to check for autocorrelation. If the residuals are independently distributed (no autocorrelation), it suggests that the model has captured the primary change points effectively[7]. Conversely, significant autocorrelation might indicate that some change points have been missed or that some detected points may be false positives.

The following code is based on the implementation of the Ljung-Box's statistic on **statsmodels** library[8]:

```
from statsmodels.stats.diagnostic import acorr_ljungbox
```

```
# Segmenting the signal based on detected breakpoints and analyzing
residuals
for i, bkpt in enumerate(result[:-1]):
    segment = data[result[i-1]:bkpt]
    # Assuming the model under null hypothesis is a constant (mean of the
segment)
    residuals = segment - np.mean(segment)
    # Ljung-Box test for each segment
    df_test_stat = acorr_ljungbox(residuals, lags=[max_lags], return_df =
```

6 i.e. the dotted vertical bars in the previous graphic.
7 If no autocorrelation is found in the residuals, it implies that the model has identified the main change points, indicating that no additional statistical relationships remain in the residual analysis.
8 https://www.statsmodels.org/stable/index.html

```
True)
    p_val = df_test_stat.loc[df_test_stat.index[-1] , 'lb_pvalue' ]


    print(f"Segment {i+1} (index pos: {bkpt})| Ljung-Box test p-value: {p_
val}")
    # Interpretation
    if p_val < 0.05:
        print("Significant autocorrelation detected in residuals -> poor
CPD.\n")
```

This code outputs the following results:

```
Segment 1 (index position: 10)| Ljung-Box test p-value: 0.6132004582354784
Segment 2 (index position: 25)| Ljung-Box test p-value: 0.7610265642130016
Segment 3 (index position: 35)| Ljung-Box test p-value: 0.5437320316542755
...
Segment 8 (index position: 97)| Ljung-Box test p-value:
0.028073716949534897
Significant autocorrelation detected in residuals -> poor CPD.
Segment 9 (index position: 107)| Ljung-Box test p-value: 0.7441227622887603
...
Segment 11 (index position: 134)| Ljung-Box test p-value:
0.02712131034835348
Significant autocorrelation detected in residuals -> poor CPD.
...
Segment 18 (index position: 226)| Ljung-Box test p-value:
0.9391197784597746
```

For the **cosine** kernel algorithm, **segment #8** and **segment #11** are incorrectly identified as change points. These segments do not exhibit significant changes in the underlying distribution and their detection as change points was likely due to false positives or errors in the detection algorithm.

For the other change points, the algorithm seems to correctly detect the breakpoints in the series of increments in future copper prices. The following graph shows the CPDs accepted (vertical bars) and those rejected (dotted vertical bars) by the statistical test:

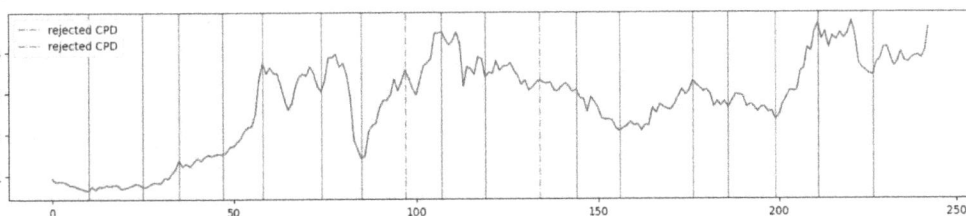

Figure 9.5: Accepted and rejected CPD

We are satisfied with this first result obtained with the analysis library. We have detected, identified, and ranked the change points and shifts according to their statistical significance, providing a clear understanding of the strength of each of them.

However, we can further explore the data by asking: Are all segments[9] homogeneous, or can they be categorized into distinct groups based on their characteristics? Can we identify clusters of segments that share similar traits, allowing us to group them into natural families?

Clustering sequences

The next logical step is to apply methods to group similar segments together, uncovering the underlying patterns and relationships that define these segments.

Data preparation for clustering

Before we can apply clustering algorithms, we need to prepare our data. The first step in this process is to preprocess our sequences and segments. This involves two key steps: **padding** our sequences to ensure they are uniform in length, and **standardizing** our segments to prevent any individual feature from dominating the analysis. We will begin by applying **padding** to our sequences.

In the context of sequence data, padding refers to the process of adding extra values to a sequence to make it a uniform length. This is often necessary when working with sequences of varying lengths, as many machine learning algorithms require fixed-length input data. Without padding, sequences of varying lengths would not be compatible with these algorithms. Furthermore, if sequences have different lengths, the model may be biased towards the longer sequences, which could lead to inaccurate results.

The following is the code to standardize (**pad_sequences**) the input segments (**seqs** is a list of sequences), ensuring they are all of uniform length[10]:

```
from keras.preprocessing.sequence import pad_sequences
padded_seqs = pad_sequences(seqs, padding='post', dtype='float32')
```

---

9 Segments are bounded by the identified change points.
10 The following is an example of applying padding on four toy sequences :
# Example sequence data
sequences = [np.array([1, 2, 3]),
                np.array([4, 5]),
                np.array([6,7,8,9,10,11])]
# Padding sequences to the same length
pad_sequences(sequences , padding='post', dtype='float32')

It give the following formatting:
array([[1., 2., 3., 0., 0., 0.],
    [4., 5., 0., 0., 0., 0.],
    [6., 7., 8., 9., 10., 11.]], dtype=float32)

After ensuring uniform length, we need to **standardize** the input segments statistically. To achieve this, we apply a standard scaler (**StandardScaler()** function), which transforms all inputs to have a similar scale, characterized by a zero mean and unit standard deviation.

This step (**scaler.fit_transform**) enables the machine learning algorithm to more easily compare the different sequences, facilitating the discovery of recurring patterns:

```
from sklearn.preprocessing import StandardScaler
# padded_seqs :array of padded sequences
scaler = StandardScaler()
# Standardize the sequences
seqs_scaled = scaler.fit_transform(padded_seqs.reshape(len(padded_seqs),
-1))
```

Before clustering, we apply a critical preprocessing step: **dimensionality reduction**. Experience shows that this improves the analysis of complex financial data. We will use the **Uniform Manifold Approximation and Projection algorithm (UMAP)** algorithm, which is known for preserving local data structure while reducing dimensionality.

Applying UMAP algorithm

With our data now standardized, we could move on to clustering. However, from my experience with financial data analysis, I know that it is often necessary to refine the data to make it more analyzable. To do this, we will use a dimensionality reduction technique that preserves the local structure of the data called UMAP algorithm[11]. We have already introduced this algorithm in *Chapter 6, Improving Model Capability with Features*. By applying UMAP, we can distill complex, high-dimensional data into a more manageable, lower-dimensional representation called **projection** (typically one or two dimensions). The algorithm ensures that the relationships between neighboring data points are preserved during the projection step, so that data points that were originally close together remain close together.

This step simplifies the data and preserves its inherent characteristics, a feat that UMAP accomplishes with remarkable precision:

```
from umap import UMAP
trsf = UMAP(n_neighbors = 2, min_dist = 0.1, n_components = 2)
seqs_reduced = trsf.fit_transform(seqs_scaled)
```

With UMAP reducing dimensionality, we can now group similar sequences. Using **kMeans**, we will identify patterns and structure within the data.

Clustering sequences with KMeans

The UMAP-transformed data are fed into the clustering algorithm, which groups similar data points together. In essence, we are not analyzing the original data, but rather the

---

11 We have already presented and used UMAP algorithm in chapter 6 devoted to feature engineering.

UMAP-transformed data, which allow for more effective pattern recognition and clustering.

The heavy lifting is done by UMAP, which projects the complex data into a lower-dimensional space while preserving its essential characteristics. This sets the stage for the k-Means clustering algorithm to group the points based on their proximity to each other.

In short, **k-Means** is an unsupervised algorithm that groups data points into clusters based on their similarities, allowing us to identify natural families within the data. It works by iteratively refining the cluster assignments until the data points are grouped into coherent clusters that share common characteristics.

By doing so, k-Means provides a way to uncover hidden patterns and structures in the data, allowing us to better understand and describe the underlying relationships between the data points:

```
# CLUSTERING
n_clusters = 4
clst = KMeans(n_clusters = n_clusters ,  n_init = 'auto')
clusters = clst.fit_predict(seqs_reduced )
```

The following graph illustrates the result of applying k-Means clustering to the data that has been transformed by UMAP, showing the resulting groupings into four distinct clusters.

We annotate the points with their label based on their order in the original list and highlight the last (most recent one) subsequence with a distinct color and label (16), as follows:

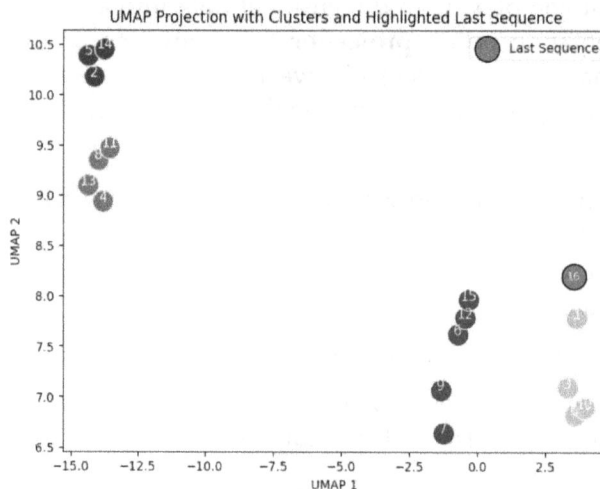

Figure 9.6: *Visualization of clustered sequences*

This graph shows the categorization of sequences into their inherent groups, with each group represented by a different color. For example, the initial two sequences (0 and 1) and the latest one (**'last sequence'**) are clustered together, as indicated by the orange color assigned to this group.

While this scatter plot of clustered sequences provides a useful visualization of how they interact with each other, it lacks a critical dimension: **time**. To fully capture the dynamics of these sequences, we need to incorporate the temporal aspect into our graph. Instead of positioning the sequences relative to each other, we will **reorder** them according to their appearance in time.

In the following figure, we will display each sequence, labeled by the clustering algorithm, in its correct position on the time scale, providing a more comprehensive understanding of their relationships:

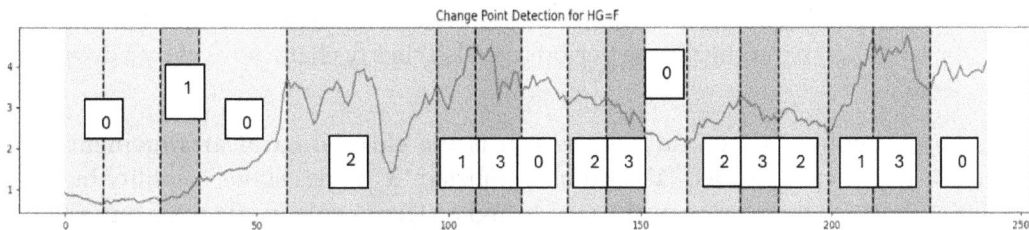

Figure 9.7: Clustering of ordered sequences

The graph shows the closing prices for copper futures segmented into four clusters, each indicated by a different color: [**'orange'**: labeled '**0**', **'purple'**: labeled '**1**', **'green'**: labeled '**2**', **'blue'**: labeled '**3**']. The algorithm identifies each cluster as a distinct regime characterized by its own unique dynamics and behavior.

Interpreting clustering

The clusters identified by the algorithm reveal a complex dynamic that will permit us to guide our interpretation and analysis of the market's dynamic.

Specifically, we need to do undertake the following steps:

1. Characterize each cluster in terms of its underlying dynamics, revealing the unique patterns and behaviors that define each regime.

2. Examine the chronological arrangement of the sequences, seeking to understand whether there is a specific order in which each type of sequence emerges in relation to others.

3. Finally, we will explore whether the insights gained from this analysis can be used to predict the next type of sequence that is likely to occur, following the last observed sequence (labeled **'orange'**, numbered **16,** cluster '**0**').

Let us start with the first step[12] which is to characterize each cluster in terms of its **underlying dynamics**. We can observe the following facts:

- **'orange' zones (labeled '0')**: These segments generally represent periods of **relative stability** or minor fluctuation in copper prices.

- **'purple' zones (labeled '1')**: These periods show a trend of **increasing volatility** or rising prices.

- **'green' zones (labeled '2')**: These segments are characterized by significant **fluctuations**, possibly indicating periods of market uncertainty or correction phases.

- **'blue' zones (labeled '3')**: These periods also display volatility with noticeable peaks, possibly suggesting reactionary movements to external market influences or speculative trading. These periods are also clearly characterized by a **downward trend**.

Let us now examine the second step, which is the **chronological arrangement** of the sequences. The purple (labeled '1') and blue (labeled '3') zones show volatility but differ in the frequency of their price peaks and troughs. The purple zones may represent the build-up to a market event or the anticipation of a trend change, while the blue zones may indicate the aftermath or a stabilization period following volatility. This refinement helps to understand not only the presence of volatility, but also its potential causes, and the market cycle positional, which is thought to represent stability, may occasionally precede more volatile periods (as seen transitioning into the purple and green zones), suggesting they may be the calm before significant market movements.

Recognizing these patterns helps predict future trends and identify potential investment or trading opportunities based on historical market behavior following these stable periods.

To answer the last point, predicting the **next probable regime** in the cluster sequence based on the observed patterns. We first need to analyze the transitions between different clusters and understand these regimes' underlying market dynamics. From the analysis, observing the sequence, there appears to be a cyclical pattern where periods of stability (orange '0' zones) often precede volatility (purple '1' and green '2' zones). Additionally, after significant volatility (blue '3' and green '2' zones), there is a return to more stable or less volatile periods (orange '0' zones).

We can summarize these insights in the sequence of regimes:

Stability regime (**'orange'** '0' zones) -> **Volatility** (purple '1' or green '2') -> **Stability** (**'orange'** '0')

CPD is a powerful technique for uncovering hidden patterns and anomalies in financial time series data. By understanding the principles, methods, and applications of CPD, you

12 The interpretation of a clustering is a subjective process that cannot be automated. At this stage of the analysis, it is not the algorithm itself, but rather human insight and interpretation that are essential for gaining an understanding of the results and uncovering meaningful patterns and relationships.

can gain a competitive edge in the markets, optimize your trading strategies, and improve the associated risk management practices.

Conclusion

By the end of this chapter, we gained practical skills in applying unsupervised learning techniques to financial data and analyzing patterns that are often outside the traditional scope of data science. We explored CPD, a powerful tool for identifying regime shifts in market behavior, both online and offline methods, learning to separate meaningful changes from noise.

Beyond detection, we applied dimensionality reduction with UMAP, refining high-dimensional sequences into a structured representation that enabled k-means clustering to segment financial data into distinct phases. But we went further: instead of relying solely on standard CPD techniques, we trained an architecture that integrates CPD detection, non-linear mapping, and clustering to create a storytelling method that captures market dynamics.

This structured approach enables an intuitive understanding of financial sequences and helps predict future trends by analyzing entire market movements rather than isolated events. Ultimately, we developed a complete, data-driven strategy that goes beyond traditional statistical methods by combining unsupervised learning and pattern recognition to anticipate financial market evolution.

Having explored clustering and CPD, we now turn to another critical aspect of unsupervised learning: pattern matching. Financial markets are full of recurring structures, and identifying them can provide a strategic advantage.

In the next chapter, we will cover distance matrices and recurrence plots, essential tools for visualizing and quantifying time series dynamics. We will also examine the Matrix Profile, a powerful method for uncovering hidden patterns and detecting anomalies in financial data. These techniques will help us move far beyond static clustering to dynamic pattern recognition, enhancing our ability to identify, compare, and exploit market behavior.

Join our book's Discord space

Join the book's Discord Workspace for Latest updates, Offers, Tech happenings around the world, New Release and Sessions with the Authors:

https://discord.bpbonline.com

CHAPTER 10
Unsupervised Learning with Pattern Matching

Introduction

In this chapter, we focus on the practical application of unsupervised learning techniques, using pattern matching methods and their ability to detect **patterns**, **recurring motifs**, or distinct anomalies. We begin by examining fundamental unsupervised techniques, such as **Distance Matrix (DM)** and **recurrence plot (RP)**, that are used to visualize and quantify the dynamics of time series data. These methods allow us to uncover hidden patterns and *structures* in financial data that might otherwise go unnoticed. In addition, we will explore the use of the matrix profile, a powerful tool for pattern matching that allows the identification of both recurring patterns and *outliers* within time series data.

Structure

In this chapter, we will cover the following topics:

- Understanding unsupervised learning
- Introduction to recurrence plot and Distance Matrix
- Trading with recurrence plot and Distance Matrix
- Pattern matching

Objectives

The purpose of this chapter is to reinforce our knowledge of unsupervised techniques that we started with in the previous chapter, and to guide readers in mastering pattern matching using the matrix profile, including how to compute and interpret it to identify recurring patterns (motifs) and anomalies (discords) in financial data. In addition, we will understand how features derived from recurrence plots of the matrix profile can be integrated into machine learning models to predict market trends and enhance trading strategies. Moreover, we will cover the practical application of these unsupervised learning methods to real-world financial data, which will be demonstrated, offering insights into how to implement these techniques within algorithmic trading systems.

Understanding unsupervised learning

Unsupervised learning is a type of machine learning in which the algorithm learns patterns and relationships from unlabeled data. Unlike supervised learning, where the algorithm is trained on labeled data to make predictions, unsupervised learning does not rely on pre-defined labels or outcomes. Instead, it discovers hidden structures, relationships, and patterns in the data itself.

The power of unsupervised learning lies in its ability to identify novel and unexpected insights in data. In the context of algorithmic trading, unsupervised learning can help traders and analysts uncover hidden trends, anomalies, and correlations that may not be immediately apparent using traditional analysis methods.

Unsupervised learning techniques

Unsupervised learning includes several techniques. The following are some **key** unsupervised learning techniques relevant to algorithmic trading:

- **Clustering,** which is the subject of *Chapter 9, Unsupervised Learning Methods for Trading*, involves grouping similar data points into clusters based on their characteristics. This technique is useful for identifying[1] together, uncovering the underlying patterns, and relationships that define this input.

- **Dimensionality reduction** techniques, such as **Principal Component Analysis (PCA)**, help simplify complex data by reducing the number of features while preserving essential information. This is particularly useful in trading, where high-dimensional data can be overwhelming. For details on this technique, see *Chapter 6, Improving Model Capability with Features*.

- **Anomaly detection** techniques are used to identify unusual patterns that do not conform to expected behavior. In trading, this can be useful for detecting outliers or unusual market activities, such as identifying sudden price movements that

---

1 cf Chapter 9, Unsupervised Learning Methods for Trading

could indicate a significant market event. For details on this technique, see *Chapter 12, Advanced Unsupervised Learning, Anomaly Detection, and Association Rules*.

- **Association rules** help discover relationships between different variables in trading data. This technique is useful for identifying hidden correlations between different assets or indicators that can be used to make trading decisions. See *Chapter 12, Advanced Unsupervised Learning, Anomaly Detection, and Association Rules*, for an implementation of this powerful and underutilized technique in trading.

- **Independent Component Analysis (ICA)** is a computational method for separating a multivariate signal into additive, independent non-Gaussian components. In trading, ICA can be applied to separate mixed signals into independent sources, such as isolating different factors influencing stock prices, which can help in understanding underlying market dynamics. We do not explore this topic further here, but interested readers can refer to the excellent **Scikit-learn** documentation, **https://scikit-learn.org/stable/modules/decomposition.html#ica**.

- **Pattern matching** involves identifying specific patterns in trading data. This technique is described in detail in the last part of this chapter.

- **Recurrence plot** is a graphical representation used to analyze patterns, structures and the recurrence of states in a dynamical system. It is essentially a graph showing instances where the trajectory of the dynamical system revisits the same area. recurrence plot reveals patterns that can indicate periodicities, chaos, or other hidden structures in dynamical behaviors. This technique is described in detail in the last part of this chapter.

Understanding these techniques leads us to the relevance of unsupervised learning in algo trading, where these principles of identifying hidden patterns and structures are applied.

Relevance of unsupervised learning to algo trading

Unsupervised learning techniques can identify **novel trading opportunities** by revealing hidden patterns and relationships in the data that may not be immediately apparent through traditional analysis methods. Additionally, they can aid in the development of **trading strategies** clusters of similar[2] trading days, detect anomalies, and discover correlations between different assets or indicators. Enhancing **risk management** is another benefit, as unsupervised learning can identify potential risks and anomalies in trading data, allowing traders to take proactive measures to mitigate them. Furthermore, unsupervised learning can facilitate the **automation of trading decisions** by identifying patterns and relationships that can be used to develop systematic trading strategies.

Unsupervised learning techniques extend well beyond algorithmic trading and are essential for developing high-performing AI systems in any sector.

---

2 cf Chapter 9, Unsupervised Learning Methods for Trading

Importance of unsupervised learning

Let us open the discussion to a wider context than algorithmic trading. *Yann LeCun*[3] consistently emphasizes the importance of unsupervised learning for advancing AI systems. He argues that it is critical for machines to acquire **common sense** and develop a true understanding of the world, like human learning. LeCun proposes that learning **world models** through **unsupervised** methods is key to building human-level AI. This approach would allow machines to learn vast amounts of background knowledge about how the world works through observation, with **minimal task-specific training**.

Unsupervised learning could become the mainstream technique for future AI systems that can learn from raw, unlabeled data, leading to robust and adaptable intelligence that more closely resembles human cognition.

Researchers argue that current supervised learning approaches, while successful in specific domains, are limited in their ability to **generalize** and acquire common sense knowledge.

We now turn our attention to the specific applications of these insights through pattern matching and pattern detection. In the rest of this chapter, we will examine in detail two techniques we briefly mentioned in the list of unsupervised learning techniques. We start with **recurrence plot (RP)** and **Distance Matrix**[4] **(DM)**, and then we will finish with pattern matching.

Introduction to recurrence plot and Distance Matrix

To explore and understand RP and DM, we begin by answering three basic questions: What is an RP? What can it be used for? How is it computed? After establishing these basics, we will move on to using RP and DM as features for machine learning algorithms.

Understanding recurrence plot

An RP is a tool introduced by *Eckmann*[5] and others, to visualize the time-dependent behavior and the temporal stability of a dynamical system.

Natural processes often show distinct recurrent behaviors, such as the periodicities seen in seasonal cycles or irregular cyclic patterns. Biological systems also exhibit behavioral patterns and activity dynamics, like those observed in ant colonies.

RP plots the number of times, the system revisits **approximately** the same state, highlighting patterns and structures in the data. Each point on the RP represents a time pair where the **state** at time is close to the state at time with closeness defined by a chosen threshold.

---

3 **Yann LeCun** is one of the most prominent AI researcher in the world, he heads the AI research in Meta.
4 Distance Matrix is also known as unthresholded RP, Distance Plot or Self-Similarity Matrix
5 Eckmann, J. P., Kamphorst, S. O., & Ruelle, D. (1987). Recurrence plots of dynamical systems. *Europhysics Letters (EPL)*, 4(9), 973-977.

Capabilities of an RP

The RP is valuable for detecting hidden periodicities, non-stationarity, and dynamic changes in the data that may not be apparent from the original time series alone. Its applications range from physics and astronomy to finance and neuroscience, providing insights into the dynamics and stability of complex systems. By analyzing patterns, such as diagonal lines or clusters in the plot, data scientists can infer the **nature of recurrences and the system**, dynamics, including chaos and regular cycles.

Computing a recurrence plot

The first step in computing an RP is the generation of the DM, which quantifies the pairwise distances between all points in the time series. DM is a comprehensive snapshot of how each point in the time series relates to every other point in terms of distance.

To create an RP, and DM we need to follow these steps:

1. **Select a DM**: Select an appropriate metric (e.g., Euclidean or Manhattan) to measure the distance between points in the time series. This metric determines how close the points are to each other in phase space.

2. **Compute DM[6]**: The matrix DM provides a visual representation of the distance between all pairs of points of a time series.

3. **Set a threshold**: Decide on a threshold[7] which determines how close the points must be to each other to be considered recurrent.

4. **Construct the recurrence matrix[8]**: Create a binary matrix where each element is defined as, , if and 0 otherwise. $R = 1$ indicates that the states at times *i* and *j* are **similar**. It is important to note that systems rarely return to an **identical** past state. Instead, the resulting matrix visually represents instances where the time series revisits **similar** states.

Here is the complete function to compute both DM and RP:

```
# Function to create a Distance Matrix and a recurrence plot
def dist_matrix_rec_plot(data, threshold=0.1):
    # Calculate the distance matrix
    dist_matrix = np.abs(data[:, None] - data[None, :])
    # Create the recurrence plot using the threshold
```

---

6 Here is the code to compute a distance matrix (associated with Manhattan distance):
dist_matrix = np.abs(data[:, None] - data[None, :])
7 Determining an appropriate value for this parameter is not straightforward. The practice has come out with a few heuristics. For instance, a threshold can be set to 10% of the largest observed distance.
8 Here is the code to compute a Recurrence Plot :
# Create the recurrence plot using the threshold
rp = dist_matrix <= threshold

```
rp = dist_matrix <= threshold
return rp , dist_matrix
```

The DM highlights **distance-based patterns**, while the RP reveals the **temporal recurrence**.

Examples of RPs and DM

We will begin with a simple simulated time series to demonstrate how DMs and RPs help visualize patterns such as cycles, trends, and chaotic behavior inherent in the data. This will help us understand how to interpret both the DM and the RP.

Linear function

We will start with the linear function:

The plot of this function alongside associated DM and RP is as follows:

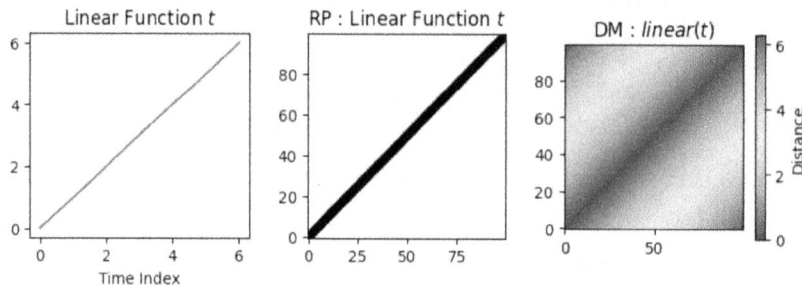

Figure 10.1: DM and RP for a Linear Function

For a linear function   and a threshold   value of 0.2, it shows a single diagonal line from bottom-left to top-right. This represents the line of identity where each point is perfectly recurrent with itself.

For RP plot the color scheme is as follows, **black** indicates recurring system states where the distance between points is below the threshold, while **white** represents non-recurring states where the distance exceeds the threshold.

The DM displays a gradient pattern that represents both shorter and longer distances. The diagonal is zero, representing no distance between a point and itself. Moving away from the diagonal, the distance increases linearly, creating a gradually symmetrical pattern. This reflects the **constant rate of change** in the linear function, with **no periodic** or complex patterns.

The **absence of other patterns indicates no periodic behavior** or complex dynamics, reflecting the simple, consistent nature of the linear function.

To further our understanding of the interpretation of both RP and DM, we now examine a piecewise function that offers more complexity than the previous linear function.

Piecewise function

A piecewise function is a function defined by different expressions or formulas for different intervals of its domain. Linear and piecewise functions can be viewed as **simplified trends** for the time series of a financial asset.

The following code defines a piecewise function where the function follows one rule for values of t less than to 3 and another rule for other points:

```
def piecewise_function(t):
    return np.where(t <= 3, t, -t + 6)
```

The following are the DM and RPs associated with this function:

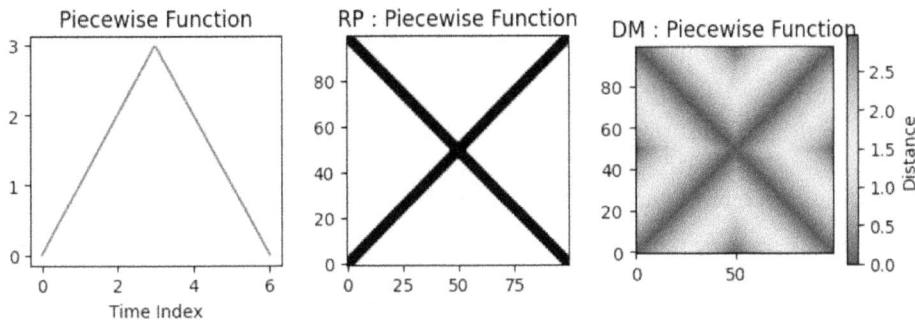

Figure 10.2: RP and DM for a piecewise function

The RP for this piecewise linear function shows a distinctive X-shaped pattern. This pattern reflects the two linear segments of the function that meet at a peak. The diagonal line from the bottom left to the top right represents points that repeat back to themselves. The additional diagonal lines that cross in the middle highlight the symmetry of the function around its peak.

The DM displays a butterfly-like pattern. The dark diagonal represents zero distance between each point and itself. The other areas show maximum distances between points at opposite ends of the time series. The V-shaped dark region reflects the function's peak, where nearby points have small distances.

Both plots effectively capture the function's **key characteristics**, its linear structure, symmetry, and the presence of a distinct peak.

Now, let us understand how periodic cycles will affect both the DM and the RP.

Periodic function

In this section, we explore how **periodic cycles** influence both the DM and the RP. By analyzing a periodic function, we can observe how its repetitive nature is reflected in these visualizations.

The following are the representation plots for a periodic function:

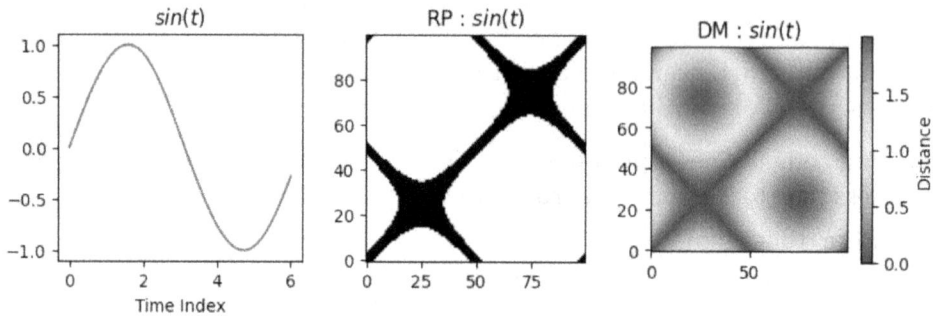

Figure 10.3: *RP and DM for a periodic function*

The RP for sine function displays a distinct pattern of lines and shapes, which is typical for a periodic function. Here is how to interpret this plot. The diagonal line running from the bottom-left to top-right is the line of identity showing perfect recurrence. The X-like patterns repeating across the plot are characteristic of the wave's nature. Each point on these lines indicates a recurrence of the wave at different times.

The implications of this pattern are the following:

- The **periodic gaps** between the distinct high-distance regions along the diagonal indicate the **regular periodicity** of the sine function. These gaps correspond to the function's consistent amplitude and frequency, reflecting how similar states reappear at regular intervals.

- The **symmetry around the center line** reflects the **symmetric nature** of the sine wave over time.

Periodic linear function

To complete our analysis of simplified dynamic representations found in financial markets, here are the DM and RP for a linear trend combined with a (damped) oscillation:

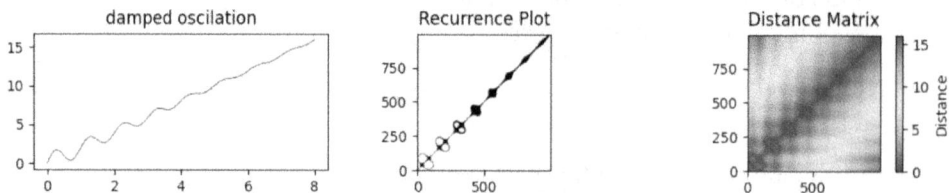

Figure 10.4: *RP and DM for a periodic linear function*

For RP, the recurring black dots and short diagonal segments off the main diagonal indicate periodic returns to similar states, reflective of the damped oscillation. The recurrence of patterns shows how the system revisits similar states periodically with diminishing intensity due to the damping effect. This adds complexity to the recurrence structure compared to a simple periodic function.

For the DM plot, the alternating bands along and parallel to the diagonal suggest the combined effect of the linear trend and the damped oscillation. The oscillatory pattern is visible in the periodic bands, reflecting the regular recurrence of the oscillatory component superimposed on the linear trend.

Now that we have mastered the interpretation rules for trends, periodic patterns, and combinations of these elements, we will apply them to analyze the typical random walk path of a financial asset.

Stock price

As the stock, we choose Reliance, the largest Indian stock in terms of capitalization (around $250 billion). This conglomerate operates in energy, petrochemicals, textiles, natural resources, retail, and telecommunications.

The following are the DM and RPs for their stock price:

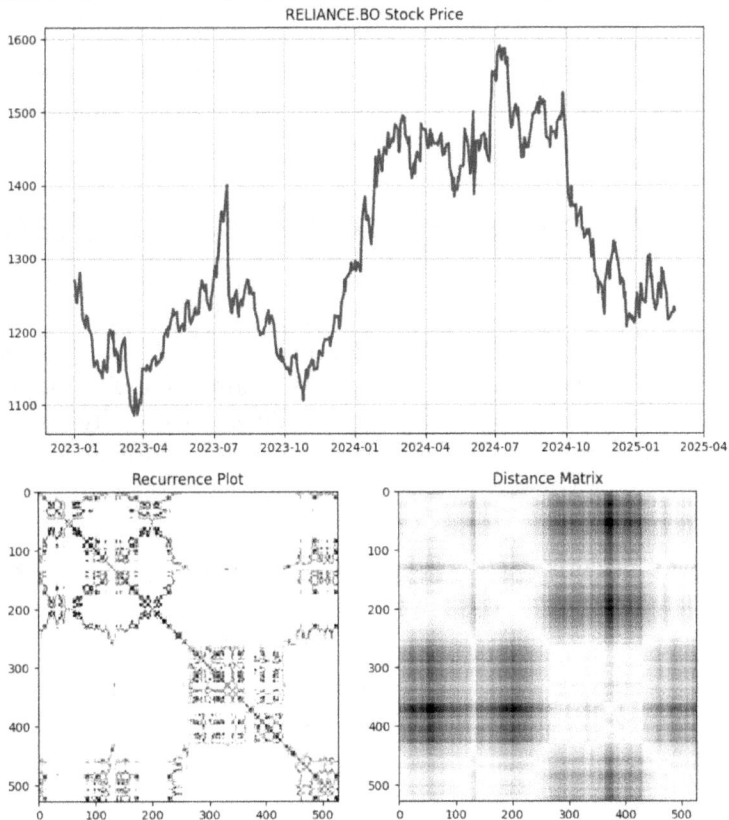

Figure 10.5: RP and DM for Reliance stock price

For the RP, the scattered patterns away from the diagonal show complex dynamics. Areas of dense black dots indicate periods where the stock revisits similar states. These clusters suggest repeated stock price behaviors. The RP reveals that the Reliance stock exhibits both trending and recurring behaviors, indicating periodic revisits to certain price levels amidst overall movement.

For the DM plot, the alternating bands represent changes in price similarities over time. The presence of cross patterns and alternating bands indicates fluctuating similarities, with closely related prices and larger price shifts. We can infer that Reliance stock has periods of stability interspersed with significant price changes. The DM helps identify when the stock was in similar price ranges and when it experienced substantial deviations.

Nonetheless, the DM shows varied shades throughout, which indicates fluctuations in the differences between the time series values at different times. This variability in shade suggests stochastic behavior, as the time series does not follow a **strictly uniform pattern of change**. The further suggests that the series does not repeat its values in a regular, predictable manner. Instead, it shows a more random variation, typical of stochastic processes. The **varied and inconsistent shading** throughout the rest of the matrix indicates that while there is a **general trend**, the exact changes from one point to another are **not predictable**.

All these patterns offer valuable insights into the dynamical system; however, interpreting them **visually** requires experience and expertise. Next, we will examine how to extract **direct numerical quantifications** through RPs or DMs.

Trading with recurrence plot and Distance Matrix

A more objective method for analyzing RPs is **Recurrence Quantification Analysis (RQA)**, a non-linear data analysis technique that quantifies the number and duration of recurrences within a dynamical system. RQA simplifies the challenge of visually interpreting RP and DM visually and is a critical step toward using them as features in a machine learning algorithm.

Introduction to Recurrence Quantification Analysis

Several RQA measures have been developed, including the percentage of recurrence points (recurrence rate), the average length of diagonal lines, and the length of the longest diagonal line among others. These measures are useful for characterizing and comparing different types of RPs. For example, researchers[9] computed RQA measures from electromyogram[10] data and utilized them as features to train a Support Vector Machine classifier to detect normal and abnormal neuromuscular disorders.

We can consider financial asset prices as a dynamic system. Therefore, we will draw inspiration from this cutting-edge scientific research that uses RQA derived from RP and DM to gain insights. To assess randomness and predictability in a time series using RQA, the two most important metrics are **Recurrence Rate** and **Determinism**.

Here is an explanation of these metrics:

- **Recurrence Rate (RR)**: RR is the fraction of points in the recurrence plot that are recurrent (i.e., below a certain threshold distance). It quantifies the **density** of the recurrence plot and gives an overall idea of the state repetition in the system. High RR indicates frequent recurrence of states, suggesting less randomness. While low RR suggests infrequent recurrence, indicating more randomness.

- **Determinism (DET)**: DET measures the proportion of recurrent points that form diagonal lines of at least a given length in the recurrence plot. It reflects the predictability of the time series. High DET indicates more predictable and less random behavior as the system evolves in a deterministic manner. Low DET suggests more stochastic or complex behavior with less predictability.

These two statistics (RR and DET), along with their product and ratio, provide a means to assess information about the dynamics (such as quantifying trend and randomness).

For instance, these statistics computed for the simulated dynamics (linear, periodic, and damped oscillations) and Reliance Industries stock price introduced previously yield the following results:

Dynamics	Recurrence Rate	Determinism	Product (RR x DET)	Ratio (DET / RR)
Linear	0.069	49.638	3.415	721.484
Periodic	0.190	21.586	4.093	113.850
Damp	0.158	76.379	12.075	483.131
Close Price	0.035	14.644	0.519	413.525

Table 10.1: RQA for determinist and random dynamics

For linear dynamics, RR and DET suggest low recurrence with moderate predictability. For the periodic (Sin) dynamic, RR is higher, indicating more frequent recurrences typical of periodic behavior. DET is lower, suggesting less predictability in cyclic patterns. For the

9 Sultornsanee et al., P. (2015). Classification of electromyography (EMG) signals using Recurrence Quantification Analysis (RQA) and Support Vector Machine. *2015 8th Biomedical Engineering International Conference (BMEiCON)*
10 Electromyogram: Measures muscle electrical activity during contraction and rest.

Reliance's stock price, RR and DET suggest low recurrence and moderate predictability. Product and ratio highlight the high variability and stochastic nature of stock prices.

Can the RP and DM matrices, along with the derived RQA statistics, provide sufficient information for a machine learning algorithm to predict market movements? If so, how can these recurrence-based representations improve predictive models?

In the next section, we will explore how integrating RP, DM, and RQA as features can enhance the predictive power of trading models.

RP as a feature for trading system

What if we incorporate RP, DM, and RQA as features in a machine learning algorithm? In this section, we will explain and illustrate how unsupervised and supervised techniques can be effectively combined. Such an approach is valuable because it leverages the strength of DMs in capturing complex relationships in an **unsupervised** manner. The **supervised** classifier then learns to make predictions based on these **rich, unsupervised features**. This combination leads to more robust and interpretable models, especially in financial data where underlying structures are complex.

To understand how to incorporate RP and DM into a machine learning pipeline, we will start with a basic benchmark. By establishing a simple yet effective foundation, we can assess the feasibility of using RP and DM in a machine learning framework before exploring more advanced techniques.

Baseline based approach

The baseline approach consists of finding the minimum necessary actions to train a machine learning algorithm (either an unsupervised or a supervised algorithm) using a DM or a RP. This baseline method provides ample room for improvement, if successful. A baseline represents the **simplest version**, aiming to demonstrate its capability to deliver consistent returns (Sharpe ratio > 0.5), rather than achieving state-of-the-art results. If the baseline proves effective, there are numerous ways to enhance and augment this initial attempt.

The following are the minimum steps to iterate through the initial signal, compute the initial DM at each time step, then derive RQA statistics and transform these 2D matrices into data structures suitable for training with a standard ML algorithm:

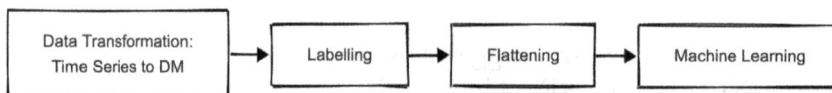

Figure 10.6: Pipeline to use RP and DM in machine learning

The sequence of operations to use RP and DM in machine learning, as described in the previous figure, is as follows:

1. **Data transformation**: Compute DM for each time step and derive RQA statistics. Iterate through initial signal, slide through the time series data to generate multiple time steps.

2. **Labelling**[11]: For each matrix, create a label (classification or regression).

3. **Flattening**: Transform 2D matrices. Convert the derived statistics and matrices into a 1D flatten feature vectors or data structures compatible with standard machine learning algorithms.

4. **Training ML algorithm**: Use these data structures to train a classification or regression model.

In the following sections, we will take a closer look at each of these stages and implement them with an asset. To put our methodology into practice, we apply it to a real financial asset. Our selected asset is the Teucrium Corn ETF Fund, which trades under the ticker **CORN**:

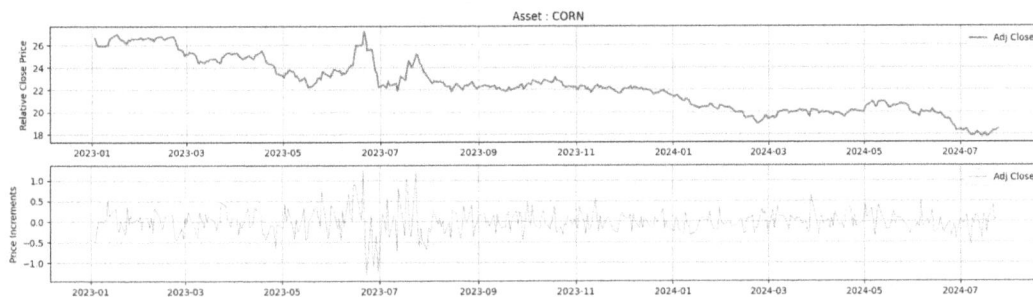

Figure 10.7: *Close and Price increments for Teucrium Corn Fund ETF*

It is a commodity **Exchange-Traded Fund** (**ETF**) that trades on the NYSE Arca. This fund is designed to track the price of corn futures and offers investors a convenient way to gain exposure to the corn market without needing to engage directly in futures trading. Now that we have our dataset, we can begin the initial stage of the analysis.

Data transformation

First, we specify which matrix to choose, RP or DM, as this choice will influence the subsequent results. One **limitation** of RP analysis is the need to **specify a threshold** value, which can be challenging to determine. The current approach relies on local heuristics, where the threshold is set based on a single RP. However, this can lead to inconsistent results when analyzing multiple plots.

To overcome this issue, we utilize information embedded in DM. This approach **eliminates** the need for a threshold value and allows for a more direct analysis of the distance between each pair of subsequences.

---

11 This step is required only in case of supervised learning.

We employ a windowing approach to extract small segments of the closing price time series as depicted in the following figure:

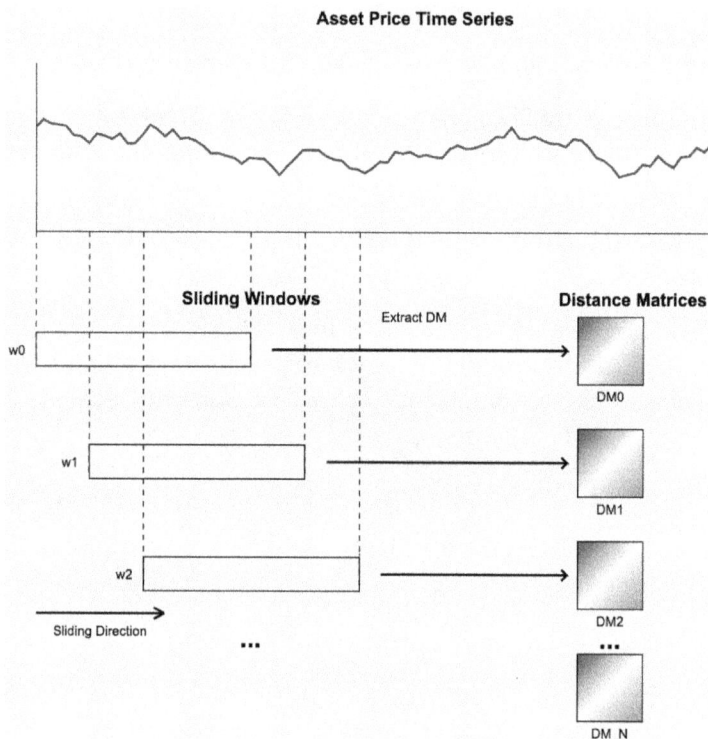

Figure 10.8: Data transformation

A sliding window[12] (**window**) browses through the chronology (**series**), extracting values from each segment and sending them to calculate the DM (**distance_matrix**) for that specific segment:

```
def create_distance_matrix(series, window_size:
    matrices = []
    for i in range(len(series) - window_size + 1):
        window = series[i:i+window_size]
        distance_matrix = np.abs(window[:, None] - window[None, :])
            matrices.append(distance_matrix)
    return matrices
```

The previous code used a sliding window approach to extract successive segments from the time series and compute a DM for each segment. This helps to capture the local structure of the time series within each window.

12 Another common challenge with the windowing approach is determining the optimal value for the sliding window parameter. A short window size can capture local structures, while a longer window size can reveal more global patterns. This choice of window size impact the results of analysis and modeling.

Labelling

If we perform a supervised learning task, we must provide a label. In supervised learning, each DM that serves as a feature corresponds to a specific target to learn. Unsupervised DMs can be used in both supervised and unsupervised contexts and can be integrated into various learning paradigms in trading.

The following code defines the labels needed for a supervised learning task. Since we decide to predict market movements, we use the direction of the price movement: a positive value indicates an upward movement and a negative value indicates a downward movement:

```
# Create labels
labels = np.sign(np.diff(close_prices[window_size - 1:]))
labels[labels == 0] = -1
```

Before feeding the DMs into a machine learning model, we first **split** them into **training** and **test** sets, then flatten them into 1D arrays for proper ingestion.

Splitting and flattening

The splitting step, a necessary step that we have consistently applied since the very beginning of the book, require splitting the DM into a training set and a test set.

```
# Split into train and test sets
train_matrices, test_matrices, train_labels, test_labels = train_test_
split(
    distance_matrices[:-1], labels, test_size=0.2, shuffle=False)
```

This provides structured inputs and corresponding goals for learning. After separation, these two sets (train and test sets) are **flattened** into 1D structures (arrays) for ingestion by the machine learning algorithm:

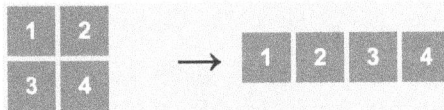

Figure 10.9: Transforming a 2D matrix into a 1D array

As shown in the preceding figure, each DM (from **train** and **test** sets) is converted into a 1D array:

```
train_matrices_flat = np.array([matrix.flatten() for matrix in train_matrices])
test_matrices_flat = np.array([matrix.flatten() for matrix in test_matrices])
```

The original and unconventional feature engineering is now complete. At this point, we continue with the conventional steps of training the machine learning algorithm on the training set and evaluating it on the test set.

Train a machine learning algorithm

As we have already stated and explained, the baseline requires an algorithm to demonstrate the proof of concept that even a basic machine learning algorithm (**LogisticRegression**, for instance) can learn the features we have and deliver consistent predictions. This is the preliminary step in the quest for the best algorithm. The data structures (**train_matrices_flat**) are well-shaped and were prepared during the previous step. All that remains is to instantiate the classifier and train (**fit**) it to predict (**predict**) our target based on the unsupervised DM features:

```python
from sklearn.linear_model import LogisticRegression
clf = LogisticRegression(max_iter = 1000, solver = 'liblinear')
clf.fit(train_matrices_flat , train_labels)
test_predictions = clf.predict(test_matrices_flat)
```

Evaluate the baseline

Let us now see how the baseline model performs. We know the metrics to compute. Initially, the confusion matrix and Scikit-Learn classification report (**classification_report**) will provide all the necessary information to evaluate this machine learning algorithm's ability to predict return signs:

```python
# Print detailed classification report
print(classification_report(test_labels, test_predictions))
```

```
Classification Report:
              precision    recall  f1-score   support

        -1.0       0.56      0.61      0.58        41
         1.0       0.43      0.38      0.40        32

    accuracy                           0.51        73
   macro avg       0.49      0.49      0.49        73
weighted avg       0.50      0.51      0.50        73
```

For class **-1.0**, **precision** is **0.56**, meaning that 56% of the predicted negative returns were correct. **recall** is **0.61**, meaning that 61% of actual negative returns were correctly identified and the same analysis applied to the positive class.

The model performs better at predicting negative returns than positive ones, as indicated by higher precision, recall, and F1-scores for the negative class -1.0. These results suggest that there is significant room for improvement, particularly in the prediction of positive returns. Further tuning and the inclusion of additional features or more sophisticated algorithms may improve performance. To further assess its effectiveness, we will now backtest the baseline model to evaluate its performance in terms of financial decision-making for buying and selling.

Backtest the baseline algorithm

By backtesting the unseen test set data with the same code, generating predictions using the baseline algorithm, and simulating investments with a 3-basis-point transaction cost, we obtain the following equity curve:

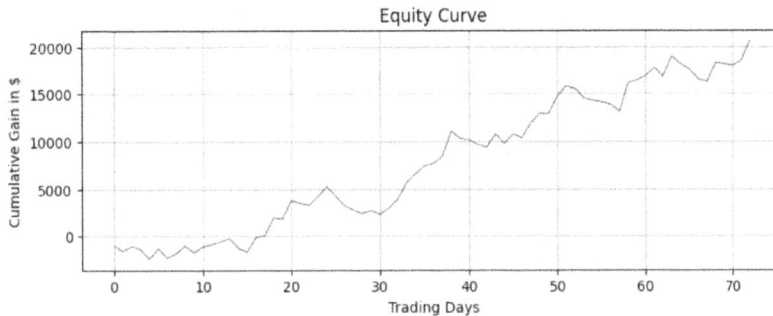

Figure 10.10: Equity curve from baseline algorithm

These performance metrics summarize the effectiveness of our strategy over the backtest period. The associated metrics are as follows:

```
Initial Capital: $100000
Final Capital: $120580
Annualized Return (on 0.3 years): 71.0%
Sharpe Ratio: 2.1
```

The results indicate a good performance, with a high annualized return and a Sharpe ratio suggesting a favorable risk-adjusted return. While the baseline approach provides a starting point, there are several ways to improve its performance.

Improve the baseline version

Regarding **features**, the classifier has only seen the DM and not any close prices. Including close prices (or any combination of OHLC data) would be a good idea. Additionally, there are many other interesting **features** to provide to the ML algorithm, as covered in *Chapter 6, Improving Model Capability with Features.*

As discussed in *Chapter 7, Advanced Machine Learning Models for Trading*, we should explore more **advanced methods** such as boosting, bagging, ensemble, and voting algorithms instead of the basic logistic regression used for the baseline. We can also utilize automatic methods, as highlighted in *Chapter 8, AutoML and Low-Code for Trading Strategies*, to improve feature engineering. **Automated feature engineering** libraries can streamline the creation of relevant features, and **AutoML** platforms automate the process of selecting the best machine learning algorithm for a given dataset and problem.

With a solid understanding of DM and RP, we now move on to another unsupervised technique called Pattern Matching, which allows us to identify and extract meaningful patterns in data.

Pattern matching

Pattern matching is the process of identifying similar patterns within a dataset. It helps find recurring sequences or anomalies. For example, in quantitative finance, pattern matching can detect similar price movements across different stocks, aiding in predicting future price trends. A lot of patterns matching methods exist, among them we can cite the most powerful: **Dynamic Time Warping (DTW)**, **Hidden Markov Models (HMM)**, **Fourier Transform (FT)** and Matrix Profile. After a brief introduction demonstrating DTW, we will briefly introduce **HMM** and **FT** methods but focus on a detailed exploration of the latter.

After installing the required library, the following code demonstrates how **DTW** helps with pattern matching by measuring the similarity between two time series, even if they vary in speed or timing:

```
!pip -q install fastdtw

from fastdtw import fastdtw
from scipy.spatial.distance import euclidean

# Create two time series time_series_1 and time_series_2 with oscillations
# Compute DTW distance
distance, path = fastdtw(time_series_1, time_series_2, dist=lambda x, y:
euclidean(x.flatten(), y.flatten()))
for (map1, map2) in path:
    plt.arrow(map1, time_series_1[map1], map2 - map1, time_series_2[map2]
-          time_series_1[map1], color='black', length_includes_head=True,
head_width=0.05)
```

The next figure illustrates how DTW flexibly adjusts sequences, aligning patterns even when they are out of sync or of different lengths. This makes it useful for detecting similar patterns in time series data, even when there are time differences:

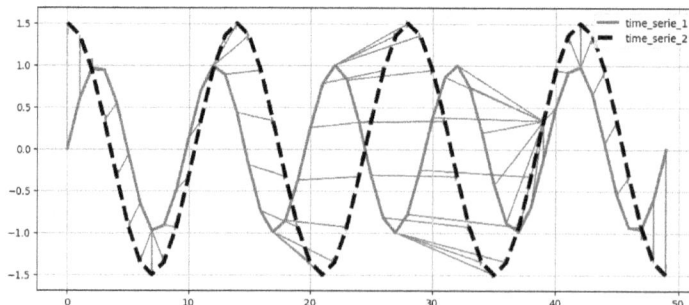

Figure 10.11: Dynamic Time Warping

 The lines joining the time series illustrate the alignment and help to understand the DTW path. This example demonstrates how DTW can match complex, oscillating time series even with phase shifts and noise.

We will briefly introduce three other prominent methods and make a comparison between them.

HMMs help in pattern matching by modeling time series data as sequences of states with probabilistic transitions. They can identify hidden states and their transitions, effectively capturing temporal patterns and allowing for the recognition of complex, recurring sequences within the data. HMM are more complex to tune than Pattern matching method with matrix profile.

The FT for pattern matching involves converting a time series into the frequency domain to identify and compare periodic[13] patterns. FT can detect similarities and recurring cycles within different sections of the data, but FT is limited in capturing non-stationary patterns and local anomalies.

We do not describe FT or HMM in detail because **modern pattern recognition using state-of-the-art libraries,** such as the one introduced in the next section is both more powerful and more flexible. It handles large datasets, adapts to dynamic structures, and provides richer insights into time series patterns.

Pattern matching with **matrix profile** involves identifying and ranking the most similar subsequences within a time series. In the following section, we apply this technique to both the **normalized spread** and the **asset price**, allowing us to detect recurring patterns in price movements and deviations from the historical mean.

Fast pattern matching with matrix profile

Matrix profile is the key data structure for achieving pattern matching. It calculates the distances[14] between all subsequences in a time series, creating a profile that highlights areas with repeating patterns and anomalies. This makes it easier to identify and analyze similar sequences within the data. We use a Python library called **Stumpy**[15], which is a highly optimized implementation for computing matrix profiles and is likely the best tool

---

13 FT is primarily used for periodic time series. For non-periodic time series, pattern matching techniques like Dynamic Time Warping or Hidden Markov Models are more appropriate as they can handle varying time scales and irregular patterns effectively. FT is less effective for non-periodic patterns as it focuses on frequency domain analysis.

14 Matrix Profiles are calculated by determining the distance between all subsequences in a time series, often leveraging the Fast Fourier Transform (FFT) for efficient computation. The primary steps involve:
- Subsequence Extraction: Extract all subsequences of a given length from the time series.
- Distance Calculation: Use the FFT to efficiently calculate the distance between subsequences. The convolution theorem allows the Euclidean distance to be computed in a very efficient way, making the whole process much more efficient. By using FFT, we can calculate these similarities much faster than traditional methods. Hence the name "Fast Pattern Matching Method"
- Profile Creation: For each subsequence, record the minimum distance to any other subsequence. This minimum distance forms the Matrix Profile.

15 https://stumpy.readthedocs.io

in this field. This approach surpasses the simplistic implementations commonly used. **Stumpy** employs advanced mathematical techniques to deliver a highly efficient library, capable of processing big data, high-frequency trading, and massive streams of real-time data.

We will now take a first hands-on tour with this tool to explore its capabilities in practice. This code installs and imports **Stumpy**:

```
!pip -q install stumpy
import stumpy
```

We will experiment with the daily closing price time series of **Bitcoin** (**BTC** ticker) from Yahoo Finance, covering the period from 2015 to 2024:

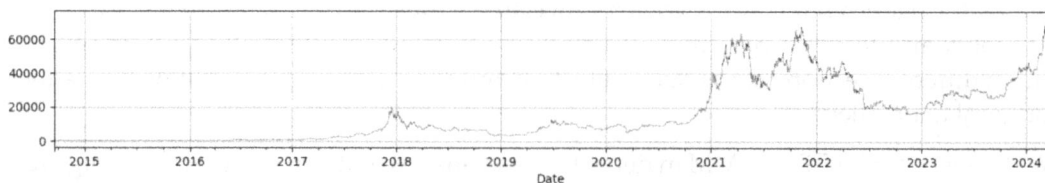

Figure 10.12: Bitcoin Daily Closing Price

In the following sections, we will use the matrix profile to first explore similarities and then identify specific patterns in time series data.

Find similarities and anomalies with matrix profile

This section explores the **Matrix Profile**. We will compute the profile and identify key patterns, **motifs** (similar sequences) and **discords** (dissimilar sequences). Normalization is introduced to refine comparisons by focusing on shape rather than scale.

By the end, you will see how this approach reveals hidden structure in financial data, aiding in pattern recognition and forecasting, as follows:

1. The first step is to define a window length (**m**) for the analysis: **m = 640**

2. The second step is to compute the matrix profile, which will contain the distance information between all subsequences within the entire time series, as shown:

   ```
   ts = df.iloc[-1500:]['Close']
   mp = stumpy.stump(ts, m)
   plt.plot(mp[:, 0])
   ```

The following graph represents the matrix profile:

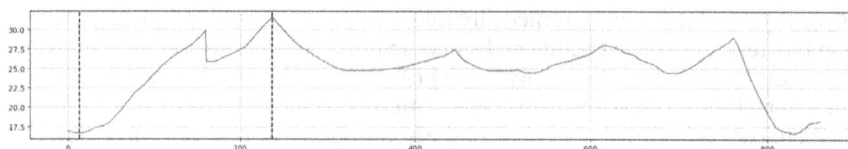

Figure 10.13: Matrix profile

The matrix profile plot displayed shows the similarity of subsequences within the closing prices. Lower distance values in the matrix profile (like those at around index 200 and index 800) indicate subsequences that are **similar** to each other, suggesting the presence of motifs or recurring patterns.

On the other hand, higher peaks (like the one located at index 237 on the graph), indicate subsequences that are **less similar** to any other part of the time series, potentially highlighting unique or anomalous events. The dashed lines might mark significant points where motifs or discords are detected.

After that, we can extract the corresponding pairs of subsequences based on our goal: finding the **most similar** pairs, known as **motifs**, and identifying the **most distinct** pairs, referred to as **discords.** Pairs are sorted in increasing order based on distance.

To identify the most dissimilar pair, we look for the subsequence with the **largest distance** in the Matrix Profile to identify the most dissimilar pair. The following code extracts and locates this discord within the time series.

The **last** index (**motif_idx_1**) represents the largest distance, indicating   the following:

```
motif_idx_1 = np.argsort(mp[:, 0])[-1]
print(f"The discord is located at index {motif_idx_1}")
discord_idx = mp[motif_idx_1, 1]
```

The following output displays the result of the subsequent code, highlighting the identified discord in the time series:

```
The discord is located at index 237
```

This code has identified the largest discord among all subsequences in the Matrix Profile. The corresponding subsequences (located at index **motif_idx_1** and **discord_idx**) are highlighted in the following graph:

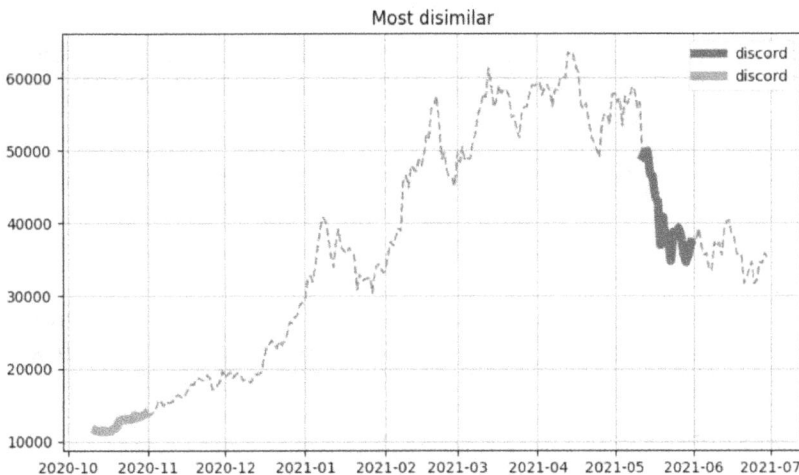

Figure 10.14: Dissimilar sequences

Unlike simple similarity measures, discord detection does not rely on sequences being of the same length or **perfectly aligned**. Instead, it standardizes them for optimal comparison, ensuring that the most meaningful differences are captured, **regardless of scale or position** in the time series.

Conversely, the **first** index (`motif_idx_2`) represents the minimal distance, indicating the most similar pair (motif):

```
motif_idx_2 = np.argsort(mp[:, 0])[0]
nearest_idx = mp[motif_idx_2, 1]
print(f"The motif is located at index {nearest_idx}")
```

This is the output for the aforementioned code block:

```
The motif is located at index 830
```

This code has identified the largest motif among all sequences. The corresponding sequences are highlighted in the following graph:

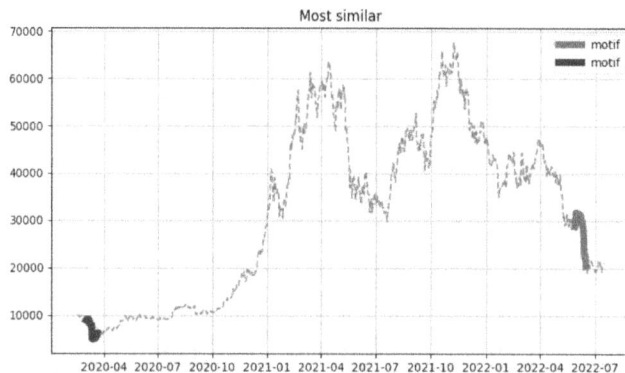

Figure 10.15: Similar sequences

Motif detection, like discord detection, standardizes sequences to ensure the best possible comparison. This allows it to identify meaningful repetitions in the data, regardless of their position or exact scale.

As noted above, it can be difficult to fully appreciate how similar or dissimilar the extracted patterns are because they do not occur at the same time. For example, the most similar sequences might be separated by several years. This is particularly significant for an asset like Bitcoin, which behaves like a bubble. To correct this effect, we must normalize subsequences. Normalizing the sequences allows for a more precise comparison, reducing the effect of scale differences and focusing on the shape and pattern similarities or differences.

Normalization is done with the following code:

```
df_norm = stumpy.core.z_norm(df['Close'].values)
```

The following plot compares the discord and motif subsequences **after** normalization:

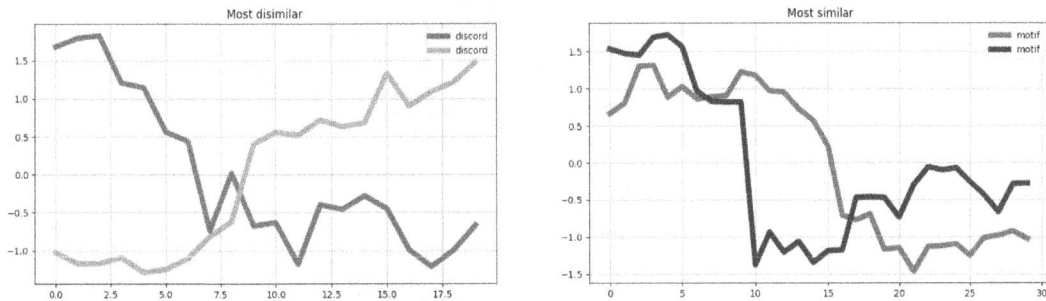

Figure 10.16: Normalized Motif and Discord Sequences

On the left, the discord plot shows the two most dissimilar subsequences. Despite normalization, these subsequences display clear differences in their shapes and trends, indicating significant divergence in the time series behavior during these periods. On the right, the motif plot presents the most similar subsequences. These subsequences closely resemble each other in their overall shape and patterns, reflecting recurring behavior in the time series data. This could be of particular interest for pattern recognition or forecasting in a financial context.

Searching for motifs or discords is not the only task we can perform with the matrix profile. In the next section, we will explore how to search for a specific pattern or signature within the data.

Search for pattern with matrix profile

Using the matrix profile, we can search for subsequences in the time series that are most like a specific pattern of interest. For example, we should identify periods in the past that most closely *resemble*[16] the last 80 days of data. By setting the last days as our reference sequence, the matrix profile can identify similar patterns throughout the time series, allowing us to identify past events that might be indicative of future trends. This technique is especially useful for forecasting or recognizing **key signatures** in the data that align with particular market conditions.

It is important to note that our analysis is performed using the normalized spread **z-score**, a normalization technique described in detail in *Chapter 1, Algorithmic Trading and Machine Learning in a Nutshell,* and discussed in subsequent chapters. As a reminder, the z-score[17] represents the spread between the closing price and the moving average, expressed in

---

16 Obviously, we are not looking for exact matches, as that type of search does not require machine learning or advanced analysis capabilities. Instead, we aim to find patterns that are similar enough to be significant, with the goal being to identify the closest possible matches. The closer the match, the more valuable the insight.

17 , is the rolling mean (20 days in our experiment) and is the standard-deviation (same length than the rolling mean).

terms of standard deviation. This method provides monitoring the z-score spread helps identify periods when the asset's price deviates significantly from its historical average, signaling overbought or oversold conditions. A **high positive z-score** suggests that the price is **unusually** high relative to its historical behavior, indicating a possible mean reversion or correction, while a **low negative z-score** suggests the opposite. Traders use this information to anticipate reversals or confirm trend strength, thereby improving the timing of entry and exit points.

To enhance this analysis, we leverage the matrix profile to identify similar sequences within historical data, allowing us to detect recurring patterns that may signal profitable trading opportunities. We will use the matrix profile to identify the most similar sequences (pattern matching) within the entire historical data.

To apply this concept, we calculate the rolling mean and standard deviation over a defined window. This allows us to compute the z-score, which standardizes the closing prices based on **local trends**.

The following code performs these calculations:

```
window = 20
df['rolling_mean'] = df['Close'].rolling(window=window).mean()
df['rolling_std'] = df['Close'].rolling(window=window).std()
# Compute z-score
df['z_score'] = (df['Close'] - df['rolling_mean']) / df['rolling_std']
```

This figure represents the z-score calculations for Bitcoin for the last ten years:

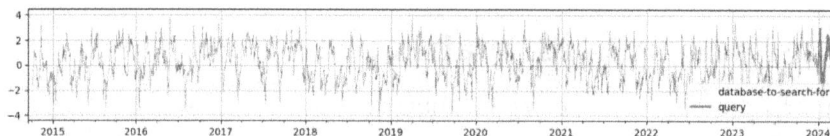

Figure 10.17: Z-score Normalized Close Price

The highlighted sequence represents the last 80 days, which we will use as a query (**Q_df**) to search for similar patterns throughout the historical data.

The following is the code to define this query search:

```
length_hint = 80
#locate the start of the sequence you are looking for
idx_begin_query = df.shape[0] - length_hint

# Q query (what to search) and T target (where to search):
T_df = df.iloc[ : idx_begin_query]['z_score']
Q_df = df.iloc[idx_begin_query :]['z_score']
print(f'query to search begin at position : ' , df.iloc[idx_begin_query].name)
```

Output of the aforementioned code is as follows:

```
query to search begin at position :  2024-01-08 00:00:00
```

Next, we will compute the matrix profile with the following code:

```
distance_profile = stumpy.core.mass(Q_df, T_df)
```

We then plot the matrix profile in the following graph:

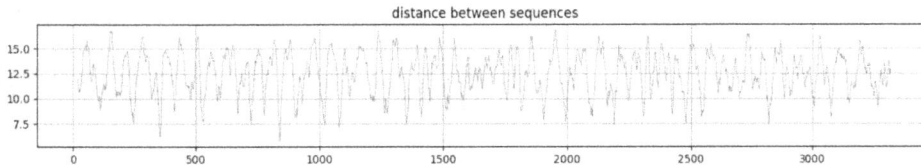

Figure 10.18: Matrix Profile for the Z-score Normalized Close Price

The dips, which indicate the minimum distances, represent the location of all the recurring patterns, while the peaks, indicating the greatest distances, represent the discords.

In the following graph we will compare the query (last 80 days of the Bitcoin time series shown in red) with its most similar past patterns, identified using the matrix profile:

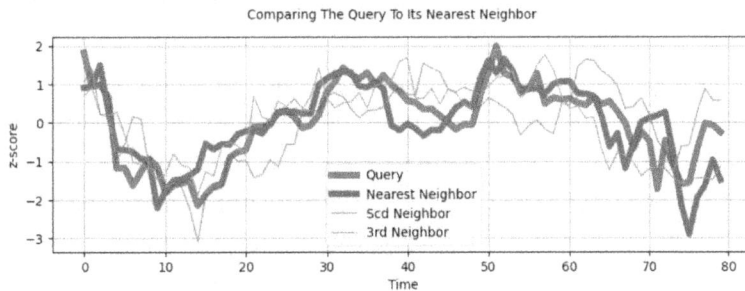

Figure 10.19: Closest matches to the specific pattern

In the plot shown, we have the query sequence together with the nearest neighbor subsequence found in the historical data, identified using the matrix profile. The fine lines represent the second and third closest matches (neighbors). As we can see, the nearest neighbor closely tracks the query sequence, indicating that a very similar pattern has occurred in the past. This suggests that there may be recurring behavior in the time series that could be of interest for forecasting or analysis.

The second and third nearest neighbors are somewhat less similar but still follow the general trend of the query, providing additional context and confidence in the pattern matching. This approach allows us to not only identify similar patterns but also compare multiple instances to understand the variability and robustness of these patterns over time. The Matrix Profile technique, combined with z-score normalization, makes it easier to compare and analyze these patterns across different time periods and market conditions.

This approach is particularly useful for detecting recurring behaviors or patterns, such as identifying periods in the past where the market behaved similarly to the recent trend. Once the most similar patterns are found, they can be analyzed to gain insights into potential future movements.

In the following figure, the visual representation of the matching subsequences helps in identifying areas of interest within the historical data:

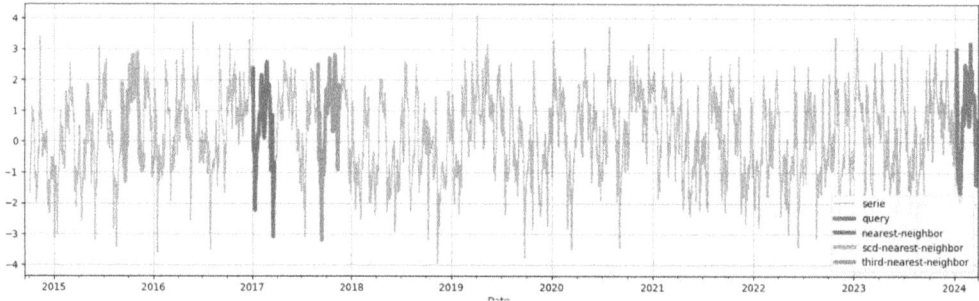

Figure 10.20: *Matching sub-sequences*

In this graph, we show the query again, along with its neighbors. It is interesting to note that the temporal order is not at all relevant to the search for recurrent patterns; in fact, the closest sequence is not the most recent.

The nearest neighbor shows the highest similarity to the recent trend, suggesting a possible repetition of market behavior. The other two neighbors are slightly less similar but still show a recognizable pattern that matches the query.

These visualizations help understand how past events in the time series relate to current trends. By identifying these similar periods, we can gain insights into potential future movements based on historical patterns. The ability to spot such recurring patterns and understand how the market has reacted in similar past situations is valuable for forecasting in financial markets.

In the following graph, we represent the various subsequences throughout the historical data that most closely match the query pattern:

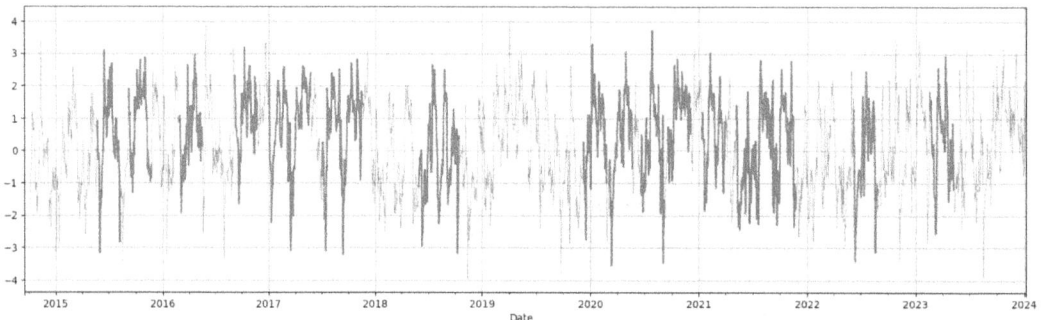

Figure 10.21: *All matching sub-sequences*

The concentration of segments across different years indicates that similar market behaviors have occurred multiple times in the past. This visualization allows us to see how often and when these similar patterns have emerged.

Conclusion

This chapter demonstrated the practical applications of unsupervised learning techniques in quantitative trading, focusing on unorthodox, state-of-the-art, and original tools such as DM, RP, and Matrix Profile. These methods, widely used by sophisticated professional traders yet largely ignored by the majority, offer a unique edge in financial markets. Their ability to detect recurring patterns and anomalies within time series data provides deeper insights into market behavior and allows traders to place trades that do not mimic the rest of the crowd.

By integrating these techniques into machine learning models, traders can improve the precision of **market trend forecasts** and develop more **robust** trading strategies. Beyond simply identifying structure in time series data, these methods allow for **pattern-based trading**, helping to uncover hidden market dynamics that traditional indicators often miss. Understanding motifs and anomalies enables the creation of original, non-consensus strategies that stand apart from mainstream approaches.

These insights maintain a distinct edge over conventional strategies used by the majority.

We now focus on another underutilized yet powerful approach, analyzing financial text using Natural Language Processing. While most quantitative strategies rely solely on numerical data like prices, modern machine learning techniques allow us to extract valuable trading insights from financial news, reports, and textual information.

In the next chapter, we will explore how to process and structure text-based financial data, map relationships between companies, and visualize these connections in a way that enhances decision-making. We will also demonstrate how these insights can be directly applied to portfolio construction, offering a fresh perspective on diversification and risk management beyond traditional price-based methods.

Join our book's Discord space

Join the book's Discord Workspace for Latest updates, Offers, Tech happenings around the world, New Release and Sessions with the Authors:

https://discord.bpbonline.com

## CHAPTER 11

Trading Signals from Reports and News

Introduction

Modern **Natural Language Processing** (**NLP**) algorithms have become invaluable tools for analyzing data beyond traditional numerical inputs like **Open, High, Low, Close** (**OHLC**) prices. These advanced algorithms enable us to process and interpret information in its **most natural form**, text, speech, and voice, the primary mediums[1] through which humans communicate. In this chapter, we will explore several possibilities for utilizing machine learning to analyze these textual inputs. Specifically, we will demonstrate how to automatically analyze and interpret financial news and reports, and how to leverage a vast repository of publicly available information to map out the relationships among S&P 500 companies. By applying these techniques, we can construct diversified portfolios to outperform a naïve, equal-weighted approach.

Structure

In this chapter, we will cover the following topics:

- Introduction to trading from news and reports
- Data collection
- Reading Wikipedia pages with API

---

1 In fact, it is estimated that 80% of the information available on the internet exists in these formats.

- Text preprocessing
- Building a similarity matrix
- Portfolio construction

Objectives

This chapter explores the extraction of trading signals from financial news and reports using advanced **unsupervised** NLP techniques. We will look at how to create data structures (word embeddings and similarity matrices) from textual data, and how to visualize these structures through clustermaps and tree graphs. The chapter then demonstrates how to leverage these insights for portfolio construction, comparing novel approaches like dissimilarity-based selection and **Hierarchical Risk Parity** (HRP) with traditional methods.

Our goal is to showcase how integrating textual analysis into quantitative finance can offer fresh perspectives and enhance portfolio optimization strategies.

By the end of this chapter, you will have hands-on experience with state-of-the-art **unsupervised** methods for scrapping and integrating **raw text** and **web data** into financial pipelines. These techniques allow you to extract market-moving insights **directly** from textual sources without relying on labelled data, making them a powerful complement to traditional supervised learning approaches. Since powerful news first appears in text form, you will learn how to react to important developments **before** they are fully reflected in asset prices - giving you a **decisive advantage** over other traders.

Introduction to trading from news and reports

Trading signals derived from news and reports have become a critical edge in financial markets. The power of machine learning allows us to extract signals from unstructured data, opening new frontiers in algorithmic trading.

News events and financial reports trigger rapid price movements within seconds of publication. *Traditional manual analysis simply cannot keep up with the volume and velocity of information flow.* This is where machine learning algorithms excel, parsing vast amounts of text data to identify patterns and sentiment shifts that human traders might miss.

Consider the impact of a surprise earnings report or an unexpected geopolitical event. These can cause immediate volatility, creating both risks and opportunities. Machine learning models can be trained to recognize these patterns across multiple data sources, from official company filings to social media chatter, providing a comprehensive view of market sentiment.

The challenge is to turn raw text into quantifiable signals. NLP techniques form the basis of this process, enabling algorithms to understand context and sentiment, and to detect linguistic clues that may indicate insider knowledge or market manipulation.

The potential applications are vast: from near high-frequency trading strategies that capitalize on breaking news, to longer-term portfolio[2] allocation decisions based on trend analysis of company reports.

Let us start with the first stage, data collection. The quality and scope of our data sources will directly impact the effectiveness of our machine learning models and the reliability of our trading signals.

Data collection

Data is the foundation of any successful machine learning-driven trading strategy. When extracting signals from news and reports, this process involves aggregating vast amounts of textual information from diverse sources, each offering unique insights into market dynamics and sentiment. It is not enough to simply amass data; we must also ensure its relevance, timeliness, and quality to feed our algorithmic models effectively.

Besides this, unlike *numerical* market data, which can be readily fed into algorithms, **textual** information is unique. It is *unstructured*[3] and of a completely different **nature** to digital data. This requires specific preprocessing techniques (refer to the *Text preprocessing* section) to transform raw text into machine-readable formats.

Source of financial news

Algorithmic traders use a variety of news feeds to capture market-moving information. These include real-time news APIs from providers like *Bloomberg* and *Reuters*, which offer comprehensive coverage but often come at a premium cost.

RSS feeds from financial websites are a more accessible alternative. *SEC EDGAR*[4] filings offer corporate disclosures, while social media platforms like *Twitter-X* can signal sentiment shifts.

Specialized data providers aggregate and structure news from multiple sources, offering pre-processed feeds tailored for algorithmic consumption. Each source has its own update frequency, data format, and potential for alpha generation, so it is essential to evaluate and integrate them carefully into trading systems.

---

2 This chapter contains a comprehensive, real-world example that illustrates the entire process of developing and implementing a portfolio based on internet pages. This hands-on case study highlights each stage, from data collection and preprocessing to model development and backtesting implementation.
3 **Unstructured** data refers to information that does not conform to a *predefined* data model or organizational structure, which lacks the orderly arrangement of structured databases or spreadsheets making it challenging even impossible for traditional programs to interpret.
4 For a complete example of how to retrieve data from this provider, see Chapter 2, *"Data Feed, Backtests, and Forward Testing"*.

Extracting news data

In this section, we will provide code examples to extract financial news using two different sources: **Yahoo Finance RSS** feed and the **BizToc** platform. These tools will help you automate the retrieval of real-time market information to feed our machine learning algorithms.

Scrapping BizToc platform

BizToc is an online[5] platform that aggregates and curates business news from professional and highly credible sources (*Google News, Wall Street Journal, Financial Times, Reuters*, and so on…), providing quick access to the latest financial and market updates. It offers a streamlined view of current events, helping users stay informed about trends, company news, and industry insights. As the internet site says, *the Entire Business World on a Single Page*.

Here is a minimal example using the **requests** library already used in *Chapter 2, Data Feed, Backtests, and Forward Testing,* to scrape news headlines from BizToc. This example shows how to make a simple request to their website and parse the response using **BeautifulSoup**:

```python
import requests
from bs4 import BeautifulSoup


url = "https://biztoc.com/"
# Send request to the website
response = requests.get(url)
# company name and ticker we are interested in
company_name = "NVIDIA"
ticker = "NVDA"
# request successful ?
if response.status_code == 200:
    # Parse the HTML content of the page
    soup = BeautifulSoup(response.content, 'html.parser')
    # Find all 'a' tags that contain news headlines
    news_items = soup.find_all('a', attrs={'data-p': True})
    # Extract and print the headline text and the corresponding URL
    for item in news_items:
        headline = item.get_text(strip=True)
        # Check company name, ticker is mentioned in headline or data-p content
        if company_name.lower() in headline.lower() or company_name.lower()
in item['data-p'].lower() or ticker.lower() in item['data-p'].lower():
```

5 https://biztoc.com

```
url = item['href']
print(f"Headline: {headline}")
print(f"URL: {url}\n")
```

This code filters the news headlines to show only those that mention the specific company or ticker you are interested in (**nVIDIA**, ticker **NVDA**) in this example.

The aforementioned code will give the following output:

```
Headline: New Nvidia research shows AI can predict local weather
URL: https://www.marketplace.org/2024/08/20/new-nvidia-research-shows-ai-
can-predict-local-weather/?ref=biztoc.com
Headline: Nvidia earnings preview: Blackwell commentary
URL: https://www.investing.com/news/stock-market-news/nvidia-
earnings-preview-blackwell-commentary-to-overshadow-guidance-numbers-
3578640?ref=biztoc.com
Headline: AMD Steps Up Nvidia Rivalry With $4.9 Billion Acquisition
URL: https://www.investors.com/news/technology/amd-stock-rises-on-zt-
systems-acquisition/?ref=biztoc.com
Headline: Can Ukraine Survive a Second Trump Term?
URL: https://247wallst.com/investing/2024/08/20/can-ukraine-survive-a-
second-trump-term/?ref=biztoc.com
Headline: AMD Makes a $4.9B A.I. Acquisition to Challenge Nvidia's
Dominance
URL: https://observer.com/2024/08/amd-acquires-zt-data-center-
ai/?ref=biztoc.com
Headline: AMD buys server maker ZT Systems in bid to compete with Nvidia
URL: https://www.siliconvalley.com/2024/08/19/amd-buying-server-maker-zt-
systems/?ref=biztoc.com
Headline: Storm chasers: Nvidia builds new AI weather model
URL: https://www.bizjournals.com/sanjose/news/2024/08/19/nvidia-and-ai-and-
weather-forecast.html?ana=brss_3891&ref=biztoc.com
```

Sentiment analysis with Yahoo! RSS feed

Yahoo Finance provides RSS feeds that can be easily accessed and parsed.

The following is an example of how to use the **feedparser** library to analyze sentiment from Yahoo Finance RSS feeds:

```
!pip install -q feedparser
import feedparser
from textblob import TextBlob


# Function to get sentiment score
```

```
def get_sentiment(text):
    return TextBlob(text).sentiment.polarity
```

Using **feedparser** library, the script fetches the RSS feed for a specified stock symbol and parses the feed to extract the publication date and title of each news item:

```
stock_symbol = 'AAPL'
rss_url = f'https://finance.yahoo.com/rss/headline?s={stock_symbol}'


# Fetch and parse the RSS feed
feed = feedparser.parse(rss_url)
data = []
for entry in feed.entries:
    data.append([entry.published_parsed, entry.title])
df = pd.DataFrame(data, columns=['date', 'title'])
df['date'] = df['date'].apply(lambda x: datetime(*x[:6]))
df.head()
```

The aforementioned code outputs the following table:

date	title
2024-08-20 14:41:48	Apple has 'enormous expectations' in its AI-tied valuation
2024-08-20 14:15:17	Is It A Sign? Warren Buffett's Latest Move With Apple Stock Is Still Puzzling Investors. But There May Be More Behind It
2024-08-20 13:55:15	Warren Buffett Stocks: What's Inside Berkshire Hathaway's Portfolio?
2024-08-20 13:34:42	Amazon's AI Spending Plans Keep Stock From Joining Tech Rebound
2024-08-20 13:17:00	It Isn't Just Apple: Warren Buffett Could Be Souring on This Other Megacap Stock
2024-08-20 10:00:09	Microsoft's dominant 21st century offers a key lesson for stock market investors: Morning Brief
2024-08-20 08:44:00	The Best "Magnificent Seven" Stock to Buy Right Now, According to Wall Street
2024-08-19 20:29:06	Apple Inc. (AAPL): This AI Stock Is Trending Right Now
2024-08-19 20:19:33	Apple iPhone 16: Speculation abounds about the latest phone and announcement date
2024-08-19 20:16:51	Dow Jones Surges As Trump Stock Breaches Key Level; These Warren Buffett Picks Are Near Entries (Live Coverage)

Table 11.1: *Fetch the Yahoo Finance RSS News*

The table displays recent news articles for a given stock, with the date of publication and the title summarizing each article. This helps quickly identify relevant market-moving news. Using **textblob** library, it then performs sentiment analysis on the news titles and calculates the sentiment using a pre-trained model based on movie reviews. It also analyzes text for polarity (positive or negative) and subjectivity. Polarity ranges from **-1** (very negative) to **1** (very positive):

```
# Analyze sentiment
df['sentiment'] = df['title'].apply(get_sentiment)
df.head(14)
```

The output for the aforementioned code is as follows:

date	title	sentiment
2024-08-20 14:41:48	Apple has 'enormous expectations' in its AI-tied valuation	0.0
2024-08-20 14:15:17	Is It A Sign? Warren Buffett's Latest Move With Apple Stock Is Still Puzzling Investors. But There May Be More Behind It	0.2
2024-08-20 13:55:15	Warren Buffett Stocks: What's Inside Berkshire Hathaway's Portfolio?	0.0
2024-08-20 13:34:42	Amazon's AI Spending Plans Keep Stock From Joining Tech Rebound	0.0
2024-08-20 13:17:00	**It Isn't Just Apple: Warren Buffett Could Be Souring on This Other Megacap Stock**	**-0.125**
2024-08-20 10:00:09	Microsoft's dominant 21st century offers a key lesson for stock market investors: Morning Brief	0.025
2024-08-20 08:44:00	The Best "Magnificent Seven" Stock to Buy Right Now, According to Wall Street	0.76
2024-08-19 20:29:06	Apple Inc. (AAPL): This AI Stock Is Trending Right Now	0.29
2024-08-19 20:19:33	Apple iPhone 16: Speculation abounds about the latest phone and announcement date	0.5
2024-08-19 20:16:51	Dow Jones Surges As Trump Stock Breaches Key Level; These Warren Buffett Picks Are Near Entries (Live Coverage)	0.08
2024-08-19 19:02:03	Apple Podcasts launches on the web	0.0
2024-08-19 17:50:42	**Magnificent Seven Stocks: Nvidia Stock, Tesla Rally**	**1.0**
2024-08-19 14:27:00	GM Is Cutting More Than 1,000 Workers From Its Software Business	-0.05

date	title	sentiment
2024-08-19 14:03:00	Apple Is Set to Win in AI. How That's 'Already Priced In.'	0.8

Table 11.2: Sentiment analysis

The RSS feed for a specific stock symbol (in this case, **AAPL**) does not exclusively contain news about that stock. It often includes broader market news or news about related companies or sectors. The article with the highest sentiment score (line in bold in the table) is about the **Magnificent Seven** stocks, which **implicitly** include Apple, but also other major tech companies like Nvidia, Tesla, and Google. The sentiment analysis is being performed on the entire title, regardless of whether it specifically mentions **AAPL**.

We print the **minimum** and **maximum sentiment ratings** along with the corresponding news titles:

```
print('minimum sentiment rating : ',np.min(df['sentiment']))print(df.
iloc[np.argmin(df['sentiment']) , :]['title'])


print('maximum sentiment rating : ',np.max(df['sentiment']))
df.iloc[np.argmax(df['sentiment']) , :]['title']


minimum sentiment rating :  -0.125
It Isn't Just Apple: Warren Buffett Could Be Souring on This Other Megacap
Stock


maximum sentiment rating :  1.0
Magnificent Seven Stocks: Nvidia Stock, Tesla Rally
```

The average sentiment score for positive news is much higher (approximately 0.39) than the average sentiment score for negative news (around -0.09), reflecting an overall optimistic sentiment in the news items analyzed. More generally speaking, sentiment analysis provides valuable input for machine learning algorithms that analyze news feed alongside sentiment ratings. It is an example of **feature engineering** that we are already familiar with.

While news feeds remain an essential component of trading decisions, unconventional sources such as Wikipedia pages can also provide valuable perspectives on market dynamics and company profiles as we will demonstrate in next sections.

Reading Wikipedia pages with API

Before analyzing Wikipedia pages, the first step is to obtain this information programmatically. This can be done using tools (web scraping libraries and APIs) that allow automated retrieval of Wikipedia content. Once collected, the data is cleaned and preprocessed, as we will see in the next section *Text preprocessing*, to ensure usability.

Since Wikipedia pages often summarize key financial details, including those from **U.S. SEC Form 10-K filings** (financial statements, business overview, management's discussion & analysis (MD&A), and risk factors), they provide a structured way to extract both qualitative and quantitative insights from regulatory disclosures. This allows us to leverage Wikipedia as a complementary source of financial intelligence while ensuring the extracted information is grounded in official reports.

To demonstrate this, we install the `wikipedia-api` package, which allows us to programmatically access and extract data from internet pages:

```
!pip install -q wikipedia-api
```

We then retrieve the text from a Wikipedia page[6] that serves as a portal for all S&P 500 companies listed in the index and extract all company links from the following table. While Wikipedia may not always be considered a primary source, it provides a structured starting point for automated data extraction and offers convenient access to company information in a centralised format:

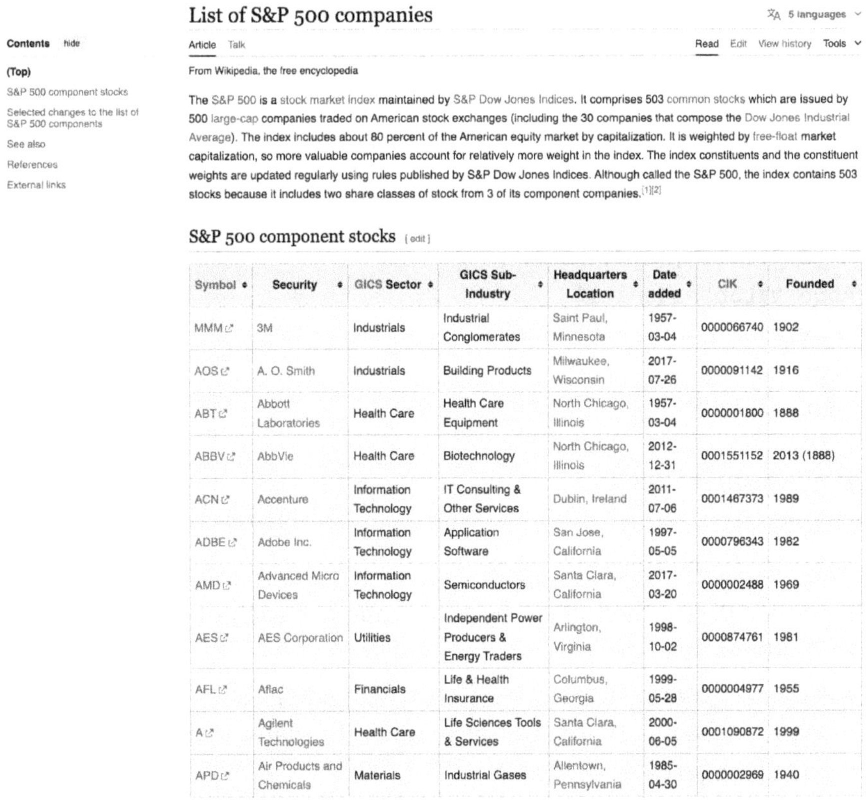

List of S&P 500 companies

ᴬ 5 languages ⌄

Contents hide	Article Talk					Read Edit View history Tools ⌄	

(Top)

S&P 500 component stocks

Selected changes to the list of S&P 500 components

See also

References

External links

From Wikipedia, the free encyclopedia

The S&P 500 is a stock market index maintained by S&P Dow Jones Indices. It comprises 503 common stocks which are issued by 500 large-cap companies traded on American stock exchanges (including the 30 companies that compose the Dow Jones Industrial Average). The index includes about 80 percent of the American equity market by capitalization. It is weighted by free-float market capitalization, so more valuable companies account for relatively more weight in the index. The index constituents and the constituent weights are updated regularly using rules published by S&P Dow Jones Indices. Although called the S&P 500, the index contains 503 stocks because it includes two share classes of stock from 3 of its component companies.[1][2]

S&P 500 component stocks [edit]

Symbol ◆	Security ◆	GICS Sector ◆	GICS Sub-Industry	Headquarters Location ◆	Date added ◆	CIK ◆	Founded ◆
MMM ⌝	3M	Industrials	Industrial Conglomerates	Saint Paul, Minnesota	1957-03-04	0000066740	1902
AOS ⌝	A. O. Smith	Industrials	Building Products	Milwaukee, Wisconsin	2017-07-26	0000091142	1916
ABT ⌝	Abbott Laboratories	Health Care	Health Care Equipment	North Chicago, Illinois	1957-03-04	0000001800	1888
ABBV ⌝	AbbVie	Health Care	Biotechnology	North Chicago, Illinois	2012-12-31	0001551152	2013 (1888)
ACN ⌝	Accenture	Information Technology	IT Consulting & Other Services	Dublin, Ireland	2011-07-06	0001467373	1989
ADBE ⌝	Adobe Inc.	Information Technology	Application Software	San Jose, California	1997-05-05	0000796343	1982
AMD ⌝	Advanced Micro Devices	Information Technology	Semiconductors	Santa Clara, California	2017-03-20	0000002488	1969
AES ⌝	AES Corporation	Utilities	Independent Power Producers & Energy Traders	Arlington, Virginia	1998-10-02	0000874761	1981
AFL ⌝	Aflac	Financials	Life & Health Insurance	Columbus, Georgia	1999-05-28	0000004977	1955
A ⌝	Agilent Technologies	Health Care	Life Sciences Tools & Services	Santa Clara, California	2000-06-05	0001090872	1999
APD ⌝	Air Products and Chemicals	Materials	Industrial Gases	Allentown, Pennsylvania	1985-04-30	0000002969	1940

Figure 11.1: Wikipedia page for S&P 500 companies

6 https://en.wikipedia.org/wiki/List_of_S%26P_500_companies

The code reads content from the **Security** column, which contains URLs for each company. These URLs lead to pages that aggregate reliable information from official sources, including regulatory filings and financial reports already mentioned:

```python
def get_sp500_company_links(wikipedia_url):
    response = requests.get(wikipedia_url)
    soup = BeautifulSoup(response.content, 'html.parser')
    table = soup.find('table', {'class': 'wikitable sortable'})
    rows = table.findAll('tr')
    links = []
    for row in rows[1:]:
        link = row.find('td').find_next('td').find('a')['href']
        links.append(link)
    return links
```

We use **requests** to get the HTML content and **BeautifulSoup** to parse, extract and return the URLs for each company's Wikipedia page from the table:

```python
wikipedia_url = 'https://en.wikipedia.org/wiki/List_of_S%26P_500_companies'
#get a link for all companies
sp500_company_links = get_sp500_company_links(wikipedia_url)
sp500_company_links
```

The preceding code produces the following output, which shows the address for each company:

```
['/wiki/3M',
 '/wiki/A._O._Smith',
 '/wiki/Abbott_Laboratories',
 '/wiki/AbbVie',
 '/wiki/Accenture',
 '/wiki/Adobe_Inc.',
 '/wiki/AMD',
 '/wiki/AES_Corporation',
 '/wiki/Aflac',
 '/wiki/Agilent_Technologies',…]
```

Using Wikipedia API, we then fetch the text content of each of the corresponding page based on its address:

```python
def get_wikipedia_text(page_title, language='en'):
    wiki = wikipediaapi.Wikipedia(language , headers = headers)
    page = wiki.page(page_title)
    if page.exists():
        return page.text
```

As an example, here is the content of the page for NVIDIA, extracted by executing the code:

```
text = get_wikipedia_text(page_title)
if text:
  page_content[page_title] = text
page_content.get('Nvidia')[:550]
```

```
'Nvidia Corporation (, en-VID-ee-ə) is an American multinational
corporation and technology company headquartered in Santa Clara,
California, and incorporated in Delaware. It is a software and fabless
company which designs and supplies graphics processing units (GPUs),
application programming interfaces (APIs) for data science and high-
performance computing, as well as system on a chip units (SoCs) for the
mobile computing and automotive market. Nvidia is also a dominant supplier
of artificial intelligence (AI) hardware and software.\nNvidia's pr'
```

We now have the **full content** of the Wikipedia file for each company in the SP500 index, which we will analyze in the upcoming sections.

In the next section, we will cover text preprocessing, focusing on key steps like cleaning, tokenization, and creating word embeddings to prepare the data for further analysis.

Text preprocessing

Text **preprocessing** is an initial step in **NLP**[7], involving cleaning and tokenization to prepare raw text data for analysis by removing irrelevant elements, breaking text into manageable units, and ensuring consistency across the dataset.

Cleaning

Cleaning in NLP involves preparing text data by removing irrelevant elements, such as special characters, numbers, or inconsistent formatting, to ensure the data is in a uniform and usable state for analysis. This process often includes the removal of **stop words**. Stop words are common words, like **and**, **the**, or **is**, that are removed during preprocessing because they appear frequently and do not carry **significant meaning**. For example, in the sentence "*The cat sat on the mat*," removing stop words would leave **cat**, **sat**, and **mat** as the key terms.

In recent years, NLP has advanced significantly, making this step less critical and reducing the importance of removing stop words. For the latest algorithms, such as embeddings

---

7 NLP is a field within machine learning that focuses on enabling computers to understand, interpret, and generate human language. It combines computational techniques with linguistic knowledge to process and analyze large amounts of natural language data for various applications.

with Transformers[8] or **Global Vectors for Word Representation (GloVe)**[9], stop words are less of a concern because these models are designed to capture the full context of words, including the roles that stop words play in sentence structure and meaning.

Tokenizing

After cleaning the text, tokenization breaks the cleaned data into individual words (tokens) or phrases, transforming it into structured units that can be more easily analyzed by machine learning models. Tokenizing is a common method before converting text into numbers, making it suitable for processing by machine learning algorithms. For instance, a text prompt like *"a cute and adorable bunny"* would be split into tokens such as *a, cute, and, adorable,* and *bunny*:

```
import nltk
nltk.download('punkt')
text = "a cute and adorable bunny"
nltk.word_tokenize(text)
```

Following is the output for the preceding code:

```
[nltk_data] Downloading package punkt to /root/nltk_data...
[nltk_data]   Unzipping tokenizers/punkt.zip.
['a', 'cute', 'and', 'adorable', 'bunny']
```

Introduction to word embeddings

Word embeddings are a way to represent tokens (words) as numerical vectors, capturing the meaning and relationships between words in a form that machine learning models can understand. Think of it as a way to map words into a high-dimensional space where similar words are closer together.

The following figure gives an illustration of word embeddings:

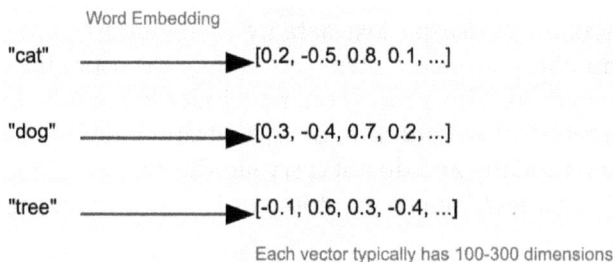

Word Embedding

"cat" ⟶ [0.2, -0.5, 0.8, 0.1, ...]

"dog" ⟶ [0.3, -0.4, 0.7, 0.2, ...]

"tree" ⟶ [-0.1, 0.6, 0.3, -0.4, ...]

Each vector typically has 100-300 dimensions

Figure 11.2: Word embeddings

---

8 Transformers are a type of machine learning models designed for processing sequential data, particularly natural language. They use self-attention mechanisms to capture relationships between words in a sentence, enabling efficient and effective language understanding and generation tasks.
9 GloVe is an unsupervised learning algorithm used to generate word embeddings by analyzing word co-occurrence statistics in a large text corpus, capturing the semantic relationships between words.

This transformation of words into vectors allows us to feed machine learning algorithms with structured numerical data. However, that is not all, these embeddings do more than just represent words as numbers. As we will explain in detail, they encode the meaning of words in a mathematical form, capturing semantic relationships and contextual nuances that enable more advanced text analysis.

For example, in a word embedding model, the words **buy** and **purchase** would be positioned near each other because they have similar meanings. This allows machine learning models to understand and analyze text data more effectively by recognizing patterns and relationships between words.

The meaning and relationships of words are **encoded** within the numerical vectors representing each word, allowing models to understand the context and semantics of language, as follows:

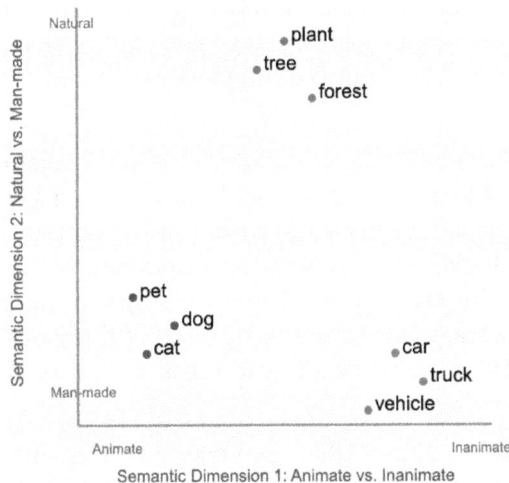

Figure 11.3: Word representations with word embeddings

The visualization shows two axes representing semantic dimensions in a 2D space, several words plotted as points in this space and words with similar meanings clustered together. The illustration demonstrates how word embeddings can capture semantic relationships:

- Animal-related words (cat, dog, and pet) are clustered together at the bottom-left.
- Vehicle-related words (car, truck, and vehicle) are grouped at the top-right.
- Nature-related words (tree, plant, and forest) are placed in the middle.

The axes can be interpreted as follows, **Semantic Dimension 1** (x-axis) represents **Animate vs. Inanimate** and **Semantic Dimension 2** (y-axis) represents **Natural vs. Man-made**. This illustration shows how word embeddings can capture multiple semantic dimensions simultaneously. It is important to note that in actual word embedding models, there are usually many more dimensions, and the interpretations of these dimensions are often not as clear-cut as in this simplified 2D example.

In this section, we covered the fundamentals of word embeddings. We will now extend this concept beyond individual words and apply it to entire companies. Just as we compute embeddings for a word or term, we can generate an embedding for an **entire document**, summarizing all available information about a company, 10-K reports, Wikipedia data, client relationships, market positioning, products, and more.

All these highly valuable sources will be transformed efficiently by the embedding API we will use. The result will be a company embedding vector, a **compact numerical representation that captures the essence of a company** beyond just historical price data.

Creating company embeddings with GloVe

GloVe is an advanced technique used to compute word embeddings by analyzing the co-occurrence of words in a large text corpus. As we explained in the previous section, it captures the relationships and similarities between words in a high-dimensional space, allowing for a deeper understanding of language and context in text data. GloVe enhances the ability to extract information by representing words in a way that reflects their semantic relationships.

GloVe uses a **pre-trained** model that has already learned the relationships between words based on a vast amount of text data. This model provides word embeddings that capture the general meanings and associations of words. In the context of the current text, we use these pre-trained embeddings to analyze and understand the specific content we are working with, **applying the learned word relationships to our particular dataset**. This approach allows us to leverage the extensive training of the model while focusing on the unique context of our text without needing to retrain the model on our specific text as demonstrated in the following code:

This code installs and loads the pre-trained (**'average_word_embeddings_ glove.840B.300d'**) GloVe model using the highly recommended **Huggin Face** API which serves, among other things, as a repo for curated and high-flying pre-trained machine learning models:

```python
!pip install -qU sentence-transformers
from sentence_transformers import SentenceTransformer
# Load the SentenceTransformer model with GloVe embeddings
model = SentenceTransformer('average_word_embeddings_glove.840B.300d')
```

We then feed the pre-trained model with the **S&P 500 company pages** (refer to the previous section, *Reading Wikipedia Pages with API*) and obtain company embeddings for each of them in return:

```python
# Get embeddings for each text article
for title, content in page_content.items():
    embeddings[title] = model.encode(content, convert_to_tensor=True)
```

We are arranging all the embedding vectors into a DataFrame for easier manipulation and to provide a concrete view of what these embeddings look like by displaying an extract:

```
df_embeddings = pd.DataFrame(embeddings)
```

The following is the output from the aforementioned code:

	3M	AMD	American_Airlines_Group	Apple_Inc.	AT&T
0	-0.014903	-0.047319	-0.055452	0.007243	-0.072743
1	0.072532	0.069450	0.031295	0.051805	0.060159
2	0.021636	0.043283	0.090286	0.086281	0.018121
3	-0.021050	-0.029598	-0.024121	-0.006353	-0.014126
4	-0.024960	-0.028327	-0.000651	0.029981	-0.025551
...	...	...	...	...	...
295	-0.046276	-0.055258	-0.095426	-0.051326	-0.063740
296	-0.040526	-0.034594	0.028350	-0.014783	-0.031071
297	-0.006549	-0.009413	-0.094267	-0.030501	-0.035756
298	0.005902	0.051357	0.006496	0.041917	0.013778
299	0.038869	0.017541	0.048115	0.086058	0.014192

Table 11.4: Word embeddings vectors

Visualizing word embeddings with UMAP

Since it is not possible to directly visualize such complex multi-dimensional arrays (300D), we utilize the sophisticated UMAP[10] algorithm to help visualize a subset of 30 company embeddings in the following figure:

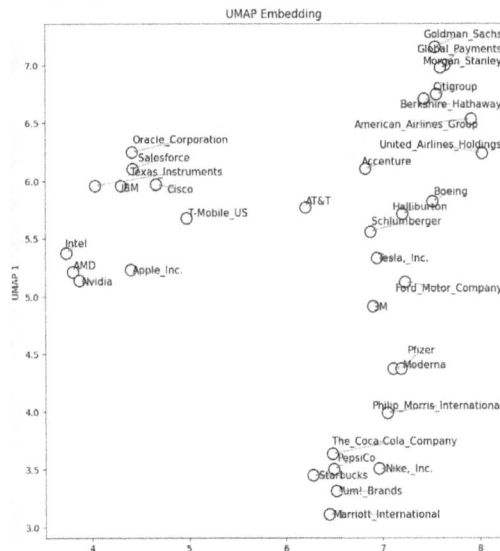

Figure 11.4: Visualize embeddings with UMAP

---

10 See chapter 6, *Improving Model Capability with Features*, for an introduction to UMAP algorithm and chapters 9, *Unsupervised Learning Methods for Trading*, and 10, *Unsupervised Learning with Pattern Matching*, for using UMAP in a different context.

The embeddings projected with UMAP provide a visual representation of the relationships between S&P 500 companies *Intel, AMD,* and *Apple,* which are grouped closely together, indicating a strong contextual similarity, due to their involvement in similar industries. On the other hand, companies like Tesla and Ford Motor Company are positioned near each other, reflecting their shared focus in the automotive sector, and so on for the rest of the companies.

This visualization offers traders and economists a unique perspective on the clustering of companies based on their underlying characteristics extracted and calculated from web pages. It can be used to identify sectors and groups of companies which are not accessible through traditional financial analysis. Such elements could inform portfolio diversification strategies.

Now that we have converted the articles into numerical vectors (embeddings), we have the flexibility to perform a variety of computations on this data. Specifically, since these vectors represent the essence of each company, we will apply, in the following section, arithmetic operations to them, including comparisons and similarity measurements, to prepare for the forthcoming portfolio construction based on these measurements.

Building a similarity matrix

We construct a similarity matrix between companies. It allows us to quantify how closely related different articles, and therefore companies, are to each other based on the content of their web pages.

Before performing this computation, we illustrate the concept of a similarity matrix using a simple example involving four elements: car, cat, dog, and flower. Each of these terms is represented by its respective word embedding (left side of the following figure), and we then compute the similarity matrix (right side of the following figure) directly based on these embeddings using the **Cosine Similarity** method. If two vectors (representing words, sentences, or companies) point in the same direction, they are very similar (cosine similarity close to 1). If they point in opposite directions, they are completely different (cosine similarity = -1). In simple terms, it checks how much two things **align** in meaning rather than just comparing raw numbers.

The following visualization illustrates how word vectors relate to similarity scores and the inverse relationship[11] between semantic distance in vector space and similarity score:

11

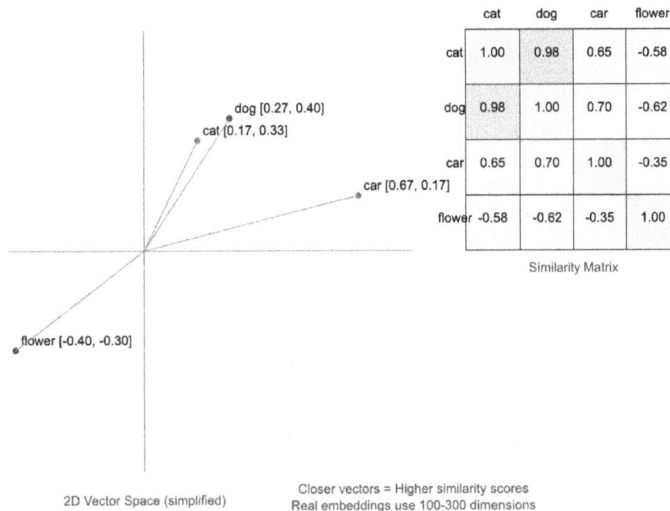

	cat	dog	car	flower
cat	1.00	0.98	0.65	-0.58
dog	0.98	1.00	0.70	-0.62
car	0.65	0.70	1.00	-0.35
flower	-0.58	-0.62	-0.35	1.00

Similarity Matrix

dog [0.27, 0.40]
cat [0.17, 0.33]
car [0.67, 0.17]
flower [-0.40, -0.30]

2D Vector Space (simplified)

Closer vectors = Higher similarity scores
Real embeddings use 100-300 dimensions

Figure 11.5: Word embeddings vectors and similarity matrix

We can see that **dog** and **cat** share a lot of common concepts (pets, classification as mammals, etc.), resulting in a very high similarity score (0.98). On the other hand, **car** and **flower** share nothing and therefore have a score (-0.35) that reflects this semantic distance.

Similarity matrix with Cosine Distance offers great advantages like the ability to measure semantic similarity between assets. It is less sensitive to outliers than the covariance matrix (widely used in portfolios construction). It captures non-linear relationships and is more stable over time than correlation coefficients.

Let us now consider the application of this to our S&P 500 companies. To compute the similarity matrix between companies, the procedure is repeated in the same way. We start with the representation of each company as a vector (company embeddings). Then, we compare these vectors with each other, to measure how similar they are, using the Cosine Similarity formula. The result is a symmetric matrix where each cell shows the similarity score between two items, indicating how closely related they are based on their vector representations.

We do not perform these computations manually; instead, we use the high-level library **Scikitlearn** to handle the similarity calculations, such as cosine distance.

In the following code, the **cosine_similarity** function takes embeddings (**df_embeddings**) as input and outputs a similarity matrix:

```
from sklearn.metrics.pairwise import cosine_similarity

cosine_sim_matrix = cosine_similarity(df_embeddings.T)
df_cos_sim = pd.DataFrame(cosine_sim_matrix ,
```

```
                    index = df_embeddings.columns,
                    columns = df_embeddings.columns)
df_cos_sim.iloc[:6, :6]
```

It outputs an extract (first six elements) of the similarity matrix:

	3M	Accenture	AMD	American_ Airlines	Apple	AT&T
3M	1.000000	0.911221	0.754084	0.854462	0.900515	0.882236
Accenture	0.911221	1.000000	0.728500	0.893048	0.902334	0.919001
AMD	0.754084	0.728500	1.000000	0.654434	0.842097	0.713088
American_ Airlines_ Group	0.854462	0.893048	0.654434	1.000000	0.831370	0.898130
Apple_Inc.	0.900515	0.902334	0.842097	0.831370	1.000000	0.880814
AT&T	0.882236	0.919001	0.713088	0.898130	0.880814	1.000000

Table 11.5: Similarity matrix

The following code gives the top companies most similar to AMD based on cosine similarity:

```
# pick a label
lbl = df_cos_sim.columns[2]
print('similarities for: ',lbl)
df_cos_sim.loc[lbl].sort_values(ascending=False)[1:5]
```

Preceding code gives the following output:

```
similarities for:  AMD
Intel                0.947384
Nvidia               0.941569
Texas_Instruments    0.850835
Apple_Inc.           0.842249
```

Intel and *Nvidia* are the closest, indicating that their text embeddings share significant similarities with *AMD's*, followed by *Texas Instruments* and *Apple*. These companies are major players in the semiconductor industries, which explains the high similarity scores. The similarity matrix rightly suggests that their **business descriptions**, **market roles**, and **technological focuses** are closely related. It appears to be an effective tool for **mapping company relationships** and **identifying clusters** within the industry landscape.

To validate the effectiveness of the cosine similarity matrix, we examine the landscape for Goldman Sachs to check for any anomalies:

```
lbl = 'Goldman_Sachs'
print(lbl)
pprint(df_cos_sim.loc[lbl].sort_values(ascending=False)[1:5])
```

The following is the output from the aforementioned code:

```
Goldman_Sachs
Citigroup              0.981535
Morgan_Stanley         0.969291
Berkshire_Hathaway     0.927531
Accenture              0.921569
```

The results show high similarity with *Citigroup, Morgan Stanley,* and *Berkshire Hathaway,* which are all major financial institutions. Accenture also shows a strong similarity, likely due to its significant involvement in financial consulting, indicating that the similarity matrix is accurately capturing relationships within the financial sector.

The similarity matrix is a valuable tool for identifying proximities between individual companies. However, to visualize the relationships among a selection of 30 S&P 500 companies more effectively, we can use more powerful tools: a clustermap and a tree graph.

Building a clustermap

The clustermap not only visualizes similarities but also adds a structured **perspective** to the entire landscape. It automatically orders all companies based on their proximities, creating a **hierarchical clustering** that reveals the underlying structure and relationships among the companies, making it easier to identify sectors and groups with similar characteristics. The clustermap and tree graph (see next section, *Building a tree graph*) derived from Wikipedia pages are inspired by Gautier Marti's excellent blog post, available at, **https://gmarti. gitlab.io/quant/2023/05/07/wikipedia-network-companies-sentence-transformers.html.**

This code outputs the clustermap:

```
import seaborn as sns
sns.clustermap(df_cos_sim)
```

Unlike a similarity matrix, the clustermap ranks each company based on their similarities and organizes them into **hierarchical clusters** as we can see in the following graph:

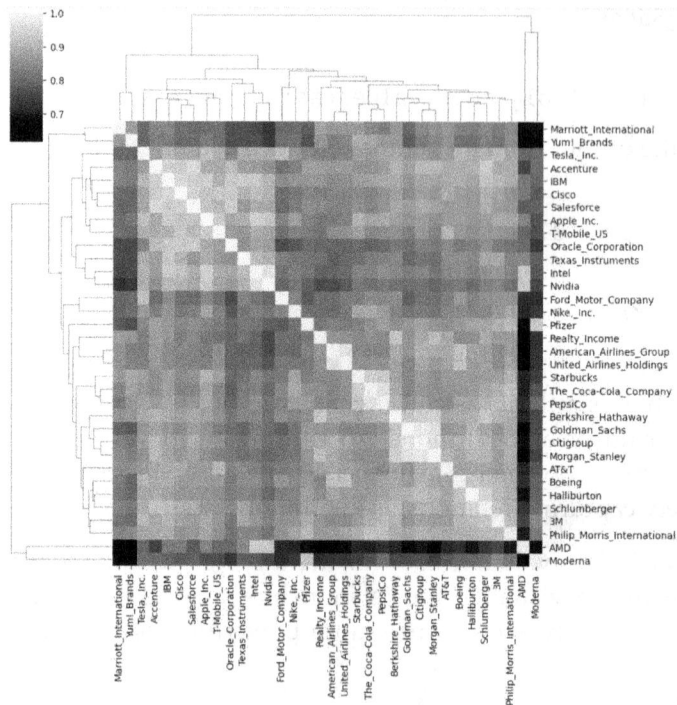

Figure 11.6: *Clustermap for S&P500 companies*

The gradient of colors indicates varying degrees of similarity, with closely related companies forming distinct clusters.

In concrete terms, for example in the preceding figure, **Goldman Sachs** and **Morgan Stanley** are positioned very close to each other in the clustermap, reflecting their strong similarity. Both companies operate in the investment banking and financial services industry, and their proximity on the clustermap suggests that their pages describing their activities discuss overlapping topics such as financial markets, investment strategies and global economic impact.

Moving one level up in the hierarchy, Goldman Sachs and Morgan Stanley cluster with **Citigroup** and **Berkshire Hathaway**. This grouping is logical, as these companies are also key players in the financial sector. Citigroup, with its extensive global banking operations, and Berkshire Hathaway, with its significant financial investments, share common themes with Goldman Sachs and Morgan Stanley in terms of their influence on financial markets and global economies.

At the next hierarchical level, this financial cluster merges with **IBM** and **Accenture**, companies known for their involvement in technology and consulting services, respectively. The connection is through their shared focus on providing high-level business and financial solutions. The cluster expands to incorporate companies that provide essential services and solutions to the financial sector.

Uncovering hidden connections through similarity analysis

In financial analysis, companies are typically grouped based on traditional classifications such as industry sector or revenue stream. However, text-based embeddings and similarity analysis allow us to uncover relationships that go **beyond simple industry labels**. By analyzing how companies are described in different sources, we can uncover unexpected connections based on common themes such as **market positioning, brand influence, business strategies,** and **customer engagement**.

This approach is particularly valuable in portfolio construction, where understanding hidden similarities between companies can help with risk diversification, factor-based investing and alternative clustering approaches. Instead of relying solely on predefined industry categories, we can now use data-driven relationships to structure investment strategies.

The following example illustrates this concept in action. By examining a cluster map of company embeddings, we can see how companies that appear to be unrelated share meaningful characteristics based on their descriptions in textual sources.

We will now look at an example of *American Airlines* and *United Airlines* to illustrate how embeddings and similarity analysis can uncover less obvious connections:

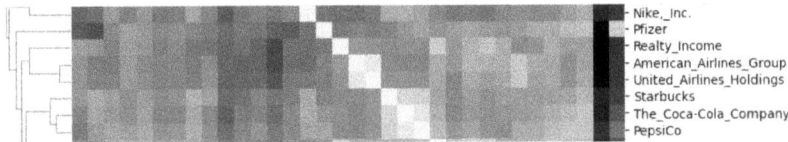

Figure 11.7: Hidden connections with clustermap

As we see in the preceding cluster map magnification, the two airlines (**American** and **United**) are positioned very close to each other in the clustermap, reflecting their shared industry and business model. However, when we move levels up, they are clustered with *Starbucks*, *PepsiCo*, and *The Coca-Cola Company*. This might seem surprising at first, but it highlights how these companies, despite being in different sectors, share common themes like **global brand presence**, **customer service**, and **consumer engagement**.

As we move further up the hierarchy, the cluster expands to include other major consumer brands like *Nike* and *Marriott International*. This broader grouping suggests that, while American Airlines and United Airlines are airline companies, the way their market strategies and global operations are described has significant overlaps with how **consumer-oriented** companies are portrayed.

This example demonstrates that **advanced machine learning algorithms** (company embeddings combined with similarity analysis) can **reveal unexpected connections**, uncovering hidden relationships not apparent through traditional analysis and that go beyond obvious industry ties.

Having examined the information provided by the similarity matrix and cluster map, we can now turn our attention to another effective tool, tree graph structures derived from a Distance Matrix.

Building a tree graph

Unlike a similarity matrix, which indicates how close entities are, a Distance Matrixemphasizes the differences, enabling us to construct a tree structure that visually represents the relative distances between companies. This approach provides an **alternative perspective** on the relationships within the dataset, revealing how companies are positioned in relation to each other based on their distance.

In the following code, we use *NetworkX*[12] library to process the input data (**distance_matrix**) into a tree as expected:

```
import networkx as nx


distance_matrix = 1 - df_cos_sim
graph = nx.from_numpy_array(distance_matrix.values)
# Compute the minimum spanning tree
mst = nx.minimum_spanning_tree(graph)
```

NetworkX also offers the necessary tools (**nx.draw**) for visualizing tree graphs:

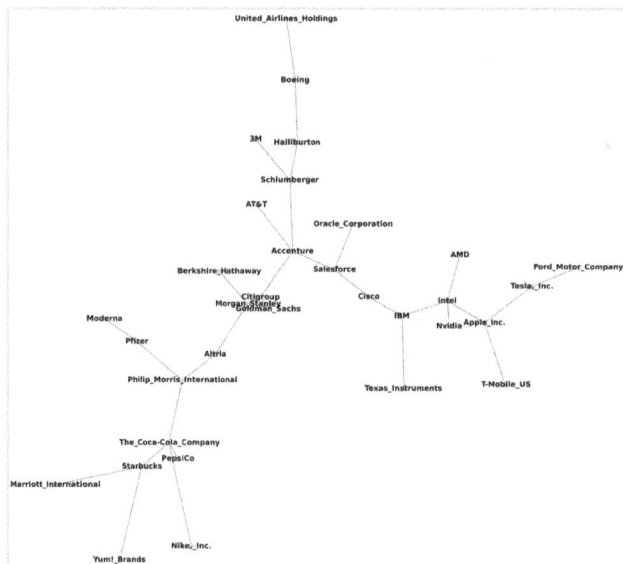

Figure 11.8: Tree graph for SP500 companies

---

12 NetworkX, Software for Complex Networks, is a Python package for the creation, manipulation, and study of the structure, dynamics of complex networks. It provides tools for the study of the structure and dynamics of social networks and the ability to painlessly work with large nonstandard data sets. https://networkx.org

The tree graph visually represents the relationships between companies based on their dissimilarities, derived from a Distance Matrix. Each connection (edge) between companies shows the **distance** between them. This structure informs us the most significant connections and paths between companies, offering a clear and hierarchical view of how these entities are related in a broader context, based on the textual data extracted from their internet articles.

We are using a **minimum spanning tree**[13] (**MST**) graph. It connects all the nodes (in our case, companies) together with the minimal total edge weight, ensuring that there are no cycles and only the most critical connections are highlighted. The utility of the MST in displaying a graph tree lies in its ability to **simplify highly complex networks** by focusing on the most important relationships, reducing the visual clutter that comes from fully connected graphs with less significant connections. This makes it easier to identify key clusters and paths within the data, offering a concise view of the overall structure.

We will explore how data structures (company embeddings, similarity matrix and tree graph) can be used to construct an optimally diversified portfolio - entirely based on the text-derived insights from web pages. This approach demonstrates how machine learning can extract meaningful financial signals without relying on traditional numerical price data.

Portfolio construction

A portfolio approach is more interesting than focusing on **individual** trades because it allows for the management of risk and return across a diverse set of assets, optimizing overall performance rather than relying on the success of single positions. By diversifying across different asset classes and sectors, portfolio construction reduces the impact of any single asset's poor performance on the overall portfolio. We will explore an example of this technique in the next section, where methods like optimization algorithms are employed to construct portfolios.

Advantages of allocation based on similarity matrix

Portfolio construction with a similarity matrix enables the identification of assets that are less correlated, promoting diversification and helping to minimize risk while maximizing potential returns. Moreover, portfolio selection using similarity matrix identifies truly diverse assets based on **semantic relationships**, it uncovers non-obvious diversification opportunities and adapts more quickly to changing market conditions. Then, the advantages over traditional *Markowitz*[14] optimization are its ability to incorporate

---

13 https://en.wikipedia.org/wiki/Minimum_spanning_tree
14 Markowitz portfolio theory, also known as Mean-Variance Portfolio, aims to optimize the balance between risk and return in a portfolio by selecting a combination of assets that minimizes risk (variance) for a given level of expected return and asset weights

qualitative information (news, reports, or sentiment) that we simply **cannot**. It is more forward-looking than historical returns, may be more robust to market regime changes, and it could identify diversification opportunities missed by correlation analysis.

Maximizing asset diversity through dissimilarity ranking

We write a function (**select_and_rank_dissimilar_pairs**) that identifies and ranks asset pairs based on their level of dissimilarity. By highlighting the most divergent pairs, it enables a targeted approach to portfolio construction by focusing on truly distinct assets. The key point in the **select_and_rank_dissimilar_pairs** function is, for each company, finding the other company that is **least** (**Numpy argmin** function) similar to it with the following code:

```
min_indices = np.argmin(similarity_matrix, axis=1)
```

Subsequently, the function is executed with the similarity matrix as the input, resulting in the generation of a list of the most dissimilar companies:

```
top_n_pair = 3
lst_dissim = select_and_rank_dissimilar_pairs(df_cos_sim.values ,
df_cos_sim.columns , top_n_pair)
print(lst_dissim)
```

The complete code returns a diverse set of ticker pairs that are **maximally** dissimilar to each other:

```
['MAR', 'YUM', 'MS', 'AMD']
```

The following are the companies corresponding to the given ticker symbols:

- **MAR**: Marriott International
- **YUM**: Yum! Brands
- **MS**: Morgan Stanley
- **AMD**: Advanced Micro Devices

We use the tree graph to assess whether these companies are dissimilar by evaluating if their positions are **sufficiently** distant from each other. We highlight their positions in the following graph:

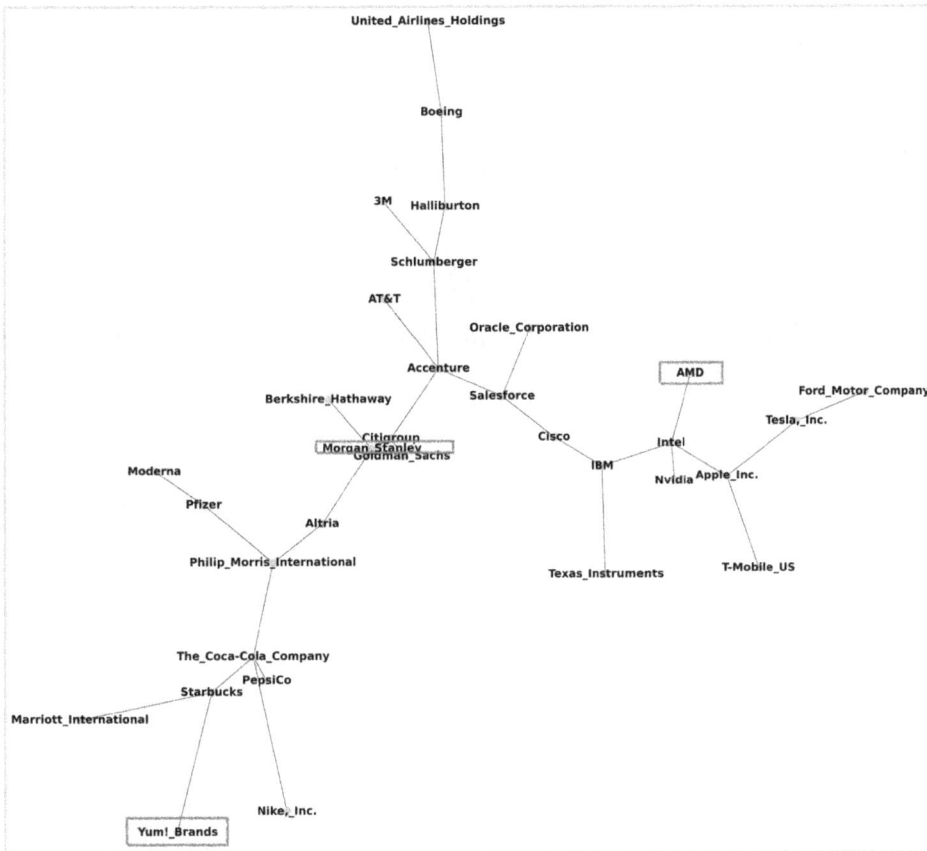

Figure 11.9: *Diversified portfolio tree graph*

The selected companies identified as the most dissimilar **appear distant from each other** in the MST structure, emphasizing their lack of similarity. This demonstrates how graph-based approaches can effectively highlight structural differences between companies beyond traditional industry classifications.

Looking ahead, we can envisage a broader application of these techniques, where **portfolio selection could be performed directly from a graph**, exploiting the relationships encoded in company embeddings. This would provide a data-driven diversification strategy that automatically identifies companies with minimal similarity to optimize risk diversification.

Once this has been checked, *normalized*[15] historical prices of the selected dissimilar assets are used to compute the portfolio value over time, and an **equal weight** is assigned to each asset in the portfolio, as shown:

```
# portfolio with most dissimilar assets
normalized_data = data[lst_dissim] / data[lst_dissim].iloc[0]
```

15 The asset prices are normalized by dividing each series by its initial value, which allows for comparison on the same scale

```
portfolio_dissim = np.sum(normalized_data * np.ones(len(lst_dissim)) * 1/
len(lst_dissim) , axis=1)
```

The code constructed an equal-weight portfolio by normalizing the historical prices of the selected most dissimilar assets and assigning equal allocations to each. Now, we compare its performance against a broader equal-weight portfolio to evaluate the impact of this selection strategy.

Comparison with equal weight portfolios

Next, we display the portfolio value over time alongside its natural benchmark, which is an equal-weight portfolio consisting of the thirty S&P 500 companies we have analyzed from the start:

Figure 11.10: Equity curve of the most dissimilar companies

The chart shows that the portfolio constructed from the most dissimilar companies (in red) outperforms the equal-weight S&P 500 portfolio (in black) over time, particularly during periods of market strength. However, it also experiences higher volatility, reflecting its concentration in highly uncorrelated assets. To further enhance this strategy, implementing a stop-loss mechanism could help manage risk during downturns, and expanding the portfolio beyond the initial four companies could improve diversification, potentially leading to more stable returns while maintaining the benefits of holding dissimilar assets.

While identifying four dissimilar assets offers a straightforward method for diversification, it may not fully capture the complex relationships within the entire asset universe. To address this, we will now extend our use of the similarity matrix to a more sophisticated approach.

Hierarchical Risk Parity allocation

HRP is a recent, sophisticated, innovative portfolio optimization technique that addresses some of the limitations of traditional covariance-based methods. Unlike traditional approaches, which rely heavily on expected returns and are sensitive to estimation errors, HRP focuses primarily on the risk structure of the portfolio. It uses **hierarchical clustering** to group assets based on their similarities, creating a tree-like structure that represents the relationships between different investments. *This hierarchical approach allows HRP to consider both the risk of individual assets and the risk relationships between different clusters of assets.* By allocating risk rather than capital, HRP aims to create well-diversified portfolios that are robust to estimation errors and market changes.

From a machine learning perspective, HRP is essentially an unsupervised machine learning approach applied to portfolio optimization.

HRP as an unsupervised algorithm

HRP[16] does not rely on predefined labels or target outcomes but instead discovers **inherent risk structures** within the data. By using hierarchical clustering, an unsupervised technique, HRP autonomously groups assets based on their similarity, allowing it to uncover multi-level relationships in the portfolio without the need for explicit return forecasts or predefined asset classifications.

In this section, we explore how HRP aligns with clustermap visualization, revealing the underlying structure used for portfolio optimization.

Connecting HRP with clustermap

The clustermap visualization is like HRP, both methods group assets based on similarities. As we see in section *Building a clustermap*, a clustermap groups assets into clusters that can be shown in a tree-like structure. This shows the hierarchical relationships between assets, helping to identify diversification opportunities and reduce concentration risk in portfolio construction.

HRP uses this structure to allocate portfolio weights. This ensures that assets within the same cluster do not dominate the portfolio. This improves diversification. The process used in HRP to determine clusters and allocate weights is similar to how clusters are formed and shown in a clustermap.

Building the HRP portfolio

We will use a modern analytic tool called *Riskfolio-Lib*[17] library to build an HRP portfolio. It handles complex calculations, allowing any quantitative trader to benefit from it without needing an in-depth understanding of the underlying mathematical principles.

---

16 Here is an overview of the key steps in the HRP algorithm:
   1. Similarity matrix: Compute correlations between assets
   2. Hierarchical clustering: Group assets into a tree structure based on similarities
   3. Matrix reorganization: Reorder correlation matrix to visualize asset clusters
   4. Risk allocation: Recursively divide portfolio, allocating risk from top to bottom of the tree
   5. Weight calculation: Convert risk allocations to portfolio weights, considering asset volatilities

17 Riskfolio-Lib is a library for making portfolio optimization and quantitative strategic asset allocation. Its objective is to help practitioners build investment portfolios based on mathematically **complex models with low effort**, https://riskfolio-lib.readthedocs.io

Let us start with installing and importing the required library:

```
!pip3 install -q riskfolio-lib
import riskfolio as rp
```

Then, build and optimize a portfolio based on hierarchical clustering. Initialize the hierarchical clustering portfolio with the similarity data (**df_cos_sim**) and set up for optimal portfolio:

```
port = rp.HCPortfolio(returns = df_cos_sim)
```

The aforementioned code tuns the optimization process and outputs desired optimal weights (**w**):

```
w = port.optimization(model=model,
                      codependence=codependence,
                      rm=rm,
                      rf=rf,
                      linkage=linkage,
                      max_k=max_k,
                      leaf_order=leaf_order)
```

RiskFolio-Lib also supports visualization tools and the disclosure of allocation weights as they are calculated:

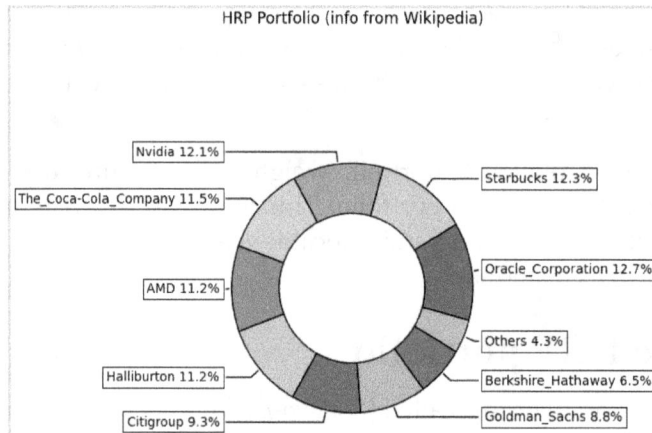

Figure 11.11: Optimal weights given by HRP

The portfolio is spread across different sectors, giving exposure to different areas of the economy:

- **Technology**: Oracle, Nvidia, and AMD represent the tech sector. This sector exhibits high potential returns that come with volatility.

- **Consumer discretionary**: Starbucks reflecting consumer spending trends. This sector is sensitive to economic cycles.

- **Consumer staples**: Coca-Cola is known for its stability and consistent demand regardless of economic conditions. It adds a defensive aspect to the portfolio.

- **Energy**: *Halliburton* (major player in the energy sector), provides exposure to global energy prices (oil and gas) and geopolitical factors.

- **Financials**: *Citigroup, Goldman Sachs, Berkshire,* and *Morgan Stanley* represent the financial sector. This sector's performance is closely tied to interest rates and economic growth.

We highlight the selected assets in the MST graph, as follows:

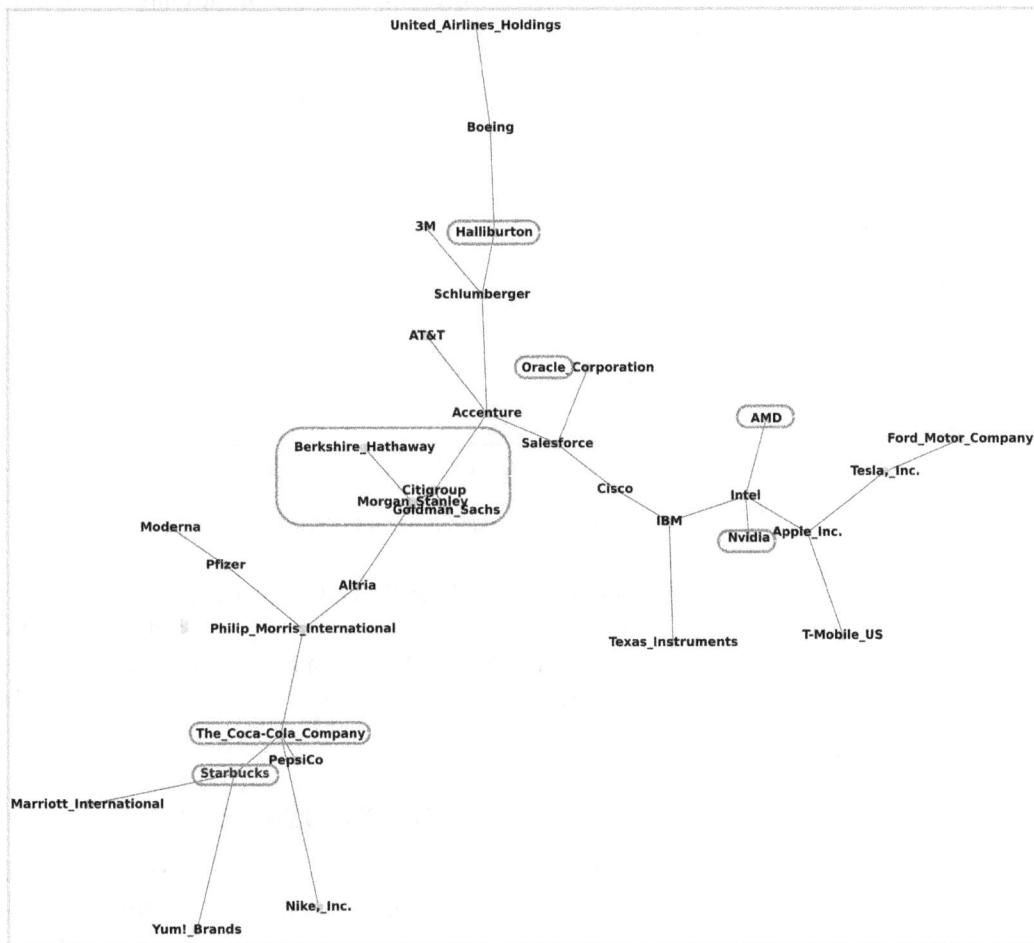

Figure 11.12: Portfolio given by HRP

As we can see, the selected assets are spread across distant branches of the MST, confirming that they are structurally dissimilar based on their text-derived embeddings. This reinforces the idea that portfolio diversification can be achieved directly from a graph, without relying on traditional sector labels. The technology stocks cluster together, while the financials form a separate group, reflecting their common industry characteristics. Starbucks and Coca-Cola, although in different industries, are positioned closer together due to common themes in global branding and consumer engagement. Halliburton stands apart, emphasizing its unique role in the energy sector.

The MST structure visually confirms that the portfolio is made up of assets that are far apart in the network, ensuring low similarity and strong diversification. *This demonstrates how machine learning and text embedding can directly guide asset selection by identifying relationships beyond traditional metrics.*

In the following figure, we compare the HRP portfolio against an equal-weight portfolio, with the clear objective of outperforming the neutral equal-weighted approach:

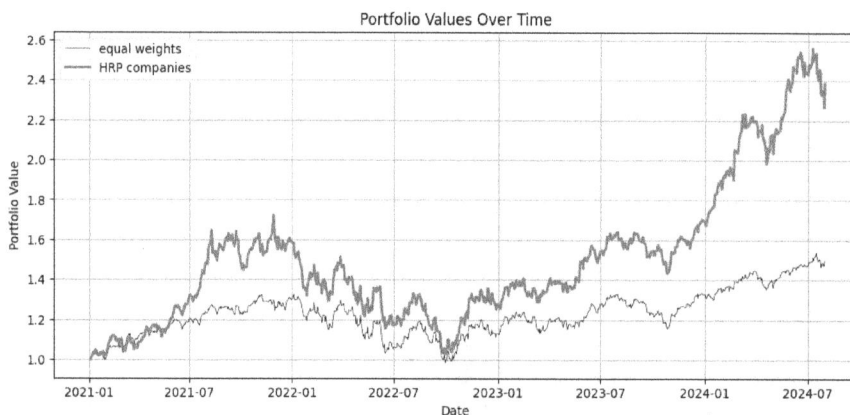

Figure 11.13: Equity Curve for HRP portfolio based on text data

The chart illustrates that the HRP portfolio **significantly** outperforms the equal-weight portfolio over the observed period. The HRP portfolio shows higher growth during market upswings, reflecting the effectiveness of leveraging textual data for portfolio construction. This performance suggests a more profitable investment strategy compared to a neutral equal-weighted approach.

Weight allocation based on Sharpe metric

We built the HRP portfolio solely based on a similarity matrix extracted from text analysis (company embeddings and distances) of the internet pages, making the portfolio directly connected to the underlying content of those pages. It would be valuable to compare this NLP-based portfolio with a traditional financial approach centered on asset returns.

To do this, we construct a portfolio aimed at maximizing the Sharpe[18] Ratio in the upcoming period, following a training phase where the model identifies the best-performing assets to achieve this objective, as shown:

18 See chapter 3 *"Optimizing Trading Systems, Metrics, and Automated Reporting."* for details about Sharpe Ratio metric.

1. The algorithm is trained for about four years (2020 to the end of 2023). It represents eighty percent of the dataset (**data**):

```
idx_train = int(80/100 * data.shape[0])
```

2. We calculate the returns (**ret**) for the period to feed into the optimization algorithm in a later step:

```
ret = data.iloc[:idx_train].pct_change().fillna(0)
print(f'Training end @ {data.iloc[idx_train].name}')
```

3. The code output is as follows:

```
Training end @ 2023-11-10 00:00:00
```

4. Set up portfolio objective, i.e. minimize risk (Variance) and **maximize sharpe ratio**:

```
# Building the portfolio object
port = rp.Portfolio(returns = ret)
rf = 0 # Risk free rate
port.rf = rf
# Calculate expected returns and covariance
port.assets_stats(method_mu='hist', method_cov='hist')
# Set up optimization parameters
#'MV'   # Minimum Variance and max sharpe ratio:
port.rm = 'MV'
port.obj = 'Sharpe'
```

5. Run optimization and create bar plot (six largest weights):

```
w_sharpe = port.optimization(model='Classic')
```

Once the algorithm has been trained, we identify and display the assets with the largest weights, highlighting the most influential companies in the portfolio, as follows:

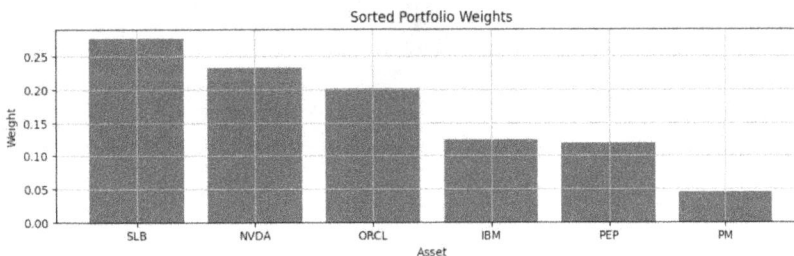

Figure 11.14: Portfolio largest weights

The bar chart shows the portfolio weights assigned to each asset to achieve the desired risk-adjusted returns (maximize the Sharpe Ratio). The largest weight is given to **Schlumberger (SLB)**, **Nvidia**, and **Oracle (ORCL)**. These are the top candidates identified by the model during the training period.

Other assets like **IBM**, **PepsiCo (PEP)**, and **Philip Morris (PM)** are also included but with smaller weights, reflecting their relative contribution to the overall portfolio's expected performance. This distribution indicates the model's preference for a mix of technology, energy, and consumer staples sectors to balance growth with stability.

Compared to the HRP portfolio, the weights are larger, resulting in a less diversified portfolio that is more concentrated on a smaller set of assets.

Let us compare this portfolio with the HRP portfolio, which is based on textual information only. Compared to the HRP portfolio, the weights are larger, resulting in a less diversified portfolio that is more concentrated on a smaller set of assets.

In the following chart, we position both portfolios within the MST structure for direct visual comparison. The HRP allocations are indicated by **surrounding** the asset names, while a star around the asset names indicates the Max Sharpe Ratio allocations:

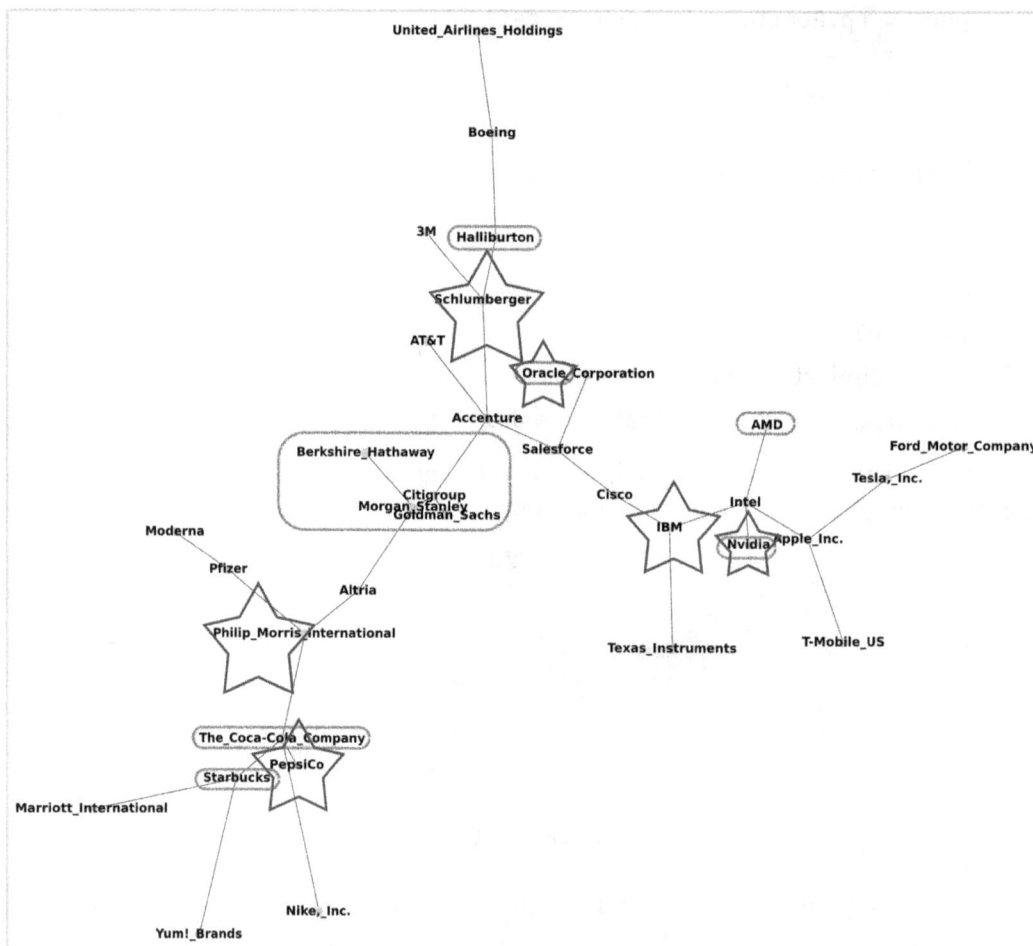

Figure 11.15: Traditional portfolio vs. text-based HRP portfolio

The Max Sharpe Ratio portfolio is more concentrated, with higher weights in a smaller number of assets, while the HRP portfolio is more broadly diversified, using textual similarities for diversification. The MST visualization highlights this contrast, the **HRP allocations are spread** across different industries, while the **Max Sharpe Ratio allocations tend to cluster** around a few selected high-return assets. This reinforces the trade-off between risk-adjusted returns and diversification, with HRP offering broader exposure and Max Sharpe favoring efficiency over balance.

We will now analyze the equity curves to compare the risk-return profiles of the two portfolios over time, assessing their returns, volatility and diversification effects, as shown:

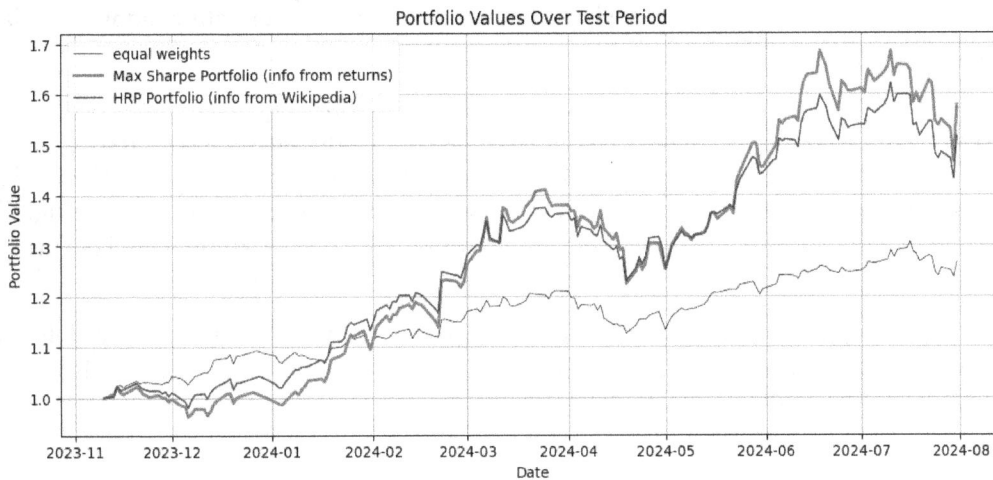

Figure 11.16: Max Sharpe Portfolio and HRP portfolio

The chart compares the performance of the HRP portfolio (in blue), constructed using text analysis, with the Max Sharpe Ratio portfolio (red line), which is based on financial returns, over the test period. The Max Sharpe Ratio portfolio shows a slightly higher growth, outperforming both the HRP portfolio and the equal-weight portfolio (in black). This suggests that the HRP approach, grounded in text analysis from Wikipedia, is a strong contender, offering a diversified and **data-driven alternative** that effectively captures asset relationships and mitigates risk.

Despite its higher performance, the **HRP equity curve** aligns with our MST tree analysis. The **Max Sharpe Ratio portfolio** is more concentrated and less diversified, resulting in a higher maximum drawdown.

Conclusion

By the end of this chapter, we were introduced to advanced unsupervised NLP-driven portfolio construction, demonstrating how purely text-based data can be transformed into meaningful financial insights. Using company embeddings, similarity matrices and graph-based structures, we built alternative asset allocation strategies that go beyond traditional numerical data.

Through HRP, we showed how unsupervised learning can create diversified portfolios from text alone, while the Max Sharpe Ratio approach, focused on return optimization, produced a more concentrated portfolio with higher drawdowns.

Readers will now have **practical experience** in extracting and processing financial text from professional sources like *The Wall Street Journal* and *Reuters* via the *BizTok* API, computing company embeddings using *Hugging Face,* and applying machine learning to portfolio selection. More broadly, this chapter demonstrated how **graph theory**, **clustering**, and **NLP** can uncover hidden relationships between companies, enabling adaptive, data-driven investment strategies.

Next, we turn to **anomaly detection** and **association rule mining**. These are powerful yet underutilized techniques in finance. We will explore how unsupervised anomaly detection reveals market inefficiencies, unusual trading patterns, and trend reversals. This is done without relying on labelled data. Additionally, we introduce association rule mining. This is a technique widely used in retail and industry but rarely applied to finance. This method offers a systematic approach to generating predictive trading signals.

In the next chapter, we will have hands-on experience in building anomaly detectors, extracting association rules from market data, and transforming these insights into actionable trading strategies.

Join our book's Discord space

Join the book's Discord Workspace for Latest updates, Offers, Tech happenings around the world, New Release and Sessions with the Authors:

https://discord.bpbonline.com

## CHAPTER 12

Advanced Unsupervised Learning, Anomaly Detection, and Association Rules

Introduction

In this chapter, we look at advanced unsupervised learning techniques aimed at uncovering **hidden patterns** and **anomalies** in financial markets. We begin by addressing the challenges of anomaly detection, where market inefficiencies, **anomalous behavior** and unusual events often signal both risks and opportunities. While statistical methods lay the groundwork, machine learning approaches, such as **Isolation Forest**, provide more sophisticated detection.

We then introduce a **hybrid approach** that combines **sequence clustering** with **non-linear projections**, offering a more effective way to identify distinct **market regimes** and **detect trend reversals**. This is followed by an exploration of **association rule mining**, where relationships between market events are discovered and used to shape long-only trading strategies.

By integrating these advanced unsupervised techniques, the chapter provides a practical toolkit for navigating complex financial data and building more informed, data-driven strategies for market analysis.

Structure

In this chapter, we will cover the following topics:

- Introduction to anomaly detection in finance

- Sequence clustering and projection for anomaly detection
- Clustering-based strategy with association rule

Objectives

This chapter concludes our exploration of advanced techniques of unsupervised learning, focusing on **clustering**, **association rules** and **anomaly detection** in financial markets. It equips readers with the skills needed to identify market inefficiencies and unusual events using statistical approaches such as Z-score, **Interquartile Range (IQR)**, and **Change Point Detection (CPD)**, as well as machine learning methods such as Isolation Forest for more sophisticated anomaly detection.

The chapter introduces hybrid approaches that integrate **sequence clustering** with non-linear **dimension reduction** to enhance the ability to detect market **regimes** and **trend reversals**. It also explores **association rule mining** - an undervalued and unorthodox algorithm that is largely ignored in finance, but widely used for pattern discovery in retail, industry and engineering. By applying it to financial data, the chapter shows how association rules can uncover meaningful relationships between market events, providing a basis for constructing data-driven trading strategies. By working through the chapter, readers will gain a practical toolkit for analyzing complex financial data, making informed decisions, and using cutting-edge data science to gain a competitive edge in market analysis.

Introduction to anomaly detection in finance

Anomaly detection in financial markets is a critical application of unsupervised learning, focusing on identifying data points, events, or sequences and patterns that **deviate significantly from expected behavior**. These anomalies range from individual outliers to complex collective deviations.

Anomalies come in a variety of forms, each requiring different detection methods to reveal market inefficiencies and risks. **Point anomalies** appear as **sudden spikes** in trading volume or unusual price movements, often linked to isolated events such as earnings surprises or news-driven shocks. **Contextual anomalies** occur when otherwise typical trading volumes become abnormal within certain time frames, reflecting shifts in market behavior that may indicate **structural changes** or hidden risks. Beyond individual events, **collective anomalies** occur when groups of data points exhibit unusual correlations, often signaling broader market stress or **systemic disruption**. Recognizing these differences allows for more precise application of anomaly detection techniques and improves the accuracy of financial models.

The **importance of anomaly detection in finance** lies in its ability to uncover market inefficiencies, detect manipulation and provide early warning of significant events such as crashes, liquidity crises, flash crashes, speculative bubbles, coordinated market manipulation, sudden regime changes and major geopolitical or macroeconomic shocks. By **identifying these anomalies early**, traders and analysts can better anticipate risks, adjust strategies and take advantage of market dislocations before they fully unfold. By leveraging unsupervised learning techniques, we can identify these anomalies without relying on labeled data.

Challenges in detecting financial anomalies

Imagine a trading algorithm suddenly detecting a 10% price jump in a blue-chip stock within seconds. Is this a true anomaly signaling a major market event or just a data glitch? This scenario illustrates the complex difficulties in anomaly detection, particularly when using unsupervised learning techniques:

- The **high dimensionality** of financial data poses a significant hurdle. Markets generate vast amounts of data across multiple assets, timeframes, and indicators. Unsupervised algorithms must sift through this multidimensional space to identify meaningful anomalies, a task we will address through dimensionality reduction techniques in our machine learning approaches.

- The **non-stationary** nature of financial time series complicates anomaly detection. Market regimes shift, volatilities change, and what is anomalous today might be normal tomorrow. Our proposed clustering *algorithm*[1] tackles this by identifying distinct market regimes, allowing for context-specific anomaly detection.

- True anomalies in financial markets are **rare**, creating a severe class imbalance. This makes it challenging for standard methods to distinguish between significant anomalies and noise. We will explore how association rules can help establish **normal** patterns within each regime, making anomaly identification more robust.

- The fine line between noise and significant anomalies in finance demands sophisticated detection methods. A small price movement might be normal noise for a low-volatility stock but a significant anomaly for a stable cryptocurrency. Our integrated approach combines multiple techniques to navigate this complexity.

These difficulties underscore the need for advanced, adaptable unsupervised learning techniques in financial anomaly detection. As we progress through statistical methods, machine learning approaches, and our novel integrated algorithm, we will see how each technique addresses these challenges, providing a comprehensive way for identifying and interpreting anomalies.

Overview of unsupervised approaches to anomaly detection

Unsupervised methods offer significant advantages due to their independence from labelled data, eliminating the need for **expert-driven annotation**. This is particularly

---

1 See last section, *Clustering-based long-only strategy*

valuable in scenarios where labelled datasets are scarce, expensive or non-existent. Instead of relying on predefined categories, unsupervised techniques, **autonomously identify hidden structures** and patterns in complex, high-dimensional data. This ability enables them to uncover relationships and anomalies that rule-based systems and traditional supervised learning approaches miss.

Building on these advantages, we can explore the core categories of unsupervised approaches that are particularly effective in financial anomaly detection. The first of these is **statistical methods**.

Statistical methods

These methods leverage statistical measures such as **Z-scores**, to detect abnormal price movements or unusual market behavior. For instance, statistical methods are applied to pinpoint unusually high trading volumes that precede significant market events, like earnings announcements, insider activity, anticipation of an event, or general market sentiment, **before** it is reflected in the stock price.

We use **Tiingo**[2] API in conjunction with the **request** API to extract close price and transaction volume data:

```
import requests
from google.colab import userdata
# Your Tiingo API key
TIINGO_API_KEY = userdata.get('TIINGO_API_KEY')
```

For anomaly detection with **Tiingo** API, we use the **volume** column, as it represents the actual number of shares traded on a given day, reflecting real trading activity. The **adjVolume** column, adjusted for corporate actions like stock splits, is useful for historical comparisons but **not** for detecting real-time anomalies. Therefore, the focus is on the **volume** column to capture actual trading patterns. We know that Z-score represents the number of standard deviations a data point (**volume**, in this case) is from its mean[3]:

In the following code, we calculate the Z-score:

```
# Calculate Z-scores for trading volume
# rolling mean and std are adaptive
window_size = 20
stock_data['Z-Score'] = (stock_data['volume'] -stock_data['volume'].
rolling(window_size).mean()) / stock_data['volume'].rolling(window_size).
std()
```

---

2 As we previously introduced this library in Chapter 2, "*Data Feed, Backtests, and Forward Testing*" readers seeking an introduction to Tiingo's services and API should refer to that chapter. Note that you will need an **API key** to request Tiingo.

3 For example, a Z-score of 1 means the data point is 1 standard deviation above the mean.

We start presenting statistical methods with the **IQR method** to detect anomalies in a dataset. The IQR method is one of the *simplest* statistical techniques for outlier detection. It works by calculating the range between the **1st quartile (Q1)** and the **3rd quartile (Q3)** and then identifying data points that fall outside this *interval*[4], as shown:

```
# Step 2: Use trading volume for anomaly detection
volume_data = stock_data['volume']
# Step 3: Calculate Q1, Q3, and IQR
Q1 = np.percentile(volume_data, 25)  # 25th percentile
Q3 = np.percentile(volume_data, 75)  # 75th percentile
IQR = Q3 - Q1  # Interquartile Range
# Step 4: Define the lower and upper bounds for anomalies
lower_bound = Q1 - 0.3 * IQR
upper_bound = Q3 + 1.5 * IQR
```

We have set **lower_bound = Q1 - 0.3 * IQR** and **upper_bound = Q3 + 1.5 * IQR**. The lower bound is adjusted to be less strict, allowing us to capture **more** low-end anomalies than the standard approach:

```
#
 Step 5: Identify anomalies (values below lower_bound OR above upper_bound)
stock_data['Anomaly'] = (volume_data < lower_bound) | (volume_data > upper_bound)
```

Then plot the volume points flagged as anomalous (red dot):

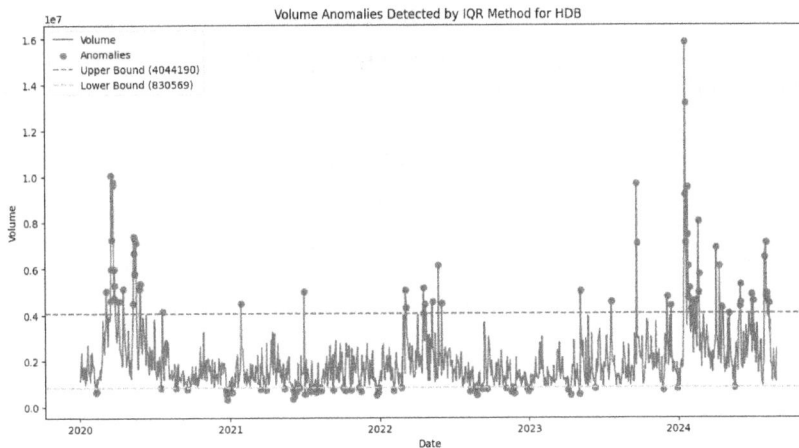

Figure 12.1: Statistical method for anomaly detection

Both the IQR and Z-score methods are similar in that they identify anomalies by focusing on data points that deviate from central tendencies. However, the IQR method uses the spread between the 25th and 75th percentiles to find outliers, while the Z-score detects

4 This means below Q1 - 1.5 * IQR or above Q3 + 1.5 * IQR.

anomalies based on how far data points are from the mean, typically flagging points beyond 1.96 standard deviations.

A Z-score of 1.96 corresponds to a point where approximately 95% of the data lies within this Z-score range (between -1.96 and 1.96). Therefore, the remaining 5% of the data lies outside this range. To identify anomalies, we set a Z-score threshold of 1.96, **flagging** data points that fall outside the typical 95% confidence range.

The following code applies this threshold to detect anomalies in trading volume:

```
# Set a Z-score threshold for anomalies
threshold = 1.96
stock_data['Anomaly'] = stock_data['Z-Score'].apply(lambda x: True if
abs(x) > threshold else False)
# visualize Anomalies
stock_data[stock_data['Anomaly'] == True]
```

In terms of probability, this means there is only a 5% probability that a randomly selected data point will have a Z-score greater than 1.96. In practical terms, data points with Z-scores beyond ±1.96 are considered *anomalies*[5].

Then, using a Z-score threshold of 1.96 is a way to flag data points that are unlikely to occur by chance (only 5% of the time). This threshold is commonly used in statistics to identify outliers or anomalies, as it indicates that the data point is **significantly different** from most of the dataset.

The following graph illustrates the anomalies detected in HDB's trading volume using the Z-score method. *HDFC Bank* (ticker **HDB**) is a prominent financial institution, one of India's largest private sector banks, and is actively traded on the US market. As mentioned above, historical market data is sourced from Tiingo API. The chart provides a multi-layered view: the first panel highlights trading volume anomalies, the second overlays these anomalies on the adjusted closing price, and the third shows daily returns, as follows:

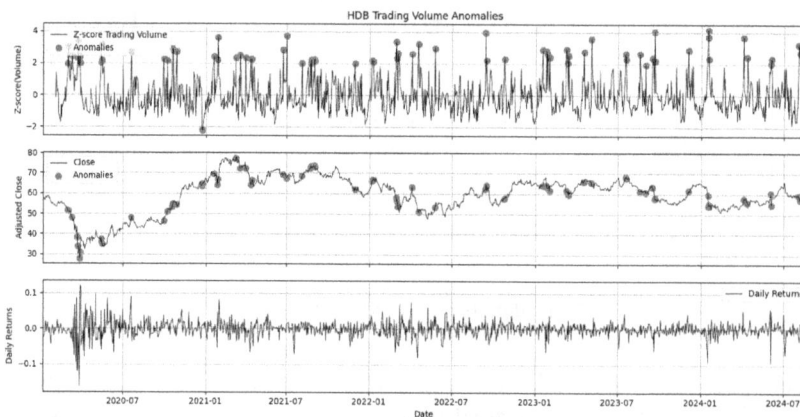

Figure 12.2: Z-Score for anomaly detection

_____

5 in the context of a normally distributed dataset

In the chart aforementioned, the red dots mark points where volume exceeded the anomaly threshold. The second graph overlays these volume anomalies on the adjusted closing price, and the third graph shows daily returns, allowing us to observe **correlations between abnormal volume activity and price or return movements**. The graph suggests that many anomalies occur **before** sharp price changes or trend reversals, suggesting that volume anomalies could act as early warning signals of market trends and reversals.

The following chart illustrates how CPD enhances anomaly detection by identifying structural shifts in trading volume trends. Unlike Z-scores, which highlight isolated **spikes**, CPD tracks broader **regime changes**, providing a more comprehensive view of market dynamics. The first graph illustrates CPD scores, which quantify the significance of detected shifts, alongside identified change points. The second chart overlays these anomalies on the adjusted closing price, helping to assess their impact on market movements. For a deeper understanding of CPD methods, see *Chapter 9, Unsupervised Learning Methods for Trading*.

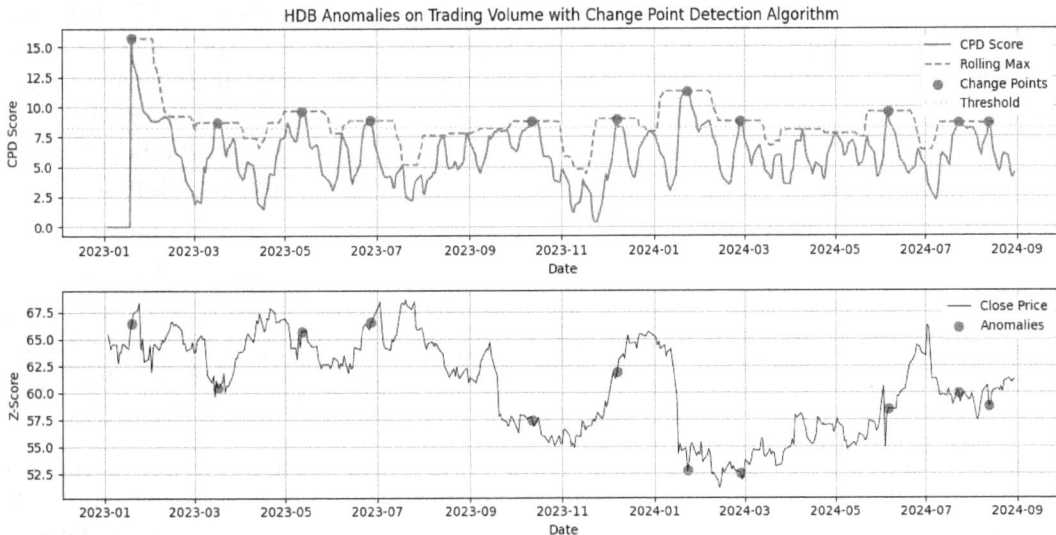

Figure 12.3: CPD for anomaly detection

By comparing the timing of volume anomalies (upper graph) with price movements (lower graph), we can assess whether the volume anomalies **lead to significant price changes**.

In many cases, the detected change points in volume coincide with price ruptures. In early 2023, a volume anomaly (detected by CPD[6]) correlates with a downward shift in price. In mid-2023, another volume anomaly is followed by a decline in the price. There are multiple CPD spikes (late 2023 to early 2024), and each time, the price undergoes a **notable change in direction**. In conclusion, the CPD algorithm effectively **detects** significant shifts in trading volume, many of which precede notable price movements. By capturing these

6 CPD is primarily a statistical approach, though some advanced implementations can incorporate machine learning techniques to enhance detection accuracy.

structural changes, CPD serves as a valuable tool for identifying potential price ruptures ahead of time, offering traders and analysts an early signal for market shifts.

Statistical methods provide valuable evidence of anomalies and trend shifts, while machine learning approaches, such as Isolation Forest, provide more sophisticated tools by learning patterns from the data itself, enabling more dynamic and adaptive anomaly detection.

Machine learning approach

Statistical methods like Z-scores use predefined rules or thresholds to detect anomalies and shifts in data. They analyze patterns based on historical averages, standard deviations, or other fixed statistical properties. These methods are effective for identifying outliers or sudden changes in trends but can be limited when the **data patterns are complex or evolving over time**.

On the other hand, machine learning approaches go beyond fixed thresholds by **learning the underlying patterns** from the data itself. These models adapt to the data's structure and can detect more subtle, complex, or evolving anomalies. Since they learn from the data, they can handle more dynamic scenarios and provide better detection in cases where the data does not follow simple statistical norms. In short, while statistical methods offer clear, rule-based information, machine learning models provide **flexibility and adaptability** by detecting more data-driven anomalies.

In the following example, we will implement an **Isolation Forest** (i.e. machine learning approach) for anomaly detection, focusing on analyzing volume to detect early price moves. The features include daily volume, rolling average volume, and volume ratios. This unsupervised method is particularly good at identifying rare events or outliers and could potentially detect unusual volume spikes before significant price movements.

Isolation Forest is a good starting point for the following reasons. It has **few hyperparameters** to tune and it is **computationally efficient**, making it faster to train and predict, especially on large datasets. It works effectively with smaller datasets and does not require labeled data, which is a challenge for many anomaly detection tasks. The results are interpretable, and it handles high-dimensional data without requiring significant feature engineering. Additionally, it provides a **built-in anomaly score** for each data point. An implementation of Isolation Forest is available in the *Scikit-learn*[7] library, making it accessible without complex setup.

Isolation Forest isolates observations by splitting data points. It works by constructing trees[8] where anomalous points, which are rare and different, get isolated faster with fewer splits. The algorithm assigns an **anomaly score** to each data point based on how quickly

7 https://scikit-learn.org/stable/modules/outlier_detection.html
8　　While both **Isolation Forest** and **Decision Trees** split data to make predictions, Isolation Forest focuses on isolating anomalies quickly, making it more efficient for detecting outliers, whereas Decision Trees are primarily used for supervised learning (classification and regression tasks). For details on Decision Trees see Chapter 5, *Supervised Learning for Trading Systems*.

it was isolated, making it effective at detecting outliers in high-dimensional datasets. Its efficiency and simplicity make it a widely used tool for anomaly detection.

To implement the Isolation Forest algorithm on our data, we create a set of features for volume analysis. We will use daily volume, rolling average volume, and volume ratios as features for the Isolation Forest:

```
# Calculate rolling averages and volume ratios
stock_data['Rolling Volume Mean'] = stock_data['volume'].
rolling(window=10).mean()
# Ratio of current volume to rolling mean
stock_data['Volume Ratio'] = stock_data['volume'] / stock_data['Rolling
Volume Mean']


# Drop NaN values (caused by rolling calculations)
stock_data.dropna(inplace=True)


# Select features for Isolation Forest
features = stock_data[['volume', 'Rolling Volume Mean', 'Volume Ratio']].
values
```

Then, we fit the Isolation Forest model:

```
isolation_forest = IsolationForest(contamination=0.1, random_state=42)
```

We clearly indicate anomalies by applying the **fit_predict()** function:

```
stock_data['Anomaly Score'] = isolation_forest.fit_predict(features)
```

The following chart shows the anomalies detected by the Isolation Forest marked as red Xs:

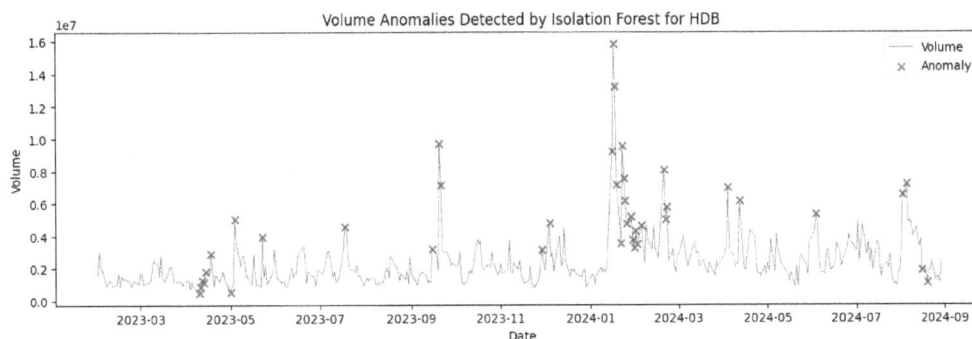

Figure 12.4: Machine learning method for anomaly detection

To further analyze how volume anomalies relate to price movements, we plot the adjusted close price along with detected volume anomalies:

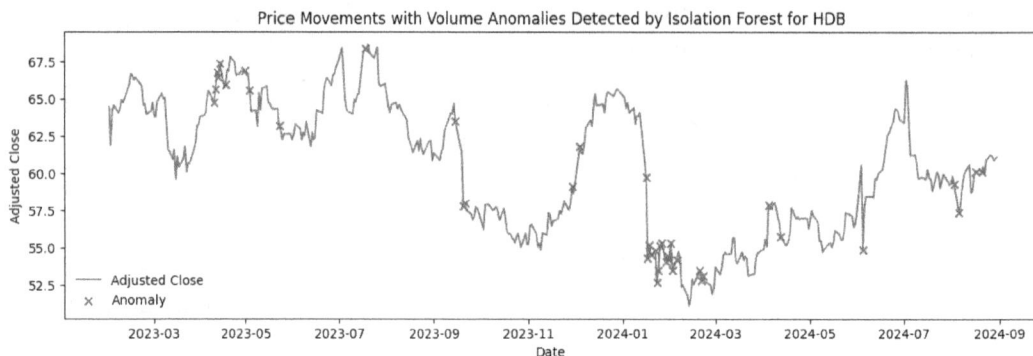

Figure 12.5: *Machine learning method for anomaly detection in price*

Several volume anomalies appear **before significant price shifts**, suggesting that these anomalies might signal upcoming price changes. For example, in mid-2023, a series of volume anomalies is detected before a noticeable rise in price, and a similar pattern can be observed before a drop later in the year (late November to early January 2024).

There are **clusters of anomalies** around critical price inflection points, such as early 2024, where a sharp price drop is observed. This suggests increased market activity or irregular trading patterns prior to significant price movements. Notably, several anomalies appear immediately after the drop, potentially signaling a shift in market dynamics and an **imminent rebound**. The pattern suggests that volume anomalies detected by Isolation Forest serve as early warning signals of both trend reversals and potential recovery phases.

This exploration of the Isolation Forest algorithm concludes our introduction of anomaly detection techniques. We have now gained a good understanding of the different approaches in the field, including both statistical methods and machine learning algorithms.

Moving forward, our focus will turn to the implementation of an integrated approach. This method combines the clustering of chronological sequences with a dimension reduction algorithm.

Sequence clustering and projection for anomaly detection

The objective is to map normal and abnormal sequences based on their positions within the proposed projection space. The hybrid technique we proposed aims to exploit the strengths of both sequential clustering and dimensionality reduction for improved anomaly detection. Distinguishing financial chronological sequences is our primary objective. To effectively map these sequences, we first construct meaningful features that capture temporal patterns.

Feature engineering

Previously introduced in *Chapter 6, Improve Model Capability with Features*, the Hurst exponent offers an efficient method to characterize markets based on trend persistence. We will incorporate this information into the chronological price sequence (day 1, day 2, day 3, etc.).

The selection of the Hurst exponent as a feature aligns with its fundamental purpose. This metric categorizes time series into **three potential regimes**, trending, purely stochastic, or anti-persistent (mean-reverting). Consequently, each chronological sequence will be paired with the Hurst exponent calculated for its corresponding period.

Let us start by calculating the Hurst:

```
!pip install -q hurst
from hurst import compute_Hc
window_size = 100  # Set a window size >= 100
# Make sure to apply the rolling only on windows with enough data
stock_data['hurst_price'] = stock_data['adjClose'].rolling(window=window_
size).apply(lambda x: compute_Hc(x, simplified=True)[0] if len(x) >= 100
else np.nan, raw=False)
```

We plot the resulting calculations of the Hurst exponent, as shown:

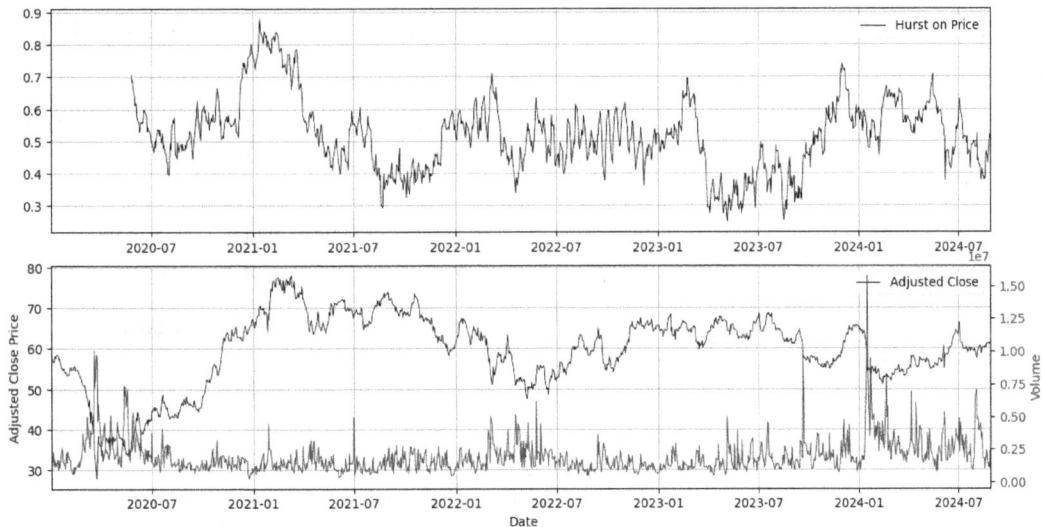

Figure 12.6: Hurst exponent on price

The first graph shows the *Hurst exponent* (noted **H**) over time (the window size is 100 days), which fluctuates between 0.3 and 0.9, indicating varying periods of mean-reverting behavior (H < 0.5) and trending behavior (H > 0.5). There are noticeable peaks in Hurst values around mid-2021, suggesting strong persistent market trends, followed by a drop, implying increased randomness or mean reversion.

The second graph shows **Adjusted Close Price** (black line) alongside **Volume** (blue line). There are a few significant spikes in volume, particularly around early 2024, which may suggest important market events or increased trading activity.

Overall, the combined analysis of Hurst and Volume suggests alternating market regimes, with periods of trending behavior followed by randomness, but price stability in reaction to high-volume spikes.

We then create a set of lagged features[9]. Their purpose is to enrich the dataset (OHLC values) with **historical information and memory**, allowing for the capture of **temporal patterns** and trends. We will generate lagged versions of several key metrics (closing prices, Percentage changes in closing prices, Z-scores, percentage changes in trading volume, and Hurst exponent values):

```
for i in range(1 , 4):
    stock_data[f'close_{i}'] = stock_data['adjClose'].shift(i)
    stock_data[f'close_pct{i}'] = np.round(stock_data['adjClose'].pct_
change().shift(i) , 3)
    stock_data[f'zscore_{i}'] = np.round(stock_data['Z-Score'].shift(i) , 2)
    stock_data[f'volume_pct{i}'] = np.round(stock_data['volume'].pct_
change().shift(i) , 3)
    stock_data[f'hurst_{i}'] = np.round(stock_data['hurst_price'].shift(i),2)
```

The feature set comprises the following elements:

```
1st_col = ['open','high',  'low', 'close', 'adjClose', 'volume', 'Z-Score',
'hurst_price', 'close_1', 'close_pct1', 'zscore_1', 'volume_pct1',
'hurst_1', \
            'close_2', 'close_pct2', 'zscore_2','volume_pct2', 'hurst_2', \
            'close_3', 'close_pct3', 'zscore_3','volume_pct3', 'hurst_3']
```

With these engineered features, we proceed to clustering to identify distinct market regimes and anomaly patterns.

Clustering algorithm

In the following code we apply a basic clustering algorithm to the prepared sequences to identify patterns and market regimes. We choose *default parameters*[10] and **do not try to optimize anything**, as we did before with hyperparameter optimization, allowing a quick and iterative approach to testing ideas. Refinements and parameter tuning are left for later to improve preliminary results and focus on the most promising insights:

9 We have used this method several times and explained the purpose of lagged values in Chapter 6, *Improving Model Capability with Features.*

10 https://scikit-learn.org/stable/modules/generated/sklearn.cluster.KMeans.html

```
from sklearn.cluster import KMeans
clst = KMeans(n_init = 'auto' , n_clusters = 8)
clst.fit(stock_data[lst_col])
np.unique(clst.labels_ , return_counts = True)
```

The aforementioned code will have the following output:

```
[0, 1, 2, 3, 4, 5, 6, 7],
[223, 102,  10, 240,  46,   2, 279, 170]
```

This output represents the results of the **KMeans** clustering. It shows the cluster labels (0 through 7) and the number of data points assigned to each cluster (223, 102, 10, and so on), indicating the distribution of trading days across different market regimes or patterns identified by the algorithm.

The challenge involves **interpreting** each of these clusters to understand the underlying market regime it represents. For instance, we need to determine whether cluster 0, containing 223 market sequences, corresponds to trending markets, mean-reverting behavior, or low volatility periods. This interpretation requires in-depth analysis of the cluster characteristics.

Non-linear projection and visualizations

To address the other challenge of visualizing high-dimensional data, we employ **Uniform Manifold Approximation and Projection** (UMAP[11]), a state-of-the-art dimensionality reduction technique. This allows us to project our multi-feature dataset onto a 2D map, facilitating easier visualization of the market sequences and their cluster associations.

```
!pip install -q umap-learn
from umap import UMAP
trsf = UMAP(n_neighbors = 7, min_dist = 0.1, n_components = 2)
```

We then project sequences and clusters onto the optimal 2D map calculated by UMAP:

```
seqs_reduced = trsf.fit_transform(stock_data[lst_col])
# Transform cluster centroids using the same UMAP transformation
centroids_reduced = trsf.transform(clst.cluster_centers_)
```

After positioning sequences and clusters on the 2D map, we can calculate the distance of each sequence from its assigned cluster center as follows:

```
factor = 1.3
# Step 1: Calculate distances to assigned cluster centroids
distances = np.array([np.linalg.norm(point - centroids_reduced[label])
                    for point, label in zip(seqs_reduced, clst.labels_)])
```

11 Since its introduction in Chapter 6, already quoted, on Feature Engineering, UMAP has become an indispensable tool in our data science toolkit. We have utilized this algorithm numerous times, recognizing its growing importance in solving visualization challenges. UMAP's effectiveness in dimensionality reduction has made it an essential technique for tackling complex data visualization problems.

This computation is a fundamental approach to anomaly detection. Essentially, an anomaly is identified as a point that **significantly deviates** from other points in its cohort, and more importantly, from its **cluster center** (which serves as a reference point). This method effectively highlights outliers by quantifying their dissimilarity from the expected behavior represented by their cluster, providing a robust framework for identifying unusual or potentially anomalous market sequences.

To go into more detail, we apply a threshold to determine which point is an anomaly. The threshold is adaptive to each cluster and is calculated as follows:

```python
# Step 2: Define threshold for anomalies for each cluster
thresholds = {}
for label in np.unique(clst.labels_):
    cluster_distances = distances[clst.labels_ == label]
    thresholds[label] = np.mean(cluster_distances) + factor *
np.std(cluster_distances)
```

Anomalies are identified as sequences that deviate significantly from their assigned cluster center, surpassing a predefined threshold and indicating potential irregular market behavior:

```python
# Step 3: Identify anomalies in top cluster
anomalies = np.array([distance > thresholds[label] and (label in top_
clusters)
                     for distance, label in zip(distances, clst.labels_)])
```

To assess the prevalence of anomalies in the dataset, we calculate the proportion of sequences that exceed the threshold and classify them as anomalies:

```python
print(f"Anomalies: {100*np.sum(anomalies)/len(seqs_reduced):.2f}%")
```

The following is the output:

```
Anomalies: 9.33%
```

The analysis reveals that approximately 10% of the sequences are classified as anomalies. This proportion aligns well with **standard practices** in anomaly detection, falling within the typical range of 1% to 10%. Such a percentage suggests a **balanced approach** to identifying unusual market behaviors, capturing significant deviations without being overly sensitive.

The next step involves plotting the data points on a two-dimensional map. This visualization will allow us to observe the distribution of market sequences, their cluster associations, and potentially identify anomalies within the reduced dimensional space. We focus on the points belonging to the **top four crowded clusters**, as shown:

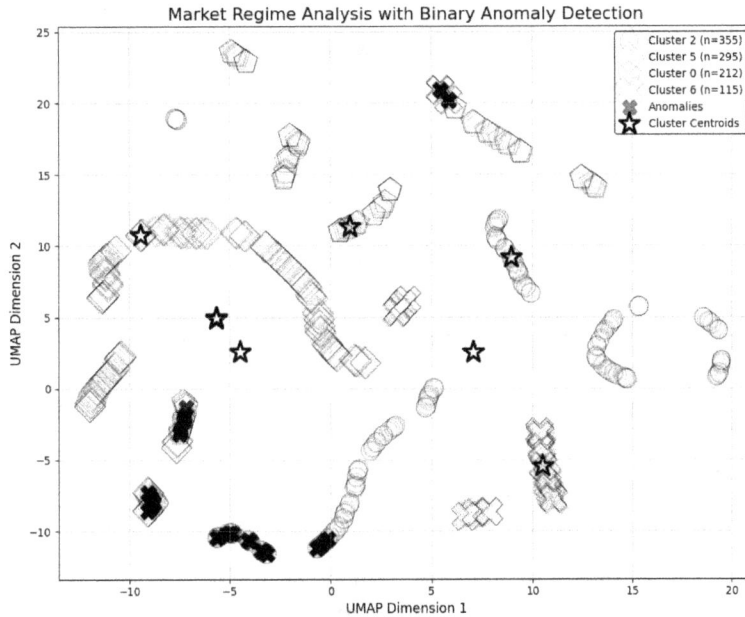

Figure 12.7: Visualization of market regime

This graph confirms that UMAP is an incredible tool for comprehensively mapping highly complex and high-dimensional datasets. In this UMAP visualization of market regimes, the **top four clusters** represent different regimes based on the underlying market features (e.g., OHLC, Volume, Hurst, etc.). Each cluster shows distinct groupings of sequences, with centroids marked by stars. The tightness and spread of the clusters suggest differing market stability and variability across these regimes. **Anomalies** are marked with a black cross and represent sequences where the distance from their cluster is greater than the threshold.

The following graph provides additional context for interpreting the clusters by mapping detected anomalies onto **price movements**:

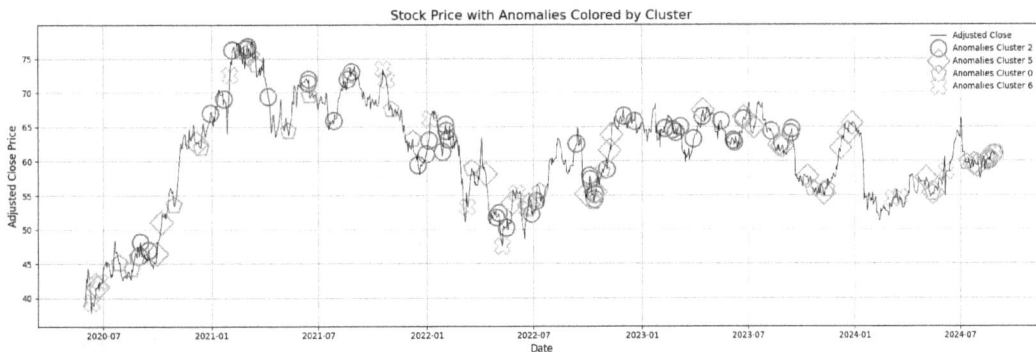

Figure 12.8: Visualization of market anomalies

We visualize the anomalies on the price chart using the same symbols (circle, diamond, pentagon, and cross) from *Figure 12.7*, to determine whether the four anomaly clusters correspond to distinct types of market events. What is immediately striking in the graph is that the algorithm has automatically detected peaks and troughs with high accuracy. Almost all anomalies align with critical market levels, highlighting key support and resistance zones, widely monitored by traders. These levels act as pivots, where price reactions often determine the next market move. When breached, they serve as entry or exit points for trades, reinforcing the significance of anomaly detection in identifying high-impact moments in the market.

Different clusters highlight anomalies with **distinct behaviors**. Some clusters appear near strong **upward momentum**, while others coincide with **consolidations**. This suggests that anomaly classification could further refine trading strategies by distinguishing **continuation** patterns from **reversal** signals.

The fact that an unsupervised algorithm naturally detects areas that traders manually identify as key support and resistance zones is particularly significant.

This demonstrates that machine learning can objectively quantify what many traders subjectively analyze, paving the way for systematic trading strategies based on detected anomaly points. This combined approach of clustering, projection, and anomaly detection offers numerous opportunities to be translated into well-informed trading systems.

Anomaly detection for trend reversals

This approach leverages anomaly detection to anticipate potential trend changes before they become apparent through traditional technical analysis.

When an anomaly is *detected*[12], indicating unusual market behavior, we open a position in the **opposite direction of the current trend**. The reasoning here is based on our previous findings: most anomalies act as early warning signs for trend reversals in the market.

These unusual data points often precede significant shifts in market direction:

```
# Compute trend by moving average
def detect_trend(prices, window=20):
    ma = prices.rolling(window=window).mean()
       # positive slope ? -> 1 else -> -1
    trend = np.where(ma.diff() > 0, 1, -1)
    return trend


# Apply trend detector :
trend = detect_trend(stock_data['adjClose'], window)
```

The current market trend is determined using a short-term **Moving Average (MA)**. A negative slope of the MA indicates a downtrend, while a positive slope indicates an

12 Points far from their cluster centroids in UMAP space.

uptrend. Then, the system goes short if the market is currently in an uptrend and an anomaly is detected, or long if the market is in a downtrend and an anomaly is detected.

```
for i in range(window, len(stock_data)):
    if anomalies[i] and clst_labels[i] in top_clusters:
        # If anomaly detected, take opposite position of the trend
        positions[i] = -trend[i]
```

As parameters, a trading window of 120 days is set up and a stop-loss of 2% is defined to limit potential losses. Again, we are not going to optimize the parameters. Rather, our aim is to **validate the core concept** as it stands and assess whether it delivers promising results even in its initial, unpolished form:

```
# Apply the strategy
window = 120
stop_loss = -2/100
positions, returns = trading_strategy(stock_data, anomalies, clst.labels_,
list(top_clusters) , window)
returns = np.where(returns < stop_loss , stop_loss , returns)
```

We calculate cumulative returns, total return, annualized return, and Sharpe ratio:

```
# Calculate cumulative returns
cumulative_returns = np.cumsum(returns)


print(f"Total Return: {cumulative_returns[-1]:.2%}")
print(f"Annualized Return: {(1 + cumulative_returns[-1]) ** (252/
len(returns)) - 1:.2%}")
print(f"Sharpe Ratio: {np.mean(returns) / np.std(returns) *
np.sqrt(252):.2f}")
```

This code gives the following output:

```
Total Return: 28.45%
Annualized Return: 6.06%
Sharpe Ratio: 1.02
```

The following graph shows the cumulative returns of the strategy (solid line) and the benchmark buy-and-hold strategy (dotted line), which consists of buying at the beginning and holding the asset for the entire period:

Figure 12.9: Equity curve of anomaly detection

The anomaly-based strategy d capitalizes on trend reversals, showing steady gains while avoiding prolonged drawdowns. Compared to the **Buy & Hold** approach, **it adapts dynamically to market shifts**, reinforcing the value of anomaly detection in trading decisions.

Compared to many other techniques, the methods and algorithms used here have fewer and untuned parameters and are unsupervised, very significantly reducing the risk of overfitting compared to traditional systematic trading strategies.

There is significant potential to enhance this strategy: expanding it to include all clusters, not just the major ones, refining how we differentiate between anomalies instead of treating them equally, and improving trend detection, as the current MA is quite basic.

In any case, we will be introducing a powerful data science tool that will allow us, among other things, to validate pre-defined data patterns. This tool is called association rules.

Clustering-based strategy with association rule

The idea is to maintain clustering as the foundation of our work while adding a validation tool to mine data and identify associations between events, which we can then turn into actionable trading strategies.

Association rules

Association rules identify relationships between different events in the data, highlighting patterns that occur together frequently.

Association rule mining is a powerful tool that can transform data into valuable insights. Take supermarket sales data, for instance. By analyzing this data, we can spot patterns that reveal buying **habits**. For example, we might discover that customers who buy onions and potatoes together are also likely to purchase hamburger meat: {**onions, potatoes**} ⇒ {**burger**}. These patterns may not be immediately obvious, but by mining transactional data, businesses can uncover hidden relationships and use them to optimize product placement, promotions, or recommendations.

Association rule mining identifies **frequent co-occurrences** between items or events. It is a data-driven approach that businesses in various domains, including retail and finance, can use to make more informed decisions.

In the financial world, we use the same approach to uncover hidden connections between market behaviors. By recognizing recurring patterns, such as a spike in volume followed by a spike in price, we can turn these insights into actionable trading strategies.

Association rule *learning*[13] is an **unsupervised learning technique** that automatically uncovers hidden relationships. Association rule mining explores the data without predefined outcomes. **It searches for frequent item sets that often occur together**, and extracts **if-then** relationships, known as rules. These rules, expressed as **if event A occurs, event B is likely to follow**. We are not finding a perfect rule that fits every event and is always true. It is important to understand that association rules only find a correct correlation, not the perfect truth.

Data preparation

We will apply association rule mining to extract actionable rules from our dataset of sequences and clusters, aiming to uncover hidden relationships that can be turned into trading strategies. To achieve this, we need to convert the numerical values in our dataset into **boolean True/False indicators**. This is necessary because **association rule algorithms work by finding patterns between binary variables**. This simple transformation is the only preparation required before feeding the data into an association rules library, enabling us to seamlessly discover meaningful connections that can inform trading decisions.

Ideally, using association rules, we would like to correlate events such as **is_cluster_A -> positive_return**. In this fictional example, the rule should be read as follows: sequences belonging to Cluster A **likely to follow** a positive return.

In this example, **is_cluster_A** is the *antecedent*[14]. It is the condition or event that must occur first. **Positive_return** is the **consequence**. The **consequence** is the resulting event that is likely to follow.

How can we use this rule? Obviously, this rule suggests buying (going long) whenever a sequence belongs to cluster A.

To implement this approach, we first transform numerical values into **boolean (True, False)** indicators, allowing the association rule algorithm to identify meaningful patterns, as shown:

13 https://en.wikipedia.org/wiki/Association_rule_learning
14 Antecedent and consequent part of the rule: antecedent (LHS) -> consequent (RHS)

```
lag = 1
# Compute daily returns
asset_ret = stock_data["close"].pct_change().shift(-lag)
# boolean True/False indicators
asset1_bins_pos = asset_ret > 0
asset1_bins_neg = asset_ret < 0
```

We work with lagged returns (**lag = 1**) because our goal is to anticipate future returns using current information. We have flagged positive and negative returns and created a **bag of events** with other notable factors such as **is_cluster_A** to **is_cluster_D, is_anomaly, is_trend**, and **is_not_trend**:

```
is_cluster_A = pd.Series(clst.labels_ == top_clusters[0] )
is_anomaly = pd.Series(anomalies)
is_hust_trend = stock_data['hurst_price'] > 0.5
is_hurst_notrend = stock_data['hurst_price'] < 0.5
```

This builds on our previous work constructing sequences with these features. Now, as mentioned, we need to convert these features into logical (**True/False**) indicators. This is the **human part** of applying association rule algorithms, deciding which events are significant enough to be included in the analysis. It is essential to fill this bag of events carefully, as the quality of the input directly affects the output (**garbage in, garbage out**). Once prepared, the association rule learning algorithm will extensively mine these events to reveal **correlations** between them:

```
# Create a dataset with discretized returns
dataset = pd.concat([asset1_bins_pos, asset1_bins_neg, is_cluster_A, is_
cluster_B, is_cluster_C, is_cluster_D,is_anomaly , is_hust_trend, is_hurst_
notrend], axis=1)
```

The following is an extract of the dataset:

date	asset_ret_pos	...	is_anomaly	is_hust_trend	is_hust_not_trend
2020-05-29 00:00:00+00:00	1	...	0	1	0
2020-06-01 00:00:00+00:00	1	...	0	1	0
2020-06-02 00:00:00+00:00	1	...	0	1	0
2020-06-03 00:00:00+00:00	1	...	0	1	0
2020-06-04 00:00:00+00:00	1	...	0	1	0

Table 12.1: Data preparation for association rules

With the dataset prepared, we can now move on to mining association rules to uncover meaningful relationships between market events.

Search for association rules

The data preparation is complete; now we just need to import the appropriate *library*[15] and feed it the dataset:

```
from mlxtend.frequent_patterns import apriori
from mlxtend.frequent_patterns import association_rules

# Perform association rule mining
frequent_itemsets = apriori(dataset, min_support = 0.05, use_colnames =
True)
rules=association_rules(frequent_itemsets, metric="confidence",min_
threshold=0.5)
```

Hundreds of rules can potentially be generated by the association rules algorithm as it outputs all the rules it finds, but many of these lack meaningful insight or are not actionable. The human role is to filter all these rules and focus on those that are of interest.

Rules like **x -> asset_ret_pos** or **y -> asset_ret_neg** are a good starting point, as they involve the sign of the return as a consequence (right part of the rule):

```
# Filter rules where 'asset_ret' is in the consequents
asset_ret_rules = rules[rules['consequents'].apply(lambda x: 'asset_ret_
pos' in x or 'asset_ret_neg' in x)]
```

Once we have focused on precise rules, we need to effectively prioritize and evaluate the discovered rules. We need a reliable metric to rank them in terms of importance and relevance.

Understanding the lift metric in association rule learning

Lift[16] metric shows how strongly two events are connected compared to if they happened randomly. A lift **above** 1 means the events occur together more often than by chance, suggesting a meaningful relationship. A lift *below* 1 indicates the events happen together less often than expected, while a lift of exactly 1 means there is no connection.

The following figure helps understand the lift metric:

---

15 Mlxtend (machine learning extensions) is a Python library of useful tools for the day-to-day data science tasks. https://rasbt.github.io/mlxtend
16 Rule : A -> B, **Lift** measures how much more likely B is to occur when A occurs, compared to B's overall likelihood.

Lift = P(B|A) / P(B) = (Joint occurrences of A and B / Total A events) / (Total B events / Total events)

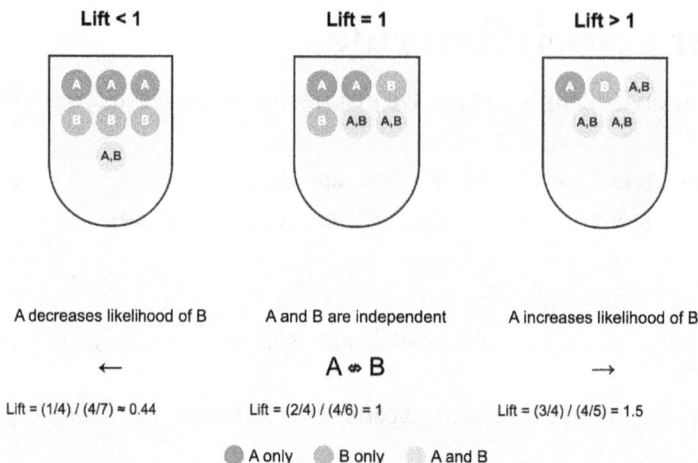

Figure 12.10: Lift metric

The library carries out all these calculations, all we must do is order (**sort_values**) the results according to the lift criterion we are discussing:

```
# Sort by lift
asset_ret_rules = asset_ret_rules.sort_values(['lift'], ascending=False)
asset_ret_rules
```

We look for rules that support a long-only strategy based on cluster information. The reason is that long-only strategies are easier to implement and are a good starting point. Of course, once we gain confidence in using this promising association rule tool, we will go further and look for much better (and potentially complex) rules.

The following are the three rules from the data that support long-only strategies:

- **(is_cluster_A) → (asset_ret_pos), Lift: 1.005305**
- **(is_cluster_C) → (asset_ret_pos), Lift: 1.037014**
- **(is_cluster_D) → (asset_ret_pos), Lift: 1.002947**

These rules suggest that Clusters C, A and D are associated with positive returns, with a lift above 1, which aligns with a long-only strategy. This supports an approach of going long when in certain clusters (like C, A or D) and staying out of the market otherwise.

Now, we will turn all this into the following code:

```
# Trading logic
for i in range(1, len(data)):
    # cluster A : 0, C : 2 or D : 3
    if cluster_labels[i-1] == top_clusters[0] or\
```

```
        cluster_labels[i-1] == top_clusters[2] or\
         cluster_labels[i-1] == top_clusters[3]:
            positions[i] = 1  # Go long
    else:
            positions[i] = 0  # Exit position
    # Update portfolio value
        portfolio_value[i] = portfolio_value[i-1] * (1 + positions[i] *
returns[i])
```

```
# Calculate performance metric
sharpe_ratio = np.mean(strategy_returns) / np.std(strategy_returns) *
np.sqrt(252)
print(f"Sharpe Ratio: {sharpe_ratio:.2f}")
```

The following is the output of the aforementioned code:

```
Sharpe Ratio: 1.55
```

This is a good performance statistic that is confirmed by the following equity curve:

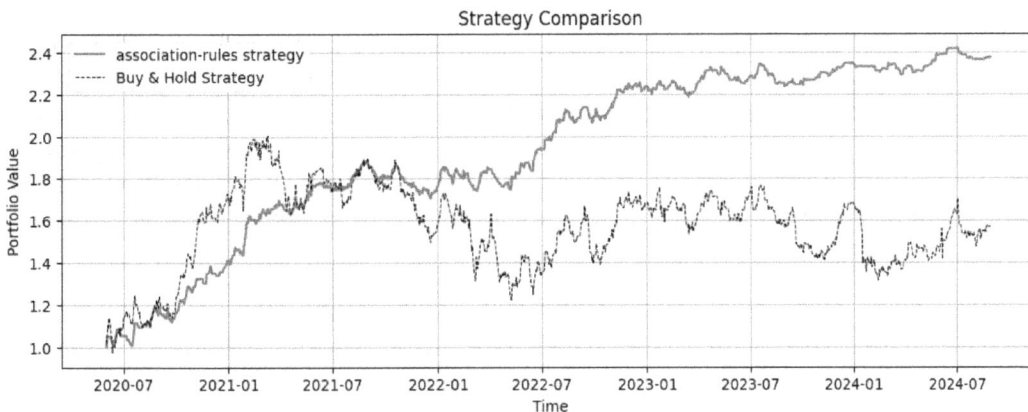

Figure 12.11: Equity curve of rules-based detection

The clustering-based strategy enhanced with association rules delivers consistent gains with lower volatility, outperforming the Buy & Hold approach. A Sharpe ratio of 1.5 confirms good risk-adjusted returns, demonstrating the effectiveness of combining unsupervised learning with rule validation in trading.

Conclusion

By the end of this chapter, we explored the advanced unsupervised learning techniques for financial markets, moving beyond traditional statistical anomaly detection to more sophisticated machine learning-driven methods. We consider Isolation Forest and CPD, followed by a hybrid approach combining sequence clustering and non-linear projections (UMAP) to detect market regimes and trend reversals.

A particularly original contribution of this chapter is the integration of clustering and association rule mining in anomaly detection. Association rule mining is underutilized in finance, despite its success in retail (recommendation engines) and engineering (predictive maintenance). By applying it to financial markets, we have demonstrated how it can automatically validate and refine anomaly-based signals, adding an extra layer of robustness.

The final equity curve confirms the effectiveness of the strategy, outperforming buy-and-hold with a Sharpe ratio of 1.5 and demonstrating strong risk-adjusted returns. While further refinements in parameter tuning and noise filtering could improve results, this chapter offers a cutting-edge, data-driven approach to financial analysis. By combining advanced anomaly detection, clustering and association rules, traders can systematically anticipate market shifts and develop more robust trading strategies based on data rather than intuition.

Note to the reader

Reaching the end of this book is more than just completing a technical journey, it marks the beginning of your ability to apply state-of-the-art AI techniques to the financial markets. From basic trading strategies to advanced supervised and unsupervised learning, feature engineering, automated machine learning, and integrating text analytics into financial pipelines, this book has equipped you with the tools to go beyond conventional market analysis and leverage cutting-edge machine learning for a real competitive advantage.

We not only explored key methods and algorithms but also provided concrete implementations to bridge theory and practice. Whether you are a quantitative trader, data scientist or researcher, we hope these methods inspire further exploration, refinement and innovation in algorithmic trading.

Join our book's Discord space

Join the book's Discord Workspace for Latest updates, Offers, Tech happenings around the world, New Release and Sessions with the Authors:

https://discord.bpbonline.com

APPENDIX

APIs and Libraries for each chapter

Chapter 1: Algorithmic Trading and Machine Learning in a Nutshell
- Basic Data Science: Pandas, NumPy
- Data Sources: yfinance
- Machine Learning: scikit-learn

Chapter 2: Data Feed, Backtests, and Forward Testing
- Macroeconomic Data APIs: wbdata (World Bank), fredapi (Federal Reserve), quandl
- Fundamental Data APIs: requests (for Tiingo, Financial Modeling Prep)
- Market Data: yfinance

Chapter 3: Optimizing Trading Systems, Metrics, and Automated Reporting
- Hyperparameter Optimization: hyperopt
- Financial Functions and Metrics: ffn, empyrical
- Analytics and Reporting: quantstats

Chapter 4: Implement Trading Strategies
- Backtesting Frameworks: BackTrader, Zipline, PyAlgoTrade
- Data Feeds and Brokers: yfinance, Alpaca, QuantRocket, InteractiveBrokers API

Chapter 6: Improving Model Capability with Features

- Feature Engineering & Selection: scikit-learn, statsmodels
- Technical Indicators: pandas_ta
- Information-Theoretic Features: pyinform, hurst
- Dimensionality Reduction: umap

Chapter 7: Advanced Machine Learning Models for Trading

- Hyperparameter Optimization: skopt (BayesSearchCV)

Chapter 8: AutoML and Low-Code for Trading Strategies

- Feature Engineering: Feature-engine, autofeat
- AutoML Frameworks: FLAML, H2OAutoML, auto-sklearn, TPOT, pyCaret, RapidMiner, KNIME, BigML

Chapter 9: Unsupervised Learning Methods for Trading

- Change Point Detection: changefinder, ruptures
- Statistical Testing: statsmodels (acorr_ljungbox)
- Clustering and Scaling: scikit-learn (KMeans, StandardScaler)
- Sequence Handling: keras.preprocessing.sequence (pad_sequences)
- Dimensionality Reduction: umap

Chapter 10: Unsupervised Learning with Pattern Matching

- Pattern Matching & Time Series: stumpy, fastdtw
- ML and Clustering: scikit-learn (LogisticRegression, KMeans, train_test_split)
- Sequence Processing: keras.preprocessing.sequence (pad_sequences)
- Visualization: umap

Chapter 11: Trading Signals from Reports and News

- Web Scraping & Data Collection: requests, BeautifulSoup, feedparser, wikipedia-api
- NLP: TextBlob, NLTK, sentence-transformers, Hugging Face
- Similarity & Visualization: scikit-learn, UMAP, NetworkX
- Portfolio Optimization: riskfolio-lib

Chapter 12: Advanced Unsupervised Learning, Anomaly Detection, and Association Rules

- Data Acquisition: requests (Tiingo API), Google Colab userdata
- Clustering & Anomaly Detection: scikit-learn (KMeans, IsolationForest)
- Statistical Tools: hurst, umap-learn
- Association Rule Mining: mlxtend (apriori, association_rules)
- Financial APIs: Tiingo

Index

www.ingramcontent.com/pod-product-compliance
Lightning Source LLC
Chambersburg PA
CBHW061800210326
41599CB00034B/6829

* 9 7 8 9 3 6 5 8 9 3 8 9 2 *